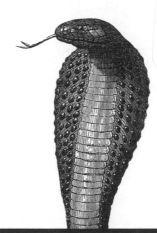

DREAMWEAVER
IN A NUTSHELL

A Desktop Quick Reference

DREAMWEAVER
IN A NUTSHELL

A Desktop Quick Reference

Heather Williamson & Bruce Epstein

O'REILLY®

Beijing • Cambridge • Farnham • Köln • Paris • Sebastopol • Taipei • Tokyo

Dreamweaver in a Nutshell

by Heather Williamson and Bruce Epstein

Published by O'Reilly & Associates, Inc., 1005 Gravenstein Highway North,
Sebastopol, CA 95472.

O'Reilly & Associates books may be purchased for educational, business, or sales
promotional use. Online editions are also available for most titles (*safari.oreilly.com*).
For more information, contact our corporate/institutional sales department at
800-998-9938 or *corporate@oreilly.com*.

Editor: Bruce Epstein

Production Editor: Ann Schirmer

Cover Designer: Ellie Volckhausen

Printing History:

> January 2002:   First Edition.

ISBN: 0-596-00239-4
[M]

To all who sleep, eat, and dream
Dreamweaver

—H.W.

To Frank Willison (1948–2001)

—B.E.

Table of Contents

Part II: Managing Dreamweaver

Part III: Behaviors and Interactive Elements

Preface

Macromedia Dreamweaver (DW) is the must-have tool for professional web developers. This book covers the features and usage of Dreamweaver 4 (DW4) on both Windows and Macintosh systems as distilled from my own experience, plus tips gleaned from mailing lists, user groups, beta testers, and my fellow Dreamweaver developers.

This book will address your questions and needs with a minimum of verbiage. Its instructions, notes, tips, and warnings apply to both Dreamweaver and Dreamweaver UltraDev. (Although this book does not cover features exclusive to UltraDev, UltraDev is implemented atop Dreamweaver and shares the same core feature set.)

Dreamweaver's tools include standard HTML objects such as tables and frames, plus prebuilt scripts and behaviors, timeline-based activities, XML support, CSS support, and a JavaScript debugger. For webmasters, Dreamweaver includes site-management tools such as File Check In/Out and Design Notes. This book will help you use Dreamweaver to:

- Develop HTML pages using both basic and advanced objects
- Design and manage templates for individual pages and complete sites
- Define and manage your site's overall structure
- Create cross-browser, cross-platform, standard-compliant HTML without a lot of hand coding

This book is not a step-by-step tutorial, nor does it attempt to teach HTML or web design. Instead, it helps you leverage your existing skills within the Dreamweaver environment. Instead of explaining how to make your site popular, it explains how to efficiently create and maintain a site using Dreamweaver. This book assumes a basic understanding of web page development tools and concepts, but no particular knowledge of Dreamweaver. If you are completely unfamiliar with

Dreamweaver, keep the application open while you read the book and consult the excellent Help files that accompany the product. Use the Help → Welcome option for a quick visual overview of Dreamweaver.

For assistance with peripheral issues or for further details on Dreamweaver itself, see "Suggested Reading" and "Other Resources." Reference material from O'Reilly & Associates covering HTML, CSS, and JavaScript is also included within the Dreamweaver 4 Reference panel (Window → Reference).

The Big Picture

Dreamweaver is the dominant WYSIWYG (What You See Is What You Get) software program for professional web development. Dreamweaver can help you build and manage complex web sites that work appropriately with Netscape Navigator (NN), Internet Explorer (IE), and other browsers.

Although Dreamweaver 4 includes an integrated HTML editor, it is much more than just an HTML tool. Yes, Dreamweaver allows you to work with all of the normal HTML formatting structures such as tables, frames, and layers, but it also provides many tools for managing web sites, whether they use HTML only, or server-side languages such as ASP or ColdFusion as well.

 Refer to Appendix C for a good overview of the issues you'll need to consider before, during, and after developing your site.

Here is a quick rundown of Dreamweaver's primary features.

Tables
> Dreamweaver has two ways of looking at tables: the traditional way and the Layout view (new in DW4). The traditional table (Standard) view allows you to configure each cell of a table individually, but is hard to use for complex tables. Layout view uses visual tools, which would be available in a desktop publishing program, to lay out complex tables. For more information, see Chapter 3.

Frames
> Dreamweaver easily creates the most popular frames configurations, such as equally centered left and right frames, top and bottom frames, and thin frames on the left, top, right, or bottom of your screen. For more information, see Chapter 4.

Layers
> Layers originated with Cascading Style Sheets and are supported in the 4.0+ versions of the most popular browsers. Layers allow you to format information without setting up a grid and allow you to superimpose multiple layers of information in one page location. For more information on layers in Dreamweaver, see Chapters 4, 14, and 17.

Styles, Libraries, and Templates

Dreamweaver offers several time-saving ways to standardize pages and reuse components. Dreamweaver helps you use formatting standards such as Cascading Style Sheets, but also implements its own system of templates (on which you can base similar pages), libraries (for reusing and updating commonly needed components), and HTML styles (to help you apply formats easily). See Chapters 8, 9, 10, and 11.

Assets and History

The Assets panel makes it easy to find and reuse elements throughout your site. The History panel allows you to undo, record, and automate almost any step or process.

Roundtrip HTML

Dreamweaver has various tools that make it easy to work with HTML documents created in Dreamweaver and other HTML editors. The Roundtrip HTML feature allows you to modify your Dreamweaver documents in any HTML editor, with little or no change to your document's structure. For more information about Dreamweaver's HTML tools, including Roundtrip HTML, see Chapter 7.

Site Management

Dreamweaver includes advanced site-management tools to synchronize the local copy of your web site files with those on the web server. Dreamweaver's collaborative tools also allow teams of developers to work on a site simultaneously. Checking files in and out as they are being edited prevents two team members from working on the same document concurrently. Design Notes allow workgroups or single developers to track changes that have been made or need to be made to individual files. For information on defining sites, managing sites, and the Dreamweaver Site window, see Chapter 6.

 You can use Dreamweaver to create and manage a new site from scratch or to manage an existing site originally created with other tools.

Site Checking

Broken links are an offense punishable by death, or at least the death of sales. Dreamweaver incorporates checks for broken links, external links, and orphaned files. Site checking and error reports are covered in Chapter 6.

Behaviors

Dreamweaver includes a wide variety of ready-made JavaScript behaviors that run properly in most web browsers. Dreamweaver's Behaviors panel allows you to select the level of browser support you need and then limits access to only the events that work in the selected web browser versions. For details on the behaviors shipped with Dreamweaver, see Part III.

Firework Integration

Fireworks is bundled with Dreamweaver in the Macromedia Dreamweaver 4 Fireworks 4 Studio bundle. This book covers how to integrate Fireworks with Dreamweaver in Chapter 5. Chapter 13 explains how to import Fireworks roll-over images, sliced tables, and other effects into Dreamweaver.

 I highly recommend that you use Fireworks for your web-based graphics. Its powerful features and integration with Dreamweaver make it an indispensable companion tool. This books cover a few Fireworks techniques to get you started, and you'll be hooked once you get your feet wet. For developers who use Photoshop, I recommend the PhotoWebber utility available at *http://www.medialab.com*. PhotoWebber lets you use Photoshop to create many of the effects described in this book using Fireworks.

Integration of Server-Side Languages

Dreamweaver recognizes tags associated with server-side languages, such as Active Server Pages (ASP) and ColdFusion Markup Language (CFML). It won't change their contents even if you modify the other HTML code on the page. For more details on Dreamweaver's support for server-side languages, see Chapter 21.

Dreamweaver Customization

Dreamweaver is highly configurable. See Chapters 18, 19, and 20 for details on making Dreamweaver work the way you want it to.

Dreamweaver Extensions

Extensibility is one of Dreamweaver's key features. With a little knowledge of JavaScript, HTML, and XML, you can add your own functionality to Dreamweaver. For those without such knowledge, Dreamweaver 4's built-in Extension Manager and the Dreamweaver Exchange web site (*http://www. macromedia.com/exchange/dreamweaver/*) provide easy access to many existing extensions from Macromedia and third parties. For more details, see Chapter 22.

New Features in Dreamweaver 4

For those of you familiar with earlier versions of Dreamweaver, this book will bring you up to speed on the features added in Dreamweaver 4 (DW4). Also see the introduction to new features under Help → What's New (in DW's Help menu).

New features include:

- An integrated text editor used to edit HTML code manually
- Customizable keyboard shortcuts for greater productivity
- A JavaScript debugger, which helps to find and fix bugs in your scripts
- Integrated editing of non-HTML code (such as code for ColdFusion and Active Server Pages)

- Improved graphics editing tools and closer integration with Fireworks
- A Table Layout view, which facilitates the use of tables for page layout
- Improved template functionality, which allows greater control over how templates display dynamic information
- The standard Macromedia User Interface, which leverages your familiarity with other Macromedia products and allows multiple panels to be docked inside one floating window
- Simplified insertion of Flash and Shockwave documents
- Better asset management through the Assets panel
- Integrated email in the Site window for improved workgroup communication
- Integration with version control systems, including Microsoft Visual SourceSafe and WebDAV (Web-based Distributed Authoring and Versioning)
- Site-wide reporting tools used to coordinate files within workgroups (File Check In and Check Out)
- Improved Extension Manager (formerly the Package Manager) and enhanced extensions from the Macromedia Exchange

---

 Download and install the free Dreamweaver 4.01 updater from the URL cited under the "Other Resources" in this preface. It includes some minor bug fixes and enhanced support for Netscape 6.

Dreamweaver UltraDev's Features

Dreamweaver UltraDev is a superset of Dreamweaver, sold separately and built atop the Dreamweaver platform. It can read information from databases and other data sources. UltraDev is a complete development environment for creating server-side applications using JSP, ASP, and ColdFusion (future versions may support PHP). Although this book does not cover UltraDev-specific features, I mention them here to help you decide if you should develop your site using UltraDev instead of the basic Dreamweaver application. In short, if you are building a database-driven web site, you should seriously consider using UltraDev.

Luckily, all your existing Dreamweaver knowledge will transfer seamlessly to the UltraDev environment. UltraDev includes all of Dreamweaver 4's capabilities, plus the following features not covered in this book:

- Live data collection and customization
- Multiserver design environment
- Data bindings
- Remote database connectivity
- User authentication server behaviors

- Master detail, database editing, recordset navigation, and recordset status life objects
- Dynamic data formatting
- Server behavior library
- SQL Query Editor
- Code Navigation
- JavaBeans support
- Recordable server behaviors

Layers and Tables and Frames, Oh My!

You should already have a reference frame for thinking about Dreamweaver and have some idea about how you'd like to structure your site. If not, spend a few minutes sketching out your site's major areas and a typical web page from each area. This exercise will give you something to work towards and a skeleton to hang your knowledge upon as you read this book.

You may know how you want your site to look but not know the best tools to achieve the desired effect. We'll jump right in by facing some of the first decisions that confront a web site developer. Later, we'll cover techniques for creating individual pages and managing your entire site.

Whether to use layers, tables, and frames when designing your pages is a controversial topic. Issues include ease of use, compatibility with different browsers (especially older ones), performance, and the ability for search engines to index your pages.

A recent survey shows that approximately 28 percent of sites use frames (*http:// www.securityspace.com/s_survey/data/man.200107/techpen.html*).

The same survey shows that JavaScript is used in over 40 percent of sites, but far fewer sites use CSS stylesheets, Java, Flash, and Shockwave.

 Dreamweaver's Templates, Library, and HTML Styles features generate HTML supported by older browsers. Layers and Cascading Style Sheets generally require 4.0+ browsers but can be converted to tables and HTML markup using File → Convert → 3.0 Browser Compatible. Most users have 4.0+ browsers.

The best choice for your site depends on its functionality, your client's requirements, the browsers you'll be supporting, and the connection speed of your users. I'll outline the issues surrounding frames, tables, and layers briefly. Later, I'll guide you through all Dreamweaver tools so you can use your chosen weapons with optimal efficiency.

Frames

Some developers are vehemently against the use of frames, even if the site could benefit from them. The controversy surrounding frames makes it imperative to educate your clients and may force you to offer a no-frames alternative. You can use frames to add a menu or table of contents for your entire site; this technique prevents the same information from reloading on every page, yet keeps that information readily available. Frames also allow you to combine documents from multiple sources into a single cohesive page.

Frames are supported by Version 2.0 and later of the major browsers, so almost all current users can view frames. Frames also have a built-in fallback system; the `<noframes>` tag allows browsers without frames support, or browsers with disabled frames support, to access an alternative version of a web page.

Although frames can simplify some aspects of site maintenance, such as updating a toolbar frame used on every page, they can also complicate site management. Because frames use multiple documents to construct each page, you must keep track of multiple documents for each page and contend with more complicated screen layout issues. For some users, especially those using a keyboard for navigation, frames complicate site navigation. It is also relatively difficult for users to bookmark individual pages in a framed document, although newer browsers allow you to bookmark pages by using the command menu associated with each frame. Finally, to ensure that your pages are indexed by search engines, avoid using frames, as they make your pages more difficult to index. You can ameliorate the problem by avoiding frames on your home page and on other entry points but still using frames on the other pages. See Chapter 4 for details on using frames in Dreamweaver.

Tables

As with frames, the use of tables has its advocates and detractors. Some developers argue that tables add bulky tags to your document, make it harder for search engines to index your pages, and restrict pages to a grid-based design. Other developers feel that tables are the best way to create a highly structured web site that can be viewed by any browser.

Tables add download time to web pages due to the large number of tags used to create a table, and slow machines may take a long time to render large tables. But tables are the most reliable way to design complex page layouts, display data, align text, create a page template, or incorporate a multipart image. See Chapter 3 for details on using tables in Dreamweaver, including the new Layout view. Although they can accomplish similar things as tables, layers have their own benefits and drawbacks.

Layers

Like tables, layers allow precise alignment, but they also offer capabilities that tables do not. Tables are "flat" (only one piece of content can occupy a given area), whereas layers can display images and text stacked on top of one another. This feature can add depth to your pages and incorporate more information into the same page space.

However, layers should be used only if visitors have a 4.0+ version of one of the major web browsers. Older browsers don't recognize layers—they simply display the information the layer contains in the order it appears in the document, or not at all. Over 95 percent of users have 4.0+ browsers, so using layers is usually a safe choice. See Chapter 4 for details on using layers in Dreamweaver.

Contents

By now you should have a rough mental picture of your web site, its typical pages, and the navigation between the pages. The rest of this book will show you how to use Dreamweaver to refine and realize that vision.

The book is separated into five parts.

Part I: The Content Objects

Part I introduces all the core elements you'll use to create pages, insert objects, and navigate Dreamweaver's user interface.

Chapter 1, *Dreamweaver UI*
> Gives a quick orientation to Dreamweaver's Document window and major user interface (UI) panels including the Objects panel, Property inspector, and Launcher.

Chapter 2, *Core Objects*
> Explains the core objects you'll use throughout your development, including page options, meta tags, hyperlinks, images and image maps, text, lists, and hidden elements.

Chapter 3, *Tables and Form Objects*
> Covers tables and forms, including importing tabular data, form objects, and jump menus.

Chapter 4, *Frames and Layers*
> Whether you like or dislike HTML frames, this chapter details their use within Dreamweaver. Likewise, it covers layers and their appropriate usage. See Chapter 14 for more information about using layers with JavaScript behaviors.

Chapter 5, *Using External Resources*
> Covers working with external resources, such as those created in Flash, Shockwave, Fireworks, and Generator. It also covers server-side includes, ActiveX controls, plugins, and Java applets.

Part II: Managing Dreamweaver

Part II covers the broader issues of site management and document management using templates, libraries, and stylesheets.

Chapter 6, *Managing a Web Site*
> Covers site management, including FTP access, Web-based Distributed Authoring and Versioning (WebDAV) file tracking and manipulation systems, Design Notes, and File Check In/Check Out. The chapter also covers file synchronization, updating links, and checking for broken links and orphaned files.

Chapter 7, *Managing HTML Documents*

Covers document management features, including cleaning up poor HTML code, using the Quick Tag Editor, performing browser checking, and automating tasks with the History panel.

Chapter 8, *Templates*

Covers using templates to create multiple documents that share a uniform layout. The chapter also discusses important tips and traps to keep in mind when using templates.

Chapter 9, *The Library*

Covers the benefits and traps of the Library feature, including details on updating items and sharing items with a development team.

Chapter 10, *Cascading Style Sheets*

Covers using Cascading Style Sheets to format documents, with special attention paid to their use in Dreamweaver.

Chapter 11, *HTML Styles*

Covers HTML styles to format commonly used elements—such as headings, copyright notices, paragraph text, and other elements of your own creation—that can be used to standardize style and reduce page creation time.

Part III: Behaviors and Interactive Elements

Part III covers the use of JavaScript behaviors to perform commonly needed functions.

Chapter 12, *Behaviors and JavaScript*

Covers the use of JavaScript within your HTML documents. The chapter includes a general discussion of behaviors and the use of standard behaviors to identify the browser and manipulate browser windows.

Chapter 13, *Image Behaviors and Fireworks*

Covers built-in image-related behaviors, such as image rollovers, image preloading, and image swapping, that are useful for navigation bars and other effects. The chapter also covers how to create effects in Fireworks and import them into Dreamweaver.

Chapter 14, *Layer Behaviors*

Covers creating multidimensional HTML documents with layers. The chapter details built-in behaviors used to move, set, and change the properties associated with layers.

Chapter 15, *Text Behaviors*

Discusses behaviors that manipulate the text content of objects in your document or in the browser's window.

Chapter 16, *Miscellaneous Behaviors*

Discusses strategies for using behaviors with links and covers miscellaneous built-in behaviors.

Chapter 17, *Timelines*

Covers the configuration of frames, keyframes, behaviors, and objects to animate page content over time using the Timelines panel.

Part IV: Configuring and Extending Dreamweaver

Part IV covers ways to configure, customize, and extend Dreamweaver to meet both your needs and your work style.

Chapter 18, *Dreamweaver Preferences*
Covers all Dreamweaver preference settings.

Chapter 19, *Customizing the Interface*
Explains how to customize menus and keyboard shortcuts and how to add objects to your Objects panel.

Chapter 20, *Customizing the Document Template and Dialog Boxes*
Covers modifying the default document template and dialog boxes in the Dreamweaver interface.

Chapter 21, *Displaying Third-Party Tags*
Discusses Dreamweaver's support for and integration with the predominant server-side programming languages.

Chapter 22, *Extending Dreamweaver*
Covers extending Dreamweaver by using the Macromedia Dreamweaver Exchange. The chapter also covers some useful extensions.

Chapter 23, *CourseBuilder*
Covers the CourseBuilder extension, including installation, configuration, and use of CourseBuilder interactions.

Part V: Appendixes

Part V includes reference information you'll need throughout site development.

Appendix A, *Keyboard Shortcuts*
Lists keyboard shortcuts, sorted by function for easy reference.

Appendix B, *HTML Character Entities*
Lists the HTML character entities supported by the primary web browsers.

Appendix C, *Site Construction Checklist*
Aggregates a list of information you'll need when developing a web site. Includes a Dreamweaver checklist to create a well-functioning site, plus tips on creating graphics and getting your site listed in search engines.

Conventions

The following typographical conventions are used in this book:

Menu options
Menu options are shown using the → character, such as File → Open.

`Constant Width`
Indicates code examples, functions, variables, HTML elements, attributes, and events.

`Constant Width Bold`
Indicates items that the user must enter exactly as shown, such as in a dialog box. In some tables, the default option is shown in bold.

Constant Width Italic

Indicates variables in code or dialog boxes that should be replaced with user-supplied information.

Italic

Indicates filenames, online addresses (URLs), items that need emphasis, and newly introduced technical terms.

 Notes highlight important information related to the current topic.

 Warnings alert you to ill-advised techniques or irrevocable choices that could be destructive.

Screenshots and Keyboard Shortcuts

Although Dreamweaver's user interface is nearly identical on Macintosh and Windows, I've incorporated screenshots from both platforms. When the user interface differs markedly between the two platforms, I've included screenshots of both the Macintosh and Windows interface.

Some Dreamweaver menus and shortcuts vary across the two platforms. Most keyboard shortcuts require you to press one or more indicated function keys (such as F5), modifier keys (such as Shift), or alphanumeric keys (such as A) simultaneously. Keyboard shortcuts are shown using capital letters, but the Shift key should be used only when indicated explicitly (the word *Shift* is used on both platforms, even though the Dreamweaver menus on the Macintosh use an arrow symbol to indicate the Shift key).

Most shortcuts have nearly equivalent counterparts on both platforms. The counterpart of the Windows *Ctrl* key is the Macintosh *Command* key (a.k.a., the Apple, cloverleaf, or propeller key), abbreviated as *Cmd*. The counterpart of the Windows *Alt* key is the Macintosh *Option* key, shown in the menus as a bizarre character rarely reproduced in print and abbreviated as *Opt*.

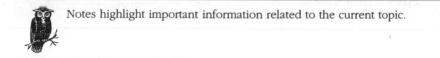 Use Edit ‣ Keyboard Shortcuts to open the Keyboard Shortcuts dialog box, which summarizes all keyboard shortcuts. Use the Export Set as HTML button in this dialog box to save the listing in an HTML file that can be printed out for easy reference. (This book uses the same keyboard shortcut notation as the exported file.)

Windows users can access any menu item using the Alt key followed by one or more letters in sequence (as indicated by underlining in the menu). For example Alt-V, W means to press the Alt key, followed by the V key (to access the View menu), followed by the W key (to access the Design View on Top option).

Keyboard shortcuts are summarized in Appendix A. Some shortcuts may not work on some computers, particularly laptops, which intercept some function keys. If a shortcut does not work on the Macintosh, turn off the Hot Function Key option in the Keyboard Control Panel.

Suggested Reading

Beginners who are unfamiliar with basic concepts regarding web site development, or users in need of an introductory tutorial, should consider the following books from O'Reilly & Associates:

- *Dreamweaver 4: The Missing Manual* by David Sawyer McFarland
- *Learning Web Design* by Jennifer Niederst
- *Web Navigation: Designing the User Experience* by Jennifer Fleming

For more insight into web design, HTML, Cascading Style Sheets, and JavaScript, consider these other O'Reilly books:

- *HTML/XHTML: The Definitive Guide* by Chuck Musciano and Bill Kennedy
- *Cascading Style Sheets: The Definitive Guide* by Eric A. Meyer
- *Web Design in a Nutshell* by Jennifer Niederst
- *Webmaster in a Nutshell* by Stephen Spainhour and Robert Eckstein
- *Perl in a Nutshell* by Ellen Siever, Stephen Spainhour, and Nathan Patwardhan
- *JavaScript: The Definitive Guide* by David Flanagan
- *Programming ColdFusion* by Rob Brooks-Bilson
- *ASP in Nutshell* by A. Keyton Weissinger
- *ActionScript: The Definitive Guide* by Colin Moock
- *XML in a Nutshell* by Eliotte Rusty Harold and W. Scott Means

Other Resources

Consult these online resources for more information about Dreamweaver, HTML, web standards, and web scripting languages. Also see the *ReadMe.htm* and *ResourcesOfInterest.htm* files located in the folder where Dreamweaver is installed. Other useful links can be found by searching for "HTML and Web Technologies Resources" under Help → Using Dreamweaver (F1).

Author's home page for Dreamweaver in a Nutshell
    http://www.dwian.com/

O'Reilly catalog page for Dreamweaver in a Nutshell
    http://www.oreilly.com/catalog/dreamweavernut/

Macromedia Dreamweaver Home
    http://www.macromedia.com/software/dreamweaver/

Macromedia Dreamweaver Support
    http://www.macromedia.com/support/dreamweaver/

Macromedia Dreamweaver Download Center (Dreamweaver 4.01 updater)
    http://www.macromedia.com/support/dreamweaver/downloads/

Macromedia Dreamweaver Exchange
    http://www.macromedia.com/exchange/dreamweaver/

Macromedia UltraDev Home
    http://www.macromedia.com/software/ultradev/

Macromedia UltraDev Support
    http://www.macromedia.com/support/ultradev/

Macromedia UltraDev Exchange
    http://www.macromedia.com/exchange/ultradev/

UD Zone (UltraDev Resources)
    http://www.udzone.com/

WebDAV
    http://www.webdav.org/

Visual SourceSafe
    http://msdn.microsoft.com/ssafe/

Web Review
    http://www.webreview.com/

Web Reference
    http://www.webreference.com/

ColdFusion
    http://www.coldfusion.com/

World Wide Web Consortium's documents on the HTML standard
    http://www.w3.org/MarkUp/

World Wide Web Consortium's documents on the CSS standard
    http://www.w3.org/StyleSheets/

Reference materials for all major Internet related technologies
    http://www.internet.com/

CGI scripting examples and resources
    http://www.cgiresourceindex.com/

Matt's Script Archive
    http://www.worldwidemart.com/scripts/

Moock.org—Flash and ActionScript examples and resources
    http://www.moock.org/moockmarks/

How to Contact Us

We have tested and verified the information in this book to the best of our ability, but you may find that features have changed (or even that we have made mistakes!). Please address comments and questions concerning this book to the publisher:

O'Reilly & Associates, Inc.
1005 Gravenstein Highway North
Sebastopol, CA 95472
1-800-998-9938 (in the United States or Canada)
1-707-829-0515 (international/local)
1-707-829-0104 (fax)

To ask technical questions or comment on the book, send email to:

bookquestions@oreilly.com

The web site for this book lists examples, errata, and plans for future editions. You can access this page at:

http://www.oreilly.com/catalog/dreamweavernut/

For more information about our books, conferences, software, resource centers, and the O'Reilly Network, see our web site:

http://www.oreilly.com

Heather's Acknowledgments

My hat goes off to the great teams at O'Reilly and Studio B for their constant faith in me throughout the demanding task of publishing this book. I definitely couldn't have done it without their help. A special thanks to Tim O'Reilly, Bruce Epstein (my editor at O'Reilly), and Neil Salkind (my agent at Studio B), who saw me through writing this book while I was trying to build a house (not a task for the faint of heart or those with low stress tolerance). The team at O'Reilly—including Ann Schirmer, Claire Cloutier, Rob Romano, and Cathy Record—was wonderful to work with and should be commended for their contributions to this project.

I would like to thank my primary technical reviewer, Chip Dunbar, for his diligence on this project, including heroic assistance with the Macintosh screenshots. My thanks also to Brian Hall, Mary Ann Brown, and Massimo Foti (*http://www. amila.ch*) for their feedback and technical edits to the manuscript. Their help was invaluable to the completion of this project.

I would also like to thank Ann for being such a wonderful, understanding daughter while I was working on this book. There is no one better than you. Mom and Dad, thank you for encouraging me to keep up the hard work and for giving me a "never quit" attitude. And Luis, whatever you do, just never change. My thanks also to my many friends whose support makes light work out of the heaviest load.

Bruce's Acknowledgments

My thanks to Tim O'Reilly and his outstanding staff.

My love to my wife Michele for her patience, understanding, and willingness to listen to me talk endlessly.

PART I

The Content Objects

Part I introduces all the core elements you'll use to create pages, insert objects, and navigate Dreamweaver's user interface (UI).

CHAPTER 1

Dreamweaver UI

Dreamweaver's rich feature set makes it an indispensable tool for professional web developers. Its visual interface offers easy access to standard HTML objects such as tables and frames, plus prebuilt scripts and behaviors, timeline-based activities, CSS support, and a JavaScript debugger. For webmasters, Dreamweaver includes site-management tools such as File Check In/Check Out and Design Notes.

This book covers Dreamweaver's practical usage, including its site management features. Reference material from O'Reilly & Associates covering HTML, Cascading Style Sheets (CSS), and JavaScript is also included within the Dreamweaver 4 (DW4) Reference panel (Window → Reference).

This chapter will familiarize you with Dreamweaver's Document window and some common elements you'll use within it. These topics will help orient those who are familiar with HTML or earlier versions of Dreamweaver, but may be new to Dreamweaver 4. Although you should plan your site before beginning serious production work, this chapter will help you perform quick edits on existing pages and get immediate hands-on experience. For those who prefer the "top-down" approach, refer to Part II, which covers site management.

Your use of Dreamweaver will rely heavily on the Dreamweaver user interface (UI) objects discussed in this chapter. Macromedia's documentation variously refers to Dreamweaver's UI components as *panels*, *inspectors*, *editors*, *bars*, *windows*, and *palettes*, and we follow those conventions when referring to them individually. For convenience, we use the term *panels* to refer to them collectively.

This chapter covers:

* The Document window in its various views, plus its Toolbar and status bar

* The Objects panel and its respective categories

* The Property inspector and its selection of options

- The Reference panel and its vast selection of HTML-, JavaScript-, and CSS-related information

- The Launcher bar used to access other Dreamweaver panels, such as the Behaviors, CSS Styles, HTML Styles, and Timelines panels.

In later chapters, we'll cover the interface options that control such things as tables, layers, frames, forms, markers, rulers, gridlines, and tracing images. With these options, Dreamweaver stands above other visual development tools.

 Hidden *contextual pop-up menus* can be accessed using right-click on Windows or Ctrl-click on the Macintosh. Use this shortcut when the book tells you to choose an option from the contextual menu. These menus vary, depending on which window or object you click.

The Document Window and Views

Web pages are composed in the Dreamweaver *Document window*, which can be viewed in several modes:

- Code view (View → Code) allows you to edit HTML source code directly.

- Design view (View → Design) is Dreamweaver's WYSIWYG mode.

- Code and Design view (View → Code and Design), shown in Figure 1-1, shows the Code and Design panes simultaneously. Resize the two panes by dragging the horizontal line that separates them. Use the View → Design View on Top option to reverse the location of the panes.

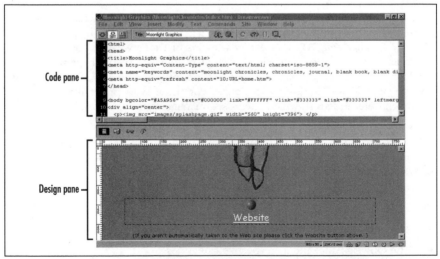

Figure 1-1: Code and Design view

You can switch view modes using the View → Switch Views command, Ctrl+Tab (Windows), or Opt+Tab (Macintosh). While in Code and Design view, the Switch Views command moves the cursor into the other pane; otherwise, it toggles between Code view and Design view.

Text can be typed directly into the Design pane. Dreamweaver automatically creates the necessary HTML when you insert objects using, say, the Objects panel. Edits performed in the Design pane are reflected immediately in the Code pane.

You can hand-edit the HTML code directly in the Code pane, but the visible results, if any, won't appear in the Design pane until it is refreshed. The Design pane refreshes automatically when switching from Code view to Design view, but not when switching from Code view to Code and Design view.

 After hand-editing HTML, use View → Refresh Design View, F5, Ctrl+Space (Windows), or Cmd+Space (Mac) to reevaluate the HTML in the Code pane and refresh the Design pane.

You can configure the following Code pane options under View → Code View Options:

Word Wrap
Turn on this option to wrap long lines of HTML code (this option does not affect text in the Design pane).

Line Numbers
This option provides line numbers for easier debugging.

Highlight Invalid HTML
This option helps to avoid hand-coding errors by highlighting unsupported and unmatched tags in yellow. Reevaluate the HTML in the Code pane by using the shortcuts in the preceding tip. The Design pane always highlights errors.

Syntax Coloring
This option highlights HTML tags and body text according to the settings under Edit → Preferences → Code Colors.

Auto Indent
This option indents text automatically according to the settings under Edit → Preferences → Code Format.

While in Code view, some menu options that are ordinarily available in Design view are inactive. You can use some menu options, such as those under the Insert menu in Code view. Use caution, however, because they'll insert HTML wherever your cursor is, which may put the HTML in an invalid place, such as outside the <html> tags.

Code view is convenient for viewing and editing other types of non-HTML documents, such as JavaScript (.js) files. Each document window has its own Code view, so you can use Code view for one page while using Design view for another

---

page. The older Code Inspector, opened using Window → Code Inspector (F10), shows the code of the current page. The Code Inspector is a legacy from earlier versions of Dreamweaver and has been superceded by Code view.

Toolbar

The Document window has a convenient *Toolbar* with icons for commonly used operations. Use View → Toolbar, Ctrl+Shift+T (Windows), or Cmd+Shift+T (Mac) to ensure that the Toolbar is visible. The Toolbar, which changes according to the type and contents of your document, lets you switch among view modes and access other common functions as indicated in Figure 1-2.

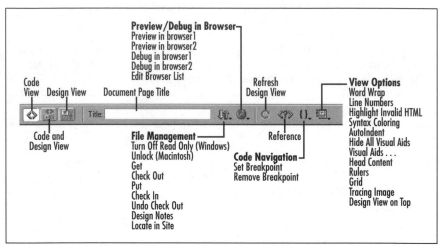

Figure 1-2: Toolbar buttons

Status Bar

The *status bar* at the bottom of the Document window, as shown in Figure 1-3, contains the Tag Selector, Window Size pop-up menu, and the Mini-launcher bar. It also shows the current document's size and estimated download time. The status bar can be configured under Edit → Preferences → Status Bar or by clicking the Edit Sizes option in the Window Size selector as described in Chapter 18.

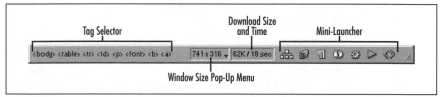

Figure 1-3: The status bar

Tag Selector

> The *Tag Selector* is visible only in Design view or when the Design pane is active in Code and Design view. It displays the HTML tags that control the currently selected item. The tag of the exact selection is shown in bold, and you can change the selection by clicking the other tags that appear in the Tag Selector. See "Tag Selector" in Chapter 7.

Window Size pop-up menu (Design view only)

> The *Window Size pop-up menu* makes it easy to preview your pages at various screen sizes. The usable screen area is usually less than the monitor resolution due to the toolbars and borders associated with typical browsers. Because HTML window sizes are fluid, this setting has no bearing on the window size when the document is viewed in the user's browser. Use frames or JavaScript to control the size of the window in which your HTML page is displayed.

Document size and estimated download time

> The document size shown in the Status bar is the size of the HTML page plus the size of any images or media files used in the document. The download time estimate is based on a 28.8 Kbps connection, but the target connection speed can be configured under Edit → Preferences → Status Bar. Most users have a 56 Kbps connection, but a more limited number have faster connections (ISDN, DSL, cable, satellite, and T1).

Mini-launcher

> The *Mini-launcher* is a much more compact and convenient version of the Launcher bar, discussed later in this chapter.

Objects Panel

The *Objects panel* offers quick access to the primary objects, such as images and tables, that you typically place within your HTML document. To insert text, simply click in the Document window and start typing. Dreamweaver inserts <p> tags whenever you press the Enter key or Return key.

The Objects panel has seven different categories—Characters, Common, Forms, Frames, Head, Invisibles, and Special—each providing links to tools and objects specific to that category. The Objects panel, shown in its Common category mode in Figure 1-4, is accessed via Window → Objects, Ctrl+F2 (Windows), or Cmd+F2 (Macintosh). You can switch categories by using the panel category selector menu indicated in Figure 1-4. The Objects panel can be customized as discussed in Chapter 19.

Clicking an icon in the Objects panel places the chosen object at the current cursor location (or you can drag the icon to the desired location in the Document window). Some objects require additional information to be entered via a dialog box before the object can be inserted. To insert an empty placeholder object (and bypass the dialog box), disable the Edit → Preferences → General → Show Dialog When Inserting Objects option, or hold down the Ctrl key (Windows) or Option key (Macintosh) while inserting the object. Properties of existing objects can be modified using the Property inspector.

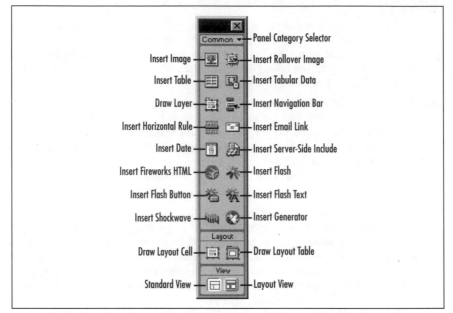

Figure 1-4: The Objects panel's Common category

> Use Ctrl-drag (Windows) or Opt-drag (Macintosh) to quickly dupli-
> cate an element on the page.

Table 1-1 lists the options available in each category of the Objects panel. See Chapter 19 for details on adding custom objects to the Objects panel. The Objects panel can also be configured to show icon labels using Edit → Preferences → General → Objects Panel → Icons and Text.

Table 1-1: Objects panel categories

Category	Inserts these objects	Notes
Characters	Line break	` `
	Nonbreaking space	` `
	Copyright	`&copy;`
	Registered trademark	`&reg;`
	Trademark	`&#153;`
	Pound	`&pound;`
	Yen	`&yen;`
	Euro	`&euro;`
	Left double quotes (")	`&#147;`
	Right double quotes (")	`&#148;`
	Em dash (—)	`&#151;`
	Other characters	Other ASCII characters, such as single quotes (see Figure 2-22)

Table 1-1: Objects panel categories (continued)

Category	Inserts these objects	Notes
Common	Image Rollover Image Table Tabular Data Draw Layer Navigation Bar Horizontal Rule Email Link Date Server-Side Include Fireworks HTML Flash Flash Button Flash Text Shockwave Generator	See Chapters 2, 3, and 5
Forms	Form Text Field Button Checkbox Radio Button List/Menu File Field Image Field Hidden Field Jump Menu	See Chapters 2 and 3
Frames	Left Frame Right Frame Top Frame Bottom Frame Left, Top-Left Corner, and Top Frames Left and Nested Top Frame Top and Nested Left Frame Split Frame Center	See Chapter 4
Head	Meta Keywords Description Refresh Base Link	See Chapter 2
Invisibles	Named Anchor Script Comment	See Chapter 2
Special	Applet Plugin ActiveX	See Chapter 5

Many of the objects inserted via the Objects panel can also be inserted using the keyboard shortcuts listed in Table 1-2.

Table 1-2: Object shortcut keys

Object	Windows	Macintosh
Line Break	Shift+Enter	Shift+Return
Nonbreaking Space	Ctrl+Shift+Space	Cmd+Shift+Space Opt+Space (Design pane only)
Image	Ctrl+Alt+I	Cmd+Opt+I
Table	Ctrl+Alt+T	Cmd+Opt+T
Flash Movie	Ctrl+Alt+F	Cmd+Opt+F
Shockwave Director Movie	Ctrl+Alt+D	Cmd+Opt+D
Make a Link	Ctrl+L	Cmd+L
Named Anchor	Ctrl+Alt+A	Cmd+Opt+A
Any external file	Drag the file from Explorer or Site window to the Document window	Drag the file from Finder or Site window to the Document window

Property Inspector

Use the *Property inspector* (PI) to display or edit properties of the currently selected element. There are several ways to open the Property inspector (if it is already open, most of the gestures close it):

- Select Window → Properties or Modify → Selection Properties.

- Press Ctrl+F3 (Windows) or Cmd+F3 (Macintosh).

- Double-click on an HTML element (this gesture does not open the Property inspector for some element types, such as text, and opens the file selection dialog box for other element types, such as images).

- Right-click (Windows) or Ctrl-click (Macintosh) and choose Properties from the contextual pop-up menu.

Figure 1-5 shows the Property inspector's appearance when a text object within a table is selected. The upper half of the Property inspector is the same for all text objects, but the lower half may differ. You can show or hide the lower half of the Property inspector using the Expand/Contract button indicated in Figure 1-5, or simply by double-clicking an unoccupied area within the Property inspector.

Table 1-3 lists the properties that are most commonly needed and available from the Property inspector at almost all times (and are also available via menu choices).

 To create a hyperlink, highlight an item, such as a piece of text, in the Document window and specify the destination document in the Link field of the Property inspector. You can drag-and-drop a file into the Link field or select a file using the Browse icon in the Property inspector.

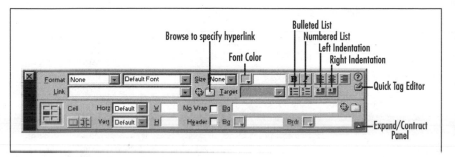

Figure 1-5: The Property inspector

We'll cover properties that modify images, layers, tables, and frames in later chapters. See Chapter 7 for coverage of the Quick Tag Editor (QTE), which is accessible from the Property inspector.

Table 1-3: Property inspector options

Menu option	Windows	Macintosh	Description
Window → Properties	Ctrl+F3	Cmd+F3	Opens or closes the Property inspector
Help → Using Dream-weaver	F1	F1	Provides context-sensitive help
Text → Paragraph Format	Ctrl+Shift+P	Cmd+Shift+P	Sets paragraph formatting
Text → Font	Alt-T, N	N/A	Selects font, reverts to default font, or adds a new font to the menu
Text → Style	Alt-T, S	N/A	Selects bold, italic, emphasis, or code style
Text → Color	Alt-T, R	N/A	Opens the Color dialog box to set text color
Text → Style → Bold	Ctrl+B	Cmd+B	Bolds selected text
Text → Style → Italic	Ctrl+I	Cmd+I	Italicizes selected text
Text → Align → Left	Ctrl+Alt+Shift+L	Cmd+Opt+Shift+L	Left-aligns text
Text → Align → Center	Ctrl+Alt+Shift+C	Cmd+Opt+Shift+C	Centers text
Text → Align → Right	Ctrl+Alt+Shift+R	Cmd+Opt+Shift+R	Right-aligns text
Text → List → Unordered List	Alt-T, I, U	N/A	Formats text as bulleted list
Text → List → Ordered List	Alt-T, I, O	N/A	Formats text as numbered list
Text → Outdent	Ctrl+Alt+[	Cmd+Opt+[	Removes any existing indentation
Text → Indent	Ctrl+Alt+]	Cmd+Opt+]	Indents text

Table 1-3: Property inspector options (continued)

Menu option	Windows	Macintosh	Description
Modify → Quick Tag Editor	Ctrl+T	Cmd+T	Edits tag for current element
Modify → Make Link	Ctrl+L	Cmd+L	Creates a hyperlink
Modify → Link Target	Alt-M, G	N/A	Changes a link's target. Specify target frame name, or _blank, _parent, _self, or _top

Reference Panel

The *Reference panel*, added in Dreamweaver 4 and shown in Figure 1-6, provides detailed documentation from O'Reilly & Associates. Open the Reference panel using Window → Reference. After choosing HTML, CSS, or JavaScript Reference from the Book pop-up menu in the panel, you can look up HTML tags and their attributes, CSS properties, or details on JavaScript objects, properties, and methods.

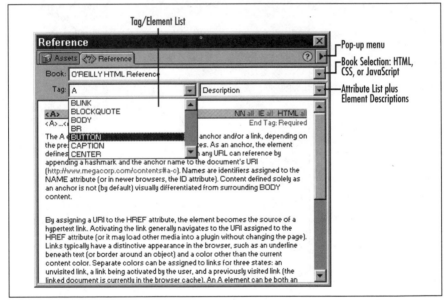

Figure 1-6: The Reference panel

For example, the O'Reilly HTML Reference provides a drop-down list of HTML tags. Selecting a tag displays its definition, compatibility, description, formatting requirements, and use within the Document Object Model (DOM) for both Microsoft Internet Explorer (IE) and Netscape Navigator (NN).

The arrow at the upper-right side of the Reference panel opens a pop-menu. The menu lets you change the font size of the text; it also includes a link to O'Reilly Books Online (the O'Reilly Safari subscription service).

Launcher Bar and Panel Shortcuts

The *Launcher,* accessible via Window → Launcher and shown in Figure 1-7, provides quick access to Dreamweaver's primary panels. The small icon in the Launcher bar's lower-right corner toggles its orientation between horizontal and vertical.

Figure 1-7: The Launcher bar

Table 1-4 lists additional ways to access all panels, not just those available on the Launcher. The Objects panel and Property inspector are not included in the Launcher bar by default but can be added using Edit → Preferences → Panels → Show in Launcher. The preferences also affect the Mini-launcher in the lower-right corner of the Document window, which is a more compact and convenient way to access the same options as the Launcher bar.

Table 1-4: Panel shortcuts

Window	Menu access	Windows	Macintosh
Objects panel	Window → Objects	Ctrl+F2	Cmd+F2
Property inspector	Window → Properties	Ctrl+F3	Cmd+F3
Launcher bar	Window → Launcher	Alt-W, U	N/A
Site Files view	Window → Site Files or Site → Site Files	F8	F8
Site Map view	Window → Site Map or Site → Site Map	Alt+F8	Opt+F8
Assets panel	Window → Assets	F11	F11
Behaviors panel	Window → Behaviors	Shift+F3	Shift+F3
Code Inspector	Window → Code Inspector	F10	F10
CSS Styles panel	Window → CSS Styles	Shift+F11	Shift+F11
Frames panel	Window → Frames	Shift+F2	Shift+F2
History panel	Window → History	Shift+F10	Shift+F10
HTML Styles panel	Window → HTML Styles	Ctrl+F11	Cmd+F11
Layers panel	Window → Frames	F2	F2
Library panel	Window → Library	Alt-W, I	N/A
Reference panel (open or close)	Window → Reference	Ctrl+Shift+F1	Cmd+Shift+F1
Reference tab	Help → Reference	Shift+F1	Shift+F1
Timelines panel	Window → Timelines	Shift+F9	Shift+F9
Templates panel	Window → Templates	Alt-W, M	N/A
Arrange panels	Window → Arrange Panels	Alt-W, G	N/A
Show/Hide panels	Window → Show Panels Window → Hide Panels	F4	F4

Table 1-4: Panel shortcuts (continued)

Window	Menu access	Windows	Macintosh
Minimize all panels	Window → Minimize All	Shift+F4	Not supported
Restore all panels	Window → Restore All	Alt+Shift+F4	Not supported
Document window	Window → *docName*	N/A	N/A
Quick Tag Editor	Modify → Quick Tag Editor	Ctrl+T	Cmd+T

Docking Panels

The number of panels in Dreamweaver can be overwhelming. Fortunately, two or more panels can be docked (combined) into a single panel with multiple *tabs*. For example the Reference and Assets panels are actually two separate tabs within a single floating panel. You can move a tab from one panel to another by dragging the tab (not the title bar of the panel), onto another panel. Figure 1-8 shows the outline of the Behaviors tab being dragged over another panel. When the mouse is released, the Behaviors tab is moved to the new panel. Drag and drop a tab outside of any existing panel to create a new, separate panel containing only that tab.

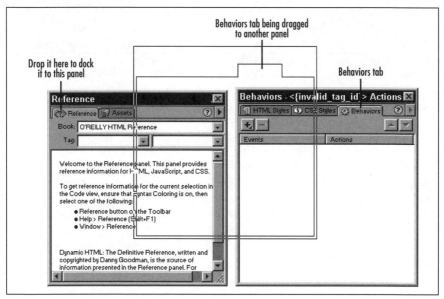

Figure 1-8: Moving the Behaviors tab from one panel to another

You can't dock the Property inspector and Launcher bar with other panels. However, you can drop other panels into the Objects panel to turn it into a dockable panel (try it!).

To arrange all of your panels neatly, select Window → Arrange Panels, which returns Dreamweaver's open panels to their original default positions.

This chapter covered the common UI elements you'll use within Dreamweaver. Chapter 2 focuses on how to create common HTML elements within a web page. It also covers issues related to the formatting, structure, meta information, and color schemes associated with documents.

CHAPTER 2

Core Objects

This chapter shows how to add common HTML elements to your web pages. The core objects included in almost every document are as follows:

- Document `<head>` objects including `<title>`, `<link>`, `<base>`, and `<meta>` tags
- Hyperlinks
- Images and image maps
- Text and page formatting options
- Characters
- Hidden comments, scripts, and line-break tags.

Head Elements

This section covers the tools that ensure proper usage of HTML elements within your document's `<head>` block. Dreamweaver 4 provides easy access to the `<title>`, `description`, and `keywords` elements (which provide information for search engines), and the `<meta>`, `<base>`, and `<link>` elements (which provide instructions to client and server software that interacts with your document).

Prior to Version 4, Dreamweaver showed `<head>` tags in Code view only. As of DW4, head content can be accessed using the Head Content bar, shown in Figure 2-1, in Design view or Code and Design view. The Head Content bar is opened using View → Head Content, Ctrl+Shift+W (Windows), or Cmd+Shift+W (Macintosh). In Code view, the Head Content bar isn't available, but you can still hand-edit the `<head>` tags.

To edit the attributes of a head element in the Property inspector, double-click the element's icon in the Head Content bar. To delete an extraneous head element, select its icon from the Head Content bar and press the Delete key (or hand-edit the HTML in Code view).

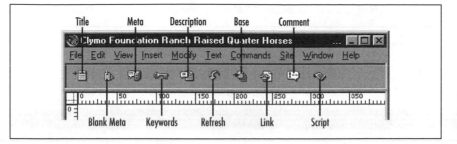

Figure 2-1: The Head Content bar

The <head> tags and their attributes are discussed in the following sections. Comment tags are discussed later in this chapter under "Hidden Objects."

Title Tag

The <title> element's text is displayed in a web browser's title bar and is used as the default filename when saving the document to disk. Search engines also use the title to index your page.

The <title> element can be set in the Page Properties dialog box (Modify → Page Properties) or in the Property inspector (accessed via the Head Content bar's Title icon).

Use Edit → Find and Replace, Ctrl+F (Windows), or Cmd+F (Macintosh) to retitle documents that use the default title ("Untitled Document"). You can generate a list of untitled documents using Site → Reports → HTML Reports → Untitled Documents.

Meta Tags

Dreamweaver can create four types of <meta> tags—*content*, *keywords*, *description*, and *refresh*—without hand-coding. (In Code view, you can create any <meta> element data you like.)

All <meta> elements follow the general format:

```
<head>
  <meta name="label" content="content associated with label">
  <meta http-equiv="instruction-name" content="instructions">
</head>
```

Do not treat the **name** and **http-equiv** attributes interchangeably. Use the **http-equiv** attribute, which is more widely read by both browsers and servers, to identify document languages and provide instructions for documents displayed using

---

HTTP response message headers. Use the `name` attribute to provide information such as keywords and document descriptions, as shown in the following example:

```
<meta http-equiv="Content-Type" content="text/html; charset=iso-8859-1">
<meta name="keywords" content="testing web site construction">
```

Content attribute

Dreamweaver automatically adds a `<meta>` element that identifies the content type (usually `text/html`) and the character set (usually `iso-8859-1`) to each HTML document.

The `<meta>` element shown in Figure 2-2 would appear in your HTML document as follows:

```
<meta http-equiv="Content-Type" content="text/html; charset=iso-8859-1">
```

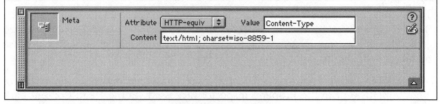

Figure 2-2: The Property inspector for the Meta element

You can insert additional `<meta>` elements using Insert → Head Tags → Meta, which opens the Insert Meta dialog box. In the dialog box, select the attribute type (either `name` or `http-equiv`), specify the attribute's value (such as `Content-Type`), and specify the attribute's content (such as `text/html; charset=iso-8859-1`). Each `<meta>` element can be edited in the Property inspector (accessed by double-clicking the corresponding icon in the Head Content bar).

Keywords attribute

The keywords element (`<meta name="keywords">`) provides a list of keywords that can be indexed by search engines (about 90 percent of web hits are generated from major search sites).

Use the Insert Keywords dialog box (Insert → Head Tags → Keywords) to enter a comma-delimited list of words and short phrases that describe the contents of your document.

The keywords element in the `<head>` portion of your HTML document might appear as follows:

```
<meta name="keywords" content="ranch raised horses, roping horses,
rope horses, rodeo horses, barrel racing, team roping, bull dogging">
```

Modify existing keywords using the Property inspector (accessed via the Keywords icon in the Head Content bar) or by hand-editing the HTML.

To modify existing keywords, do not reselect Insert → Head Tags → Keywords, as it would create a second keywords element.

Search engines often ignore secondary keywords elements. Worse, the secondary elements might be interpreted as trying to influence your search position unfairly, which would cause search services to remove your HTML document from the search results entirely. Delete an extraneous keywords element by deleting its icon from the Head Content bar (or by hand-editing the HTML).

Description attribute

Search engines use the description element (<meta name="description">) to determine a document's relevancy. However, unlike the keywords element, which is never displayed, the description element should provide a description that search engines can display along with the URLs found during a search.

 Not all search engines will use your description on their search results page. Include a similar title-like statement at the start of your page's body text so that a search engine can use whichever it prefers.

Use the Insert Description dialog box (Insert → Head Tags → Description) to enter a succinct sentence, containing as many of your keywords as possible, that describes your HTML document. Descriptions do not need to be grammatically correct, but they should express the primary point of the document. Most search engines index only the first 256 characters of the description.

The description element in the <head> portion of your HTML document might appear as follows:

```
<meta name="Description" content="Clymo Quarter Horses -
foundation, ranch raised, rodeo, rope and arena horses." >
```

Modify existing description elements using the Property inspector (accessed via the Description icon in the Head Content bar) or by hand-editing the HTML.

 To modify an existing description, do not reselect Insert → Head Tags → Description, as doing so would create a second description element. This second element would either be ignored by search engines or confuse them, so the entire page would be ignored.

Delete an extraneous description element by deleting its icon from the Head Content bar (or by hand-editing the HTML).

Refresh attribute

A refresh element will redirect a web browser to a new URL or refresh the current document after the specified delay. A refresh element is useful if an HTML page moves (to accommodate visitors with outdated bookmarks). It is also used to periodically refresh a page with updated data, such as stock quotes.

To add a refresh element, open the Insert Refresh dialog box (Insert → Head Tags → Refresh), as seen in Figure 2-3. Specify the delay in seconds and choose whether to load a new document or reload the current one.

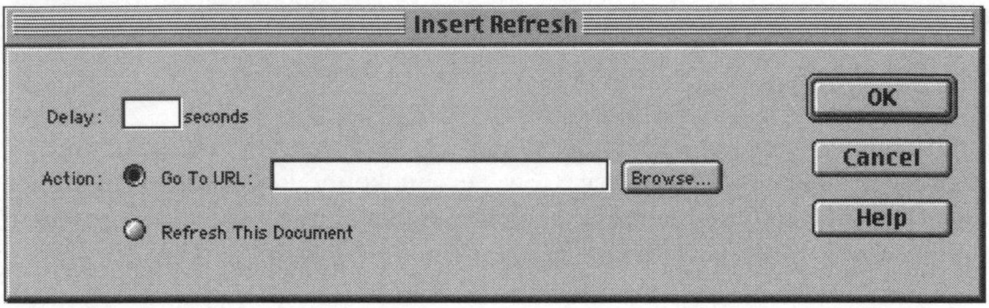

Figure 2-3: The Insert Refresh dialog box

Use the Refresh icon in the Head Content bar to modify an existing refresh tag. Reselecting Insert → Head Tags → Refresh adds a second refresh tag to your document, leading to unpredictable results.

To go to another URL immediately, specify 0 for the Delay (specify a longer delay to allow a user to read the current page before loading a new page).

Specifying a 15-second delay after which *about.htm* should be loaded creates the following <meta> tag:

```
<meta http-equiv="refresh" content="15;URL=about.htm">
```

Specifying that the current document should refresh after 60 seconds creates the following <meta> tag.

```
<meta http-equiv="refresh" content="60">
```

Avoid refreshing the current page more than every 30 seconds.

Base Tag

The optional <base> tag defines the *base folder* (reference point) from which all document-relative links in a document should be interpreted. For example, the following <base> tag causes any document-relative URL to be resolved relative to *http://clymo-quarter-horses.com*:

```
<base target=_blank href="http://clymo-quarter-horses.com">
```

Based on this information, a link that referenced *rainy.htm* would load the document *http://clymo-quarter-horses.com/rainy.htm*. The `target=_blank` attribute opens the document in a new blank window (`target` defaults to `_self`). See the "Targeting Frames" section in Chapter 4 for details on the `target` attribute. In the absence of the `<base>` tag, document-relative URLs are resolved relative to the folder containing the current web page.

To insert a `<base>` tag, use the Insert Base dialog box (Insert → Head Tags → Base). Specify a reference point in the Href field, which can be either an absolute URL, such as *http://www.clymo-quarter-horses.com/*, or a directory, such as *stallions/*. Specify the *http://* prefix only when using an absolute reference (see Table 2-3).

> Use the Base icon in the Head Content bar to adjust an existing `<base>` tag. Reselecting Insert → Head Tags → Base will add a second `<base>` tag to your document, which is erroneous and non-compliant.

Delete an extraneous `<base>` tag by deleting its icon from the Head Content bar (or by hand-editing the HTML).

Link Tag

A `<link>` tag refers to another document, such as a cascading stylesheet or a document in a different language. It should not be confused with `<a>` tags, which are used to create hyperlinks.

Use the Insert Link dialog box (Insert → Head Tags → Link), as shown in Figure 2-4, to insert a `<link>` tag. Unlike the tags discussed earlier, a document can have multiple `<link>` tags (each new `<link>` tag is represented by a separate icon in the Head Content bar).

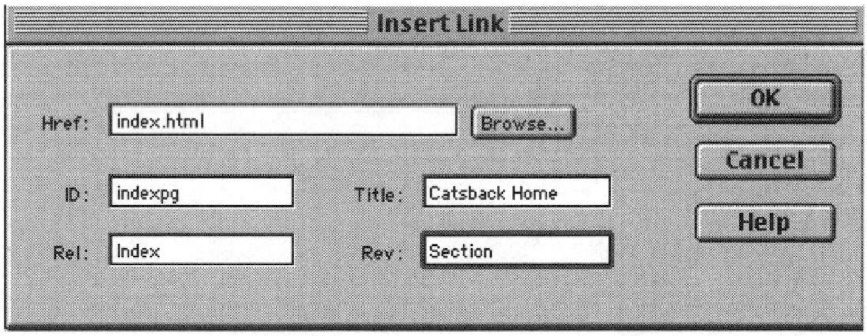

Figure 2-4: The Insert Link dialog box

Specify the fields for your <link> tag, as described in Table 2-1.

Table 2-1: The <link> tag attribute values

Attribute	Description
Href	The URL of the document to be linked.
Title	The title (name) of the document being linked.
ID	An identifier for the link, which can be used by scripts or other applications to reference the document.
Rel	The relationship when moving from the current document to the target (i.e., next would indicate that the target document is the next in a series of pages).
Rev	The relationship when moving from the target document to the current document (i.e., if Rel was next, then Rev would be prev).

The Rel and Rev attributes use the following keywords to define the relationship between the two documents:

Alternate
> A substitute document, often in a different language or media type. For example, it may be a GIF image in lieu of a Flash movie or a French translation of an English page.

Stylesheet
> An external stylesheet (typically a *.css* file).

Start
> The first in a series of documents (used by search engines).

Next
> The next document in a series of documents.

Prev
> The previous document in a series of documents.

Contents
> The table of contents.

Chapter
> One chapter in a collection of documents.

Section
> One section within a chapter.

Subsection
> One subsection within a section of a document.

Copyright
> A document containing the copyright statement for the current document.

Index
> An index for the current document.

Glossary
> A glossary of terms for the current document.

Appendix
> An appendix for a collection of documents.

Help

Help documentation for the current document or for a collection of documents.

Bookmark

A link to a key point of entry within another document.

For example, to link to a cascading stylesheet, you can set the Href to point to the *.css* file and set Rel to stylesheet. Of course, there are easier ways to create <link> tags for external stylesheets, as described in Chapter 10.

Selecting Insert → Head Tags → Link inserts a new, separate <link> tag in your document. To edit an existing <link> in the Property inspector, double-click its Link icon in the Head Content bar.

Hyperlinks

Naturally, Dreamweaver lets you create *hyperlinks* (a.k.a. *links*) that lead to other documents. Links begin with a protocol, such as *http*, as shown in Table 2-2.

Dreamweaver allows you to create and set links in several ways:

- You can insert a link using Modify → Make Link, Ctrl+L (Windows), or Cmd+L (Macintosh). This command opens the Select File dialog box in which you can select a local file or enter the link address in the URL field.

- You can also select the text to act as the link, and then provide the full address, including the protocol such as *http://*, within the Link field of the Property inspector, as shown in Figure 2-5. You can drag-and-drop a file into the Link field, or select a file using the Browse button next to the Link field in the Property inspector.

- You can right-click (Windows) or Ctrl-click (Macintosh) on a selection in the Document window and choose Make Link from the contextual menu.

- If you select an item with an existing link, you can choose Change Link, Remove Link, or Open Linked Page from the Modify menu or the contextual menu.

- Any link added to a document is automatically added to the Site list of the Assets panel's URLs category. Links can be applied to the selected item using the Apply button in the Assets panel (see Chapter 6).

- Links can also be manipulated in the Site Map window (you can use the contextual menu to access the Link to New File, Link to Existing File, Change Link, and Remove Link commands.) See "The Site Map Only View" in Chapter 6 for details.

Figure 2-5 shows a hyperlink in the Property inspector.

All links in a DW document will begin with the *file:///* protocol until the document is saved. Save your document before testing links. Test links using File → Preview in Browser (F12). URLs and anchor names are case sensitive on most web servers even though they may be case insensitive when tested locally. Links that work when tested locally may fail when uploaded to a server. (The domain name portion of a URL is not case sensitive.) You can set target frame in which a linked document opens using the Target field in the Property inspector. See the "Targeting Frames" section in Chapter 4.

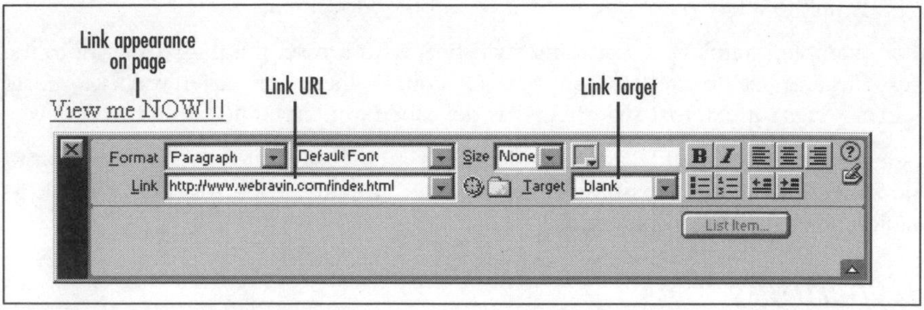

Figure 2-5: Web page link set up

Protocols

A *protocol* is the first portion of a URL. Most protocols are followed by the name of the server, such as *www.neoregon.net*, or it's equivalent IP (Internet Protocol) address, such as *192.41.42.11*. The server name is followed by the name of the file that you wish to download, such as *index.html*. Other protocols, such as *javascript* and *mailto*, are followed by a command or email address.

Table 2-2: Web protocol prefixes

Protocol prefix	Description
http://	The HyperText Transfer Protocol displays web pages. If the filename is omitted, most web servers look for a default file of the name *index. html, index.htm, home.html, home.htm, default.html,* or *default.htm.* (Some servers display a directory listing if a default file is not present in a folder. Either configure your server to not display a directory listing, or ensure that all folders contain an appropriate default file.) Specifying with an absolute URL: *http://www.macromedia.com/index.html* *http://192.41.42.11* Specifying with a relative URL: *http:subfolder/index.html* *subfolder/index.html* Specifying HTTP port (default HTTP port is 80): *http://www.macromedia.com:80/* *http://192.41.42.11:80/*
ftp://	The File Transfer Protocol is used to download files, not display them. For example: *ftp://ftp.macromedia.com/downloads/demo.zip* Specifying FTP port (default FTP port is 26): *ftp://ftp.macromedia.com/downloads:26/* Specifying a username (login name), in this case "luis": *ftp://luis@ftp.macromedia.com/downloads/* Specifying username ("luis") and password ("testing"): *ftp://luis:testing@ftp.macromedia.com/downloads/*

Table 2-2: Web protocol prefixes (continued)

Protocol prefix	Description
nntp://	The Network News Transfer Protocol is used by news servers: *nntp://news.macromedia.com:119/rec.pets/100*
news:	The News protocol accesses either an entire newsgroup or a single message from Usenet. Entire newsgroup: *news:rec.pets* Individual message: *news:1234@news.macromedia.com*
https://	The Secure HyperText Transfer Protocol is used for financial and other sensitive transactions: *https://buy.macromedia.com/placeorder.bin* Access with username ("luis") and password ("testing"): *https://luis:testing@buy.macromedia.com/order.bin*
file:////	The File protocol accesses local files on the user's disk drive: Windows: *file:///C\/Windows/testing/sample.html* Macintosh: *file:////MacHD/testing/sample.html*
javascript:	The javascript protocol executes a JavaScript/JScript command. For example: *javascript:myfunction(name)* would run the function myfunction, passing it the parameter name.
vbscript:	The vbscript protocol executes a VBScript (Visual Basic) command (supported in IE only). For example: *vbscript:myfunction(total)* would run the function myfunction, passing it the parameter total.
mailto:	The Simple Mail Transfer Protocol (SMTP) is used to send email (see Table 2-4): *mailto:book_requests@oreilly.com*
named anchors	Named anchors mark a specific location in a document. To reference a named anchor on the current page, use: *#anchorname* To reference a named anchor on another page, use: *http://www.myserver.com/index.html#top* To reference a labeled scene within a Shockwave file: *http://www.shockwave.com/coolgame.dcr#intro*
Telnet	The telnet protocol establishes a terminal session with a remote server. Telnet with username "luis" and password "testing": *telnet://luis:testing@macromedia.com*
Gopher	A connection to a Gopher server. For example: *gopher://macromedia.com:70/*

Absolute and Relative URLs

Absolute addresses specify the complete URL, including the domain name, such as *http://www.macromedia.com*. Site root-relative addresses start with a forward slash (/) and specify a file relative to the root folder of the site (the one containing the site's home page). Document-relative addresses specify the location of a file relative the current document. Several variations are shown in Table 2-3.

Table 2-3: Absolute and relative URLs

Example	Description
http://server.domain.com/home.html	An absolute URL.
/home.html	A site root-relative URL specifying the home page in the root folder.
/images/myimage.gif	A site root-relative URL specifying a *.gif* file in the *images* subfolder one level down from the root folder.
stuff/index.html	A document-relative URL specifying a document one folder below the current folder. The *http:* protocol is assumed.
./stuff/index.html	The same as the prior entry. The period (.) represents the current folder
../myimage.gif	Specifies a file in the folder immediately above the current folder. The two periods (..) indicate the parent directory.
../images/myimage.gif	Specifies an image in a subfolder adjacent to the current folder.

Email Links

Clicking on an email link opens a new message window in the user's default email program and automatically fills in the To address field. Email links can be added to your HTML document in three ways:

- By selecting Insert → Email Link and providing the link text and address in the Insert Email Link dialog box, as shown in Figure 2-6.

- By clicking the Insert Email Link button in the Objects panel's Common category, which also opens the Insert Email Link dialog box.

- By highlighting existing text in your document and specifying an email address of the form *mailto:username@domainname.com* in the Link field of the Property inspector.

 Provide the *mailto:* prefix when entering the link manually in the Property inspector, but not when using the Insert Email Link dialog box, where it is added automatically.

Email me NOW!!!

Insert Email Link

Text: Email me NOW!!!

E-Mail: heather@webravin.com

OK

Cancel

Help

Figure 2-6: The Insert Email Link dialog box

A *mailto* link merely creates a new email message. The user must send the email via her email program manually. To emulate sending email from a web page, many developers use POST to submit data to a CGI script. For example, the free FormMail CGI script available from Matt's Script Archive at *http://www.worldwidemart.com/scripts/formmail.shtml* parses the information in a form and sends it to the designated email address.

Email links can also specify a default subject, message, and addressees using the formats shown in Table 2-4. Not all email programs support all attributes of the *mailto* protocol. For example, a user's email program may not fill in the body of the email automatically. Both Netscape Messenger 6 and Microsoft's Outlook 2000 support all email attributes.

Table 2-4: Mail link attributes

Added information	Example of format
CC	*mailto:joe@macromedia.com?CC=heather@macromedia.com*
Subject	*mailto:joe@macromedia.com?Subject=This is the subject*
Body	*mailto:joe@macromedia.com?body=This is the body text*
BCC	*mailto:joe@macromedia.com?BCC=heather@macromedia.com*
To	Separate multiple recipients with a comma and space, as in: *mailto:joe@macromedia.com, heather@macromedia.com*

The following example creates an email message to be sent to *heather@macromedia.com*, with a CC sent to two additional recipients and a BCC to another recipient. It also sets the subject line and body text.

> *mailto:heather@macromedia.com?Subject=From my Web Site&*
> *CC=joe@macromedia.com, jim@macromedia.com&BCC=bill@macromedia.*
> *com&Body=this is a quick message.*

Note that the first attribute is separated from the *mailto* recipient by a question mark (?), and each subsequent item is separated with an ampersand (&) without any intervening spaces. Both CC and BCC must be in capital letters for the email to be properly addressed.

Question marks within the subject or body should be enclosed within quotation marks. If using double quotes to delimit the `href` attribute of your email link, use single quotes to delimit the subject and body strings, and vice versa. For example:

> *href="mailto:joe@macromedia.com?subject='Are you okay?' "*

Named Anchors

Named anchors define destination points within a document. After creating an anchor, you'll typically create a link that refers to it from within the same document or from another document. Place anchors *preceding* the heading or paragraph that you want to be displayed when the user follows the link.

To insert a named anchor at the cursor location, select Insert → Invisible Tags → Named Anchor, Ctrl+Alt+A (Windows), or Cmd+Opt+A (Macintosh). Provide the name of the anchor in the Insert Named Anchor dialog box, shown in Figure 2-7. In Code view, Dreamweaver indicates the anchor's location using a yellow anchor icon (see Figure 2-23).

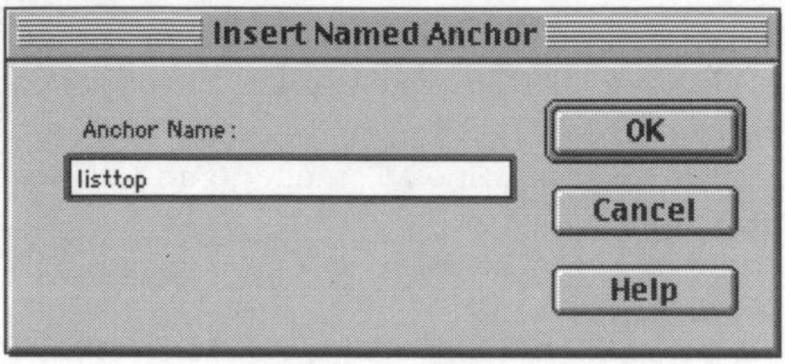

Figure 2-7: The Insert Named Anchor dialog box

To link to an anchor within the current document, create a link (as described earlier) using the following format:

> #linkname

To link to an anchor in another document, append the anchor name to the URL. The following example links to an anchor named *bottom* in the *demo.html* file, assumed to be in the same folder as the current HTML file:

> demo.html#bottom

The following example links to an anchor named *middle* in the *index.html* file at an absolute location:

> http://www.macromedia.com/index.html#middle

Anchor names and links to them are case sensitive. A link to a non-existent (or misspelled) anchor name causes the browser to jump to the top of the document (as if no such anchor exists).

Images and Image Maps

Dreamweaver allows you to work with web-compatible images (GIFs, JPEGs, and PNGs) in a variety of ways, including:

- Positioning and resizing images on a page
- Client-side image maps
- Rollover images and navigation bars
- Web photo albums

Inserting Images

Insert images using Insert → Image or by clicking the Insert Image icon in the Objects panel's Common category. In the Select Image Source dialog box, shown in Figure 2-8, select the file to link to, or enter the image's URL manually. Choose Relative To Document from the pop-up menu to create a URL relative to the current document. Choose Relative To Site Root to create a URL relative to the root folder of the site. To create an absolute URL, specify the entire path, including the server, such as *http://www.macromedia.com/images/biplane.gif*. Use the Preview Images checkbox to preview both local and remote files.

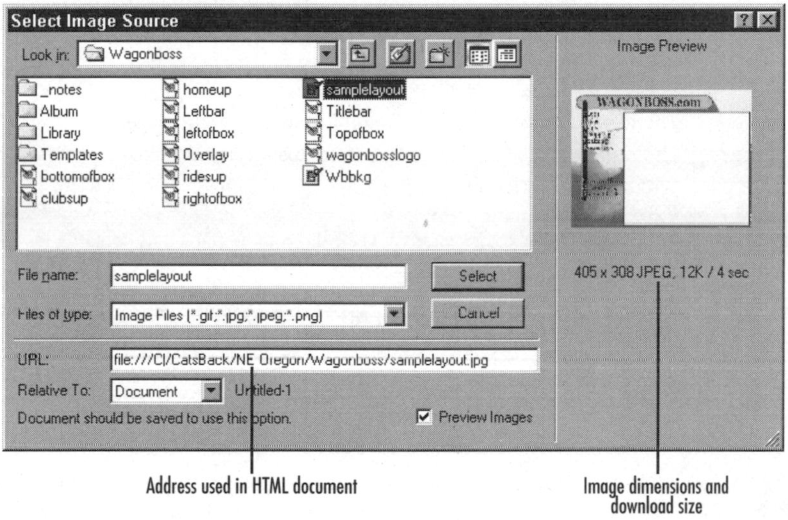

Figure 2-8: The Select Image Source dialog box

Once an image is inserted, use the Property inspector to set the <img> tag's options. Figure 2-9 shows the Property inspector when an image is selected. Double-clicking an image in the Design view opens the Property inspector and prompts you to reselect an image file for the src attribute of the <img> tag.

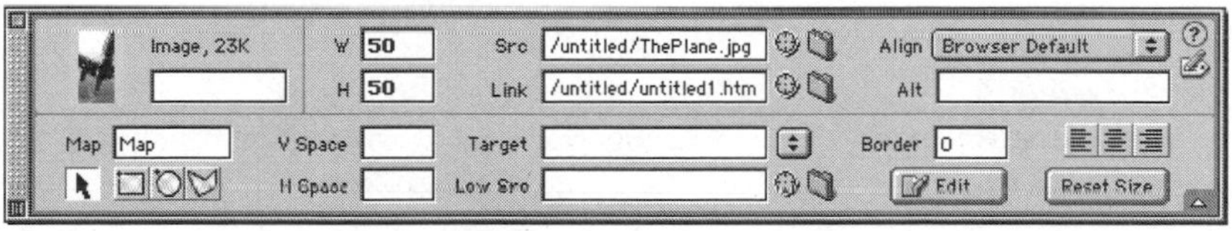

Figure 2-9: The Property inspector for images

Table 2-5 explains the Property inspector options for images.

Table 2-5: Image options

Option	Description
Name	A name for the image, which is required to reference the image in scripts or in Dreamweaver behaviors.
W (width)	The width of the image in pixels, which defaults to the image's original width, based on 72 pixels per inch (ppi) on a Macintosh and 96 ppi on Windows. An image formatted for a Windows machine appears smaller on a Macintosh.
H (height)	The height of the image in pixels, which defaults to the image's original height (based on 72 ppi on the Macintosh and 96 ppi on Windows).
Src	The absolute or relative URL of the image file. See Table 2-3.
Link	The absolute or relative URL of the file to open when this image is clicked.
Align	See details in the section following this table.
Alt	Provides a text description of the image for web browsers that don't display images. Required for HTML 4.0 compliance.
V Space	The vertical space to reserve around this image on the page.
H Space	The horizontal space to reserve around this image on the page.
Border	Width of the border, in pixels, to apply around the image. Use 0 for no border.
Map	The name of the `<map>` element (i.e., the image map) that contains instructions for providing hot links over the image.
Low Src	The URL of the image to load in low-resolution browsers. Supported by Netscape only. The preferred approach is to use interlaced images, which display at a lower resolution until the graphic is fully downloaded. The Low Src option doesn't appear in the Property inspector if the image was created in Fireworks.

 Height and Width can be specified in the Property inspector using any supported units, such as percent (%), pixels (px), picas (pc), points (pt), inches (in), millimeters (mm), centimeters (cm), font height (em), and the height of x in the current font (ex). Specify units without an intervening space, such as 50pt to indicate 50 points. Dreamweaver converts the units to pixels. For example, if you specify a dimension of 1in, Dreamweaver will convert it to 96 pixels on Windows or 72 pixels on a Macintosh.

The ten possible values for the Align option are:

Browser Default
> The default is usually bottom alignment.

Baseline
> Aligns the image's bottom with the baseline of the first line of text.

Top
> Aligns the image's top with the top of the first line of text.

Middle
> Aligns the image's middle with the baseline of the first line of text.

Bottom
> Aligns the image's bottom with the baseline of the first line of text.

TextTop
> Aligns the image's top with the top of the first line of text.

Absolute Middle
> Aligns the image's middle with the middle of the first line of text.

Absolute Bottom
> Aligns the image's bottom with the bottom of the first line of text.

Left
> Aligns the image flush left on the page. Text is shown to its right.

Right
> Aligns the image flush right on the page. Text is shown to its left.

Any image added to a document is automatically added to the Site list of the Assets panel's Images category. Images from the Assets panel can be inserted into other documents as described in Chapter 6.

Client-Side Image Maps

A *client-side image map* uses a <map> tag (see Example 2-1) to define multiple clickable areas, each with a separate link, for a single graphic image. The browser detects which link was clicked before contacting the server to fulfill the request. Each image can be tied to one <map> tag only unless it is controlled by a script. Use the Property inspector's rectangle, oval, and polygon tools to draw *hotspots* (clickable regions) for your image map, as shown in Figure 2-10.

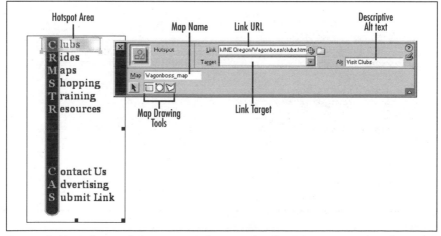

Figure 2-10: A client-side image map drawn using the Property inspector's hotspot tools

Use View → Visual Aids → Image Maps to show or hide the hotspot regions (which ordinarily appear in light blue). Enable the Edit → Preferences → Invisible Elements → Client-Side Image Maps checkbox to show a small icon representing the <map> tag.

You can specify the following settings for each hotspot:

Map
> The map name is typically the same for all hotspots on a single image. If your image has multiple states controlled by a script, each state can have a separate <map> tag; otherwise, an image should be referenced by only one <map> tag.

Link
> The URL of the document linked to this hotspot.

Target
> The target frame in which the linked document will open. The frame can be any valid document name, such as _blank, _self, _parent, or _top. It defaults to _self. See the "Targeting Frames" section in Chapter 4.

Alt
> An alternative text string for web browsers that don't display images and is also displayed before the image downloads (required to comply with the HTML 4.0 and XHTML accessibility standards).

Example 2-1 shows a simple image map using the <area> element to define the multiple clickable areas of the image. As usual, you can use Dreamweaver's visual tools while it handles the housekeeping chores for you.

Example 2-1: Client-side image map

```
<img src="/images/pagetop.gif"
     width="400" height="100"
     align="bottom" border="0"
     usemap="#cbcmap">
<map name="cbcmap">
  <area shape="rect"
        coords="4,4,55,100"
        href="logo.html"
        alt="home page"
        title="home page">
  <area shape="rect"
        coords="88,9,364,53"
        href="catsback.html"
        alt="company info"
        title="company info">
</map>
```

Rollover Images and Navigation Bars

Dreamweaver can create *rollover images* and *navigation bars* without requiring hand coding. Chapter 13 takes a deeper look at rollover images and navigation bars, but this section covers their basic use.

Rollover images

Rollover images provide a rollover state for your page's buttons and are inserted using Insert → Interactive Images → Rollover Image. The button's two states are defined in the Insert Rollover Image dialog box, as shown in Figure 2-11. If the mouse is over the image, the Rollover Image graphic is displayed; otherwise, the Original Image graphic is displayed. Rollover images work only in browsers that support JavaScript (see Table 12-1 and Table 12-3). For browsers that don't support JavaScript, or if the user has disabled JavaScript, the browser always displays the Original Image graphic.

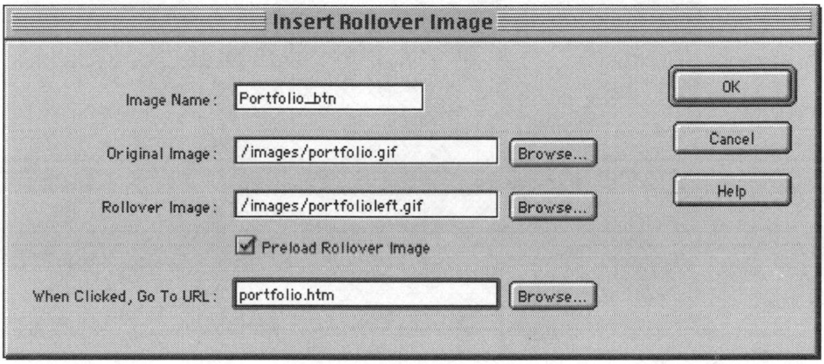

Figure 2-11: The Insert Rollover Image dialog box

The Insert Rollover Image dialog box has five options, as shown in Table 2-6.

Table 2-6: Insert Rollover Image dialog box options

Control	Description
Image Name	A required text name used to identify the image in JavaScript.
Original Image	The relative or absolute URL of the image displayed when the mouse is not over the button.
Rollover Image	The relative or absolute URL of the image displayed when the mouse is over the button.
Preload Rollover Image	This option preloads the rollover image prior to its display. Enable this option to ensure a smooth rollover transition.
When Clicked Go To URL	The relative or absolute URL of the destination to which to link.

Both images used in your rollover effect should be the same size; otherwise, the Rollover Image graphic is scaled to fit the area taken up by the Original Image graphic. Chapter 13 explains how to create so-called *disjoint rollovers* in which rolling over a button changes a separate page element.

Navigation bars

You can create a navigation bar with multiple buttons, as shown in Figure 2-12, by using Insert → Interactive Images → Navigation Bar.

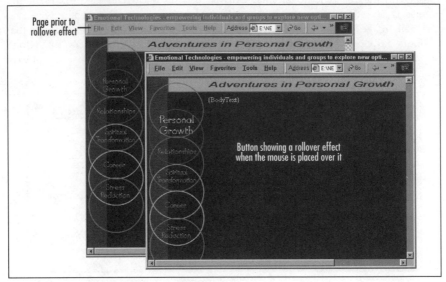

Figure 2-12: An example navigation bar

A navigation bar automatically shows the button for the current page in the highlighted (down) state to indicate which page the user is viewing.

 Navigation bars are intended for frames-based sites. Using a navigation bar with a nonframes-based document adds excess JavaScript without the benefit of its page-tracking features.

In the Insert Navigation Bar dialog box, shown in Figure 2-13, use the plus (+), minus (–), and arrow buttons to add, remove, or rearrange elements (i.e., buttons) in the Nav Bar Elements list.

The last two options in the dialog box (and in Table 2-7) apply to the navigation bar as a whole. The rest of the attributes in Table 2-7 pertain to *each* navigation bar element. Highlight each element in the Nav Bar Elements list to set its attributes.

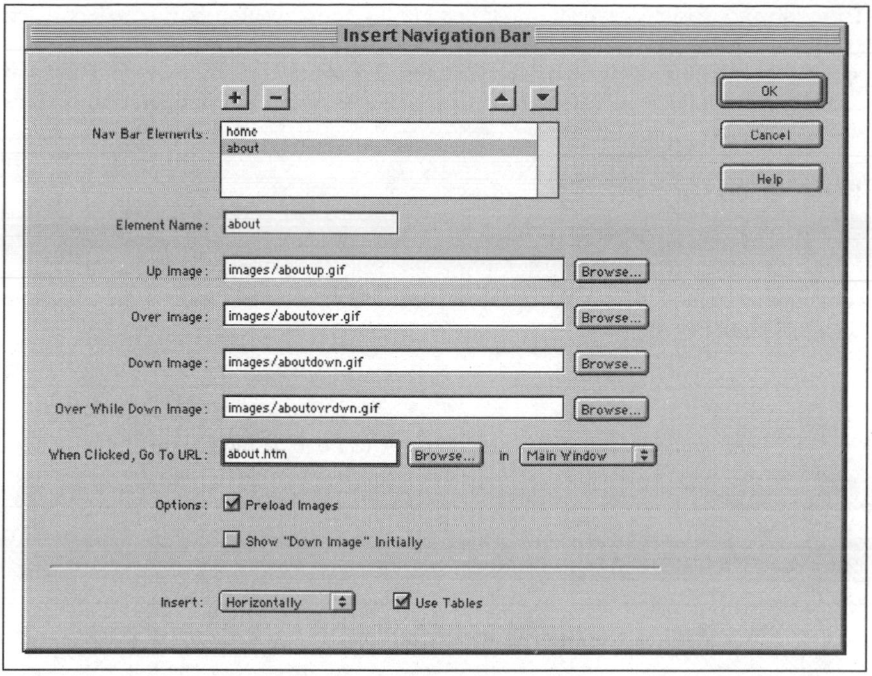

Figure 2-13: The Insert Navigation Bar dialog box

Table 2-7: Navigation bar options for each element

Control	Description
Element Name	A required text name used to identify the image in JavaScript.
Up Image	The URL of the image displayed by default when the mouse is not over the button.
Over Image (optional)	The URL of the image to display when the mouse is over the button.
Down Image (optional)	The URL of the image to display when the image button is clicked. See the Show "Down Image" Initially option.
Over While Down Image (optional)	The URL of the image to display when the mouse button was pressed before the mouse was rolled over the image.
When Clicked, Go To URL...in	The URL of the document to open when the button is clicked. Specify an optional target after the ...in prompt.
Preload Images	Enable this option to preload the image states for smoother rollovers.
Show "Down Image" Initially	Enable this option to use the Down Image instead of the Up Image as the initial state for this button. (An asterisk is shown next to Nav Bar Elements for which this option is enabled.)
Insert horizontally or vertically	This option determines whether the buttons in the navigation bar are arranged horizontally or vertically.
Use Tables	If enabled, this option uses tables to position the buttons; otherwise, layers are used (appropriate for 4.0+ browsers only).

To modify an existing navigation bar use Modify → Navigation Bar, or select Insert → Interactive Images → Navigation Bar and click OK when asked if you wish to modify the existing navigation bar. Chapter 13 explains additional navigation bar configuration options, including how to access the advanced configuration options shown in Figure 13-6.

Web Photo Album

The Web Photo Album option creates a document showing all images stored in a single directory, which is ideal for images from your latest vacation, business convention, or dog show. To create a Web Photo Album, select Commands → Create Web Photo Album.

The Create Web Photo Album option is active only if Fireworks 3 or later is installed. It requires all images to be in a single directory.

The Create Web Photo Album dialog box is shown in Figure 2-14.

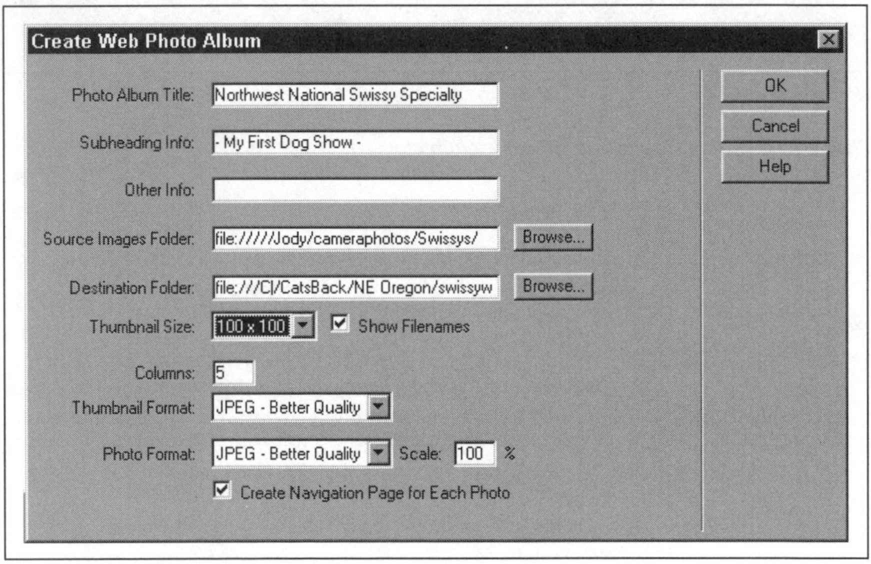

Figure 2-14: The Create Web Photo Album dialog box

Table 2-8 explains the Create Web Photo Album dialog box's options.

Table 2-8: Web Photo Album dialog box options

Control	Description
Photo Album Title	A title that appears atop your photo album and as the document title.
Subheading Info	A subheading that appears beneath the title.
Other Info	This option adds notes, such as a short description of a series of vacation photos, below the subheading.
Source Images Folder	The location of original images, which must all reside in a single directory. Fireworks can read GIF, JPEG, PNG, PSD (Photoshop), and TIFF.
Destination Folder	The destination directory for web-compatible versions of photos.
Thumbnail Size	Maximum dimensions, in pixels, of thumbnails, such as: 36 × 36, 72 × 72, 100 × 100, 144 × 144, or 200 × 200. The aspect ratio is maintained.
Show Filenames	If checked, the filenames are shown on the thumbnail page of the photo album.
Columns	The number of columns of thumbnails per page. Figure 2-15 shows 5 columns.
Thumbnail Format	The graphic format to use for thumbnails (Web Snap 128, Web Snap 256, JPEG-Better Quality, or JPEG-Smaller).
Photo Format	The graphic format for large photographs (same options as Thumbnail format). The PNG format is not supported.
Scale	Specifies the percentage of the original photo size to be used for the final photo size.
Create Navigation Page for Each Photo	If checked, use a separate page for each photo with the title, filename, and previous/next links; otherwise, thumbnails link to plain images.

Fireworks may take a few minutes to process the images. Figure 2-15 displays a completed Web Photo Album showing five columns of 100 × 100 thumbnails. Each thumbnail leads to a larger version of the same image.

To run the Web Photo Album command, you must have a document from the current site open in the Document window. If successful, the command creates an *index.htm* file plus three folders—named *images*, *pages*, and *thumbnails*—in the destination folder you specify. The file extension of the HTML files created by Fireworks is determined by Fireworks' preference settings, not Dreamweaver's preferences.

If you intend to change your photo album pages, you should see Chapter 8; templates are easier to update than the static pages created by the Create Navigation Page for Each Photo option.

Text Formatting

Dreamweaver supports the entire gamut of HTML page- and object-formatting elements. This section describes how to format paragraphs, fonts, and lists, plus how to create horizontal rules and set page properties. Chapter 10 discusses the augmentation of these elements with CSS properties. The HTML Styles panel, discussed in Chapter 11, can also be used to set text formatting properties.

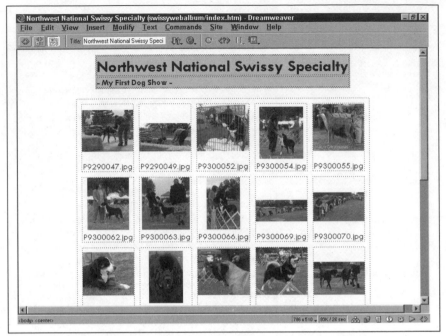

Figure 2-15: A completed Web Photo Album

Paragraph Formatting (Alignment and Styles)

Table 2-9 lists paragraph and text formatting options. These options also work on other objects, such as images, that are embedded within a paragraph. Many of these options can also be set via the Property inspector. See Table 2-11 for character formatting commands.

Table 2-9: Paragraph formatting and alignment options

HTML	Menu access	Windows	Macintosh
`<blockquote>`	Text → Indent	Ctrl+Alt+]	Cmd+Opt+]
Removes `<blockquote>`	Text → Outdent	Ctrl+Alt+[	Cmd+Opt+[
`<div>`	Text → Paragraph Format → None	Ctrl+0 (zero)	Cmd+0 (zero)
`<p>`	Text → Paragraph Format → Paragraph	Ctrl+Shift+P	Cmd+Shift+P
`<h1>`...`<h6>`	Text → Paragraph Format → Heading 1... Heading 6	Ctrl+1... Ctrl+6	Cmd+1... Cmd+6
`<pre>`	Text → Paragraph Format → Preformatted Text	Alt-T, F, R	N/A
`align="left"`	Text → Align → Left	Ctrl+Alt+Shift+L	Cmd+Opt+Shift+L
`align="center"`	Text → Align → Center	Ctrl+Alt+Shift+C	Cmd+Opt+Shift+C
`align="right"`	Text → Align → Right	Ctrl+Alt+Shift+R	Cmd+Opt+Shift+R

Use Preformatted Text (<pre>) to display verbatim text, such as a programming code example, in Courier. Use tables instead of preformatted text to align tabular data.

Horizontal Rules

Horizontal *rules* (horizontal lines used as visual separators on your page) are inserted by using the Insert Horizontal Rule icon in the Objects panel's Common category, or by selecting Insert → Horizontal Rule.

While a rule is selected, the Property inspector offers these formatting options:

Width (W)
Specifies the horizontal length of the rule in either pixels or as a percentage.

Height (H)
Specifies the vertical height (thickness) of the rule in pixels or as a percentage.

Alignment
Specifies the horizontal alignment of the rule across the page or within the left and right edges of an object containing the rule, such as in a table cell. Options are left, right, center, or default (which uses the browser's setting, usually left).

Shading
Specifies whether shading should be used to make the rule appear three-dimensional.

You can set the color of a horizontal rule by setting the color attribute in a CSS rule that customizes <hr> elements, as described in Chapter 10 (not supported in NN4).

 You can simulate a vertical rule by placing a tall, thin graphic in a table column and placing other elements in columns to either side of it.

Date and Time

To insert today's date into your web page, use the Date icon in the Common category of the Objects panel (see Figure 1-4). In the Insert Date dialog box (not shown) you can choose from a variety of date formats. You can optionally include the time and day of the week. By default, Dreamweaver inserts today's date, but if you enable the Update Automatically on Save checkbox, Dreamweaver inserts code similar to the following:

```
<!-- #BeginDate format:Am1 -->August 27, 2001<!-- #EndDate -->
```

Dreamweaver updates the date automatically each time the file is saved. This feature conveniently alerts your visitors of the day that a page on your site was last updated. Use JavaScript, as shown in Chapter 15, to display today's date. To insert a date other than today's date, just enter the text by hand.

Font Formatting

Table 2-10 lists the default font selections, accessible under Text → Font or from the Font list in the Property inspector. These fonts, or near equivalents, are available under most operating systems. If you select an option that specifies multiple fonts, such as "Verdana, Arial, Helvetica, Sans Serif," the visitor's web browser uses the first available font from the list. For example, the browser uses the Verdana font if it is available. If not, it falls back to Arial and then to Helvetica. If none of the chosen fonts are available, the default sans serif font will be used to display the indicated text.

New paragraphs will inherit the font formatting from previous paragraphs until a new font format is explicitly set.

Table 2-10: Default font options

Font	Comments
Default browser font	Typically Times New Roman or Arial
Arial, Helvetica, sans serif	Proportional, sans serif font
Times New Roman, Times, serif	Proportional, serif font
Courier New, Courier, mono	Mono-spaced, serif font
Georgia, Times New Roman, Times, serif	Proportional, serif font
Verdana, Arial Helvetica, sans serif	Proportional, sans serif font
Geneva, Arial Helvetica, sans serif	Proportional, sans serif font
Edit font list	Add more fonts to menu

There are two basic types of font styles: serif and sans serif. Characters in a serif font have *serifs*, the little "feet" and "hats" that help a reader distinguish similar letters. *Sans serif* fonts (literally "without serif") lack these embellishments. In print, sans serif font faces are typically used for headings and subheadings, whereas serif fonts are used for the body text.

 Because serif fonts are harder to read on screen, you should use a sans serif font for your web pages' body text. Consider using serif fonts, which are more legible at larger point sizes, for headings.

Fonts that are available locally or from a web server can be added to the default font list using the Edit Font List dialog box, shown in Figure 2-16. Access this dialog box using Text → Font → Edit Font List or via the Edit Font List option from the Font drop-down list in the Property inspector.

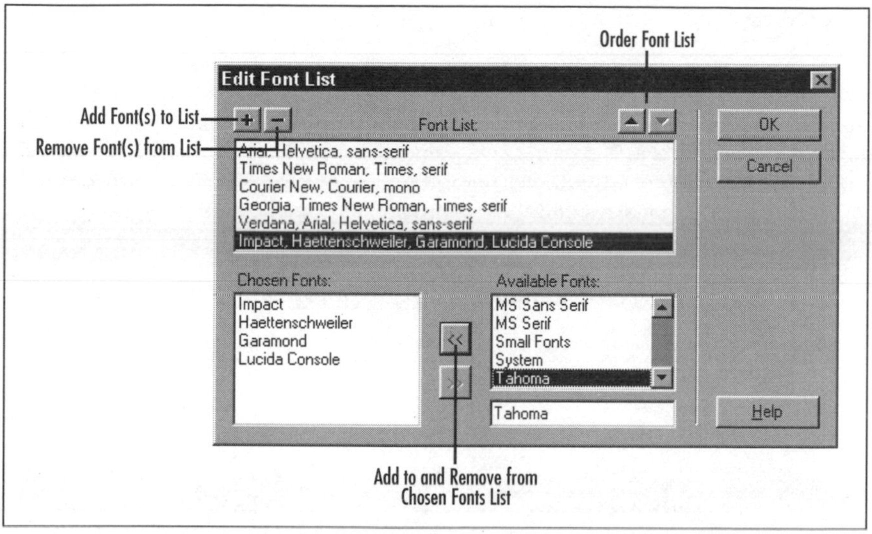

Figure 2-16: The Edit Font List dialog box

The default fonts are grouped by font style. For example, Arial, Helvetica, and Verdana are sans serif fonts, whereas Times, Georgia, and Times New Roman are serif fonts. You can group your fonts by type, size, or any other criterion. You can attempt to download a font or exercise greater control over font substitution by incorporating the CSS @font-face rule in your document, as described in Chapter 10.

Table 2-11 shows how to apply standard HTML character-formatting tags and attributes in Dreamweaver. See Table 2-9 for paragraph formatting commands.

Table 2-11: HTML text styles

HTML	Menu	Windows	Macintosh
`<b>`	Text → Style → Bold	Ctrl+B	Cmd+B
`<i>`	Text → Style → Italic	Ctrl+I	Cmd+I
`<u>`	Text → Style → Underline	Alt-T, S, U	N/A
`<s>`	Text → Style → Strikethrough	Alt-T, S, S	N/A
`<tt>`	Text → Style → Teletype	Alt-T, S, T	N/A
`<em>`	Text → Style → Emphasis	Alt-T, S, E	N/A
`<strong>`	Text → Style → Strong	Alt-T, S, R	N/A
`<code>`	Text → Style → Code	Alt-T, S, C	N/A
`<var>`	Text → Style → Variable	Alt-T, S, V	N/A
`<samp>`	Text → Style → Sample	Alt-T, S, A	N/A
`<kbd>`	Text → Style → Keyboard	Alt-T, S, K	N/A
`<cite>`	Text → Style → Citation	Alt-T, S, O	N/A
`<dfn>`	Text → Style → Definition	Alt-T, S, D	N/A
No formatting	Text ▸ Paragraph Format ▸ None	Ctrl+0 (zero)	Cmd+0 (zero)

Text Size

Dreamweaver can control the relative or absolute font size used to display text (the default font size is typically 10 pt or 12 pt). You can specify absolute type sizes from 1 to 7 and relative sizes from +1 through +4 or –1 through –3. Normal text is equivalent to a 3, so a relative value of +1 indicates an absolute size of 4 and a relative value of –1 indicates an absolute size of 2. Table 2-12 provides a list of various HTML font sizes and their approximate point sizes when displayed in a browser.

Table 2-12: Text sizes based on standard 12-pt default font

Absolute size	Relative size	Point size	Percentage of default
1	–2	8 pt	60%
2	–1	10 pt	80%
3	0	12 pt	100%
4	+1	14 pt	120%
5	+2	16 pt	140%
6	+3	18 pt	160%
7	+4	20 pt	180%

Text Color

The text color pop-up palette, shown in Figure 2-17, lets you set the color of the selected text. To limit yourself to *web-safe* colors supported across all operating systems, select the Snap to Web Safe option from the palette options arrow menu.

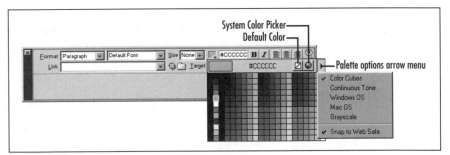

Figure 2-17: Text color pop-up palette

There are several ways to adjust the color of a selected text object:

- Type in the hexadecimal value of the color in the Property inspector's Color field.
- Select the color from the text color pop-up palette, opened using the Text Color button in the Property inspector.
- Apply a color from the Colors category of the Assets panel (see Chapter 6).
- Select Text → Color and choose the color in the Windows color selection pane (Figure 2-18) or the Macintosh color picker (Figure 2-19).

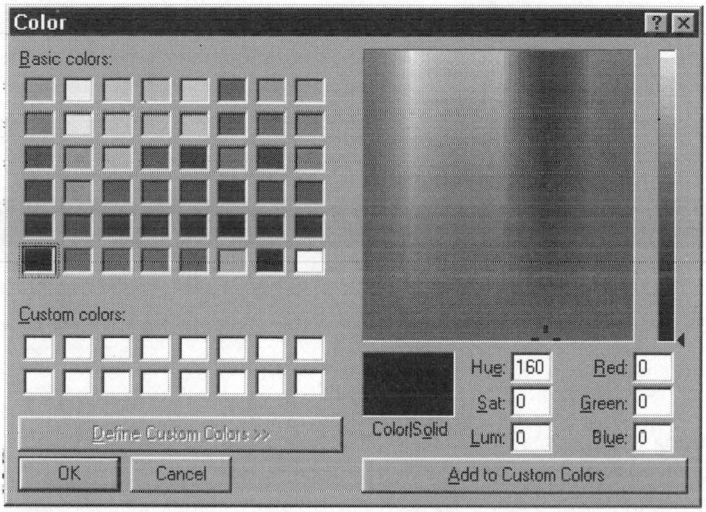

Figure 2-18: Windows color selection pane

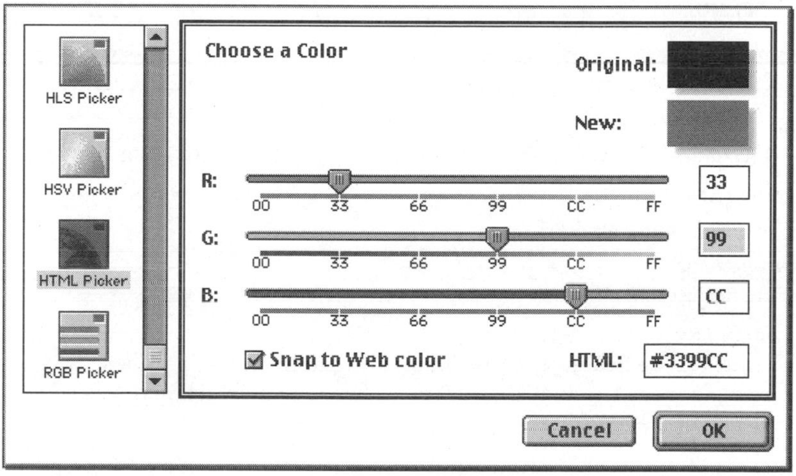

Figure 2-19: Macintosh color picker

Use web-safe colors to ensure consistent color display on all platforms. The web-safe palette is a set of 216 colors that are supported on both Macintosh and Windows. Color display on Unix and Linux is still somewhat erratic, but the web-safe palette is also the best choice for these operating systems. *Web Design in a Nutshell* (O'Reilly) contains an extensive discussion of the web color palette and color usage.

Use the web-safe palette when creating graphics in such programs as Fireworks or Photoshop to avoid *dithering* (splotchy or freckled patches of color) when they're displayed in a browser.

In the Windows color selection pane, you can select from 48 basic colors that are part of a web color palette (i.e., *web-safe palette*). Additional colors, 1 of up to 16 million, can be selected from the graduated rainbow box to the right of the basic color selectors seen in Figure 2-18. When you select a color, the gradations of that hue are shown in the selection bar on the far right of the Windows color selection pane. Click the Add to Custom Colors button to define shades for easy access.

You can maintain sets of custom colors for each web site by adding them to the Assets panel (discussed in Chapter 6) as follows:

1. If using Windows, right-click on any text that uses the desired color. (Ctrl-click if using a Macintosh.)

2. Select Add to Color Favorites from the contextual menu that appears.

3. The color will be available from the Colors category of the Assets panel.

List Styles

Dreamweaver can create numbered, bulleted, and definition-style lists. The following list-formatting options are accessed from the Text → List submenu:

None
Reverts text that was previously formatted as a list back to plain body text.

Ordered List
Creates a numbered list.

Unordered List
Creates a bulleted list.

Definition List
Creates a definition-style list from alternating items in a text block. For example, Item 1 is treated as a "term"; Item 2 is indented and acts as Item 1's "definition," etc.

You can also format the selected text as a list using the Ordered List and Unordered List buttons in the Property inspector (see Figure 1-5). You can remove list formatting by selecting the text and untoggling the appropriate button. You can also select a list type (using the buttons or menu options) prior to entering your text; the text will be formatted automatically as you type.

You can control the appearance of your list bullets or numbers using the List Properties dialog box, shown in Figure 2-20. It is accessible via the Text → List → Properties menu option, which is active only when the cursor or selection occupies a single line in an ordered or unordered list (it is not applicable to definition lists).

The List Properties dialog box includes the options shown in Table 2-13.

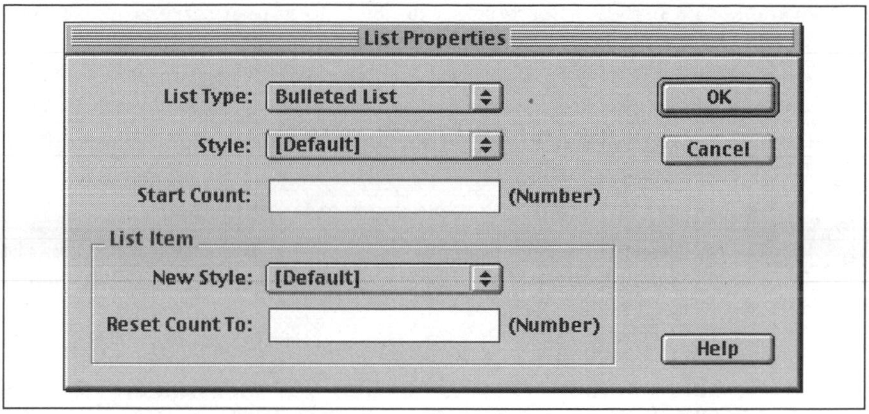

Figure 2-20: The List Properties dialog box

Table 2-13: List Properties options

Control	Description
List Type	Selects a numbered, bulleted, directory, or menu list. The last two list types are deprecated and should be avoided. (Directory lists were glossary-style lists and menu lists were one-level bulleted lists.)
Style	Select Roman, Arabic, or alphabetic (I, i, 1, A, or a) ordinals for numbered lists. Select round bullets or hollow squares for bulleted lists. Setting applies to all entries in the list (both preceding and following the selected item).
New Style	Specifies the number style or bullet style for the currently selected items and subsequent items whose New Style option is set to Default. It does not affect items preceding the selected item.
Start Count	An integer specifying the starting value for the first ordinal in a numbered list. Use an integer even if the Style setting is not Arabic. For example, the number 3 is shown as III or iii in Roman lists and is shown as C or c in alphabetic lists.
Reset Count To	Reset the item numbers in a numbered list, beginning with the selected item. It does not affect the numbering of preceding items.

Creating a list using multiple styles of numbers can be tricky. Procedure 1 creates a list that uses traditional outline nomenclature—Roman numerals (I, II, III) for the top level and capital letters (A, B, C) for the major subheadings.

Procedure 1

1. Enter the text for the list, without formatting, in the Design pane of the Document window. Select the text for the list, and use Text → List → Ordered List to convert it to an ordered (i.e., numbered) list.

2. Select the first item in the list (the entry to be designated I). Choose Text → List → Properties.

3. In the List Properties dialog box, set the Style to Roman Large. The List Type should already be set to Numbered List and the Start Count should default to 1 if left blank. Click OK.

4. Select the second item in the list (the entry to be designated A). Use Text → Indent, Ctrl+Alt+] (Windows), or Cmd+Opt+] (Macintosh) to indent the item. The numeral should default to 1.

5. Choose Text → List → Properties while this item is still selected.

6. In the List Properties dialog box, set the Style to Alphabet Large. The List Type should already be set to Numbered List and the Start Count should default to 1 if left blank. Click OK.

7. Use the Text → Indent option to indent subsequent elements (B, C, D, etc.).

8. To create a third tier to the outline (such as i, ii, iii), indent the text items twice and then repeat Step 6 using the Roman Small style.

9. Repeat Steps 4 through 8 for items to be indented under Roman numerals II, III, IV, and so on.

You must go through your list line by line, formatting the numbers for each item in sequence. If you skip a line and corrupt the numbering scheme, you must start over or correct the HTML code by hand.

Page Properties

Use the Page Properties dialog box, shown in Figure 2-21, to format your HTML documents. The dialog box includes options to set the margins, background images and colors, text and link colors, and options to control text encoding. It is accessed by using Modify → Page Properties, Ctrl+J (Windows), or Cmd+J (Macintosh).

 The Page Properties dialog box sets formatting attributes using the <body> tag, which works with 3.0 browsers but does not conform to the latest HTML standards. Chapter 10 explains how to set similar properties using CSS, when supporting 4.0+ browsers.

The Page Properties dialog box's options are detailed in Table 2-14.

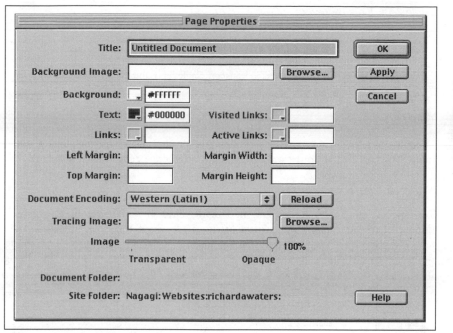

Figure 2-21: The Page Properties dialog box

Table 2-14: Page Properties options

Control	Description
Title	The title for the document—used in the browser window's title bar and used as the default name when bookmarking the page.
Background Image	If the background image is smaller than the page, it is tiled by default; otherwise it is cropped. It can also be controlled by CSS.
Background	Sets the document background color.
Text	Sets the default text color (excluding links).
Links	Sets the default color of links.
Visited Links	Sets the default color of visited links.
Active Links	Sets the default color of active links (the color that appears when clicking on a link).
Left Margin	Sets the left margin in pixels (percentages are not allowed). It is used by IE only and ignored by NN. The right margin cannot be set in IE.
Top Margin	Sets the top margin in pixels (percentages are not allowed). It is used by IE only and ignored by NN. The bottom margin cannot be set in IE.
Margin Width	Sets both the left and right margins in pixels (percentages are not allowed). It is used by NN only and ignored by IE.
Margin Height	Sets both the top and bottom margins in pixels (percentages are not allowed). It is used by NN only and ignored by IE.
Document Encoding	Sets the character encoding used in the document. Use Western (Latin1) encoding for English and Western European languages. Specify Other encoding to use the operating system's default encoding method.

Table 2-14: Page Properties options (continued)

Control	Description
Tracing Image	Specifies a layout guide image to use when designing in Dreamweaver (never visible in a web browser).
Image Transparency	Specifies the transparency level of the tracing image (0 is opaque and 100 is transparent).

Characters

Dreamweaver can insert character codes and predefined characters into a document. You can define your own characters to augment Dreamweaver's default set.

Special Characters

Ten special characters (copyright, trademark, etc.) are available in the Objects panel's Character category, shown in Figure 2-22, or via Insert → Special Characters. Use the Other Characters button (or Insert → Special Characters → Other) to open the Insert Other Character dialog box, also shown in Figure 2-22. This dialog box gives access to 99 characters (including the default 10).

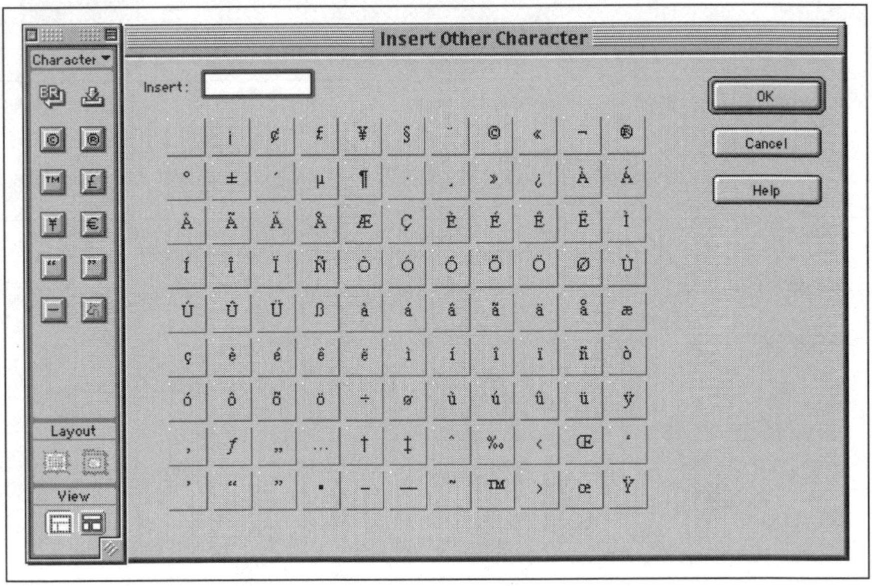

Figure 2-22: Available preconfigured characters

Use the Insert field of the Insert Special Character dialog box to specify other characters. See Appendix B for information on special characters (so-called HTML character entities). Procedure 7 in Chapter 19 demonstrates how to add new character icons to the Objects panel's Characters category.

Hidden Objects

Hidden objects (a.k.a. *invisible objects*) are objects that are not seen when the document is viewed in a web browser. Dreamweaver provides access to the following hidden objects through its interface:

- Comments
- Line Breaks and Nonbreaking Spaces
- Scripts
- Anchors (discussed earlier in this chapter)

Figure 2-23 shows the icons that act as placeholders for these and other invisible objects within Dreamweaver.

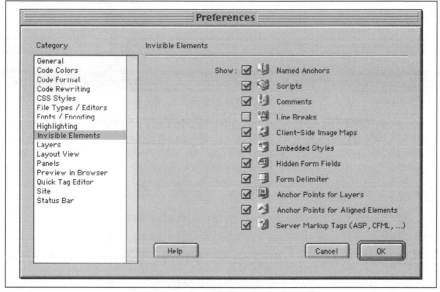

Figure 2-23: Icons for invisible objects

To make placeholders for hidden objects visible, ensure that the View → Visual Aids → Invisible Elements option is checked. Use View → Visual Aids → Hide All, Ctrl+Shift+I (Windows), or Cmd+Shift+I (Macintosh) to hide all visual aids temporarily.

Comments

Comments can be used to provide development notes about the HTML code for the benefit of future developers or for yourself, should you need to revisit some old code. Add comments to explain scripts, add instructions for use, or include notes for future development.

Comments are inserted using the Comment button in the Objects panel's Invisibles category or by selecting Insert → Invisible Tags → Comments. You can type comments directly into the Code pane, in the form:

```
<!-- This is a comment -->
```

Web browsers ignore everything between the leading `<!--` and trailing `-->` characters, which delimit the comment. Multiline comments are allowed and take the form:

```
<!-- This is another comment that takes up multiple lines.
     It keeps going and going and going. -->
```

You should not nest comments. The following code is erroneous:

```
<!-- this is a <!-- nested --> comment -->
```

If you attempt to nest comments, the text following the first `-->` character combination will be displayed to the user.

Dreamweaver uses comments to track templates, library items, and Fireworks HTML, as discussed later. Use Dreamweaver's Design Notes, described in Chapter 6, to track design issues more efficiently.

Nonbreaking Spaces and Paragraph Breaks

Extra whitespace (spaces, tabs, and line breaks) within HTML source code is generally ignored unless the text is tagged with the `<pre>` tag. You can insert nonbreaking spaces, which will be honored by a browser, using the Insert Non-Breaking Space button in the Objects panel's Characters category. You can also use Insert → Special Characters → Non-Breaking Space, or Ctrl+Shift+Space (Windows), or Cmd+Shift+Space (Macintosh).

A nonbreaking space is represented by the character entity ` `. Use tables instead of nonbreaking spaces to align text accurately.

You can also use the `<br>` and `<p></p>` tags to partially affect text placement. The `<br>` tag inserts a line break in the current line of text without creating a new paragraph, whereas the `<p></p>` tags delimit paragraphs. However, the rendering of these tags varies by browser and they are not a reliable way to control vertical whitespace. Again, use tables for more reliable formatting.

Script Tag

Dreamweaver provides its own set of JavaScript-enabled behaviors (discussed in Part III), but also provides a way to add and link to your own scripts. Add your own scripts by clicking the Script icon in the Objects panel's Invisibles category or by choosing Insert → Invisible Tags → Scripts.

The Insert Script dialog box allows you to select from four types of scripts:

JavaScript
> Specifies any version of JavaScript. Use this option as the lowest common denominator if your code will run in any version of JavaScript.

JavaScript1.1
> Use this option if your code requires JavaScript 1.1 or higher. It will be executed by browsers supporting JavaScript 1.1 or 1.2 (or higher), but not by browsers that support only JavaScript 1.0.

JavaScript1.2
> Use this option if your code requires JavaScript 1.2 or higher. Browsers that don't support at least JavaScript 1.2 will ignore it.

VBScript
> Specifies any version of VBScript. VBScript is supported by IE3+ for Windows or IE5+ on Mac. For broader compatibility, use JavaScript instead.

For JavaScript compatibility by browser, see Table 12-1.

Enter your script code within the Content area of the Insert Script dialog box, which will insert your code inside `<script>` tags as shown here:

```
<script type="text/JavaScript">
function DoItNow {
}
</script>
```

You can hide JavaScript code from older browsers by placing it in comment tags within your `<script>` tag as follows:

```
<script type="text/JavaScript">
<!--
  function WriteScreen() {
    document.writeln("This is a simple script.");
  }
-->
</script>
```

 Your page may not operate correctly in browsers (and some other HTML clients) that ignore scripts within comment tags. Furthermore, enclosing scripts within comment tags is not XHTML-compliant.

In this chapter we've covered the common elements you'll add to your HTML pages, including text, images, links, head content, and hidden objects. Chapter 3 explains how to use tables to control a web page's layout and how to use form objects to collect and submit data.

CHAPTER 3

Tables and Form Objects

Dreamweaver's tools for manipulating tables, tabular data, and forms improve with each new version. Along with the standard table-editing tools available in Standard view, DW4 offers the powerful Layout view, which uses tables to simulate page layout functionality using HTML. Dreamweaver can also import tabular data from external sources. It supports a full complement of form objects, including automated jump menu creation.

We'll discuss forms at the end of this chapter, but first we'll cover Dreamweaver's table creation tools.

Standard View Versus Layout View

Although Standard tables and Layout tables serve different purposes, both use the same familiar HTML table tags (<table>, <tr>, and <td>). Thankfully, Dreamweaver allows you to create tables visually in either mode, insulating you from the underlying complexity of the HTML. (You can switch between table modes using the View → Table View menu options or the View buttons at the bottom of the Objects panel. Don't confuse the table view modes with the unrelated Code and Design views discussed earlier.) If you're not sure whether to use tables, layers, or some other formatting element, see the section "Layers and Tables and Frames, Oh My!" in the preface.

In some cases, performing a table operation in one of the two modes is nearly, or even literally, impossible. You can switch between Standard view and Layout view when working with the same table, so use whichever mode you need. Dreamweaver creates or adjusts the HTML table tags for you automatically.

Because tables weren't originally intended for page layout, Standard view is best suited for creating simple data tables (like a spreadsheet of numbers).

Standard view and its row-and-column paradigm is ideal for displaying tabular data. Layout view merely uses tables as a means to align graphic elements on the page.

Although Layout view is better suited for complex layouts, Standard view is useful, and even mandatory, for several reasons:

- It hides some of the visual guides present in Layout view, making it easier to view the page's contents.

- It allows you to use the basic Table object and the Draw Layer tool, which are not available in Layout view.

- You can insert a table in Standard view using the keyboard shortcut Ctrl+Alt+T (Windows) or Cmd+Opt+T (Macintosh). In Layout view, you must use the mouse to create tables.

- It allows you to set the background image of a cell or table, add color to a row of cells, and sort and format tabular data (none of which can be done in Layout view).

- It allows you to easily manipulate entire rows and columns. In Layout view, you typically manipulate individual cells. There is no way to set properties of a complete row or column using Layout view.

- Cells can be merged and split easily, and rows and columns can be inserted or deleted, in Standard view. In Layout view, cells are manipulated directly and Dreamweaver automatically inserts or deletes rows and columns as needed.

Table 3-1 shows the primary table-related operations and shortcuts. Refer to Table A-8 for more table-related menu commands and shortcuts.

Table 3-1: Table shortcuts

Operation	Windows	Macintosh
Select cell (or select table, if cell is already selected)	Ctrl+A	Cmd+A
Switch to Layout view	Ctrl+F6	Cmd+F6
Switch to Standard view	Ctrl+Shift+F6	Cmd+Shift+F6
Insert Table in Standard view	Ctrl+Alt+T	Cmd+Opt+T
Draw multiple tables or cells without reselecting the tool in Layout view	Hold down Ctrl key while drawing	Hold down Cmd key while drawing
Prevent tables and cells from snapping to nearby elements (within 8 pixels) in Layout view	Hold down Alt key while drawing	Hold down Opt key while drawing
Select a multicell range in Standard view	Shift-click	Shift-click
Open contextual menu	Right-click	Ctrl-click
Nudge selected cell by one pixel in Layout view	Arrow keys	Arrow keys
Nudge cell by ten pixels in Layout view	Shift+arrow keys	Shift+arrow keys
Merge Cells in Standard view	Ctrl+Alt+M	Cmd+Opt+M

Table 3-1: Table shortcuts (continued)

Operation	Windows	Macintosh
Split Cells in Standard view	Ctrl+Alt+S	Cmd+Opt+S
Move insertion point to next cell (adds a new row if in the last cell of the last row)	Tab	Tab
Move insertion point to previous cell	Shift+Tab	Shift+Tab

Tables in Standard View

In Dreamweaver's Standard view, you can create and manipulate tables using the well-known paradigm of rows and columns. Switch to Standard view using the Standard View button in the Objects panel or by choosing View → Table View → Standard View.

Entering Standard view simply sets the drawing mode; the next step is to insert a table using Insert → Table or the Table icon in the Objects panel's Common category (these options are inactive while the program is in Layout view). Inserting a table opens the Insert Table dialog box, shown in Figure 3-1, where you can set the rows, columns, cell padding (the margin between a cell's contents and its edges), cell spacing (the space between adjacent cells), table width, and border thickness. Both cell padding and cell spacing must be set explicitly to 0 to create a seamless layout within a table. If you leave these fields empty, most browsers default to 1 pixel for cell padding and 2 pixels for cell spacing.

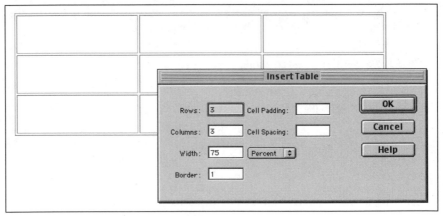

Figure 3-1: The Insert Table dialog box

Selecting Table Items in Standard View

There are several ways to select tables, cells, rows, and columns in Standard view. The following discussion applies to Standard view only. See the "Tables in Layout View" section later in this chapter for details on manipulating tables in Layout view.

Selecting tables

To select an entire table in Standard view, click on the table's upper-left corner or one of its edges when the pointer changes to a "crossed arrows" cursor.

Other ways to select a table include clicking anywhere in the table, and then:

- Selecting the `<table>` tag from the Tag Selector in the status bar.
- Choosing Modify → Table → Select Table.
- Choosing Table → Select Table from the contextual menu.
- Pressing Ctrl+A (Windows) or Cmd+A (Macintosh) twice (the first time selects a cell and the second time selects the entire table).

Selecting cells, columns, or rows

To select cells, rows, and columns in Standard view, use the following:

- Ctrl-click (Windows) or Cmd-click (Macintosh) to select an unselected cell. This gesture also selects additional cells, even discontiguous ones.
- Click inside a single cell and then drag the mouse outside of the cell to select it. (If it doesn't work, drag the mouse further.) If you drag the mouse across multiple cells, you can select a rectangular area of contiguous cells.
- Click inside a cell and the use Ctrl-A (Windows) or Cmd-A (Macintosh).
- Select a `<td>` or `<tr>` tag from the Tag Selector in the status bar to select a cell or row of cells.
- Select an entire row at once by placing your cursor to the left of the row of interest and clicking when the pointer turns into a horizontal arrow.
- Select an entire column at once by placing your cursor above the column of interest and clicking when the pointer turns into a vertical arrow.
- Select a cell and then Shift-click in another cell to select a rectangular area including all intervening cells.

Modifying Table and Cell Properties in Standard View

Table attributes differ in Standard view and Layout view. Figure 3-2 shows the Property inspector as it appears when a table is selected in Standard view, allowing you to modify table attributes. 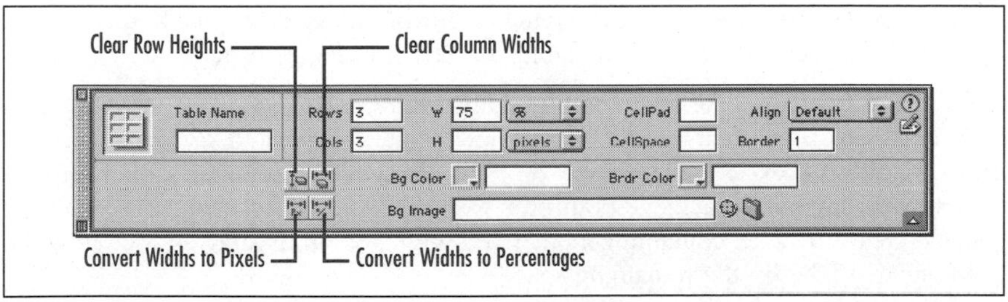

Figure 3-2: Property inspector showing table properties in Standard view

When a cell, row, or column is selected in Standard view, the Property inspector can be used to modify the attributes shown in Figure 3-3.

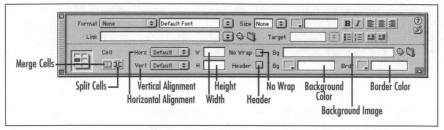

Figure 3-3: Property inspector showing cell properties in Standard view

Height and width of tables, rows, and columns

Once a table is selected in Standard view, you can resize it using the resize handles (provided it doesn't overlap with other elements on the page). Setting the table width or height to a percentage causes the table to resize dynamically based on the browser window size.

A table's rows and columns can be set to a fixed size in pixels or a percentage of the current table size. Select a row or column and then use the Height and Width fields (in the Property inspector) to set either a fixed dimension or a percentage. (Unlike the table properties, there is no pop-up menu for the units, so enter a percent sign, such as "50%".) Select the entire table and use the Convert Widths to Pixels or Convert Widths to Percentages button in the Property inspector (indicated in Figure 3-2) to convert the column widths between fixed and adjustable dimensions.

To resize a table's rows and columns manually, click and drag the border that separates adjacent rows or columns (the cursor changes to parallel lines when the pointer is positioned appropriately). Resizing columns and rows sets the height and width attributes in the HTML code to fixed dimensions (i.e., any percentage-based dimensions are converted to pixel dimensions). Select the entire table and use the Clear Height Values and Clear Width Values buttons in the Property inspector, as shown in Figure 3-2, to reset the table dimensions and start over.

The column width and height determine the wrapping of text and graphics within the table. To create a precise layout, such as that used with sliced images, you must use fixed-cell and table dimensions. If a fixed-width table is too narrow, its contents will wrap even on wide monitors; furthermore, large blank spaces may appear on one or both sides of the table, as shown in Figure 3-4.

Assigning percentages for the column widths (in Standard view) or using Dreamweaver's Autostretch feature (in Layout view) creates so-called *fluid* tables. Fluid tables avoid the excess whitespace problem; however, they don't offer precise control over layout. To achieve both precision and flexibility, Dreamweaver allows you to create a table containing both fixed-width columns and adjustable-width columns that take up the remaining space.

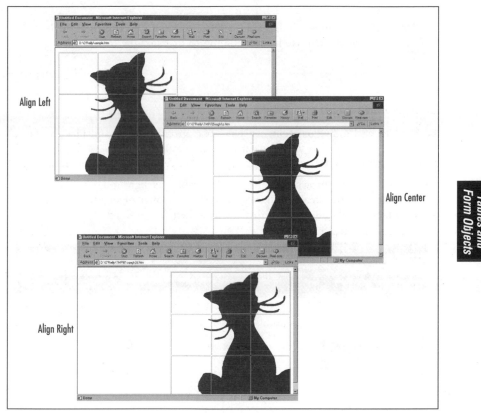

Figure 3-4: A narrow table, left-, center-, and right-justified

To make a table fill the browser window using Standard view, you must select the entire table and set its width to 100%. (As discussed in the section "Autostretch and spacer images" later in this chapter, setting one column to Autostretch in Layout view resizes the entire table to fit the browser window.)

The following code creates a table that fills the browser window. One of the columns uses all of the width remaining after the fixed-width columns are allotted their space.

```
<table width="100%">
  <tr>
    <td width="100%" height="19"> Add content here.</td>
    <td width="1" valign="top">Add content here.</td>
    <td width="1">Add content here.</td>
  </tr>
</table>
```

You can create this code by setting the table width in the Property inspector to 100%. Then, specify a fixed width for two of the columns and a percentage (100%) for the final column, again using the Property inspector.

Before adding an adjustable-width column, add content to at least one cell in each fixed-width column to maintain the desired width.

Background images and colors

Both tables and individual cells can have background colors and images applied separately. If the table is too small, the background image will be cropped. If the table is larger than the background image, the image will be tiled (i.e., repeated).

Netscape Navigator browsers don't display table background images properly; instead, they tile the image within each cell, as shown in Figure 3-5. Figure 3-6 shows a table background image displayed as intended in IE5.5.

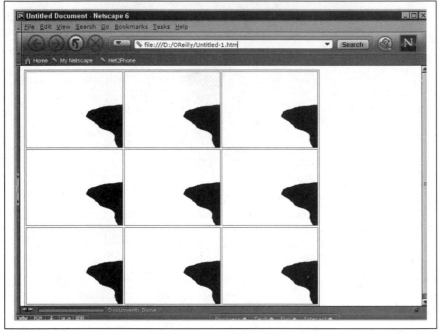

Figure 3-5: Netscape Navigator 6 with a table background image

To make a table with background images appear the same in both Internet Explorer and Netscape Navigator, you will need to split your main background image into a grid matching the cell dimensions of the table, and then apply portions of the main image to each individual cell. By converting your background image into a series of smaller images to be applied separately to each cell, your table code will appear as follows and will display correctly in the major browsers:

```
<table width="75%" border="0"
       cellspacing="1" cellpadding="0">
```

```
<tr>
  <td background="img1.gif"
      width="100" height="100"> </td>
  <td background="img2.gif"
      width="100" height="100"> </td>
</tr>
<tr>
  <td background="img3.gif"
      width="100" height="100"> </td>
  <td background="img4.gif"
      width="100" height="100"> </td>
</tr>
</table>
```

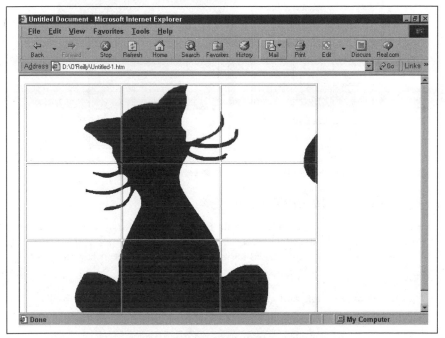

Figure 3-6: Internet Explorer 5.5 with a Table background image

When breaking an image into smaller pieces to use as a background image for table cells, be sure to specify both a height and width property for each cell to avoid cropping the images.

You can control the horizontal and vertical repetition of your background image(s) by using the stylesheet properties background-attachment, background-repeat, and background-position, as discussed in Chapter 10.

Border properties

Dreamweaver can set the colors and widths of table and cell borders, but Netscape Navigator and Internet Explorer interpret the border settings differently, as shown in Figure 3-7 (in which the border color is dark gray #333333). Prior to

DW4, the dark and light colors of the table border could be set separately using the properties `bordercolorlight` and `bordercolordark`. Because these values were interpreted differently by different browser versions and used only by Netscape Navigator, DW4 dropped this feature.

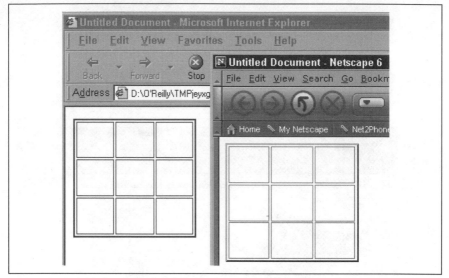

Figure 3-7: Table border color differences between browsers

Merging and Splitting Cells

Dreamweaver automatically adjusts your HTML `<table>` tag when you merge adjacent cells or split a cell in two (also known as *spanning* and *unspanning* cells). Cells can be split and merged in Standard view, but not in Layout view.

To merge table cells, select two or more adjacent cells, and then:

- Click the Merge Cells button in the Property inspector (see Figure 3-3); or
- Choose Table → Merge Cells from the cell's contextual menu; or
- Choose Modify → Table → Merge Cells; or
- Press Ctrl+Alt+M (Windows) or Cmd+Opt+M (Macintosh).

You can use merged cells to create elaborate layouts. To reduce download size, use stylesheets, background colors, or text to create graphical effects when possible. Use images only for effects that can't be created with more bandwidth-efficient techniques. See "Creating Tables in Fireworks" in Chapter 13 for an example of a complex graphical interface created using a table.

To split a table cell, select only one cell, and then:

- Click the Split Cells button in the Property inspector (see Figure 3-3); or
- Choose Table → Split Cells from the cell's contextual menu; or
- Choose Modify → Table → Split Cells; or
- Press Ctrl+Alt+S (Windows) or Cmd+Opt+S (Macintosh).

In Standard view, splitting a cell automatically creates a new row or column in your HTML code, if necessary. (In Layout view, the grid is adjusted whenever cells are resized or added with the Draw Layout Cell tool.)

Tables in Layout View

Dreamweaver 4 introduced a new Layout view for working with tables visually, but Layout view is largely unrelated to the traditional use of tables for displaying data in rows and columns. Instead, it uses legacy HTML support for tables to simulate modern page layout capabilities, even in older browsers.

Drawing Tables in Layout View

Enter Layout view using the Layout View button in the Objects panel or by choosing View → Table View → Layout View. When you first enter Layout view, Dreamweaver displays a Getting Started in Layout View overview in a dialog box. Click the dialog box's Help button to access tutorial information, or use the "Don't Show Me This Message Again" checkbox provided to prevent the dialog box from appearing the next time you enter Layout view.

In Standard view, cells are part of a row or column; in Layout view, however, the individual cells act as arbitrary layout areas. In Standard view, cells are created when you create your table (in just one step, which is easy, but doesn't offer much control). In Layout view, you must create a table manually using the Draw Layout Table tool and then add cells using the Draw Layout Cell tool (requiring multiple steps, but offering more control). The Draw Layout Cell and Draw Layout Table tools in the Objects panel, which are active in Layout view only, are shown in Figure 3-8.

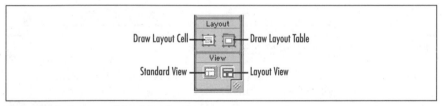

Figure 3-8: Layout table object buttons

Use the Draw Layout Table tool to create a rectangular table by clicking in the Document window and dragging the mouse cursor down and to the right. The table is placed in the upper-left corner of the page by default. To adjust the horizontal alignment of a table use the Property inspector as discussed earlier. A layout table can act as the container for subsequent (nested) tables. Additional layout tables can be added below existing tables. Each layout table is indicated by a green tab in its upper-left corner.

Use the Draw Layout Cell tool to create cells within a table.

Tables and
Form Objects

Layout tables do not automatically include cells. Cells or nested tables must be added within the unoccupied gray areas using the Draw Layout Cell or Draw Layout Table tools before you can add text or graphics to these areas. To draw multiple layout tables or layout cells without having to reselect the tool each time, hold down the Ctrl key (Windows) or Cmd key (Macintosh) while using the tool.

If you draw a layout cell prior to drawing a layout table, Dreamweaver automatically creates a layout table to enclose it, as shown in Figure 3-9. (In this case, Dreamweaver also adds a proprietary mm:layoutgroup="true" attribute to the <table> tag, which you can safely delete in Code view or by using the Quick Tag Editor.) 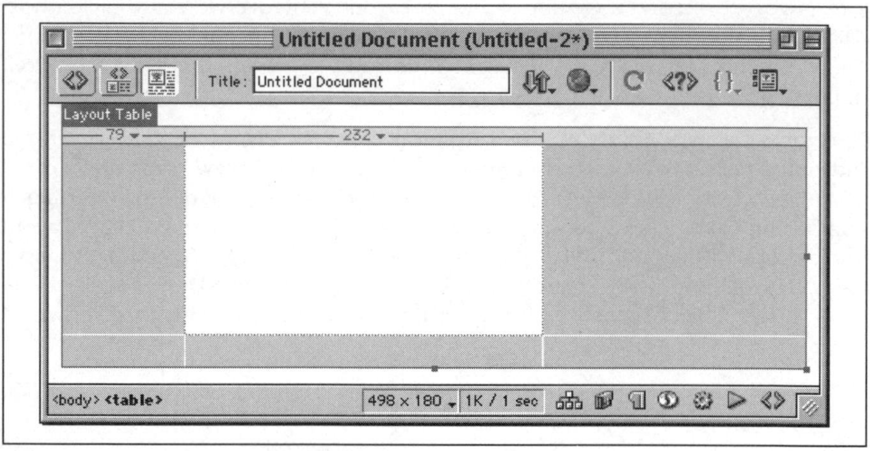

Figure 3-9: A single-cell layout table

As seen in Figure 3-10, as you add table cells, a grid is formed. Unoccupied areas remain gray. The width of each column is shown at the top of the table. Click the small arrow next to the column width number to access a pop-up menu that controls cell width.

If you are accustomed to Standard table-editing mode, the new gestures in Layout view may require some practice. Some hints about layout tables and cells may eliminate any confusion:

- You can't draw tables over existing elements such as text and graphics, so start with a blank page or place the cursor at the end of your current page.

- Tables can't overlap one another, but a table can be nested within an unoccupied gray area of another table. (However, you can't nest a table within an existing white cell.)

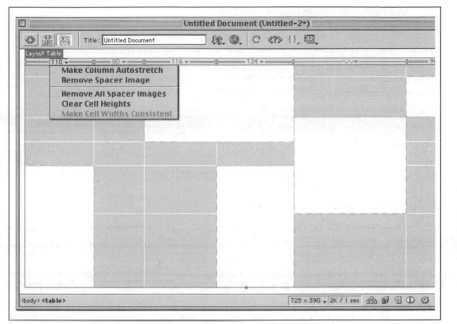

Figure 3-10: Layout table cells create a grid as they are drawn

- Cells cannot overlap one another, be drawn atop existing content, or be drawn within another cell.

- You can't merge or split cells or directly insert or delete columns in Layout view. Instead, columns and rows are created automatically and deleted as necessary when cell areas are drawn or resized. That is, if you align cells to share a common horizontal or vertical edge, Dreamweaver deletes any rows or columns that are no longer necessary to represent your grid. If cells are not aligned, Dreamweaver creates rows and columns as necessary to position them as directed.

- When cells or tables are selected, they can be resized using the resize handles that appear, but a table cannot be resized to be smaller than the area occupied by layout cells (unoccupied areas are indicated in gray).

- Cells don't need to line up in nice rows and columns. Use cells as arbitrary drawing areas. Dreamweaver automatically creates a grid to accommodate your cells. You can resize individual cells by selecting them and dragging their resize handles, provided that they don't overlap other cells.

- You can't select or set the properties of a complete row or column in Layout view.

- To select a layout cell, position the cursor over its edge until the outline turns red and then click once. The outline of the selected cell should turn blue and resize handles should appear. You can also select a cell using Ctrl-click or Ctrl-A (Windows), or Cmd-Click or Cmd-A (Macintosh).

- To delete a layout cell, select it and then hit the Delete key.

Aligning images with a tracing image

Dreamweaver can display a *tracing image* to assist in laying out a complex page or table (the tracing image appears while working in Dreamweaver, but not within a web browser). Add a tracing image using Modify → Page Properties, Ctrl+J (Windows), or Cmd+J (Macintosh). In the Tracing Image field, select the complete image of your web page and then click OK. (Because the tracing image must be a single image, use an image that hasn't already been sliced.)

The tracing image appears behind any content in the Design pane of the Document window. Use the slider in the Page Properties dialog box to control the tracing image's transparency. See "Creating Tables in Fireworks" in Chapter 13 for an alternative method of creating a complex page layout.

Table and Cell Properties in Layout View

The table and cell formatting options in Layout view differ somewhat from those available in Standard view. The options available in Layout view are explained in Table 3-2 and shown in Figure 3-11. You can also access some of these options from the pop-up menu accessed by clicking the small arrow button next to the column width measurement at the top of each column. You can configure Layout view preferences under Edit → Preferences → Layout View. The formatting options available in Standard view are explained under the "Modifying Table and Cell Properties in Standard View" section earlier in this chapter.

Table 3-2: Properties available in Layout view

Option name	Option description
Width	The Fixed mode sets the column width in pixels. An Autostretch column expands to force the table width to match the browser window's width (only one column can be autostretched).
Height	Sets the table or cell height in pixels. If blank, height is determined automatically by the table or cell contents.
Bg	Sets the table or cell background color.
CellPad	Specifies the margin in pixels (for the entire table) between cell borders and cell contents. The margin is applied on all four sides of all cells. The default is usually nonzero, so set it explicitly to 0 for seamless tables.
CellSpace	Specifies row and column spacing for the entire table. The default is usually nonzero, so set it explicitly to 0 for seamless tables.
Clear Row Height	Clears the height attribute of all table rows (`<tr>` tags).
Make Cell Widths Consistent	Sets all columns to the width required by their content. For example, a 100-pixel-wide column containing a 150-pixel-wide image would be set to 150 pixels wide.
Remove All Spacers	Removes all spacer images used for autostretching (which may cause unoccupied columns to be deleted).
Remove Nesting	Removes any tables contained within the current cell or table.
Horiz	Sets the horizontal alignment of the contents of a single selected cell (left, right, or center).
Vert	Sets the vertical alignment of the contents of a single selected cell (top, middle, or bottom).
No Wrap	Controls text wrapping within a cell.

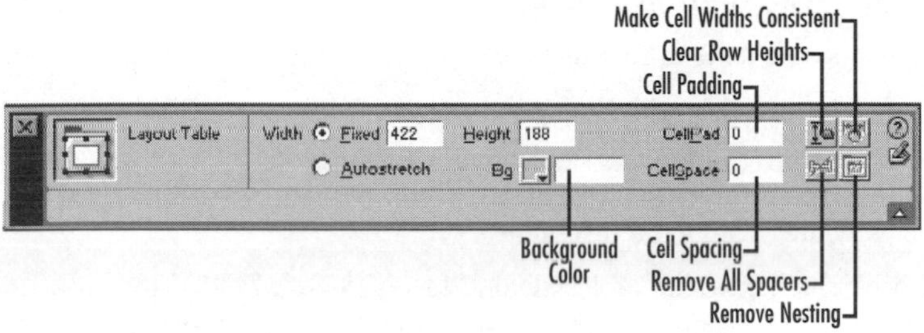

Figure 3-11: Property inspector showing table properties in Layout view

Autostretch and spacer images

Creating an autostretched column allows the width of your table to resize automatically to fit the user's browser window. If a column is set to Autostretch, its width is indicated by a wavy line (see Figure 3-10).

 Only one column in a layout table can be autostretched (setting a column to Autostretch converts any previously autostretched column to a fixed width). Add content to your fixed-width cells before setting a column to Autostretch, or the other table cells will be compressed and difficult to work with.

Dreamweaver uses *spacer images* (1 × 1 pixel transparent GIF files) in Layout view to maintain column widths. Spacer images are added in the bottom row of fixed-width columns of a table when an Autostretch column is created. The spacer added to each column is resized to the desired width so that each cell in that row maintains the column's width, regardless of the column's other contents. The spacer images prevent the autostretched column from squeezing out other columns.

When you first add an Autostretch column, you will be prompted to select a spacer image file. Either create a new one or choose an existing one (avoid the "Don't Use Spacer Images for Autostretch Tables" option).

 Use the Relative To Site Root option when saving your spacer image, or it won't work when uploaded to a server.

Double horizontal lines appear in the column heading for columns containing spacer images (see Figure 3-10). Use the options in Table 3-2 to remove spacer images from one or more columns (typically to start over when working with a table that has gotten out of control).

Creating Nested Tables in Layout View

To create a nested table in Layout view:

1. Draw a layout table with the Object panel's Draw Layout Table tool.

2. Click on the Layout Table tool again (if you didn't hold down the Ctrl key (Windows) or Cmd key (Macintosh) when drawing), and draw a table within any gray area within the first table.

You can nest tables within tables several levels deep provided that you draw the new table within the gray area of an existing table. You can also draw layout cells within nested tables or in unoccupied areas adjacent to nested tables.

You cannot draw a layout table within a layout cell. Select and delete the cell if you'd like to nest a table in that area.

Converting Between Tables and Layers

Layers provide an alternative method of laying out elements on a web page. Although web developers traditionally use tables to create documents that will work with a wide range of browsers, modern browsers (NN 4.0 or IE 4.0 or later) support layers. DW4 quickly converts between these two formatting options, using Modify → Convert → Tables To Layers and Modify → Convert → Layers to Table.

For example, if you select the table shown in Figure 3-8 and choose Modify → Convert → Tables to Layers, you will be offered options for converting your table, as shown in Figure 3-12.

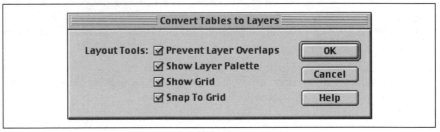

Figure 3-12: The Convert Tables to Layers dialog box

Dreamweaver creates layers from only the table cells that contain content (text, images, or a background color or image). The size of the layers created depends on the size of the cell's contents. For example, a cell with a background color applied would have the exact dimensions when rendered as a layer that it had as a table cell; a layer derived from a cell containing text would shrink to the size of the text. You can see these effects in Figure 3-13.

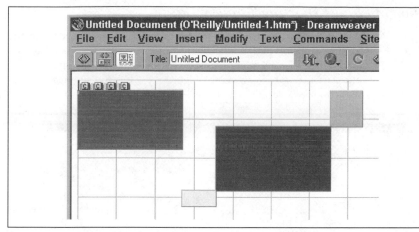

Figure 3-13: Table cells converted to layers

When converting layers to a table using Modify → Convert → Layers to Tables, the effect is essentially the same. Layers of specific dimensions have those dimensions retained when the layers are converted into a table. The Convert Layers to Table dialog box is shown in Figure 3-14.

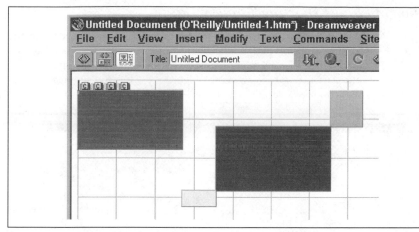

Figure 3-14: Layers converted to table cells

You can also convert layers to a table using the File → Convert → 3.0 Browser Compatible → Layers to Table command.

Tabular Data

Dreamweaver 4 can import, export, sort, and format tabular data as described in the following sections.

Importing and Exporting Tabular Data

Use File → Import → Import Tabular Data or the Insert Tabular Data icon on the Objects panel to import and format tabular data from a text file. Entries should be delimited by tabs, commas, semicolons, colons, or another delimiting character. The Import Table Data dialog box, shown in Figure 3-15, has the settings listed in Table 3-3.

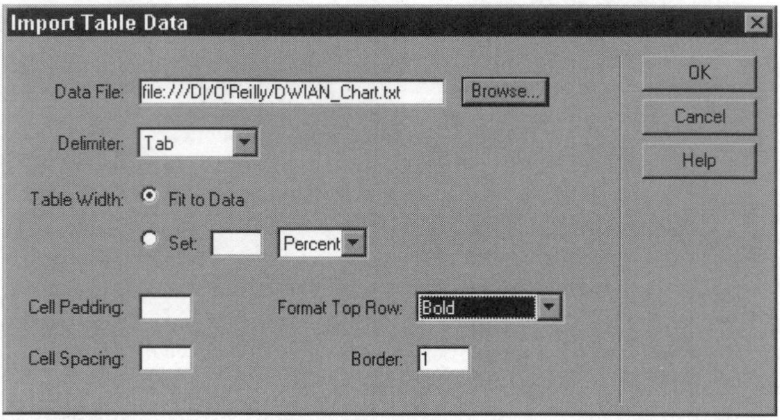

Figure 3-15: The Import Table Data dialog box

Table 3-3: Import Table Data dialog box options

Option	Description
Data File	Selects any file from the local hard drive or network.
Delimiter	Identifies the column delimiter in the file to be imported: Tab (the default), Comma, Semicolon, Colon, or Other.
Table Width	Sets the width of the overall table. The Fit to Data option adjusts the size of the table to the information being imported; the Set option sets the width to a fixed pixel size or as a percentage of the browser window.
Cell Padding	Sets the margin, in pixels, between the border of the cell and the cell contents.
Cell Spacing	Sets the amount of space, in pixels, between adjacent cells.
Format Top Row	Specifies formatting for the top row of the table (i.e., column headings). The options are No Formatting, Bold, Italic, or Bold Italic.
Border	Sets the width, in pixels, of the border around the table.

Dreamweaver can also export data from an HTML table. To export a text file containing table data:

1. Select a table in the Document window.

2. Choose File → Export → Export Table.

3. Choose the Delimiter (Tab, Space, Comma, Semicolon, or Colon) to use to separate items in the exported data.

4. Choose a Line Break style appropriate to the platform for which you are exporting the file (Windows, Macintosh, or Unix).

5. Specify the name of the text file to contain the tabular data.

6. Click OK to export the data.

Formatting and Sorting Tabular Data

You may want to sort or format tabular data to make it more comprehensible or useful to the reader. You must use Standard view to sort and format tabular data (these operations are disabled in Layout view). To format a table, select the table and then use Commands → Format Table to open the Format Table dialog box shown in Figure 3-16. You can choose from the predefined colors schemes or create your own.

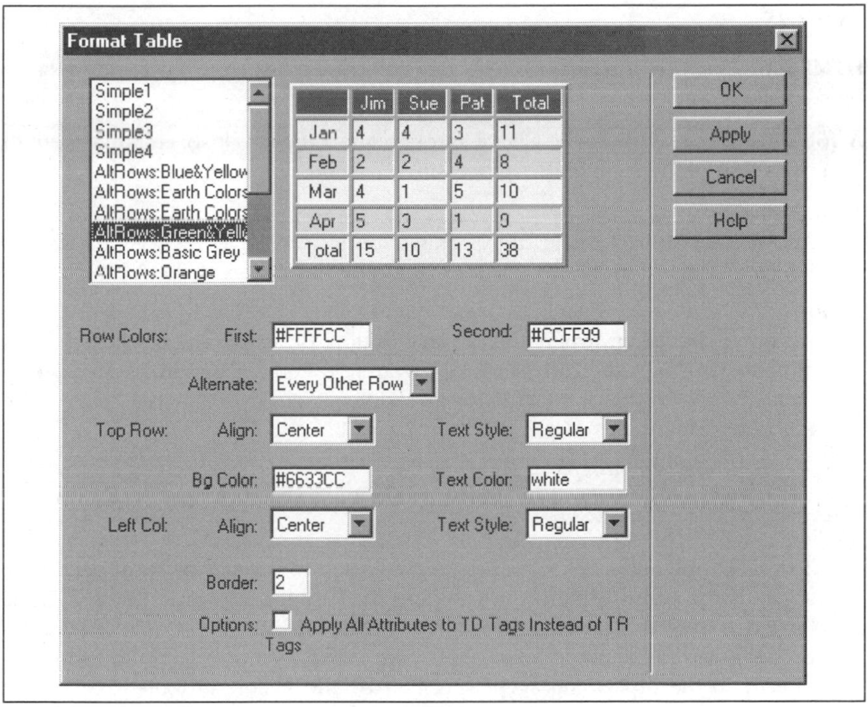

Figure 3-16: The Format Table dialog box

To sort the data in a table, select the table and then choose Command → Sort Table to open the Sort Table dialog box, whose options are explained in Table 3-4.

Table 3-4: Table sorting options

Setting	Description
Sort By	Choose a column to sort the table by.
Order	Choose either Alphabetically or Numerically. (Alphabetical sorting sorts numbers as 1, 11, 12, 2, 21, 22, 3, 4, 5, etc.)
Ascending/Descending	Select either an Ascending (A...Z, 1...100) or Descending (Z...A, 100...1) sort order.
Then By	Specify a second column to sort by when multiple rows have the same value in the Sort By column.
Sort Includes First Row	If the table includes a row of column headings, leave this option disabled.
Keep TR Attributes with Sorted Row	If enabled, row formatting is kept with the data, not the original row number, if a row of data moves.

Forms

HTML forms provide a means of collecting information, such as customer data, to be submitted to a server.

A form has three attributes available through the Property inspector that control the interaction of the form with a processing program on your server.

Form Name

Any unique alphanumeric string. This attribute can be referenced by scripts, which may perform different actions based on the entries in the form.

Action

Action to be taken when the Submit button on the form is clicked. This attribute is usually the URL of a script written in Perl (*.pl* or *.cgi*), Active Server Pages (*.asp*), ColdFusion (*.cfm*), or JavaServer Pages (*.jsp*), such as one of the following examples:

> */cgi-bin/formmail.pl*
> *http://someserver.scriptresources.com/cgi-bin/whatever.asp*

Method

The HTTP method—either GET or POST—used to submit the form data. GET appends the form fields to the URL specified by the Action attribute. GET is limited to ASCII data no larger than 8 KB (the maximum size varies by browser, but is usually at least 1 KB). The POST method sends the form data directly to the processing agent specified by the Action attribute. POST does not impose any size restriction and is required when using File Fields to upload files. Furthermore, GET is insecure, whereas POST can handle nontext data such as encrypted files.

To create a form:

1. Provide some introductory text to explain the purpose of the form and what will be done with the submitted data. Include a link to a privacy policy statement. Depending on the content, you might need to verify the user's age to comply with various laws.

2. Insert an HTML form into your document using Insert → Form. The DW form area is designated by a red dashed border, extending from the left to right

margins; it expands as form elements are added to it. (Use View → Visual Aids → Invisible Elements to ensure visibility of the form boundary.)

3. Specify the form attributes, especially Action, as described earlier in this section.

4. Add one or more form objects within the red-dashed form area using the options in the Insert → Form Objects menu or the icons in the Objects panel's Forms category.

5. Add text labels next to each of your fields to explain its purpose to the user. Consider laying out the fields within a table for greater control over formatting.

6. Include a Submit button to submit your form for processing.

7. Typically, the form Action is the URL of a server-side script that accepts the form data and (perhaps) returns an HTML page in response.

8. Ensure that your server is set up to process the form. Libraries of server-side scripts are widely available from the resources cited in the preface or can be created using UltraDev.

 Netscape Navigator browsers won't execute a script attached to a form object, such as a button, unless the form object is enclosed within a <form> tag. When you insert a form object into an HTML document, Dreamweaver prompts you to add a <form> tag if none exists. You should answer yes.

Processing Form Data

Although Dreamweaver provides you with behaviors that allow you to validate form data (see Chapter 16), it doesn't process information collected in a form, other than the jump menu discussed in the next section.

For simple data collection and manipulation, you can use one of the common CGI scripts or Java applets widely available from public resources or your ISP (and you'll need permission to run scripts on your ISP's server). See the scripting resources cited in the preface.

Note that a page can contain multiple forms or a form might span multiple pages. Forms that span multiple pages are typically processed through a ColdFusion or ASP server that automatically collates the information by writing it to a database as each page of questions is completed. Dreamweaver UltraDev includes server-side behaviors for advanced form processing with ASP, ColdFusion, and JSP.

Form Objects

DW4 provides access to all the form elements available through HTML, as listed in Table 3-5. All of these elements can be inserted using the Insert → Form Objects menu or the icons in the Objects panel's Forms category (the latter can be dragged to the desired location on the page).

Each form object on a page should have a unique name except radio buttons within the same group, which should share a common name. One name/value pair is sent for each field in the form. Names should not contain blank spaces (use underscores instead).

Table 3-5: Form objects

Form object	Attributes
Text Field	Name, Char Width, Max Chars, Wrap, Type (Single Line, MultiLine, Password), Initial Value
Button	Name, Label, Action (Submit Form, Reset Form, None)
Check Box	Name, Checked Value, Initial State (Checked, Unchecked)
Radio Button	Name, Checked Value, Initial State (Checked, Unchecked)
List/Menu	Name, Type (Menu, List), Height, List Values, Initially Selected, Selections (Allow Multiple)
File Field	Name, Character Widths, Max Characters
Image Field	Name, Width (W), Height (H), Src, Alt, Align
Hidden Field	Name, Value

Although each form object creates a typical UI element, such as a text-entry box, radio button, or checkbox (as shown in shown in Figure 3-17), each has its own quirks and caveats. Fancier UI elements can be added using Dreamweaver extensions. For example, the CourseBuilder extension, discussed in Chapter 23, offers graphically appealing radio buttons and checkboxes.

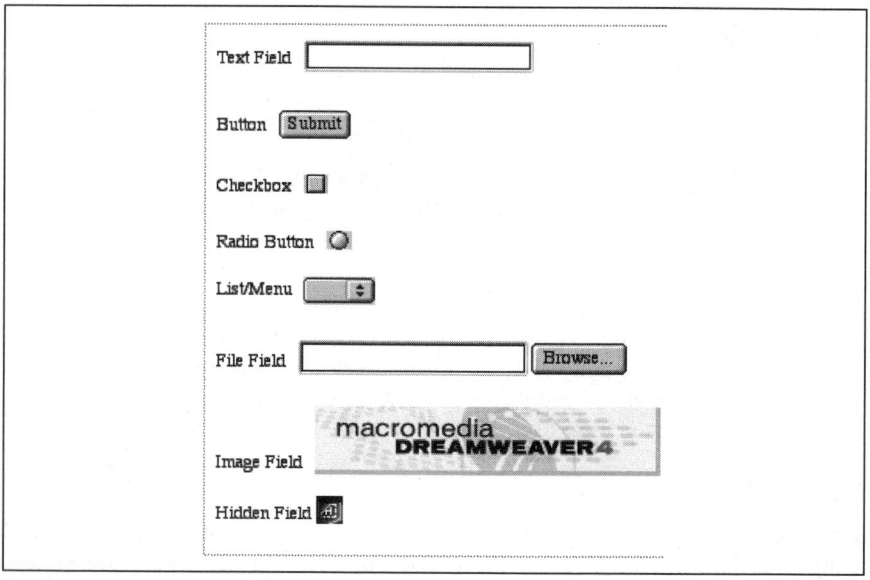

Text Field
Button **Submit**
Checkbox
Radio Button
List/Menu
File Field **Browse...**

macromedia DREAMWEAVER4
Image Field
Hidden Field

Figure 3-17: Form objects

After inserting an object, set its properties in the Property inspector. For example, to create a scrolling, multiline text area (with the `<textarea>` tag), select a text field and then choose the Multiline radio button in the Property inspector.

Text Field

Text fields can be used for single-line or multiline entries. Password fields mask the text entry with asterisks (on Windows) or bullets (on Macintosh) and are always single-line fields. Use the Num Lines option to specify the number of lines to display (the field scrolls if the user enters more data). Set the Wrap option to Virtual to allow text to wrap using "soft" line-breaks. The Validate Form behavior validates text fields only. Use a custom behavior to validate data entry such as dollars, dates, or integers. Leave the Max Char field empty to allow an entry of unlimited length.

 Don't use password-formatted text fields to collect sensitive information such as credit card numbers. The data is not encrypted when sent to the server, and is therefore not secure. For secure passwords and transfers use UltraDev or one of the eCommerce extensions available from the Dreamweaver Exchange (see Chapter 22).

Button

By default, Dreamweaver creates a Submit button when you insert a button, but you can change a button's Label and Action in the Property inspector. The Submit Form action submits the form data for processing. Set the Action to Reset Form to create a button that resets other fields to their default values. Set the Action to None when applying a custom behavior to the button (see Chapter 12 for details on applying behaviors). Assign a custom text label to the button, such as "Do It," using the Label field in the Property inspector.

Check Box

Each checkbox should have a unique Name and a different Checked Value, unlike radio buttons within a group, which share the same Name (but also have different Checked Values). The Name doesn't have to match the separate text label (which you should add beside the checkbox to indicate its purpose).

Radio Button

Radio buttons within a group must have the same Name, but should have different Checked Values. (Radio buttons in different groups must have different Names.) Be sure to add a text label for the radio button group and separate labels for each button within the group.

Use Ctrl-drag (Windows) or Opt-drag (Macintosh) to quickly duplicate a radio button or any other page element.

List/Menu

Use List/Menu fields to create pop-up menus or scrolling lists. If using List as the Type, check the Allow Multiple option to allow the user to select multiple items in the list using Ctrl-click (Windows) or Cmd-click (Macintosh). Each List Value consists of a label (shown to the user) and an optional corresponding value (submitted to the server). If a value isn't specified, it defaults to the same thing as the label.

File Field

Use a File Field to allow the user to attach a file to be uploaded (it includes a Browse button that opens a file browser when clicked). Ensure that your server allows anonymous file uploads, or incorporate a password into the URL used for the Action (which specifies the location of the file to be uploaded). Leave the Max Char field empty to allow a filename of unlimited length.

 The form submission method must be POST when using a File Field. To ensure that files are properly encoded, you must hand-edit the `<form>` tag in Code view to include the `ENCTYPE="multipart/form-data"` attribute.

Image Field

An Image Field is used to insert an image into a form. An image can also be configured to act as button, with greater graphical appeal. To use an image as a submit button, insert the image and then change the text in the name field of the Property inspector to the word Submit. Only the Submit feature is supported without the use of a custom behavior.

Hidden Field

Use hidden fields to transmit hidden data provided by the web page instead of by the user. For example, specify parameters required by generic server-side scripts, such as an email address to which you will send the form contents. Hidden fields are indicated by a shield icon if the Edit → Preferences → Invisible Elements → Hidden Form Fields checkbox and the View → Visual Aids → Invisible Elements menu item are enabled.

Jump menus

Jump menus provide a means of associating URLs with options in a menu list. Jump menus send users to the specified URL when they choose an option from the menu. You can add a jump menu to your document by selecting Insert → Form Object → Jump Menu, which opens the Jump Menu dialog box shown in Figure 3-18.

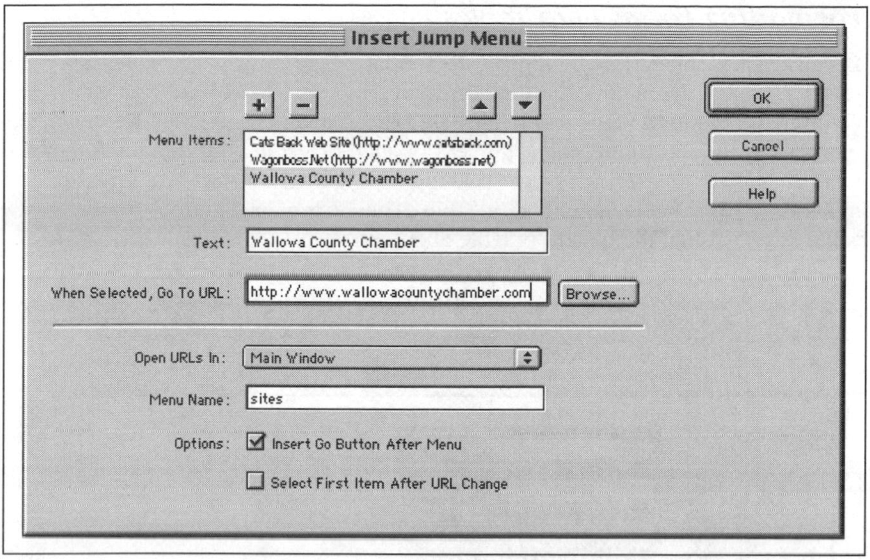

Insert Jump Menu

	OK
	Cancel
	Help

Menu Items: Cats Back Web Site (http://www.catsback.com)
Wagonboss.Net (http://www.wagonboss.net)
Wallowa County Chamber

Text: Wallowa County Chamber

When Selected, Go To URL: http://www.wallowacountychamber.com   Browse...

Open URLs In: Main Window

Menu Name: sites

Options: ☑ Insert Go Button After Menu

☐ Select First Item After URL Change

Figure 3-18: The Jump Menu dialog box

Use this dialog box to create your jump menu as follows:

1. Fill in the Text and the "When Selected, Go To URL" fields for each document, image, or other resource to which you wish to link.

2. Click the plus (+) button to create additional menu entries.

3. When you have added all your menu items, select the target window using the Open URLs In field. (This menu shows all frames plus the Main Window as selection options.)

4. Type the name of the menu in the Menu Name field.

5. Enable the "Insert Go Button After Menu" checkbox to add a Go button, which activates the menu choice. (Otherwise, the new document loads as soon as the menu selection is made.)

6. The "Select First Item After URL Change" checkbox resets the menu after each jump. It is useful only when the jump menu opens a URL in a separate frame. If the checkbox is disabled, the jump menu displays the previously selected item instead of resetting.

Jump menus, with and without a Go button, are shown in Figure 3-19. A jump menu's properties can be edited in the Property inspector.

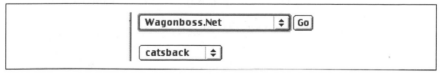

Figure 3-19: Jump menus with and without a Go button

See Chapter 16 for more details on jump menus.

Formatting Forms with Tables

Because form objects can be difficult to format neatly on a page, tables are often used to format them in columns. Typically, the text labels are placed in one column and the form fields themselves are placed in a second column. This placement allows you to control the alignment of each object in your form, whether it is text, an image, or a form object. The top of Figure 3-20 shows a series of text labels and form fields aligned in a table. The bottom of Figure 3-20 shows the same items without the benefit of table alignment.

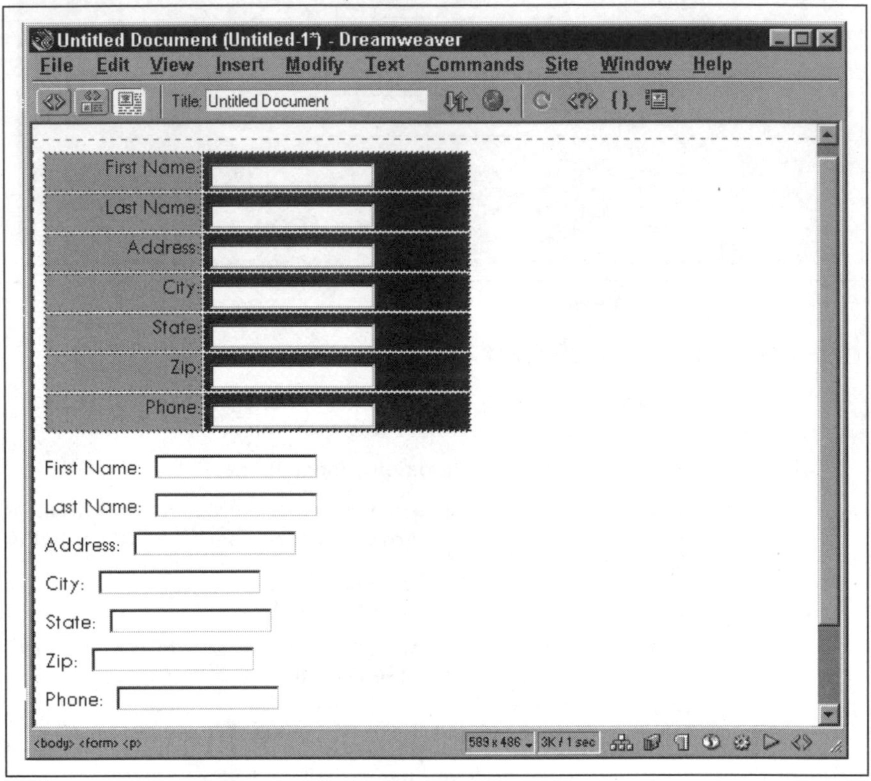

Figure 3-20: A table used to format form objects.

In this chapter, we have seen how to lay out tabular data in Standard view and lay out graphical data in Layout view. We've also seen how to retrieve user responses using forms objects. In the next chapter, we'll discuss Dreamweaver's options associated with frames and layers. Layers can be used to position items on a page or to position fields within a form.

CHAPTER 4

Frames and Layers

Frames and layers can be used to control web page formatting. Some developers consider frames and layers pure evil, whereas others accept them as an imperfect means to an end. To help decide whether you should use frames and layers, see the discussion under "Layers and Tables and Frames, Oh My!" in the preface.

Frames and Framesets

Frames can be used to split the browser window into multiple regions; each region can display a different HTML page. Frames are often used to display a table of contents or navigation bar alongside the main page. Frames are created by using one or more <frame> tags within a <frameset> tag, but as usual, Dreamweaver's visual tools handle the underlying HTML for you. (Dreamweaver does not implement the <iframe> tag in any of its frame configurations. The <iframe> tag is not supported in IE browsers prior to IE4 and is not supported in NN browsers prior to NN6.)

The Objects panel's Frames category, shown in Figure 4-1, offers an easy way to create framesets (and shows thumbnails of each configuration). You can download additional frame configurations from the Dreamweaver Exchange.

You can also insert frames by selecting Insert → Frames and choosing one of the frame configurations listed in Table 4-1 (which correspond to the icons shown in Figure 4-1, but with slightly different names).

Table 4-1 also lists commands from the Modify → Frameset menu (which split an existing frame or create a frameset if the document doesn't already contain one). No Macintosh keyboard shortcuts insert or split frames, but you can use the Alt+I, S and Alt+M, F shortcuts to access these menus under Windows. Furthermore, once a frameset is created, Dreamweaver automatically creates additional columns or rows of frames if you click and drag any edge of the frameset in the Document window.

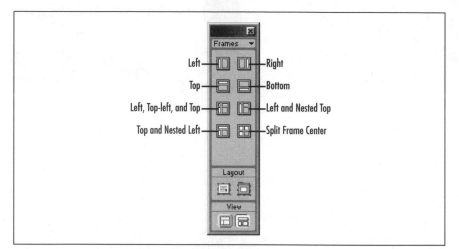

Figure 4-1: The Objects panel's Frames category

Table 4-1: Preformatted frameset options

Menu option	Layout
Insert → Frames → Left	The frame is inserted on the left side. The main window remains on the right.
Insert → Frames → Right	The frame is inserted on the right side. The main window remains on the left.
Insert → Frames → Top	The frame is inserted at the top. The main window remains on the bottom.
Insert → Frames → Bottom	The frame is inserted on the bottom. The main window remains on top.
Insert → Frames → Left and Top	Three frames are inserted on the left, the top-left corner, and the top. The main window occupies the lower right.
Insert → Frames → Left Top	Inserts left and nested top frames. The main window occupies the lower right. Compare with Top Left.
Insert → Frames → Top Left	Inserts top and nested left frames. The main window occupies the lower right. Compare with Left Top.
Insert → Frames → Split	Three square frames are inserted (the window is split into quarters), leaving the main window in the lower-right quadrant.
Modify → Frameset → Split Frames Left	The current document is moved to the left frame. A new frame is inserted on the right.
Modify → Frameset → Split Frames Right	The current document is moved to the right frame. A new frame is inserted on the left.
Modify → Frameset → Split Frames Up	The current document is moved to the top frame. A new frame is inserted on the bottom.
Modify → Frameset → Split Frames Down	The current document is moved to the bottom frame. A new frame is inserted on the top.

The Left Top and Top Left frame configurations use *nested framesets*, in which a <frameset> tag is nested within another <frameset> tag to achieve the desired layout.

For example, DW's Left Top frameset option creates code like this:

```
<frameset rows="*" cols="80,*" frameborder="NO" border="0"
framespacing="0">
  <frame name="leftFrame" scrolling="NO" noresize src="leftframe.html">
  <frameset rows="80,*" frameborder="NO" border="0" framespacing="0">
    <frame name="topFrame" noresize scrolling="NO" src="topframe.html">
    <frame name="mainFrame" src="mainframe.html">
  </frameset>
</frameset>
```

Some older browsers, such as IE3 and NN4, do not support nested framesets well and may show the top-level frames only. You can create frames in two different documents rather than using a nested frameset in a single document. For example, you could add a Left frame to a document; then click inside the right-hand frame and add a Top frame inside it. This step would simulate a Left Top frameset in a way that supports older browsers.

The HTML that defines a frameset is saved in an *.html* file. Use File → Save Frame, File → Save Frame As, and File → Save All Frames to save your frameset file and the documents that occupy the frames within it. (When saving multiple files in a frameset, Dreamweaver displays a cross-hatched border around the frame or frameset being saved.)

Frameset Properties

Just as a table contains cells, a frameset contains one or more frames that are arranged in rows and/or columns on the page. You can view and select frames within a frameset by using the Frames panel (Window ▸ Frames or Shift+F2) shown in Figure 4-2.

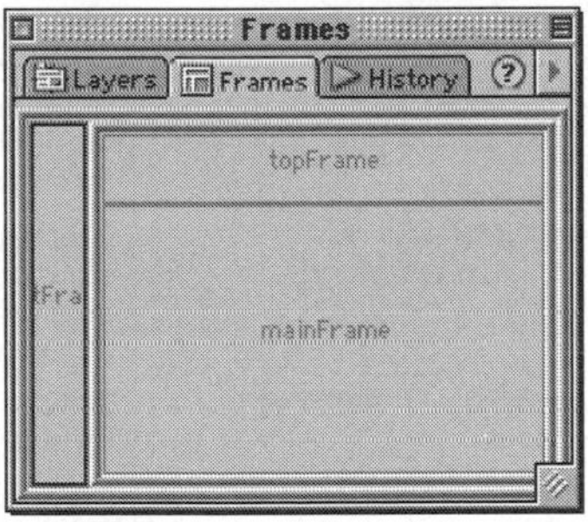

Figure 4-2: The Frames panel

Properties can be set for both the frameset and the frames within it. You should set the frameset's properties first because some affect the frame properties. Frameset properties are set in the Property inspector (see Figure 4-3) when the frameset is selected.

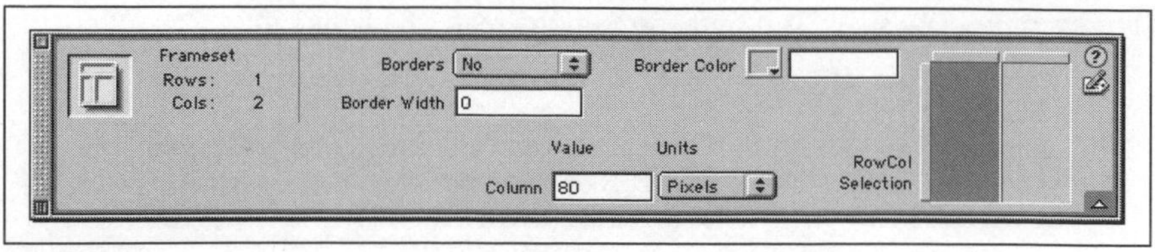

Figure 4-3: The Property inspector showing frameset properties

You can select a frameset in one of three ways:

- By selecting a frame in the Frames panel and then clicking the `<frameset>` tag in the Tag Selector.

- By clicking on the outside border surrounding the frames in the Frames panel.

- By clicking on the edge of the document or the border between any two frames in the Document window (when the cursor changes to a two-headed arrow). Use View → Visual Aids → Frame Borders to make the frame borders visible.

The frameset properties are explained in Table 4-2. Note that within the frameset Property inspector you can also set the height and width of frames within the frameset. (You can also change the height and width of frames by dragging the borders between frames in the Document window). Frame dimensions can be set as a fixed width in pixels or as a percentage of the browser window or parent frame (in the case of a nested frameset). Set the column width or row height Units to Relative to cause that column or row to autostretch to fill the necessary area when the user resizes the browser window.

Table 4-2: Frameset properties

Property	HTML attributes of <frameset>	Description
Borders	`frameborder="yes"	"no"`	Use no to hide borders between frames (and set Border Width to 0). The Border Width should be nonzero if Borders is set to yes.
Border Width	`border="length"` and `framespacing="length"`	Determines the margin around the frameset and between adjoining frames. Set it to 0 when Borders is set to no.
Border Color	`bordercolor="RGBvalue"	"colorname"`	Sets the border color (Border Width should be nonzero).
Column Width	`cols="col1width, ..., colnWidth"`	Defines the number and width of frames in a row of the frameset.
Row Height	`rows="row1height, ..., rownHeight"`	Defines the number and height of frames in a column of the frameset.
Row/Column Selector	See Column Width and Row Height entries	Selects a row or column of frames for setting height or width.

When you insert a frame, Dreamweaver adds the `cols` or `rows` attribute (or both) to the `<frameset>` tag it creates. For example, if you add a Top frame, Dreamweaver adds `rows="80,*"` to the `<frameset>` tag, which implies that there is one column containing two frames (rows) within the frameset. The top frame is 80 pixels high (the height could also be set as a percentage, such as 20%); the bottom frame's height, as indicated by the asterisk (*) expands to fill the remainder of the browser window.

Frame Properties

As with most elements, frames have their own sets of properties. You should set each frame's name and the URL of the document to be displayed within it (Dreamweaver assigns a default frame name such as leftFrame, topFrame, or mainFrame when using the predefined frame configurations). These and other properties of each frame can be set in the Property inspector (see Figure 4-4) when a frame is selected. Frame properties are explained in Table 4-3.

Note that the height and width of frames within a frameset can be set in the Property inspector when the frameset, not an individual frame, is selected. (Frame height and width are set at the frameset level because all frames in a row or column must have the same height or width.) The frame's Border and Border Color properties default to the settings for the frameset.

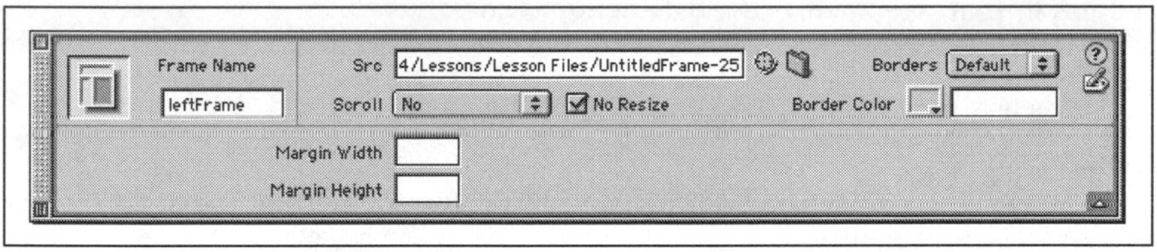

Figure 4-4: The Property inspector showing frame properties

Table 4-3: Frame properties

Property	HTML attributes of <frame>	Description
Frame Name	name="*string*"	The name used by scripts and for link targets.
Src	src="*url*"	The URL of the initial document to load.
Scroll	scrolling="auto" | "yes" | "no"	Controls the presence of scroll bars for the frame.
No Resize	noresize	See the explanation following this table.
Borders	frameborder="yes" | "no"	Shows or hides the borders between frames.
Border Color	bordercolor="*RGBvalue*" | "*colorname*"	Controls the frame border color. Uses the frameset setting if blank.
Margin Height	marginheight="*length*"	Determines vertical spacing from the adjacent frame.
Margin Width	marginwidth="*length*"	Determines horizontal spacing from the adjacent frame.

The No Resize property prevents a user from dragging the edge of a frame to resize it, but the frame may still resize when the browser window is resized. Use fixed pixel dimensions to prevent frames from resizing when the browser window is resized.

Targeting Frames

When using frames, a hyperlink can target either an individual frame or the entire document window. For example, if a frame contains a navigation bar, you'll want the navigation bar's hyperlinks to affect the contents of another frame, not the frame containing the navigation bar.

After creating a link, you can set the link's target using the Modify → Link Target menu or the Target pop-up menu in the Property inspector. The names of any frames in your document will appear in the Target menu. Setting the link target causes the new document to replace the contents of the specified frame. If no target is specified, the default is _self, (i.e., the current frame or window is replaced).

The Target menu contains four default choices (in addition to the names of any frames in your document). The default targets are:

_blank
> Opens a new browser window for the document.

_self
> The new document replaces the document into the current frame or window (this is the default).

_top
> Loads the new document into the browser window, eliminating any existing frames. This target is useful when linking from your framed site to someone else's unframed site. (The _top option is the same as _self if no frames are on the current page.)

_parent
> Loads the new document into the current frameset. If you use nested framesets, only the current frameset is affected. This option doesn't work well in NN4, which has flawed support for nested framesets. (If the page is not using nested framesets, the _parent option is the same as _top.)

Nested Frames

Although the number of frames that can be displayed within a single frameset is unlimited, there are some restrictions on how they can be arranged. You can nest frameset tags inside of other frames to create complex configurations without actually nesting framesets.

 Complicated framesets complicate surfing. Avoid using more than three frames in any document.

We saw how to simulate a Left Top frameset using nested frames in the section "Frames and Framesets" earlier in this chapter. Here's another example of how to nest framesets:

1. Create your first level of frames using one of the methods described earlier.

2. Select one of the frames to contain the nested frameset.

3. Add a new frameset inside the selected frame using:

   a. Modify → Frameset → Split Frames (and then choosing Up, Down, Left, or Right); or

   b. Insert → Frames (and choosing Left, Right, Top, or Bottom); or

   c. The Left, Right, Top, or Bottom icons in the Objects panel's Frames category.

Nesting framesets in this manner ensures that <frameset> tags are nested within <frame> tags, as shown here, and not directly within other <frameset> tags:

```
<frameset>
  <frame>
  <frameset>
    <frame>
    <frame>
  </frameset>
  <frame>
</frameset>
```

Note that nested framesets inherit the border settings of the parent frameset.

NoFrames Content

Whenever you add frames to a document, Dreamweaver automatically adds the <noframes> tag to your HTML. The <noframes> tag uses a <body> tag to display unframed data to users whose browsers don't support frames.

 According to the W3C standard, the <noframes> tag should be placed before the closing </frameset> tag, but Dreamweaver places it after the closing </frameset> tag.

The default code inserted with the <noframes> tag is:

```
<noframes>
  <body bgcolor="#FFFFFF" text="#000000">
  </body>
</noframes>
```

You can modify the <noframes> content directly using Modify → Frameset → Edit No Frames Content. When editing the <noframes> content, the words "NoFrames Content" are shown at the top of the Document window's Design pane. Select Modify → Frameset → Edit No Frames Content again to untoggle this option and return to editing your framed web page.

Layers

Layers are another alternative to frames or tables for controlling a web page's layout. Unlike other HTML elements, layers provide both compositing (i.e., two elements can occupy the same area) and absolute positioning (i.e., you can specify the coordinates of a layer relative to the upper-left corner of the browser window or relative to another layer). Layers are empty containers into which you can insert other elements, such as text and graphics.

 Unlike other HTML elements, the visual position of a layer on the page is unrelated to the location of the layer tag within your HTML code. Instead, layer positioning is controlled by the coordinate attributes specified within the tag itself.

Layers require CSS and therefore require at least IE4. Whereas NN4 supports layers, it doesn't support advanced features such as nested layers. See the discussion under "Layers" in the preface for more information. Layers can also be used for special effects and animation as described in Chapter 14 and Chapter 17. Consider using Macromedia Flash or Shockwave for more demanding animations or interactivity.

Although layers were originally designed for page layout, tables still offer more reliable alignment in most browsers. If you like, you can design your page using the layer tools and then choose Modify → Convert → Layers to Table to transform your layers to tables (however, you can't convert layers to tables if any of the layers overlap). You can also convert layers to a table using the File → Convert → 3.0 Browser Compatible → Layers to Table command. Converting tables to layers may create unnecessarily verbose HTML. Create tables using Dreamweaver's table tools for greater efficiency.

Conversely, you can convert tables to layers by using Modify → Convert → Tables to Layers. You can also export layers from Fireworks using its File → Export command and setting the Save As Type option to CSS Layers (.htm).

Layer Preferences

Dreamweaver creates layers using <div> tags by default. This default can be changed in the Layer Preferences dialog box, which is accessed using Edit → Preferences → Layers and is shown in Figure 4-5. The <layer> and <ilayer> tags are supported in NN4 only (and aren't supported in NN6), so the LAYER and ILAYER options should not be used. The <span> tag is not supported in Netscape, so use the DIV option for maximum compatibility.

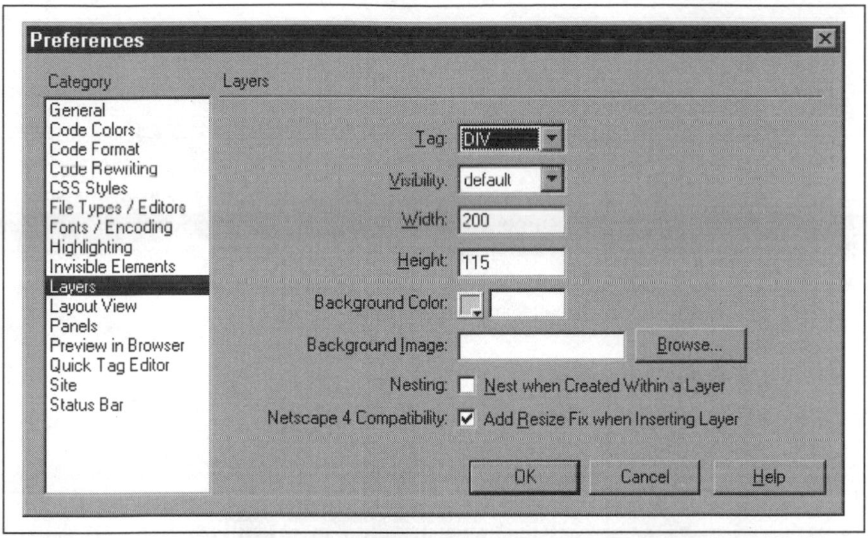

Figure 4-5: The Layer Preferences dialog box

The Layer preferences are explained in Table 4-4.

Table 4-4: Layer preferences

Preference	HTML	Description
Tag	`<div>`, `<span>`, `<layer>`, or `<ilayer>`	Creates layers using the specified tag. You should use DIV.
Visibility	`visibility:default	inherit	visible	hidden`	Controls visibility of the layer when the document loads.
Width	`width:length;`	The layer width in pixels.
Height	`height:length;`	The layer height in pixels.
Background Color	`background-color: RGBcolor	colorname;` and `layer-background-color: RGBcolor	colorname;`	The layer's background color. Both properties are used to support the major browsers.
Background Image	`Background-image: url;` and `layer-background-image: url;`	The layer's background image. Both properties are used to support the major browsers.
Nesting	N/A	Allows nested layers. It is not supported by Netscape Navigator.
Netscape 4 Compatibility	See the discussion following this table.	Refreshes layers in Netscape Navigator when the browser window is resized.

If you use layers with Netscape Navigator, turn on the "Netscape 4 Compatibility: Add Resize Fix When Inserting Layer" option under Edit → Preferences → Layers.

If you enable the Netscape 4 Compatibility checkbox, Dreamweaver inserts special JavaScript code into any document that uses layers. The JavaScript ensures that layers are properly resized by reloading the page when NN4 users resize the browser window. To add or remove this JavaScript code manually, choose Commands → Add Remove Netscape Resize Fix.

Creating a Layer

To draw a layer, use Insert → Layer or the Draw Layer tool from the Objects panel's Common category, as shown in Figure 4-6.

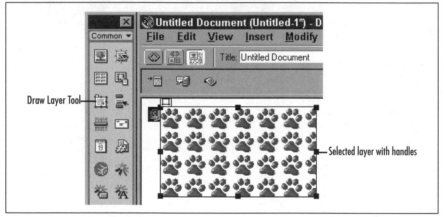

Figure 4-6: Drawing layers

Insert → Layer draws a layer (of the default size specified in the preferences) at the current cursor location. Insert → Layer doesn't set an absolute position for the layer's top-left corner, but the Draw Layer tool does.

Insert → Layer and the Draw Layer tool can be used in Standard view only; they are not available in Layout view. Hold down the Ctrl key (on Windows) or the Cmd key (on Macintosh) to retain the Draw Layer tool when drawing multiple layers.

You can also use Modify → Convert → Tables to Layers to create layers from an existing table. Layers can also be placed within a table. Be careful, however—layers nested within tables won't display properly in some browsers.

As usual, Dreamweaver automatically creates the necessary HTML for your layers, and you can adjust layer properties via the Property inspector. The HTML tag for a layer is represented by a shield icon containing a C (whose visibility depends on the View → Visual Aids → Invisible Elements setting). The icon is usually gold (see Figure 2-23), but turns blue when the layer is selected. The C on the shield icon stands for CSS, because layers implemented with the `<div>` or `<span>` tags conform to the CSS standard. If the layer is implemented using the `<layer>` or `<ilayer>` tags, which are supported by Netscape only, Dreamweaver displays an N on the shield icon instead of a C.

You can select a layer in several ways:

- Shift-click the layer. This technique can also be used to deselect a layer or select multiple layers.

- Click the shield icon representing the layer. Note that the shield icon isn't always located near the layer on the page. Moving the shield icon simply rearranges the underlying HTML code (and can be used to un-nest a nested layer), but it doesn't reposition the layer on the page.

- Click within the layer and then click on the tab that appears in its upper-left corner.

- Click the layer's border (see View → Visual Aids → Layer Borders).

- Click the layer's name in the Layers panel (discussed later in this chapter).

Layer Properties

Layers are affected by a variety of properties available through the Property inspector, as shown in Figure 4-7.

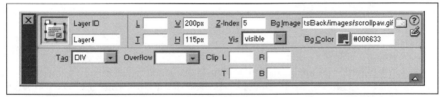

Figure 4-7: The Property inspector showing layer properties

Table 4-5 explains the layer properties that can be set in the Property inspector. If you rename a layer after applying a behavior, you'll have to edit the behavior to use the new layer name.

Table 4-5: Layer properties

Property	HTML	Description
LayerID	id="string"	The layer name (used by scripts) should start with a letter and should not contain spaces.
Left (L)	left=*integer* | *percentage* | auto | inherit	The position of a layer's left edge relative to the browser window, frame, or parent layer.
Top (T)	top=*integer* | *percentage* | auto | inherit	The position of a layer's top edge relative to the browser window or frame.
Width (W)	width=*integer* | *percentage* | auto | inherit	A layer's width in pixels.

Table 4-5: Layer properties (continued)

Property	HTML	Description
Height (H)	height=*integer*	*percentage*	auto	inherit	A layer's height in pixels.
Z-Index	z-index=*integer*	auto	Specifies the layer's stacking order. Higher-numbered layers are drawn in the foreground. (Page's z-index is 0.)
Visible (Vis)	visibility=default	inherit	visible	hidden	Controls layer visibility when the document loads (it can be modified via JavaScript).
Background Image (Bg Image)	background-image= *url*	none and layer-background-image= *url*	none;	Sets a layer's background image. Both properties are used to support major browsers.
Background Color (Bg Color)	background-color= *RGBcolor*	*colorname* and layer-background-color= *RGBcolor*	*colorname*;	Sets a layer's background color. Both properties are used to support major browsers.
Tag	<div>, <span>, <layer>, or <ilayer>	Determines the tag used to create layers. Use DIV.
Overflow	overflow=visible	hidden	scroll	auto	inherit	Controls the display when content exceeds layer dimensions.
Clip (L T R B)	clip = "*left, top, right, bottom*" or clip = "*right, bottom*"	Controls the clipping of images with the layer. Values are in pixels measured from the top-left corner of the layer.

The default Overflow option is Visible, which causes the layer to expand, if necessary, to display the elements within it. The Hidden setting crops elements that are too large to fit within a layer's dimensions. The Scroll and Auto options add scroll bars (either fixed or only when necessary) but neither works in NN4 or Opera, so avoid them.

You can specify four values for the Clip property in the L, R, T, and B fields. If you specify just the R and B values, Dreamweaver assumes that L and T should be zero. If you don't set at least the R and B values, Dreamweaver won't create the clip attribute within your HTML.

Layer Positioning

Although not accessible in the Property inspector, layers also support a position attribute that can be set to static, relative, absolute, fixed, or inherit; however, Dreamweaver always sets a layer's position attribute to absolute. To change this attribute, hand-edit the HTML code. (Subsequent changes made to the layer cause it to revert to absolute positioning). The five types of positioning are as follows.

Static

Static positioning treats a layer as a rectangular box that is rendered in the document flow as with any normal element. It allows layers to move on the page depending on the content that precedes them. This mode also causes layers to affect the position of other elements that follow them on the page

Relative

Relative positioning is the same as static positioning except that the layer's position is offset by the values of the top, right, bottom, and left attributes.

Absolute

Absolute positioning places a layer at coordinates defined by the height, width, top, right, bottom, and left attributes. This is the only mode supported by Dreamweaver. The contents of absolutely positioned elements neither affect nor are affected by the position of other content on the page. Therefore, they may obscure other content displayed on the same page. Coordinates are typically relative to the upper-left corner of the document. Internet Explorer will position nested layers relative to the upper-left corner of the parent layer; Netscape positions nested layers relative to the upper-left corner of the document (it ignores nesting).

Fixed

Fixed positioning uses window-relative coordinates. Whereas absolutely positioned layers will move if the document is scrolled, fixed layers will not, making them suitable for headers and footers. Netscape Navigator 6 is the only browser to support fixed positioning; Internet Explorer and earlier versions of Netscape do not support this mode.

Inherit

Nested layers whose position attribute is set to inherit will inherit the positioning attribute of their parent.

Layers Panel

The Layers panel shown in Figure 4-8 helps manage layers. Open the Layers panel by using Windows → Layers or F2. You can also open the Layers panel by right-clicking (Windows) or Ctrl-clicking (Macintosh) on a layer and selecting Layers Panel from the pop-up contextual menu.

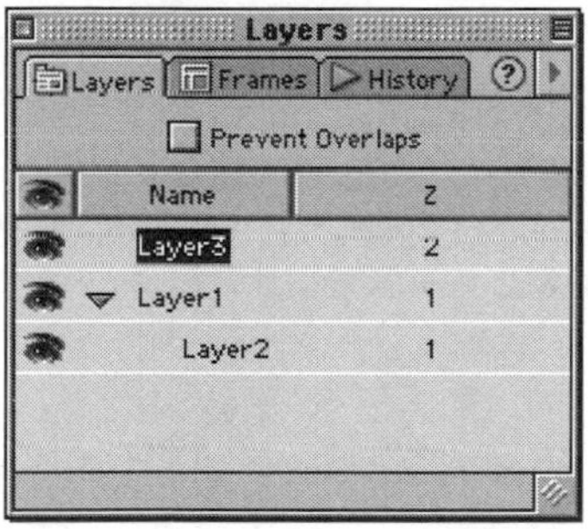

Figure 4-8: The Layers panel

The Layers panel's options are explained in Table 4-6.

Table 4-6: Layers panel options

Control	Description
Visibility	Toggles the visibility of the layer on your screen, not the default setting of the property in your document. Nested layers are hidden when the parent layer is hidden.
Layer Name	Specifies the name of the layer. You can select a layer by clicking its name.
Z-Index	Identifies the vertical stacking order of the layer. 0 is level of the document and a higher-numbered layer appears stacked above that. (The first layer in the Layers panel is in the foreground and the last one is in the background.) See Modify → Arrange → Send to Back and Modify → Arrange → Bring to Front.
Prevent Overlaps	Forces all layers to lie next to one another, preventing the creation of overlapping layers (equivalent to Modify → Arrange → Prevent Layer Overlaps). This option does not affect existing layers' unless you try to move or resize one. Nor does it prevent layers from overlapping when setting their positions via the Property inspector.

Nesting Layers

Layers can be nested inside one another, which allows a set of layers to move in unison and inherit values when the parent layer is modified by a script. Nesting layers groups them conceptually, but nested layers need not be graphically positioned within their parent layer (as in the case of nested tables and frames). Therefore, nested layers may or may not overlap on screen; only their HTML code is physically nested. Similarly, layers need not be nested to occupy the same physical space on a page.

 Netscape Navigator 4 does not handle nested layers properly and often ignores positioning and visibility settings. Avoid nested layers when supporting NN4.

You can create nested layers by:

- Dragging the Draw Layer tool within a parent layer and then releasing it.

- Clicking inside a parent layer and selecting Insert → Layer.

- Ctrl-dragging (Windows) or Cmd-dragging (Macintosh) the name of one layer onto another layer in the Layers panel. The dropped layer becomes a child of the layer you dropped it on.

If the Edit → Preferences → Layers → Nest when Created Within a Layer option is set, Dreamweaver automatically nests layers when a layer is drawn inside another layer.

After creating a nested layer, you can drag the outline of the layer to reposition it on the page; it remains nested even when its position changes.

To un-nest a layer:

- Reposition its shield icon (which moves the HTML tags, not the layer itself); or
- In the Layers panel, Ctrl-drag (Windows) or Cmd-drag (Macintosh) the layer's name to the area below any of the listed layers.
- Hand-edit the HTML code.

Layers Operations

The following layer related operations can be accomplished by hand-editing the HTML, but these gestures manipulate layers more easily.

To delete a layer, select it and then press the Delete key.

To resize or reposition a layer, select it and then:

- Use the resize handles to resize or move it.
- Use the arrow keys to move a layer one pixel (holding down the Shift key moves it by ten pixels).
- Use Ctrl-arrow (Windows) or Cmd-arrow (Macintosh) to resize a layer by one pixel (holding down the Shift key resizes it by ten pixels).
- Specify Left, Top, Height, or Width in the Property inspector using supported units, such as % (percent), px (pixels), pc (picas), pt (points), in (inches), mm (millimeters), cm (centimeters), em (font height), ex (height of x in current font). Specify units without an intervening space, as in 50pt to indicate 50 points.
- Note that negative coordinates cause the layer to be positioned outside the browser's visible area (use the keyboard or Property inspector to position layers offscreen).

You can also align and resize layers using the Modify → Align options as shown in Table 4-7. To use these alignment options, select multiple layers using Shift-click. The selected layers are aligned or resized to match the last selected layer.

Table 4-7: Modify → Align Menu Options

Align	Windows	Macintosh
Left	Ctrl+Shift+1	Cmd+Shift+1
Right	Ctrl+Shift+3	Cmd+Shift+3
Top	Cltr+Shift+4	Cmd+Shift+4
Bottom	Cltr+Shift+6	Cmd+Shift+6
Make Same Width	Cltr+Shift+7	Cmd+Shift+7
Make Same Height	Cltr+Shift+9	Cmd+Shift+9

In this chapter, you have seen how to use frames and layers to control the layout of elements on your web page. See Chapters 14 and 17 for more information on manipulating layers. The next chapter covers how Dreamweaver handles external source files such as Flash and Shockwave assets.

CHAPTER 5

Using External Resources

Dreamweaver easily incorporates external assets that provide advanced layout, multimedia, and interactive capabilities. External assets include Flash, Generator, Fireworks, and Shockwave files, plus Java applets, ActiveX controls, Netscape-style plug-ins, and server-side includes. These assets are created in other applications, not in Dreamweaver itself (although Dreamweaver can create Flash files using the Flash Button and Flash Text tools discussed later). Regardless of their origin, Dreamweaver can incorporate these external objects into your HTML documents. It inserts external objects by using icons in the Objects panel, as shown in Figure 5-1; Macromedia-related objects are found in the Common category, whereas Java applets, plugins, and ActiveX controls are in the Special category.

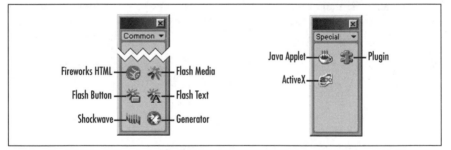

Figure 5-1: External objects in the Objects panel's Common and Special categories

Internet Explorer for Windows typically uses ActiveX controls to support external objects; other browsers on Windows and all browsers on the Macintosh use Netscape-style plugins instead. When inserting Flash and Shockwave objects, Dreamweaver automatically inserts the HTML necessary to support the major browsers on both platforms. When inserting other ActiveX controls and plugins, you may need to add separate HTML for different browsers and platforms. See the section "ActiveX Controls and Plugins" later in this chapter for important details.

Chapter 12 documents behaviors that detect the presence of plugins and ActiveX controls. If users don't have the necessary plugin installed, they have to download it to view your content (or you can provide an alternative version that doesn't require a plugin).

 External files, including images, Flash movies, and Shockwave movies, remain "linked" (i.e., external to the HTML document) and must also be uploaded to the web server in binary format. Double-clicking a linked object opens both the Property inspector and the Select File dialog box, allowing you to link to a new file.

If you haven't saved your HTML document, Dreamweaver uses absolute *file:///* paths to external assets instead of relative URLs. To avoid problems, save the current HTML file before inserting external objects.

Macromedia Source Files

Macromedia sells several graphics and multimedia authoring software packages for web delivery, including:

- Fireworks
- Flash
- Generator
- Shockwave (i.e., Director)

Macromedia sells other products, such as Authorware, but the listed products are the only ones with preconfigured insertion methods from within Dreamweaver.

Macromedia Fireworks

Macromedia Fireworks is a graphics program that uses Portable Network Graphics (PNG) as its native format. Fireworks is geared specifically for web graphics and is tightly integrated with Dreamweaver. You can even lay out web pages in Fireworks, just as you would lay out printed pages in QuarkXpress, PageMaker, or Photoshop. Fireworks is conveniently bundled with Dreamweaver in the Dreamweaver 4 Fireworks 4 Studio and can be optionally installed when you install Dreamweaver. Although Dreamweaver can work with other external graphics editors, Fireworks is required for some specialized commands, such as Commands → Optimize in Fireworks and Commands → Create Web Photo Album.

 PNG, GIF, and JPEG files created with Fireworks or another program are inserted using the Insert Image icon in the Objects panel's Common category, not the Insert Fireworks HTML icon.

The primary Fireworks features that make working with images in Dreamweaver easier include:

- Roundtrip graphics editing using a complete set of bitmap and vector tools for creating, editing, and animating web graphics.

- The creation of complex layouts using tables and sliced images, which is covered in Chapter 13.

- Controls that allow you to optimize images, add interactivity, and export images (complete with JavaScript) directly to Dreamweaver (see Chapter 13).

- Changes to HTML or image files in Fireworks automatically updates them in Dreamweaver.

Roundtrip graphics editing

Dreamweaver allows you to edit graphics in an external editor of your choice, such as Fireworks; after saving the file and returning to Dreamweaver the updated image appears in Dreamweaver's Document window.

The primary graphics editor can be set separately for PNG (.png), GIF (.gif), and JPEG (.jpg, .jpe, and .jpeg) file types under Edit → Preferences → File Types / Editors.

To edit an image in an external graphics editor automatically, select the image and click the Edit button in the lower half of the Property inspector, as shown in Figure 5-2. You can also right-click (Windows) or Ctrl-click (Macintosh) on an image and choose either Edit With Fireworks or Edit With... from the contextual menu (the primary editor and any secondary editors defined in the preferences are shown, or you can browse to pick another editor).

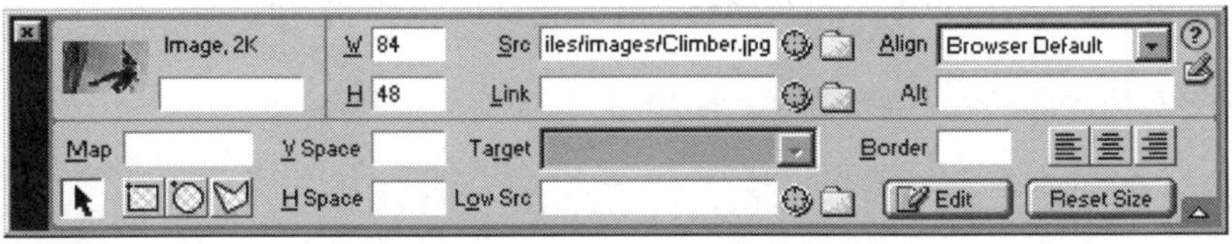

Figure 5-2: The Property inspector for Fireworks images

Make your changes in the external editor and save the file. If you don't see an updated image after returning to the Dreamweaver window, select the image and then click the Refresh button in the Property inspector.

Importing Fireworks HTML into Dreamweaver

Fireworks can create rollover images, menus, animations, and sliced images. It exports the HTML and JavaScript needed to recreate these items in Dreamweaver. Procedure 3 in Chapter 8 explains how to create a table in Fireworks.

Fireworks HTML documents can be imported into Dreamweaver using the Insert Fireworks HTML icon in the Objects panel's Common category or by using Insert

→ Interactive Images → Fireworks HTML. (HTML documents created by other applications cannot be imported this way; use the File → Open and File → Import options instead.)

Inserting Fireworks HTML opens the dialog box shown in Figure 5-3.

Insert Fireworks HTML
Fireworks HTML File: [   ] [Browse...]   [OK]
Options: ☐ Delete file after insertion   [Cancel]
[Help]

Figure 5-3: The Insert Fireworks HTML dialog box

Use the Browse button to select your Fireworks HTML file, then click OK. The Fireworks HTML document is inserted into Dreamweaver's current HTML document at the cursor location.

The Delete File After Insertion checkbox moves local HTML files to the Recycle Bin (Windows) or the Trash (Macintosh); however, files accessed over a network are deleted immediately if this option is enabled.

For more information on Fireworks integration with Dreamweaver, see Chapter 13.

Macromedia Flash

The Macromedia Flash authoring tool creates low-bandwidth animations and interactive multimedia using vector graphics and other media types. Flash uses ActionScript (a JavaScript-like scripting language) to create engaging applications including server-side connectivity. The widely deployed Flash Player is available for all major browsers and also works with some less-popular browsers. Up to 96 percent of users are capable of viewing Flash 3 content, with a somewhat lower percentage capable of viewing Flash 4 and Flash 5 content. For current adoption statistics, see *http://www.macromedia.com/software/player_census/flashplayer/*.

The free Flash Player is available as both an ActiveX control (typically installed at *C:\WINDOWS\SYSTEM\MACROMED\FLASH\Swflash.ocx*) and as a Netscape-style plugin (typically installed at *C:\Program Files\Netscape\Communicator\Program\Plugins\npswf32.dll*) under Windows. On the Macintosh, the Flash plugin is called *Shockwave Flash NP-PPC* and is stored in the *Plug-ins* folder of the major browsers.

FutureSplash (which created *.spl* files) was a product, bought by Macromedia, that subsequently evolved into Flash. Despite confusing nomenclature, the Flash Player (Shockwave for Flash) is unrelated to Shockwave for Director. Macromedia just used the same name to help promote Shockwave.com. Now that they've sold Shockwave.com to AtomFilms, the word "Shockwave" without any qualifiers once again refers to Shockwave for Director. Adding to the confusion, the Shockwave for Director installer also installed the Flash Player. When your clients ask you to create Shockwave content in Flash, chortle knowingly and refer them to Macromedia TechNote 13971 (*http://www.macromedia.com/support/general/ts/documents/sw_flash_differences.htm*).

To insert a Flash object (a document with a *.swf* extension) into your Dreamweaver document, you must first create a *.swf* file using Flash (or another third-party application that exports in the *.swf* format, such as Adobe's LiveMotion). You can create a *.swf* file from a *Flash movie (.fla)* file by using Flash 5's File → Publish command. If you don't need Flash 5's latest features, you can publish the *.swf* file in an older format, such as Flash 3 or Flash 4, for compatibility with older versions of the Flash plugin. Content authored for older Flash plugins should work with the Flash 5 plugin as well.

To detect the Flash plugin's presence and version number, see the Moock Flash Player Inspector at *http://moock.org/webdesign/flash/detection/moockfpi/*. Also see the Check Plugin behavior covered in Chapter 12.

For more information on using Macromedia Flash, consult Macromedia's *Using Flash* manual, which accompanies the software. For information on ActionScript, see *ActionScript: The Definitive Guide* by Colin Moock (O'Reilly).

See the JavaScript Integration Kit for Macromedia Flash 5, which contains various JavaScript behaviors used with Dreamweaver, to work with Flash assets (*http://www.macromedia.com/software/dreamweaver/productinfo/extend/jik_flash5.html*).

Inserting Flash Documents

Insert a *.swf* file by using Insert → Media → Flash, the Insert Flash icon in the Objects panel, Ctrl+Alt+F (Windows), or Cmd+Opt+F (Macintosh). You can also drag and drop a *.swf* file from the desktop into the Document window.

 Flash files intended for web delivery typically have a *.swf* file extension (pronounced "swif"). Dreamweaver can also import older FutureSplash (*.spl*) and Generator (*.swt*) files, but does not import Flash source (*.fla*) files. See "Configuring a Web Server for Flash" in Macromedia's *Using Flash* manual or the Flash Online Help for details on the MIME type for Flash. This MIME type is usually `application/x-shockwave-flash`.

Once a Flash asset is inserted, the Document window displays a placeholder Flash logo instead of the actual Flash movie's content. The placeholder occupies a gray box matching the size of the Flash movie, as shown in Figure 5-4. Use the Play button in the Flash Property inspector (see Figure 5-6) to preview the Flash movie in Dreamweaver, complete with interactivity. If Design Notes are enabled, changes made to a *.swf* file in Flash are automatically reflected in Dreamweaver.

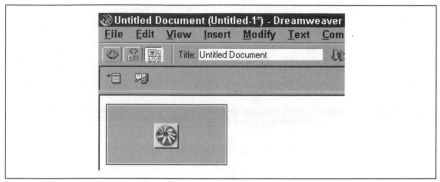

Figure 5-4: A Flash movie seen through Dreamweaver

Inserting a Flash asset adds it to the Site list in the Flash category of the Assets panel (Flash Button and Flash Text elements are not shown in the Assets panel). Flash assets can also be dragged from the Assets panel and dropped into the Document window or inserted using the Insert button in the Assets panel. The Assets panel is discussed in Chapter 6.

On the Macintosh, Flash buttons don't always refresh properly due to a bug in the Flash Player that ships with Dreamweaver. Download the latest version of the Flash plugin for Dreamweaver from *http://www.macromedia.com/downloads/*.

You can use the Play, Stop, Play All, and Stop All options under the View → Plugins menu to start and stop Flash animations and other inserted objects. Chapter 16 covers the Control Shockwave or Flash behavior, which can play and stop Flash assets at runtime under user control. You can also preview Flash objects in an external browser using File → Preview in Browser (F12), as seen in Figure 5-5.

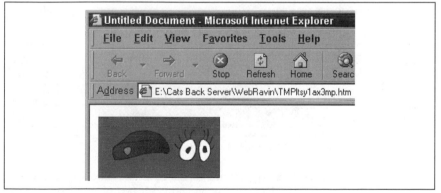

Figure 5-5: A Flash movie seen through Internet Explorer

When you insert a Flash object, Dreamweaver adds HTML similar to the code shown in Example 5-1. Note the version number of the ActiveX control specified within the `codebase` attribute. (The `<embed>` tag used for the Netscape-style plugin does not support a version mechanism; the version must be checked with a separate JavaScript behavior).

Example 5-1: Sample HTML code for inserting a Flash object

```
<object classid="clsid:D27CDB6E-AE6D-11cf-96B8-444553540000"
        codebase="http://download.macromedia.com/pub/shockwave/
                  cabs/flash/swflash.cab#version=5,0,0,0"
        width="550" height="400" id="eggplant">
  <param name="movie" value="Macromedia/Flash5/Samples/Eggplant.swf">
        <param name="quality" value=high>
        <param name="scale" value="exactfit">
        <param name="loop" value="false">
        <param name="play" value="false">
  <embed src="Macromedia/Flash5/Samples/Eggplant.swf"
        quality=high
        scale="exactfit"
        loop="false"
        play="false"
        pluginspage="http://www.macromedia.com/shockwave/
                     download/index.cgi?P1_Prod_Version=ShockwaveFlash"
        type="application/x-shockwave-flash"
        width="550"
        height="400">
  </embed>
</object>
```

Flash Properties

Double-click a Flash object to open the Select Flash File dialog box, or pick a new Flash file using the File field in the Property inspector. For Flash objects, hyperlinks are implemented in ActionScript. To attach a hyperlink to a Flash object in HTML, wrap the Flash object in a `<span>` tag and then attach the hyperlink to the `<span>` tag.

When a Flash object is selected, the Property inspector appears as shown in Figure 5-6.

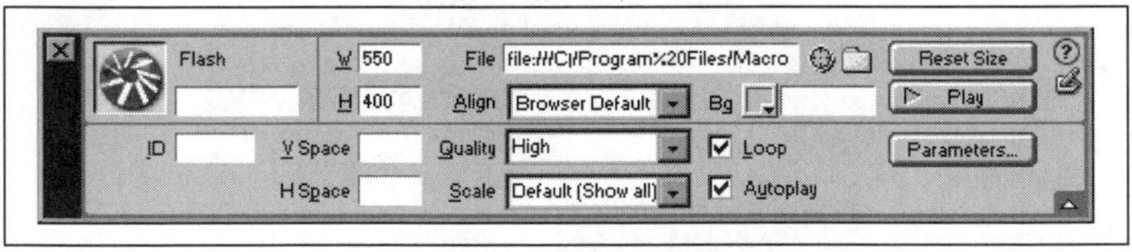

Figure 5-6: The Property inspector for Flash objects

The properties unique to Flash objects are explained in the following list. Most of these properties also apply to the Flash Button and Flash Text objects discussed later in this chapter. Refer to the HTML code in Example 5-1 for the equivalent HTML.

ID

An identification string that scripts can use to manipulate the Flash media.

Quality

Sets the antialiasing of text and graphics to control playback quality (High, Auto High, Auto Low, or Low). High uses antialiasing at all times; Low never uses antialiasing; the Auto High and Auto Low options use varying degrees of antialiasing, depending on the performance of the user's machine.

Scale

Controls scaling. Default (Show All) scales the Flash object but maintains its aspect ratio; Exact Fit stretches the Flash content to fit the object's rectangle, possibly distorting the original aspect ratio; No Border is similar to Exact Fit, but stretches the Flash content to the edges of its bounding rectangle.

Loop

Causes the Flash animation to loop continuously (loop is **true** by default). Applies to Flash objects, but not Flash Text and Flash Button objects.

Autoplay

Causes the Flash animation to play immediately upon loading (play is **true** by default). Applies to Flash objects, but not Flash Text and Flash Button objects.

The following buttons in the Property inspector are also useful for Flash objects:

Reset Size

Resets the size of a Flash object to that of the original *.swf* asset.

Play/Stop

Plays the Flash media, allowing you to preview it in Dreamweaver (use F12 to preview a Flash movie in a browser). The Play button switches to a Stop button while the Flash movie plays. Press it again to stop the Flash movie. (Also see the Play and Stop commands under the View → Plugins menu.)

Edit

Reopens the Insert Flash Button or Insert Flash Text dialog box to modify an existing Flash Button or Flash Text object (does not apply to other Flash objects).

Parameters

Allows you to add additional parameters to your objects. For more information on available parameters, see "Publishing HTML for Flash Player files" in Macromedia's *Using Flash* manual or in the Flash Help window. Use the **base** attribute to force the Flash plugin to use a specific path for resolving document-relative links within the Flash movie.

Inserting Flash Buttons

Flash Button objects are small Flash *.swf* files containing visually appealing interactive buttons that use Flash ActionScript instead of JavaScript.

Unlike most other external assets, Flash Buttons can be created directly in Dreamweaver. To create a Flash Button and add it your HTML document, use the Insert → Interactive Media → Flash Button command or the Flash Button icon in the Objects panel's Common category. Figure 5-7 shows the Insert Flash Button dialog box, which creates Flash Button objects by using the options shown in Table 5-1. Dreamweaver creates HTML code similar to Example 5-1 when you insert a Flash Button. (Flash Buttons are simply *.swf* files based on *.swt* templates).

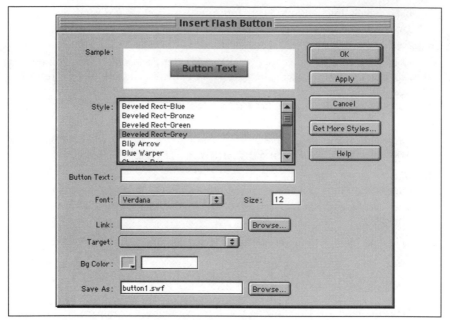

Figure 5-7: The Insert Flash Button dialog box

Other than the background color, Flash Button settings are embedded within the *.swf* file (such as *button1.swf*) created by Dreamweaver. Double-click a Flash Button object to modify its attributes in the Insert Flash Button dialog box. You can also open this dialog box by double-clicking an existing Flash Button object in the Document window. A Flash Button object's *.swf* file can also be edited in the Flash authoring tool for greater control, but it may no longer be recognized as a Flash Button object in Dreamweaver (instead, it may be treated like a straight Flash object.)

You can set the options explained in Table 5-1 in the Flash Button dialog box. Other properties can be set in the Property inspector as usual.

Table 5-1: Inserting Flash Button properties

Property	Description
Style	Select from one of the predefined Flash Buttons styles (see Figure 5-8) or download more by clicking Get More Styles…
Button Text	The text label to appear on the button (the text is always centered). This option is ignored for button styles in Figure 5-8 that don't include text.
Font	The font used for the button text. All installed fonts are available for use with Flash Buttons. Flash will embed the font in the *.swf* file if necessary.
Size	The typeface size to be used. Use a size no larger than the button can accommodate. If you scale the button in Dreamweaver, the text will scale as well.

Table 5-1: Inserting Flash Button properties (continued)

Property	Description
Link	The URL of document to load when button is clicked. Site Root Relative links are not recognized with Flash movies. Either use an absolute URL or use a document-relative URL and save the *.swf* file in the same folder as the *.html* file.
Target	The destination window or frame in which to open link document.
Bg Color	The background color, which will show through transparent portions of the button.
Save As	The filename of the newly created *.swf* file containing the Flash Button (defaults to *buttonx.swf*).
Get More Styles	A link that leads to the Dreamweaver Exchange web site, where you can download additional Flash Button styles.

The primary Flash Button styles available in Dreamweaver are shown in Figure 5-8. More styles can be downloaded from the Dreamweaver Exchange by clicking the Get More Styles button in the Insert Flash Button dialog box. Button styles are stored in *.swt* files in the folder named *Dreamweaver 4/Configuration/Flash Objects/Flash Buttons*.

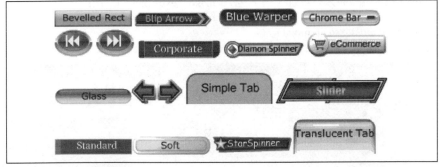

Figure 5-8: Default Flash Button styles

When a Flash Button object is selected, the Property inspector appears as shown in Figure 5-9 (likewise for Flash Text objects discussed next). Note the differences from Figure 5-6, such as the absence of the Loop and Autoplay options, the relocation of the Play button to the lower pane, and the presence of an Edit button (which reopens the Insert Flash Button dialog box to set the internal *.swf* file properties that aren't available via the Property inspector).

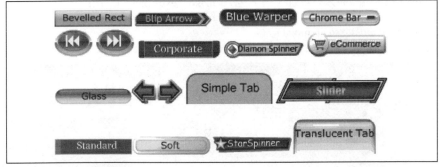

Figure 5-9: The Property inspector for Flash Buttons

To use an existing *.swf* file as a Flash Button, point to it using the File field in the Property inspector. Instead of creating a link, the Save As option in the Insert Flash Button dialog box creates a *.swf* file and overwrites any existing *.swf* file of the same name.

Inserting Flash Text

Flash Text objects are small Flash *.swf* files that can provide stylized, scalable text with an optional hyperlink. For example, if you set a Flash Text object's width to 50% in the Property inspector, the text will scale when the browser window is resized.

As with Flash Buttons, Flash Text can be created directly in Dreamweaver. To create Flash Text and add it to your HTML document, use Insert → Interactive Media → Flash Text or the Flash Text icon in the Objects panel's Common category. Figure 5-10 shows the Insert Flash Text dialog box, which creates Flash Text objects using the options shown in Table 5-2. Dreamweaver creates HTML code similar to Example 5-1 when you insert a Flash Text object. (Flash Text objects are simply *.swf* files based on the *Dreamweaver 4/Configuration/Flash Objects/Flash Text/text template.swt* template.)

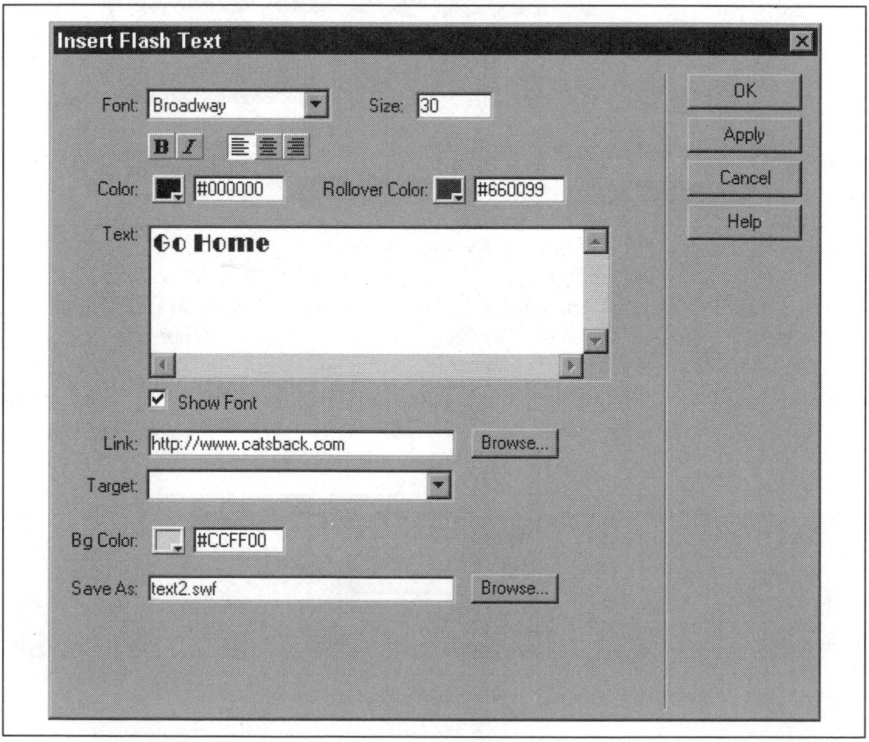

Figure 5-10: The Insert Flash Text dialog box

Other than the Bg Color, the Flash Text settings are embedded within the *.swf* file (such as *text1.swf*) created by Dreamweaver. Double-click a Flash Text object to modify its attributes in the Insert Flash Text dialog box. You can also open this dialog box by double-clicking an existing Flash Text object in the Document window. A Flash Text object's *.swf* file can also be edited in the Flash authoring tool for greater control, but it may no longer be recognized as a Flash Text object in Dreamweaver (instead, it may be treated like a straight Flash object.)

You can set the options explained in Table 5-2 in the Flash Text dialog box. Other properties can be set in the Property inspector as usual.

Table 5-2: Inserting Flash Text properties

Property	Description
Font	The font used for the text. All installed fonts are available for use with Flash Text. Flash will embed the font in the *.swf* file if necessary.
Size	The typeface size to be used. If you scale the text object in Dreamweaver, the text within it scales as well.
Bold/Italic	The text style to be used in the Flash Text object.
Alignment	Left, center, or right alignment options.
Color	The text color prior to a mouse rollover effect.
Rollover Color	The text color when the mouse pointer rolls over Flash Text.
Text	The text to appear in Flash Text object. It can be a single word or an entire paragraph.
Link	The URL of the document to load when hypertext is clicked. Either use an absolute URL, or use a document-relative URL and save the *.swf* file in the same folder as the *.html* file.
Target	The destination window or frame in which to open link document.
Bg Color	The text background color in the Flash Text object.
Save As	The filename of the newly created *.swf* file containing Flash Text (defaults to *textx.swf*).

The Property inspector's appearance is the same for Flash Text objects and Flash Button objects (see Figure 5-9). The Edit button reopens the Insert Flash Text dialog box, which is used to set the internal *.swf* file properties not available via the Property inspector.

 To use an existing *.swf* file as a Flash Text object, point to it using the File field in the Property inspector. Instead of creating a link, the Save As option in the Insert Flash Text dialog box creates a *.swf* file and overwrites any existing *.swf* file of the same name.

Macromedia Generator

Macromedia Generator is a server-based application that creates *.swf* (Flash), *.gif*, *.jpg*, *.png*, and *.mov* (QuickTime) files at runtime. Generator uses so-called template (*.swt*) files to generate files in one of these formats from dynamically changing data (for example, it could create bar charts based on real-time stock prices). The *.swt* files are like *.swf* files with placeholders for the dynamic content; *.swf* files are typically authored in Flash using the free Generator Objects included with Flash.

Your web server must be running Generator (or a third-party equivalent) to process *.swt* files, just as a web server must run ColdFusion to process *.cfm* files. In off-line mode, Generator still processes *.swt* files, but not in real-time. Macromedia offers both Generator 2 Enterprise Edition (high performance, scalable solution for enterprises) and Generator 2 Developer Edition (lower performance and lower cost). The Generator 2 Developer Edition is available separately or as part of the Macromedia Flash 5 Generator Studio. There are also third-party server applications that process *.swt* files, obviating the need to buy Generator (see, for example, JGenerator at *http://www.flashgap.com*).

Use Insert → Media → Generator or the Insert Generator icon in the Objects panel's Common category to insert a Generator object into your document. Inserting a Generator object opens the Insert Generator dialog box shown in Figure 5-11.

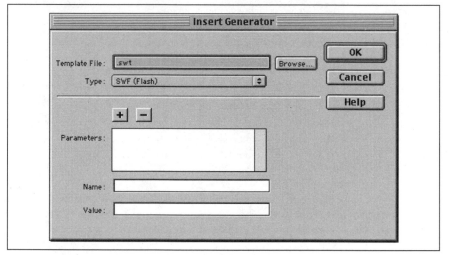

Figure 5-11: The Insert Generator dialog box

In this dialog box, select a Generator template (*.swt*) file. Specify the format that Generator should output—SWF, GIF, JPEG, PNG, or MOV (QuickTime Movie)—in the Type field. Specify additional parameters required by the *.swt* file, if necessary. See Macromedia's *Using Generator* manual or *Flash and Generator Demystified* by Phillip Torrone, Chris Wiggins, and Mike Chambers (PeachPit Press) for details on Generator.

The HTML code created by Dreamweaver when it inserts a Generator object varies depending on the output Type chosen in the Insert Generator dialog box. If the SWF format is chosen, Dreamweaver creates an <object> tag similar to that in Example 5-1; if GIF, JPEG, or PNG format is chosen, DW creates an <img> tag; if MOV format is chosen, DW creates an <embed> tag for the QuickTime plugin.

When a Generator object is inserted, the resulting HTML is similar to that of a Flash, Image, or Plugin object inserted by other means (when the object is selected, corresponding properties are reflected in the Property inspector). If you need to change the output Type, it is easier to delete and re-insert the Generator object than to hand-edit the HTML code.

Macromedia Shockwave

The Macromedia Director authoring tool (which is part of the Macromedia Director 8.5 Shockwave Studio) creates interactive multimedia by combining graphics, sound, animation, text, and video. Director's scripting language, Lingo, provides complete control over interactive learning environments, multiuser games, and 3D worlds. The free Shockwave Player (Shockwave for Director) plays back Macromedia Director content in a browser and is available as both an ActiveX control and a Netscape-style plugin. A small "stub" is installed in each browser's plugins folder, allowing it to access the large (2.5 MB) shared Shockwave libraries stored in the System folder. (The Netscape-style stub is called *np32dsw.dll* on Windows and *NP-PPC-Dir-Shockave* on the Macintosh.)

The Shockwave plugin is widely deployed, but despite being preinstalled with both Windows and the Mac OS, it is not as popular as the smaller Flash plugin. NN6 users may also have trouble viewing Shockwave content due to the buginess of the browser and its compatibility issues with the plugin. Chapter 12 explains how to use the Check Plugin behavior to test for the Shockwave plugin.

For current Shockwave browser statistics, see *http://www.macromedia.com/software/player_census/shockwaveplayer/*.

To insert a Shockwave object into your Dreamweaver document, you must first create a *.dcr* file from a *Director movie* (*.dir*) file using Director's File → Publish command. Director can't create *.dcr* files compatible with older versions of the Shockwave plugin. Therefore, unless you want to force users with older versions of the Shockwave plugin—such as 7.0 and 8.0—to upgrade, you can't use Director 8.5 for authoring. That is, if you want to support users with the Shockwave 7.0 plugin, you must author your content in Director 7.x (users with later Shockwave plug-ins, such as 8.0 and 8.5, will still be able to view content created in Director 7.0).

For more information on using Macromedia Director, consult the *Using Director Shockwave Studio* manual that accompanies the software. Also see O'Reilly's *Lingo in a Nutshell* and *Director in a Nutshell* by Bruce Epstein.

Insert a Shockwave file using Insert → Media → Shockwave, the Insert Shockwave icon in the Objects panel's Common category, Ctrl+Alt+D (Windows), or Cmd+Opt+D (Macintosh). You can also simply drag and drop a *.dcr* file from the desktop into the Design pane of the Dreamweaver Document window.

Director files intended for web delivery typically have a *.dcr* file extension, but uncompressed *.dxr* files and unprotected *.dir* files can also be played back using Shockwave. The MIME type for Director files is `application/x-director`.

Inserting a Shockwave asset adds it to the Site list in the Shockwave category of the Assets panel. Shockwave assets can also be dragged from the Assets panel and dropped into the Document window or inserted using the Insert button in the Assets panel.

Once a Shockwave asset is inserted, the Document window displays a place-holder Shockwave logo instead of the actual Shockwave movie's content. Use the Play button in the Shockwave Property inspector (see Figure 5-12) to preview the Shockwave movie in Dreamweaver, complete with interactivity. You should set the Height and Width to match the size of the Shockwave movie's stage when it was created in Director. The other Shockwave properties are similar to those of Flash objects.

Figure 5-12: The Property inspector for Shockwave objects

Chapter 16 covers the Control Shockwave or Flash behavior, which can play and stop Shockwave assets at runtime under user control. If the Shockwave plugin is installed, you can also preview Shockwave objects in an external browser using File → Preview in Browser (F12). Some Shockwave-capable browsers allow you to preview *.dcr*, *.dxr.*, and *.dir* files if they are dragged from the desktop and dropped into an empty browser window.

When you insert a Shockwave object, Dreamweaver adds the requisite HTML. The options under Director's File → Publish Settings → Format tab will also generate HTML for Shockwave objects in different scenarios. The resulting HTML can be copied into the Code pane of Dreamweaver's Document window.

Be sure that your web server is configured to recognize the MIME types for *.dcr* files. Shockwave movies can themselves use external assets such as *.gif*, *.jpeg*, and *.swa* (Shockwave audio) files, which must also be uploaded to your web server. Furthermore, Shockwave movies can use external cast files (asset libraries) with the *.cct*, *.cxt*, or *.cst* extension.

When testing Shockwave files locally, put all *.dcr*, *.cct*, and asset files used by them in a subfolder called *DSWMEDIA*; otherwise, Shockwave's security restrictions may prevent it from reading the files from your local drive.

Finally, the Shockwave plugin supports so-called Shockwave-safe *Xtras*, which are code modules that add functionality to Shockwave (Xtras are plugins for your plugin!). For example the Flash Asset Xtra allows Shockwave movies to incorporate Flash content. These Xtras use the *.X32* extension on Windows and the *Xtra* file type on the Macintosh. They are installed along with the Shockwave plugin in a folder such as *C:\WINDOWS\SYSTEM\MACROMED\Shockwave\XTRAS* (Windows) or *MacHD:System Folder:Extensions:Macromedia:Shockwave:Xtras* (Macintosh). Third-party Xtras that are digitally signed can be downloaded with the user's permission and installed automatically in the system Xtras folder.

Java Applets

Java applets are a widely supported means of adding advanced functionality to your web site without requiring multiple plugins, although Java can be slow to load. All current browsers support Java (although it creates some screen refresh problems in IE5.5), although users can turn off Java support within their browsers.

To add a Java applet to your Dreamweaver document select Insert → Media → Applet or use the Insert Applet icon in the Object panel's Special category (see Figure 5-1). Select the applet's *.class* file in the Select File dialog box. As with Flash and Shockwave objects, Dreamweaver creates the HTML for you and uses a placeholder to represent the Applet position in your document, as shown in Figure 5-13.

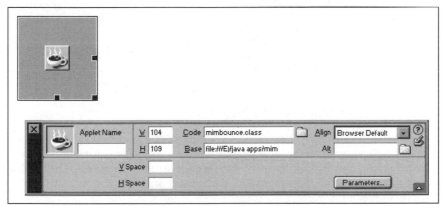

Figure 5-13: Java Applet placeholder and Property inspector

After inserting the applet, you must set up its properties. If you obtained an applet from the Internet, it probably included instructions regarding its required parameters. (If you were provided with the applicable HTML code, you can copy it into the Code pane of Dreamweaver's Document window.) If necessary, contact the applet's developer for documentation or assistance in using the applet.

If applicable, provide required parameters using the Parameters button in the Property inspector. This button opens the Parameters dialog box shown in Figure 5-14.

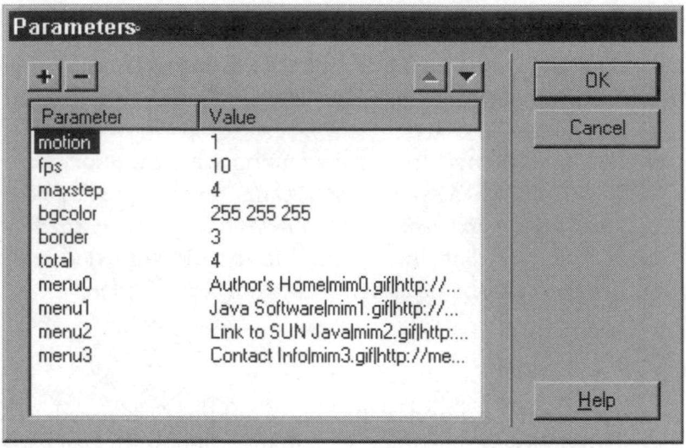

Figure 5-14: Applet Parameters dialog box

Use the plus (+) button to add each new parameter name and value pair. Once you have added all required parameters, click OK. Dreamweaver will insert HTML code that looks something like this for your Java applet:

```
<applet code="mimbounce.class"
        codebase = "/java%20apps/mim"
        width="32" height="32">
  <param name="motion" value="1">
  <param name="fps" value=10>
  <param name="maxstep" value=4>
  <param name="bgcolor" value="255 255 255">
  <param name="border" value=3>
  <param name="total" value=4>
</applet>
```

ActiveX Controls and Plugins

ActiveX controls (formerly OLE controls) are reusable components that add functionality to Internet Explorer on Windows only. Macintosh browsers and Netscape Navigator for Windows use Netscape-style plugins to provide similar functionality. Many accessories, including Flash and Shockwave, are available in both forms to support all major browsers.

Whereas prior versions of Internet Explorer for Windows supported both ActiveX controls and Netscape-style plugins, IE5.5 SP2 and IE6.0 do not support Netscape-style plug-ins. They now require ActiveX controls exclusively.

The <object> tag is used to insert ActiveX controls. For Flash and Shockwave objects (which are available as both ActiveX controls and Netscape-style plugins), Dreamweaver automatically inserts both the <object> and <embed> tags (the latter is actually included within the <object> tag). Browsers that recognize the <object> tag, such as Internet Explorer for Windows, ignore the <embed> tag; browsers that don't understand the <object> tag use the <embed> tag instead. Therefore, attributes not specific to one of the tags must be specified redundantly in both tags. (Example 5-1 demonstrates how attributes are specified, which differs slightly for each tag.)

The classid and codebase attributes are specific to the <object> tag. The classid uniquely identifies an ActiveX control, which is downloaded from the URL specified by the codebase attribute if it is not already installed. (The #version number is appended to the codebase attribute, as shown in Example 5-1, to ensure that the latest version of the ActiveX control is installed.) For more details on the <object> tag, see *http://www.w3.org/TR/REC-html40/ struct/objects.html#edef-OBJECT*.

The pluginspage attribute is specific to the <embed> tag; as with the <object> tag attributes described previously, it tells the browser where to download the missing plugin from. Attributes other than pluginspage, classid, and codebase must be specified for both tags.

Inserting ActiveX Controls

Dreamweaver lets you insert ActiveX controls and supply attributes for any required parameters. ActiveX controls have an *.ocx* or *.cab* file extension, but are typically selected by their Class IDs, not their filenames.

To insert an ActiveX control:

1. Use Insert → Media → ActiveX or the Insert ActiveX icon in the Objects panel's Special category (see Figure 5-1) to insert the object.

2. Select the ActiveX control placeholder that appears in the Design pane of the Document window.

3. Open the Property inspector (Window → Properties) for the ActiveX object, as seen in Figure 5-15.

4. Choose a ClassID from the popup menu in the Property inspector (the ClassIDs for RealPlayer, Flash, and Shockwave are preconfigured).

5. Set the additional properties as necessary.

6. Configure parameters by using the Parameters button in the Property inspector.

You can add your own ClassIDs to the Property inspector by editing the file at *Dreamweaver 4/Configuration/ActiveXNames.txt.*

Figure 5-15 shows the Property inspector as it appears when an ActiveX control is selected.

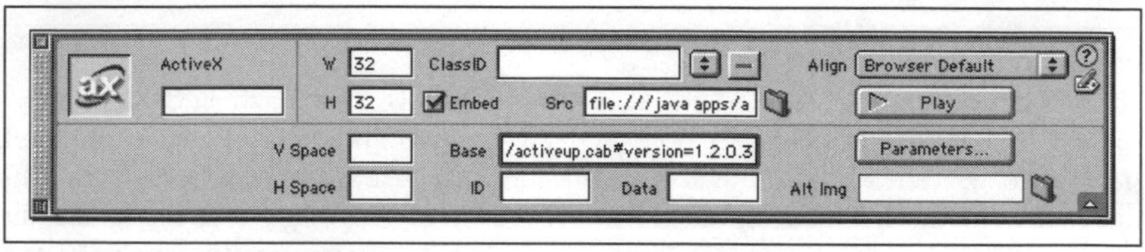

Figure 5-15: The Property inspector for ActiveX controls

Inserting an ActiveX control adds an `<object>` tag to your HTML similar to the following code:

```
<object width="300" height="300"
        classid="clsid:CFCDAA03-8BE4-11cf-B84B-0020AFBBCCFA">
  <embed width="32" height="32" src="Activeup.cab">
  </embed>
</object>
```

Prior to QuickTime 5.0.2, the QuickTime installer installed a Netscape-style plugin only. In addition to the plugin, the latest QuickTime installer includes an ActiveX control to support the latest version of Internet Explorer for Windows.

Example 5-2 shows code used to insert the QuickTime ActiveX control and Netscape-style plugin. This code must be entered by hand in Dreamweaver's Code view.

Example 5-2: HTML for inserting the QuickTime ActiveX control and plugin

```
<object classid="clsid:02BF25D5-8C17-4B23-BC80-D3488ABDDC6B"
    width="160" height="144"
    codebase="http://www.apple.com/qtactivex/qtplugin.cab">
    <param name="src"        value="sample.mov">
    <param name="autoplay"   value="true">
    <param name="controller" value="false">
<embed src="sample.mov" width="160" height="144"
    autoplay="true"     controller="false"
    pluginspage="http://www.apple.com/quicktime/download/">
</embed></object>
```

Don't change the `codebase`, `classid`, or `pluginspage` attributes. The other attributes, such as `height`, `width`, and `src`, should be changed in both places they appear. For details on other attributes of the QuickTime plugin, see *http://www.apple.com/quicktime/authoring/embed.html.* Chapter 12 explains how to use the Check Plugin behavior to test for the QuickTime plugin.

Inserting Plugins

Although ActiveX controls were preferred by Internet Explorer for Windows, until recently, all major browsers supported Netscape-style plugins. Therefore, using an <embed> tag alone to embed a document requiring a plugin was common.

 If you support IE5.5 SP2 and IE6.0, which no longer use Netscape-style plugins, you should insert plugins using HTML similar to that shown in Example 5-2.

Once the QuickTime or other ActiveX control has been installed on a user's system, IE5.5 SP2 and IE6.0 use it to display the custom asset type when encountering an <embed> tag.

If your site doesn't support the latest Internet Explorer for Windows browsers, or if an ActiveX control counterpart to the plugin is not available, use the <embed> tag alone. To insert asset types that require a plugin, use Insert → Media → Plugin or the Insert Plugin tool in the Objects panel's Special category (see Figure 5-1).

In the Select File dialog box, pick the filename of the external asset you want to insert into the page. Select an asset file that requires a plugin, such as a Quick-Time *.mov* file or an Authorware (*.aam*) file, not the plugin itself. If you select an unknown filetype, Dreamweaver inserts a Plugin placeholder icon (which looks like a puzzle piece).

Figure 5-16 shows the Property inspector as it appears when a Plugin placeholder is selected.

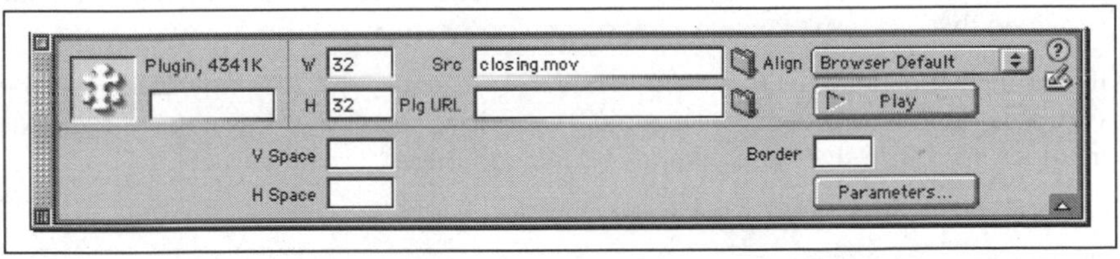

![Property inspector for Plugins showing Plugin, 4341K with W 32, H 32, Src closing.mov, Plg URL, Align Browser Default, Play, V Space, H Space, Border, Parameters fields]

Figure 5-16: The Property inspector for Plugins

Inserting a Plugin adds an <embed> tag to your HTML document similar to:

```
<embed src="/flashobjs.rm" width="32" height="32">
</embed>
```

If you select a file of one of the supported types, such as *.png*, *.swf*, or *.dcr*, Dreamweaver inserts the corresponding type of object instead of a Plugin placeholder. For example, using the Insert Plugin tool to insert a *.swf* file is the same thing as using the Insert Flash tool. In such a case, the Property inspector reflects the properties of the recognized asset type.

The Insert → Media → Plugin command inserts a generic plugin container. See the Rich Media category in the Dreamweaver Exchange for extensions that are tailored to insert plugins for QuickTime video, RealAudio, RealVideo, and other popular media types. See Chapter 22 for details on downloading and installing extensions from the Dreamweaver Exchange.

Naturally, the user must have the plugin installed to view the specialized content. If the user doesn't have the plugin installed, the browser displays a broken puzzle-piece placeholder. Netscape-style plugins under Windows typically have a *.dll* extension and are stored in the browser's *Plugins* folder. Macintosh plugins are indicated by the hidden file type NSPL (all uppercase) and are stored in the browser's *Plug-ins* folder.

Server-Side Includes

A server-side include (SSI) tells the web server to include the contents of another file before sending the requested document back to the user's browser. Although it is difficult to preview SSIs with a browser, Dreamweaver mimics the server and includes the chosen document in your HTML document.

To add an SSI to a document, use Insert → Server-Side Include.

In the Select File dialog box that appears, select the document containing the server-side include. This document could be a *.map* file for a server-side image map or any other file used for a server-directed process affecting the HTML document served to the user's browser. It can even be another file containing HTML, provided that it doesn't contain <head> or <body> tags.

If the included document contains valid HTML code, the resulting page will be viewable in Dreamweaver's Document window as well. However, server-side includes appear in the Code pane as HTML comments, as shown here:

```
<!--#include virtual="/calendar.map" -->
```

Therefore, to select a SSI, you can select the comment placeholder, as seen in Figure 5-17. When the SSI is selected in the Document window, you can set its properties in the Property inspector, also shown in Figure 5-17.

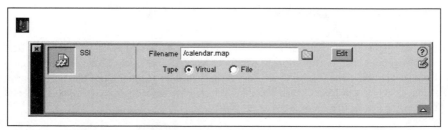

Figure 5-17: The Property inspector for server-side includes

In the Property inspector, set the Type field to Virtual if using an Apache Web Server. Set the Type to File if using a Microsoft IIS server. See "Using Server-Side Includes" in the Dreamweaver Help for more details. You can edit the included file by clicking the Edit button in the Property inspector.

 HTML documents containing server-side includes must be saved with the *.shtml* or *.shtm* file extension; otherwise, the server may not process included files.

In Part I of this book, you have seen how to use Dreamweaver to create documents and insert objects into a web page. In Part II, you'll see how to use Dreamweaver to manage sites and documents and learn to use templates, library functions, and stylesheets.

PART II

Managing Dreamweaver

Part II covers the broader issues of site management and document management, plus the use of templates, the Library, CSS, and styles.

CHAPTER 6

Managing a Web Site

Everyone knows that planning is the first step in web site development, but many people overlook the need for ongoing management. Without proper maintenance, a complex site can become riddled with broken external links, missing files, and broken CGI scripts.

Thankfully, Dreamweaver offers all the webmaster tools necessary for deployment and long-term maintenance, such as FTP, link checking, and file checking. Even better, Dreamweaver's site management tools simplify development and help reduce the likelihood of problems down the road. Dreamweaver helps you to manage and synchronize both the *local* site (the development version on your personal computer) and the *remote* site (the version on a web server that gets published on the Internet).

Site Management Overview

In this chapter we'll cover how to manage a site and the following topics:

- Setting up a site and its preferences

- Managing a site's logical structure using a *site map* (a graphical representation of the site and its links) in the Site Map view of the Site window

- Managing a site's physical structure using a *files list* (a directory listing similar to the Windows File Explorer or Macintosh Finder) in the Site Files view of the Site window

- Using File Check In/Check Out and Design Notes to manage file changes

- Finding and fixing broken links

- Uploading your site and synchronizing remote and local files

- Site-management reports

- Managing assets with the Assets panel

In the remainder of Part II, we'll discuss document management, including the use of templates, the Library, and stylesheets.

 As you work, test your pages and your site's navigation so that problems are spotted early. Use File → Preview in Browser (F12) to test your site; the Dreamweaver Document window isn't intended for meaningful testing. See Appendix C for more ideas on planning and testing your site.

Menu and File Browser Caveats

Dreamweaver's site-management operations are performed in the Site window. Although Dreamweaver operates nearly identically on the Macintosh and on Windows, the Site menu commands are an exception; the location of these menu commands varies somewhat across platforms.

 In Windows, the Site window has its own menu bar, shown in Figure 6-8, that is separate from the Document window's menu bar. On the Macintosh, a single menu is located at the top of the monitor; the Site window–related commands are under the Site submenu in this menu bar.

In Windows, some commands are duplicated on the menu bars of both the Document and Site windows. Furthermore, right-clicking (Windows) or Ctrl-clicking (Macintosh) in the Site window opens a contextual menu that duplicates the commands available elsewhere. In this chapter, we cite some, but not all, of the ways to access the commands via menus. See Table A-11 and Table A-12 in Appendix A for a complete listing.

You may also encounter some platform differences that affect how folders are chosen, as shown in Figure 6-1.

Macintosh folder selection dialog boxes contain two separate buttons—Open and Choose—used to open and select folders. Windows folder selection browser dialog boxes have a single Select button that changes to an Open button when a folder is highlighted. You can also double-click a folder's name to open it. However, if you pause too long between clicks, Windows assumes that you want to rename the folder instead and highlights the folder without opening it. Therefore, the Select button in Figure 6-1 selects the *Dreamweaver 4* folder (the last folder that was opened) on Windows, not the highlighted folder named *MySite*. On the Macintosh however, the Choose button selects the currently highlighted folder, such as the *MySite* folder in Figure 6-1. If you open the *MySite* folder on the Macintosh, you must navigate back up the directory tree before you can choose it with the Choose button.

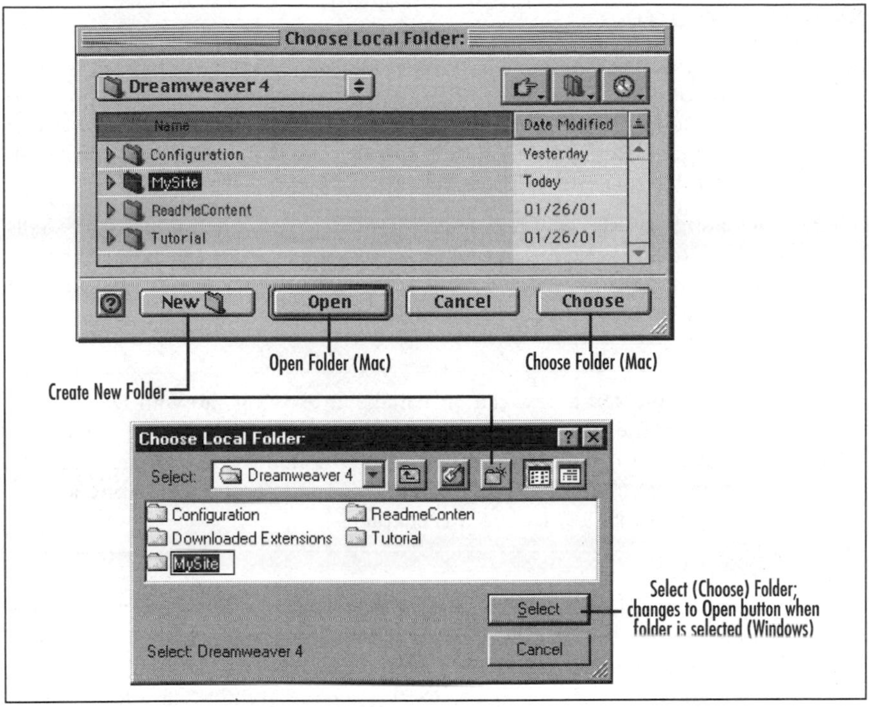

Figure 6-1: Folder selection dialog boxes on Macintosh and Windows

Choosing the wrong folder in the folder selection dialog box is very easy. On Windows, always *open* the folder that you want to choose before clicking the Select button. On the Macintosh, leave the desired folder *closed*, then highlight it and click Choose (not Open).

Sometimes you'll choose a file but not literally open it, such as when inserting an image or specifying the destination of a hyperlink. Dreamweaver sometimes displays the incorrect button (either Open or Select) in the file browser, but you can safely ignore such inconsistencies. When saving or retrieving files, Dreamweaver doesn't always reopen the file browser to the last-used folder, so check the pathname carefully.

Both Windows and the Macintosh allow you to create a new folder from within a file browser dialog box, as indicated in Figure 6-1. This feature is convenient when you want to save a file in a folder but forgot to create the folder ahead of time.

Never use the Windows File Explorer or Macintosh Finder to rename or move files within your site (Windows even allows you to rename and move files using the file browser dialog box). To avoid breaking links, move and rename files in the Dreamweaver Site window only.

Defining a Site

Before plunging into the Site window, you should *define* your site, which is done in the Site Definition dialog box. If you are a graphical thinker, you may prefer to read "The Site Window" section later in this chapter, to see how the Site window looks and operates, before returning here. As discussed in that section, you can view the Site window in several different ways.

Whereas "creating" a site entails building HTML pages, "defining" a site tells Dreamweaver to treat your collection of pages as part of a larger whole. Although you can define your site at any time, the earlier you do so, the sooner you can take advantage of Dreamweaver's site management features.

 Whether you start a new site or manage an existing site with Dreamweaver for the first time, the site definition procedure is the same. Dreamweaver can manage any set of files contained in a single local development folder and its subfolders (see the section "Preparing an Existing Site for Use" later in this chapter).

Create a separate site definition for each site you want Dreamweaver to manage. Site definitions can be created and edited under Site → Define Sites (and you can switch between existing sites using Site → Open Site). When defining a site, you specify such things as its home page, local directory, remote directory, access method, server configuration, and file tracking method.

To define a new site, use Site → New Site to open the Site Definition dialog box shown in Figure 6-2. This dialog box's options are broken down into five categories (listed on the left side and discussed in the following sections). Additional site preferences can be configured under Edit → Preferences → Site.

Local Info Category

The Local Info category of the Site Definition dialog box, seen in Figure 6-2, includes the options that tell Dreamweaver about the development version of your site residing on your local computer.

The Local Info category options are as follows.

Site Name
> A name of your choice used to identify the site in Dreamweaver; this name appears under Site → Define Sites and in the Site pop-up menu in the Site window.

Local Root Folder
> The location of the top-level folder for the site on the local machine (technically, the "local" folder could also be a networked drive). This folder should contain the Home Page, as set under the Site Map Layout category of the same dialog box. All files for a web site, including HTML files, GIF files, etc., should be placed in this folder or in subfolders beneath it. (If you link to any files outside this folder, Dreamweaver prompts you to copy the assets there.)

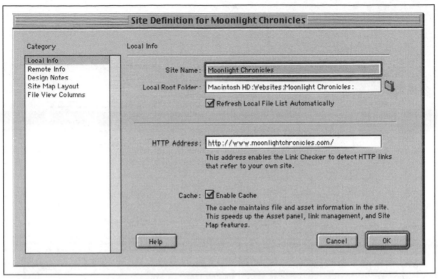

Figure 6-2: The Local Info category of the Site Definition dialog box

Whether starting a new site or managing an existing site with Dreamweaver for the first time, your Local Root Folder location should be the folder containing your home page. If your Local Root Folder pathname includes a forward (/) or backward slash (\) character on the Macintosh, it confuses Dreamweaver and prevents you from using the Site Map feature.

Refresh Local File List Automatically
If enabled, Dreamweaver automatically refreshes the Site window's local file list when copying files from the web server to the local drive.

HTTP Address
The Internet address of the web site, such as *http://www.yourdomain.com*. This setting allows the Link Checker to determine if an absolute URL refers to a file within the site or to an external site.

Cache
Enable this option to maintain a local cache file that speeds up the Assets panel, link management, and the Site Map view.

Remote Info Category

The Site Definition dialog box's Remote Info category defines the configuration of the remote server where your live site is published. The appearance of the Remote Info category pane varies, depending on the choice made for the Server Access option. Figure 6-3 shows its appearance when FTP access is selected.

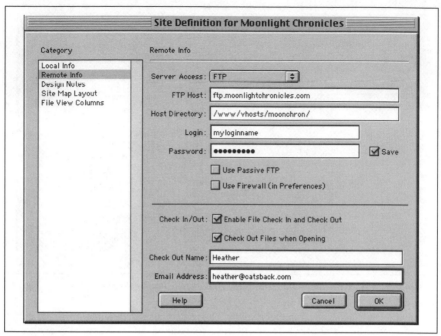

Figure 6-3: The Remote Info category of the Site Definition dialog box showing options for FTP access

Access choice

The Server Access field has five options:

None

> Choose None if you do not plan to upload your site to a server or if you don't yet have the detailed information required when using the other options.

FTP

> Use FTP access (shown in Figure 6-3) if you upload files to your web server via FTP, such as when using a typical dialup or DSL connection. You'll need additional information provided by your ISP or webmaster to complete the configuration as described in the next section.

Local/Network

> Choose Local/Network access if your web server is a machine on your local network, such as when publishing for an intranet. Instead of literally uploading files to a remote site, they'll simply be copied to the appropriate directory across the network.

SourceSafe Database

> Choose SourceSafe Database access if you're using Microsoft's Visual SourceSafe project tracking database software to collaborate with your development team.

WebDAV

> Choose WebDAV access if you're using a file-tracking and version-control system based on the Web-based Distributed Authoring and Versioning open standard.

If using the SourceSafe Database or WebDAV options, you should obtain the free Dreamweaver 4.01 update from *http://www. macromedia.com/support/dreamweaver/downloads/*.

FTP access

If you've chosen FTP access in the Remote Info category of the Site Definition dialog box (shown in Figure 6-3), you'll need to supply the following information to tell Dreamweaver how to reach the FTP server. If you've used an FTP program to transfer files in the past, use those same settings here for Dreamweaver's FTP access:

FTP Host
> Specify the address of FTP server, usually in the form *ftp.someserver.com* or *www.someserver.com*, not simply *someserver.com*. Don't include any subdirectories, slashes, or @ signs, and don't include the *ftp* protocol, such as in *ftp:// ftp.someserver.com*. If your server doesn't use the default FTP port (26) specify the FTP port, such as *ftp.someserver.com:portNum*. The ftp server name may or may not match your domain name; ask your webmaster or ISP if you're unsure.

Host Dir
> Specify the path of the folder that, with the FTP Host specified earlier, points to your site's root directory on the remote server (i.e., the one that contains your home page). The path may be something like */www/htdocs/*, */virtual_ html/*, or */home/yourdomain/*. Ask your ISP or webmaster what folder is assigned for this purpose. You must specify an existing folder on the remote site for the Host Dir. If necessary, specify another folder temporarily, create a new folder in the Remote Files pane of the Site window, and assign it as the Host Dir afterwards.

Login
> Provide the login name for accessing the FTP server; this name may not be the same login name that you use to access email from your ISP.

Password
> Provide the FTP account password. Check the Save option so you don't have to keep retyping your password (although you risk someone else gaining access to your site if you share a computer or lose your laptop).

Use Passive FTP
> Enable this option if your firewall allows passive FTP access only (ask your webmaster).

Use Firewall
> Enable this option if you connect to the remote server from behind a firewall. (Configure the firewall options under Edit → Preferences → Site.)

The following options control how Dreamweaver tracks which files are in use. All developers on a collaborative team should use File Check In/Check Out. To *check out* a file means to take ownership of it and prevent other users from making changes to it while you make changes. To *check in* a file means to submit your revisions and relinquish exclusive control of the file.

Enable File Check In and Check Out
>Enable this option to use Dreamweaver's built-in file tracking system. The next three options appear only if this checkbox is enabled.

Check Out Files when Opening
>Enabling this option causes Dreamweaver to check out a file whenever it is opened, which ensures that you don't edit a locked file. If this option is disabled, Dreamweaver prompts you whether to View or Check Out the file when you attempt to open a locked file.

Check Out Name
>Provide your name so others know to contact you if you've checked out a file but never checked it back in.

Email Address
>Provide your email address so other team members can contact you via email if you've checked out a file but never checked it back in.

Local/Network access

If you've chosen Local/Network access in the Remote Info category of the Site Definition dialog box (not shown in Figure 6-3) you'll need to supply the following information to tell Dreamweaver where to copy the files over the network for publication.

Remote Folder
>Provide the path to the network server directory that acts as the root folder for your remote site. This path might look like *G:/www/public_html/foobar/* (ask your webmaster or network administrator).

Refresh Remote File List Automatically
>Enable this option to refresh the Remote Files pane of the Site window whenever files are transferred from the Local Files list.

When using Local/Network access, the File Check In and Check Out options are the same as when using FTP access (described in the previous section). Use of Local/Network access does not require a Dreamweaver password setting. That said, to copy files to your network server, you should log into your network prior to starting Dreamweaver.

SourceSafe Database access

Visual SourceSafe is a sophisticated project tracking software package from Microsoft. If you've chosen SourceSafe Database access in the Remote Info category of the Site Definition dialog box (not shown in Figure 6-3), you'll need Dreamweaver 4.01 plus access to a Visual Source Safe (VSS) server and a VSS database. Windows users must also install Version 6 or later of Microsoft's VSS Client. Macintosh users must install the Metrowerks VSS client as described at:

http://www.macromedia.com/support/dreamweaver/site/source_safe_mac/
http://www.macromedia.com/support/dreamweaver/ts/documents/vss_on_mac.htm

These SourceSafe configuration options are accessed using the Settings button in the Remote Info category of the Site Definition dialog box (not shown). Ask your SourceSafe administrator for assistance.

Database Path
    Specifies the path to the SourceSafe database's *srcsafo.ini* file that Dreamweaver uses to initialize SourceSafe integration.

Project
    Provides the name of your project within the SourceSafe database (a single database can manage multiple projects).

Username
    Provides your SourceSafe account username.

Password
    Provides your SourceSafe account password. Enable the Save option if you don't want to keep retyping your password.

The final option determines how Dreamweaver integrates its File Check In/Check Out feature with SourceSafe.

Check Out Files when Opening
    You should enable this option to allow Dreamweaver's File Check In/Check Out feature to work cooperatively with SourceSafe. You need not supply identifying information because Dreamweaver uses your SourceSafe identity.

WebDAV access

WebDAV is an open standard for file tracking and version control supported by some web servers. If you've chosen WebDAV access in the Remote Info category of the Site Definition dialog box (not shown in Figure 6-3), you'll need Dreamweaver 4.01 plus access to a WebDAV-compatible server, such as Microsoft IIS 5.0 or the Apache Web Server.

The WebDAV configuration options are accessed using the Settings button in the Site Definition dialog box (not shown). Ask your WebDAV administrator for assistance.

URL
    The URL of the root folder on the WebDAV server, beginning with *http://*.

Username
    Provides your WebDAV account username.

Password
    Provides your WebDAV account password. Enable the Save Password option if you don't want to keep retyping your password.

Email
    Provides your email address to be used within WebDAV.

The final option determines how Dreamweaver integrates its File Check In/Check Out feature with WebDAV.

Check Out Files when Opening
You should enable this option to enable Dreamweaver's File Check In/Check Out feature to work cooperatively with WebDAV. You need not supply identifying information because Dreamweaver uses your WebDAV identity.

Design Notes Category

Design Notes provide a means to track extra file information associated with web site documents, such as the location of original artwork or comments regarding a file's status. The options available under the Design Notes category of the Site Definition dialog box are shown in Figure 6-4.

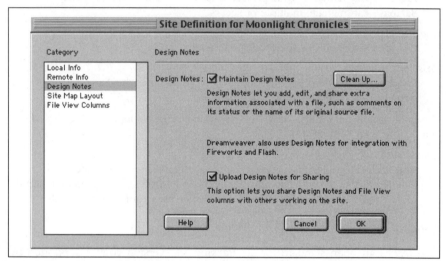

Figure 6-4: The Design Notes category of the Site Definition dialog box

Design Notes are ideal for collaboration but act as useful reminders even if you work alone. They are used for Fireworks and Flash integration and therefore should be turned on in most cases. See the section "Using Design Notes" later in this chapter for more details. The dialog box options are as follows.

Maintain Design Notes
You should enable Design Notes to take advantage of their many benefits, including File View column sharing as described under the section "File View Columns Category."

Cleanup
Use the Cleanup button to delete Design Notes associated with files that have been deleted. (Dreamweaver handles this task for you if you delete files using the Site window.)

Upload Design Notes for Sharing

Enable this option to upload Design Notes to the web server for sharing with other collaborators. The notes are *not* made available to web site visitors. This option must be enabled to support File View column sharing as described in the section "File View Columns Category" later in this chapter.

Site Map Layout Category

The Site Map Layout category of the Site Definition dialog box, shown in Figure 6-5, controls the site map's display (shown in Figure 6-9). This dialog box can be opened easily using View → Layout in the Site window (Windows) or Site → Site Map View → Layout (Macintosh); however, these menu options work only when the Site Map view is open.

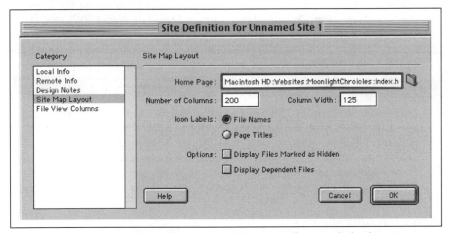

Figure 6-5: The Site Map Layout category of the Site Definition dialog box

The Site Map Layout options are described next. The most important item is the Home Page option; if it is set incorrectly, you won't be able to access the Site Map view in the Site window.

Home Page

Provides the path to the site's home page, which should be located in the Local Root Folder as specified under the Local Info category of the same dialog box. If you haven't created your home page yet, leave this option blank and set it later using Site → Set as Home Page in the Site window (Windows) or Site → Site Map View → Set as Home Page (Macintosh).

 If managing an existing site for the first time in Dreamweaver, simply browse to your home page in your site's root folder. If the path to your home page includes a forward (/) or backward slash (\) character on the Macintosh, it will confuse Dreamweaver and prevent you from using the Site Map feature.

Number of Columns

Specifies the number of file icons to display per row in the site map. If this number if large, the site map may be very wide. If the number is small, the site map will require more vertical space in the Site Map window.

Column Width

Specifies the spacing between columns in the site map (between 70 and 1,000 pixels). If the width is too narrow, items may be too crowded to read—but the width of individual columns can be set by clicking and dragging the vertical arrows in the Site Map window (see Figure 6-9). Use the Zoom pop-up menu in the lower-left corner of the Site window to change the site map's magnification.

Icon Labels

Specifies whether to display filenames or document titles below the icons in the Site Map view. Toggle this option using Ctrl+Shift+T (Windows) or Cmd+Shift+T (Macintosh). You can also run a report to detect untitled documents. The Site Files pane always shows filenames, but a document's title is shown at the bottom of the Site window when you roll over its name in the file list.

Display Files Marked as Hidden

Determines whether all files marked as hidden should be omitted from the site map. This option is also available under View → Show Files Marked as Hidden in the Site window (Windows) or Site → Site Map View → Show Files Marked as Hidden (Macintosh). To mark an individual file as hidden, use Show/Hide Link from the contextual menu in the Site window, Ctrl+Shift+Y (Windows), or Cmd+Shift+Y (Macintosh). When hidden files are displayed, their names are shown in italics.

Display Dependent Files

Determines whether to show dependent files (such as GIFs, JPEGs, and PNGs) embedded within each web page. If this option is disabled, only the files that are connected via hyperlinks are shown in the site map.

 Dreamweaver for Windows can save a picture of the site map in PNG or BMP format using the File → Save Site Map command in the Site window. Dreamweaver for Macintosh can save a picture of the site map in JPEG or PICT format using the Site → Site Map View → Save Site Map command.

File View Columns Category

The File View Columns category of the Site Definition dialog box, shown in Figure 6-6, controls the appearance of the Site Files view (shown in Figure 6-14). This dialog box can be opened by choosing View → File View Columns in the Site window (Windows) or Site → Site Files View → File View Columns (Macintosh).

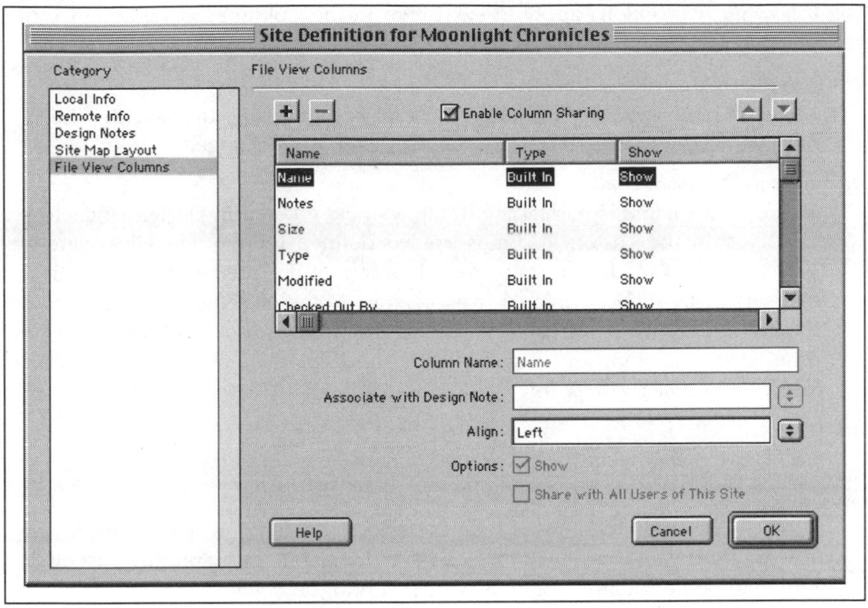

Figure 6-6: The File View Columns category of the Site Definition dialog box

The File View Columns options are described next. They can be used to show the file's name, modification date, and type, and even information from Design Notes.

Enable Column Sharing

Enabling this option allows new columns you define to be shared by other users on your development team. It also allows you to access shared columns that other users have created. After enabling sharing, you can designate specific columns to be shared using the Share with All Users of This Site option. To share columns, Design Note sharing must be enabled in the Design Notes category of the same dialog box.

Column List

The items (rows) in the scrolling Column List configure the columns shown in the Site Files window (i.e., the *row* labeled Notes controls the Notes *column* in the Site Files window as shown in Figure 6-14). Don't confuse these columns with the Name, Type, and Show columns in the Column List itself.

Select an item in the Column List to set its individual properties. Add a *Personal* (i.e., custom) item by clicking the plus (+) button (see Figure 6-6). Clicking the minus (–) button will delete an item without warning (but items can be recreated easily). The built-in items Name, Notes, Size, Type, Modified, and Checked Out By cannot be deleted (however, all but the Name column can be hidden). Use the up and down arrow buttons to control the order of the rows, which determines the order of the columns in the Site Files window. The Checked Out By column is useful for tracking who has a file checked out when using Dreamweaver's File Check In/Check Out feature.

The following five options apply to each item in the Column List (although some can't be changed for built-in items):

Column Name

A new name of your choice for the custom column when displayed in the Site Files view. The names of built-in columns cannot be changed.

Associate with Design Note

This option's name is misleading. It allows data entered in Design Notes to be displayed in the custom columns you've defined for the Site Files window. For now, you can choose Status, which is one of the predefined *fields* (pieces of data) that can be extracted from Design Notes. See the discussion under the section "Using Design Notes" later in this chapter for details on displaying other data, including the assigned, due, and priority fields. (Fields are also known as *name/value pairs*.)

Align

Controls the alignment (Left, Right, or Center) of column data.

Show

Use this checkbox to show or hide the selected column in the Site Files view. The built-in Names column cannot be hidden, but this option is useful for hiding the other built-in columns, which cannot be deleted.

Share with All Users of This Site

Enable this option to make this column available to other users who have enabled sharing. This option lets you selectively share columns, provided that Enable Column Sharing is enabled. The built-in columns are always shared by all users.

Once you've finished defining your site, click OK in the Site Definition dialog box.

Editing a Previously Defined Site

Editing a previously defined site is not the same thing as creating a site definition to manage an existing site in Dreamweaver for the first time.

 To create a site definition for an existing site, see the section "Preparing an Existing Site for Use" later in this chapter.

To transfer site definition files between computers, use the Site Import Export extension available from the Dreamweaver Exchange (as explained in Chapter 22). Dreamweaver 4 reads site definitions from earlier versions of Dreamweaver.

To edit an existing site definition, choose Site → Define Sites, which opens the Define Sites dialog box, shown in Figure 6-7.

BUSINESS REPLY MAIL

FIRST-CLASS MAIL   PERMIT NO. 80   SEBASTOPOL, CA

Postage will be paid by addressee

O'Reilly & Associates, Inc.
Book Registration
101 Morris Street
Sebastopol, CA 95472-9902

NO POSTAGE
NECESSARY IF
MAILED IN THE
UNITED STATES

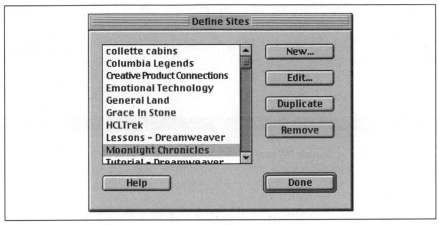

Figure 6-7: The Define Sites dialog box

From this dialog box you have four options:

New
Creates a new site definition (same as Site → New Site).

Edit
Edits an existing site definition.

Duplicate
Duplicates an existing site definition to use as the basis for a new one. Be sure to change the Local Root Folder and HTTP Address under the Local Info category, the remote server settings under the Remote Info category, and the Home Page under the Site Map Layout category. If two sites share the same Local Root Folder, Dreamweaver's file management and synchronization features may not work properly.

Remove
Deletes an existing site definition. Deleting a site definition does not delete HTML and asset files within the site, but it does delete Design Notes.

Note that the Site → Open Site command is not used to edit a site definition; instead, it "loads" an existing site definition, allowing you to switch between web site projects. You can also switch sites using the Site pop-up menu in the toolbar of the Site window (see Figure 6-8).

 Double-click the current site's name in the Site pop-up menu in the Site window's toolbar to quickly open the current site definition for editing.

Creating a New Site from Scratch

If you have an existing collection of web pages, you can create a new site definition for them by using the procedures described earlier in this chapterunder "Defining a Site." Procedure 2 shows how to define a site before creating your web pages.

Procedure 2

1. Choose Site → New Site.

2. Under the Local Info category of the Site Definition dialog box, specify the site's home directory in the Local Root Folder field. You can browse to an existing folder, or even create a new folder from within the folder selection dialog box, as indicated in Figure 6-1.

3. Set the options under the other categories of the Site Definition dialog box as desired. At a minimum, specify the remote server access information under the Remote Info category; you can temporarily set the Server Access to None if you don't have the information handy.

4. You can leave the Home Page field under the Site Map Layout category blank for now; we'll set it during Step 9.

5. Click OK to save the site definition for this site. Dreamweaver will open the Site Files view of the Site window.

6. Use File → New Window in the Site window (Windows) or File → New (Macintosh) to open an untitled Document window. Use File → Save As to immediately save the file as *home.html* in the site's local root folder, as defined in Step 2. (The filename *home.html* is an example. Your web server may prefer *home.htm, index.html, index.htm, default.html,* or *default.htm.*)

7. Add whatever content you like to the home page using the Document window, Objects panel, etc. Dreamweaver may prompt you to copy dependent files, such as GIFs, to the site's local root folder. Resave the document.

8. Use Window → Site Files (F8) to return to the Site Files window. Your new *home.html* file should appear in the Local Files pane on the right side of the window.

9. Select the *home.html* file in the Local Files list by clicking it once. Then choose Site → Set as Home Page in the Site window (Windows) or Site → Site Map View → Set as Home Page (Macintosh) to tell Dreamweaver to use this file as the site's home page.

10. Click and hold the Site Map button in the Site window's toolbar (see Figure 6-9), and choose the Map and Files option. Your home page should appear on the left in the Site Map pane of the Site window. The right pane should continue to show the Local Files list.

Congratulations! You've set up your site and defined its home page. See the next section for details on using the Site window to build and manage sites.

The Site Window

The logical map of a web site determines how visitors find information, just as the directory structure determines where developers physically organize the files. Without a well-planned logical structure, a site's appeal and usefulness is compromised; without a well-planned physical structure, development takes longer than necessary and results in a less reliable site.

There is only one Site window, but it has three different panes:

- The Site Map pane is a graphical representation of your site.

- The Local Files pane shows the files in the local (development) folder.

- The Remote Files pane shows the files on the remote (live) site.

To display these panes, the Site window has three different modes:

- The Site Map and Files view (see Figure 6-8) displays the Site Map pane and either the Local Files pane or the Remote Files pane.

- The Site Map Only view (see Figure 6-9) displays only the Site Map pane.

- The Site Files view (see Figure 6-11) displays both the Local Files and Remote Files panes.

Site Map and Files view and Site Map Only view are both variations of the Site Map view as controlled by the Site Map button in the Site window toolbar, also indicated in Figure 6-9 (click and hold the Site Map button to switch modes). The subsequent sections describe how to use and configure the Site window's various incarnations.

The Site Map and Files View

Dreamweaver represents a site's logical interconnections using a graphical *site map*. Open the Site Map window (shown in Figure 6-8) using Window → Site Map, or Alt+F8 (Windows), or Opt+F8 (Macintosh).

On the left side of the Site window is the Site Map pane showing the site map of a small site; on the right side is the Local Files pane showing the file directory structure of the same site. (You can't use Site Map view until you have specified the home page for your site. Use the Site Map Layout category of the Site Definition dialog box to do so.) You can show the Local Files pane on the left side instead of the right using Edit → Preferences → Site → Always Show Local Files on the Left. To display the Remote Files pane instead of the Local Files pane alongside the Site Map pane, use Edit → Preferences → Site → Always Show Remote Files on the Right/Left.

Although the two panes both represent the same site, the site map shows interconnections created by hyperlinks, independent of the document files' locations on the hard drive. Furthermore, some files in the Local Files pane may not be used within the site. Use the arrow button in the lower-left corner of the window (indicated in Figure 6-8) to show or hide the Site Map pane temporarily.

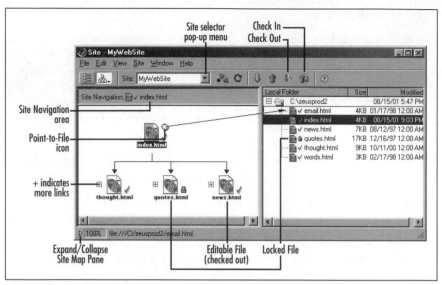

Figure 6-8: The Site Map and Files view of the Site window showing a site map and local file list

Notice that selecting a file in one pane also selects it in the other pane. When a file is selected in the Site Map pane, a Point-to-File icon appears at its upper right. Click on the Point-to-File icon and a draggable arrow appears, as shown in Figure 6-8; you can create a link to a new document by dragging this arrow to point to a file in the Local Files pane. (You can't simply drag a file from the Local Files pane to the Site Map pane, or vice-versa).

Figure 6-8 shows the Site Map window as it appears when File Check In/Check Out has been enabled in the Site Definition dialog box. The file shown with a lock icon isn't editable until it is checked out; checked out files are accompanied by checkmarks (see Figure 6-10).

Manipulating files and folders in the Local Files and Remote Files panes

You can manipulate files within the Local Files and Remote Files panes of the Site window in several ways. These options are available from the contextual menu that appears when you right-click (Windows) or Ctrl-click (Macintosh) on a document in the files list.

Operations that can be performed from the contextual menu include:

New File or New Folder
 Creates new files or folders.

Open
 Opens a document in Dreamweaver's Document window (you can simply double-click a document instead). Opening a document opens its design notes if the Show When File Is Opened checkbox is enabled in the Design Notes dialog box.

Open With (Local Files pane only)
Pick an application to open the document.

Add to Favorites (Local Files pane only)
Copies an asset to the Favorites list in the Assets panel.

Get, Check Out, Put, and Check In
Used to download and upload files and check them out and in.

Undo Check Out
Used to check in a file without updating it.

Turn Off Read Only
Used to edit a locked file that hasn't been checked out.

Locate in Remote Site or Locate in Local Site
Finds the selected local file in the Remote Files pane or the selected remote file in the Local Files pane.

Set as Home Page (Local Files pane only)
Uses the selected file as the new home page for your site (contrast with the View as Root command in the Site Map pane's contextual menu).

Preview in Browser (F12)
Tests the page in a browser.

Check Links
Verifies links for the selected file or the entire site.

Synchronize
Synchronizes the Local Files and Remote Files panes (based on file dates).

Cut, Copy, Paste, Delete, and Rename
Use these commands to move, rename, or delete files. Performing similar operations in the Windows File Explorer or Macintosh Finder would cause broken links.

Design Notes command (Local Files pane only)
Associates notes with the selected file.

To select one or more documents in the Local Files pane:

- Click on a filename.

- Click on a document and then Shift-click on another to select all files in between.

- Ctrl-click (Windows) or Cmd-click (Macintosh) to select one or more discontiguous documents.

- Selecting a folder implicitly selects all files and folders contained within it, even though they are not explicitly highlighted in the Local Files pane.

See "Finding, Selecting, and Transferring Files" later in this chapter for ways to tell Dreamweaver to automatically select files based on a specific criterion.

The Site Map Only View

Let's look at the Site Map in closer detail. Click and hold down the Site Map button on the Site window's toolbar, as shown in Figure 6-9, to switch between the Site Map and Files view and the Site Map Only view.

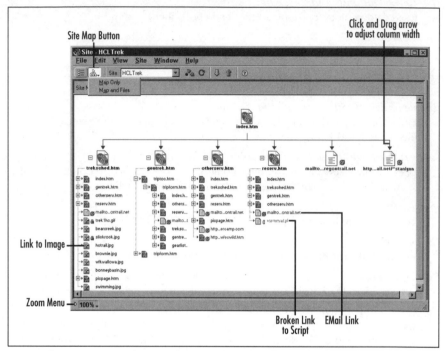

Figure 6-9: Site Map Only view showing a site's logical structure

The pages that are linked from the home page are shown in the site map using large icons. Subsequent levels below that are indicated by a plus (+) icon to the left of a file. Click the plus (+) icon next to a file to show the hyperlinks within it (hyperlinks are shown in the order in which they appear in the HTML source code). Subsequent levels in the hierarchy are shown using smaller icons to prevent the site map from rapidly becoming too large.

The site map shows only the hyperlinks implemented with the `<a href>` tag (corresponding to the Link field in the Property inspector) including both *http:* and *mailto:* links; it doesn't show hyperlinks implemented within complex objects such as Flash Text or Flash Button objects. The document icons next to each linked file indicate the file's type, if applicable. The secondary icons shown in Figure 6-10 indicate the type of file or link. Broken links are shown in red; links to email, scripts, and external sites are shown in blue; read-only (locked) files are indicated by a lock icon; files that are checked out are indicated by checkmarks. The lock and checkmark icons are used only when File Check In/Check Out is enabled.

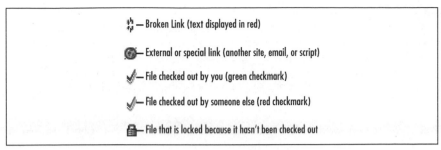

- ⌘ — Broken Link (text displayed in red)

- ◉ — External or special link (another site, email, or script)

- ✔ — File checked out by you (green checkmark)

- ✔ — File checked out by someone else (red checkmark)

- 🔒 — File that is locked because it hasn't been checked out

Figure 6-10: Interpreting icons in the Site Map window

Manipulating documents and links in the Site Map window

You can create and remove links within the Site Map window in several ways. These options are available from the contextual menu that appears when you right-click (Windows) or Ctrl-click (Macintosh) on a document in the Site Map pane:

View as Root
Temporarily changes the root of the site map tree. Also available using Ctrl+Shift+R (Windows) or Cmd+Shift+R (Macintosh).

Link to a New File
Creates a new link to a new blank document.

Link to Existing File
Creates a new link to an existing file (can be used to create a link to an image, but not to insert an image in a document).

Change Link
Alters an existing link by selecting a new destination document for it.

Remove Link
Deletes a link in the Site Map (same as selecting a file and using the Delete key). This deletion removes a link, but does not delete the file from the Local Files pane.

Show/Hide Link
Marks a link for hiding, but doesn't actually hide it unless the Show Hidden Links option is unchecked (in the View menu of the Site window under Windows or under the Site → Site Map View menu on the Macintosh).

Open to Source of Link
Opens the file that links to the currently selected file in the site map.

Check Target Browsers
Produces a report showing potential problems when displaying the page in the targeted browsers.

To display all files that link to a particular file, move the file in the Local Files pane. Dreamweaver will warn you about all files that may be affected by the move. There is no way to cancel the operation, so be sure to move the file back to its original location. (You should either update links both times you move the file or neither time.)

The Open, Open With, Add to Favorites, Get, Check Out, Put, Check In, Undo Check Out, Preview in Browser, Check Links, and Design Notes commands in the contextual menu are the same as those available in the Local Files pane and discussed in the previous section.

To select one or more documents in the Site Map pane:

- Click a document icon.
- Click and drag a selection rectangle enclosing one or more documents in the Site Map.
- Shift-click on one or more documents.
- Ctrl-click (Windows) or Cmd-click (Macintosh) on one or more documents.

Viewing and hiding pages in the Site Map window

The site map ordinarily displays HTML hyperlinks between pages; to show so-called *dependent files*, such as GIF files embedded with the <img> tag, choose View → Show Dependent Files in the Site window (Windows) or Site → Site Map View → Show Dependent Files (Macintosh). In this case, practically every file in your site map will have a plus (+) icon next to it, indicating a list of linked assets to be expanded. Double-click the plus (+) icon to expand the list of dependent assets associated with each file; double-click the minus (–) icon next to an expanded list to collapse it again. If your site uses a navigation bar on each page, it is common for two pages to link to each other. In such a case, Dreamweaver creates an infinite list of links indicated by successive plus (+) icons; you can safely ignore these redundancies.

To view a branch of the site map, select a page within the hierarchy and choose View → View as Root (Windows) or Site → Site Map View → View as Root (Macintosh). This command allows you to focus on subareas of your site by temporarily changing the root of the site map tree, but it does not change the actual home page of your site. Use the Site Navigation area indicated in Figure 6-8 to move back up the hierarchy (i.e., to restore your true home page as the root of the site map).

To hide extra links that you do not wish to see in your site map, select the file(s) you wish to hide and choose Show/Hide Link from the contextual pop-up menu.

To view or hide all links marked as hidden, use View → Show Files Marked as Hidden in the Site window (Windows) or Site → Site Map View → Show Files Marked as Hidden (Macintosh).

See the section "Site Map Layout Category" earlier in this chapter for settings that configure the Site Map view. Use the Zoom pop-up menu at the bottom of the Site window (as indicated in Figure 6-9) to enlarge or shrink the site map.

Renaming and Moving Pages

The site map can display either the title or filename of the pages in your site; toggle between the two alternatives using View → Show Page Titles in the Site window (Windows) or Site → Site Map View → Show Page Titles (Macintosh).

To change the title or filename of a page, select the file, then pause briefly before clicking the title or filename again; the text should become editable. This is a great way to fix inappropriately titled documents quickly without having to open each individually. If you double-clicked (i.e., clicked too quickly), Dreamweaver opens the document instead of allowing you to rename the file. A document can also be retitled (but not renamed) using the Modify → Page Properties option in the Document window.

The Local Files pane always shows filenames and not page titles. Another way to rename a file is to right-click (Windows) or Ctrl-click (Macintosh) on the file and choose Rename from the contextual menu that appears. If you change a file's three-letter extension while renaming it, servers will no longer recognize the file's type (Dreamweaver does not provide a warning when you change a file's extension the way the Windows File Explorer does).

You can move files in the Local Files pane by dragging them into a different folder. Dreamweaver will prompt you to update all links to or from this document to ensure their integrity. You should choose to update the links in most cases.

Set the Edit → Preferences → Update Links when Moving Files option to Always to automatically update links without prompting. Moving or renaming site-related files outside of Dreamweaver, such as in the Windows File Explorer or Macintosh Finder, breaks links. Using the Site window to move and rename files allows Dreamweaver to update all links to and from the file. Dreamweaver also updates URLs within JavaScript, if possible. However, in some cases you may need to delete and reapply the behavior or correct the problem by hand editing the JavaScript code.

You can also use the Cut, Copy, and Paste commands under the Edit menu to copy and move files in the Site window, but moving files in this way will likely break existing links and should therefore be avoided.

After renaming or moving files, be sure to refresh both the Local and Remotes Files panes using F5. Dreamweaver is not smart enough to rename the remote version of a file when you rename the local version. Instead, it attempts to upload the new file and, optionally, delete the old file when synchronizing the local and remote versions of the site. (See the Delete Remote Files Not on local Drive checkbox in the Synchronization dialog box.)

A Site's File Structure

A site's physical structure should be laid out to make life easy for the site's designers and maintainers, just as the navigational structure aids the site's visitors. With multiple developers working on a site, the directory structure and file-naming convention must be agreed upon.

Here are some hints for structuring your site and naming your files:

- Use consistent file extensions, for example all of your HTML files should use either *.html* or *.htm* as the extension, but not a mixture of both. (The default file extension for HTML documents can be set under Edit → Preferences → General → Add Extension when Saving.) Likewise, use either *.jpg* or *.jpeg* for your JPEG image extension. I prefer using three-letter extensions because they are less likely to cause problems with old network file-transfer programs.

- Except for images that are used globally throughout the site (which should be in a common directory for efficient reuse), put images in their own directory for each subdirectory in your web site.

- Use a consistent file naming scheme. For example, all press releases could be named *pr<date>.htm*, and all job descriptions could be named *jd<jobnumber>. htm*. Likewise, thumbnails images for the press release page could be named *pr<date>-<imagenum>th.gif*.

- Because URLs are typically case-sensitive, try to use either all lowercase or all uppercase letters for your filenames. I prefer all lowercase letters.

- Do not use the characters \, /, :, *, ?, ", <, >, or | in filenames. These characters are not allowed under Windows and can confuse Dreamweaver when used on the Macintosh as it attempts to translate file paths across platforms.

- Do not use the characters &, @, or ? in filenames, as they have a special meaning to web servers and may confuse the server when it manipulates your documents and document links.

- Do not use spaces in filenames or folder names, as they can confuse older browsers and many web servers. Use underscores (_) to separate words instead.

- Use a matching site structure for multiple sites on the same server. In other words, use the same system for managing files and scripts across the server.

- See the Macromedia TechNote 14610, "Naming strategies for Dreamweaver, UltraDev and various interpreters" for more tips: *http://www.macromedia.com/ support/dreamweaver/ts/documents/naming_tips.htm*.

The Site Files View

Dreamweaver can show you the physical directory structure of both the local site and the remote copy on the server using the Sites Files view, as seen in Figure 6-11. Switch to the Site Files view using Window → Site Files, F8, or the Site Files button (as indicated in Figure 6-11).

You can sort the file list in either pane by clicking on the column headings; click the column heading again to reverse the sort order.

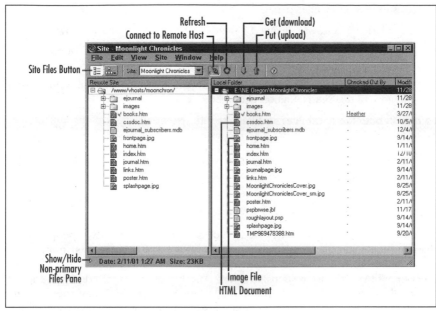

Figure 6-11: The Site Files view showing the Local Files pane on the right and the Remote Files pane on the left

To move a document within a site, simply drag and drop it into the new location. You can drag files between the remote and local panes, but if you drag and drop a file into the wrong directory in the other pane, you will often break existing links. You are better off using *Put* (upload), *Get* (download), or the Site → Synchronize command to copy files between the remote and local sites.

The position of the Local Files and Remote Files panes can be swapped using Edit → Preferences → Site → Always Show Remote Files on the Right. This preference also causes the Remote Files panel to be shown next to the Site Map pane in the Site Map and Files view. Therefore, it differs from Edit → Preferences → Site → Always Show Local Files on the Left, which causes the Local Files pane to be shown in the Site Map and Files view. Furthermore, the arrow in the lower-left corner of the Site window hides whichever pane is not given priority in the preferences.

After transferring files between the local and remote sites, be sure to refresh the file listings.

To refresh the Local Files pane:

- Use Shift+F5 while the Site window is active.

- Choose View → Refresh Local in the Site window (Windows) or Site → Site Files View → Refresh Local (Macintosh).

- Enable the Refresh Local File List Automatically option in the Local Info category of the Site Definition dialog box.

To refresh the Remote Files pane:

- Use Alt+F5 (Windows) or Opt+F5 (Macintosh) while the Site window is active.

- Choose View → Refresh Remote in the Site window (Windows) or Site → Site Files View → Refresh Remote (Macintosh).

- Enable the Refresh Remote File List Automatically option in the Remote Info category of the Site Definition dialog box.

To refresh both the Local Files and Remote Files panes:

- Use F5 while the Site window is active.

- Choose View → Refresh in the Site window (Windows) or Site → Site Files View → Refresh (Macintosh).

Checking Files In and Out

Dreamweaver's File Check In/Check Out feature prevents two people from changing the same file simultaneously. If this feature is enabled, you must *check out* a file before you can edit it. Checking out a file will Get the file and let other users know that you are responsible for it. Another user cannot edit or check out the file until you check it back in (although they can view read-only copies of the file). When you *check in* a file, you relinquish control of it. Dreamweaver will Put the revised file to the live site, and other users will again be allowed to check it out. Therefore, when File Check In/Check Out is enabled, you can edit only those files that you have checked out. Files that are not checked out, or have been checked out by other users, are locked (uneditable).

 The reference copy of a file always resides on the server. Checking out a file with Check Out initiates a revision process that ends when the file is checked back in with Check In. In a multideveloper environment, all files should be checked out before editing and checked in when completed to prevent file version conflicts. The File Check In/Check Out feature won't work properly unless all collaborators enable the feature and use it as intended.

There is no way you can perform a file check out when creating a new file, so simply use File Check In when you are ready to upload the new file for the first time.

To enable File Check In/Check Out, enable the appropriate checkboxes in the Remote Info category of the Site Definition dialog box as described earlier in the section "Remote Info Category." To check out a file, use Site → Check Out, Ctrl+Alt+Shift+D (Windows), or Cmd+Opt+Shift+D (Macintosh). To Check In a file, use Site → Check In, Ctrl+Alt+Shift+U (Windows), or Cmd+Opt+Shift+U (Macintosh).

A green checkmark icon in the Site window, as shown in Figure 6-8, indicates a file that you have checked out. Red checkmarks indicate files checked out by other developers. A lock icon indicates a file that cannot be edited until it is checked out.

Checked-out files are not actually locked by the operating system; instead, Dreamweaver puts a *lock file* (with an *.lck* extension) on the server to identify the user who has checked out each file and prevent others from editing it.

 Even though external editors ignore *.lck* files, you shouldn't edit a "locked" HTML file in an external editor. Doing so will create version control problems, causing your edits, or those of a co-worker, to be overwritten.

Use the Check Out button, shown in Figure 6-8, to download files from the server, check them out, and place *.lck* files on the server. If the Check Out Files when Opening option is enabled in the Remote Info category of the Site Definition dialog box, Dreamweaver checks out any locked file you open. If this option is disabled, Dreamweaver prompts you whether to View or Check Out the file when you attempt to open a locked file.

Use the Check In button, also shown in Figure 6-8, to upload your completed documents and remove the *.lck* files. The Check Out and Check In buttons aren't shown in the Site window toolbar if File Check In/Check Out is disabled (in which case you should use the Get and Put buttons, which download and upload files without checking them in or out, instead). Figure 6-11 shows the Get and Put buttons.

When using File Check In/Check Out, you can tell who has a file checked out by displaying the Checked Out By column in the Local Files and Remote Files panes as described under "File View Columns Category."

To email whoever has checked out a file, click on the user's name in the Checked Out By column, as seen in Figure 6-11, to open a blank message in your default email program. To override the checked-out status of a file—for example when the user is on vacation—right-click (Windows) or Ctrl-click (Macintosh) on the file in the Site window and choose Undo Check Out from the contextual menu.

For more information on uploading and downloading files, see the section "Updating Your Site" later in this chapter. To create a report that lists checked-out files, use the Site → Reports → Workflow → Checked Out By option.

Using Design Notes

Design Notes allow you to track the thoughts, difficulties, and solutions encountered by developers working on a site. Enable the Maintain Design Notes option in the Site Definition dialog box, as described earlier in the section "Design Notes Category." In a collaborative environment, all team members should use Design Notes; without full participation, you get only half the story regarding each file's status. (Enable the Upload Design Notes for Sharing option when collaborating with others.)

Macromedia SiteSpring is a new, high-end product designed to facilitate collaborative web site development. See *http://www.macromedia. com/software/sitespring/* for details.

To add a Design Note or edit an existing one, highlight the file to which the note applies and select File → Design Notes. This opens the Design Notes dialog box shown in Figure 6-12.

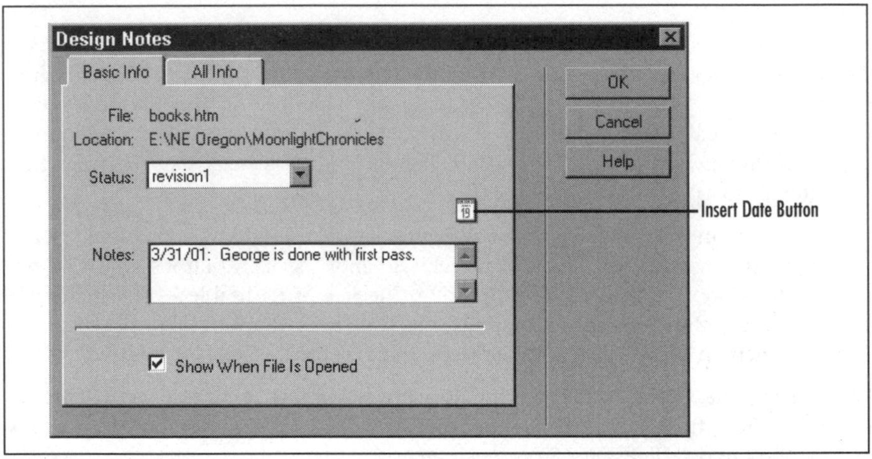

Design Notes

Basic Info	All Info

OK

Cancel

Help

File: books.htm
Location: E:\NE Oregon\MoonlightChronicles

Status: revision1

—— Insert Date Button

Notes: 3/31/01: George is done with first pass.

☑ Show When File Is Opened

Figure 6-12: The Basic Info tab in the Design Notes dialog box

Design Notes can be attached to HTML files and asset files (such as GIFs and JPEGs) in the Site Map pane, Local Files pane, or Document window. Design Notes cannot be attached to some items in the Site Map—namely broken links, external links, and read-only (locked) files; nor can Design Notes be attached in the Remote Files pane (use the Upload Design Notes for Sharing option to post design notes to the server automatically).

 You can even attach Design Notes to folders in the Local Files pane. Attach notes about the entire site to the home page or a dummy file maintained for this purpose.

Design Notes can be used informally, but if you structure your notes using *name/ value pairs*, they can be a highly effective site-management tool. Name/value pairs simply say, "This is the name of the data I want to keep track of, and here is its particular value." (Name/value pairs should sound familiar—they are used similarly in URLs when submitting form data using the HTTP GET method, as described in Chapter 2.) Luckily, Dreamweaver provides some predefined name/value pairs for you and also lets you define your own. Let's see how this concept works.

Adding Basic Info to Design Notes

In the Basic Info tab of the Design Notes dialog box, Dreamweaver provides three commonly needed name/value pairs.

Status

> Select the development status of the file related to this note from the pop-up menu. This selection creates a name/value pair with the name status and the value draft, revision1, revision2, revision3, alpha, beta, final, or needs attention.

Notes

> Enter notes of your choosing, such as "Problem fixed" or "Waiting on Joe to provide artwork." Entering notes creates a name/value pair with the name notes and the value of the text specified in the box. Use the Insert Date icon, indicated in Figure 6-12, to add today's date to the notes. The date simply becomes part of the notes text; it does not become a separate name/value pair.

Show When File is Opened

> Enable this checkbox to open the note automatically whenever the file is opened. This creates a name/value pair with the name showOnOpen and the value true.

Adding and Editing Customized Info in Design Notes

In the All Info tab of the Design Notes dialog box, shown in Figure 6-13, you can edit the existing name/value pairs or add custom ones.

The following fields control the editing of name/value pairs:

Info

> A list of the name/value pairs for this design note. You may see the status, notes, and showOnOpen name/value pairs from the Basic Info tab listed here. You can add custom name/value pairs using the plus (+) button.

Name

> Specifies the name portion of the name/value pair highlighted in the Info list. The default names are status, notes, and showOnOpen, but you can add your own custom names. We'll discuss three more pseudo-default names— assigned, due, and priority—later.

Value

> Specifies the value portion of the name/value pair highlighted in the Info list.

You can edit, add, and delete name/value pairs.

Editing an existing name/value pair

> Highlight an existing name/value pair in the Info list. Its name appears in the Name field and its value appears in the Value field. You can edit the Value, but should generally leave the Name alone. For example, if you change the name notes to myNotes, it creates a new name/value pair whose value will no longer appear under the Basic Info tab.

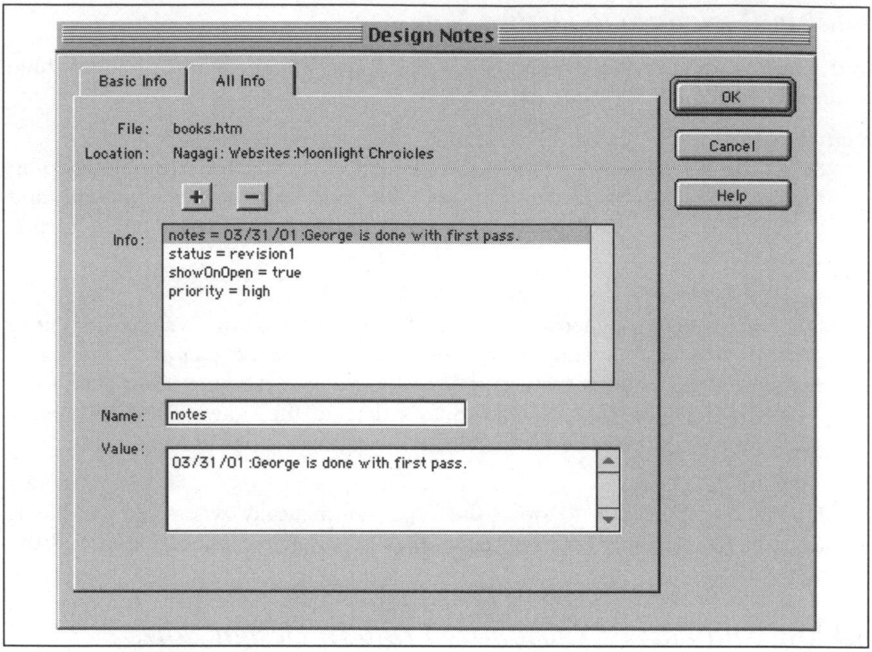

![Design Notes dialog box showing the All Info tab. File: books.htm, Location: Nagagi:Websites:Moonlight Chroioles. Info list contains: notes = 03/31/01 :George is done with first pass., status = revision1, showOnOpen = true, priority = high. Name: notes. Value: 03/31/01 :George is done with first pass. Buttons: OK, Cancel, Help, plus (+) and minus (−).]

Figure 6-13: The All Info tab in the Design Notes dialog box

To *add a custom name/value pair*

Use the plus (+) button to create a blank line in the Info list. Specify a name for your new property in the Name field and assign a value to it using the Value field. You might specify **priority** for the Name and then fill in a Value such as low. (Later, we'll see how to display custom name/value pairs in the Site Files window.)

 By using name/value pairs consistently in all your Design Notes, you'll be able to display and sort the information easily.

To *delete a name/value pair*

Select the item you wish to delete from the Info list and then click the minus (−) button. If you accidentally delete a name/value pair, use the Cancel button in the dialog box to abort the changes.

Viewing and Sorting Contents of Design Notes

If a Design Note is attached to a document, Dreamweaver displays a little balloon icon next to the document name in the Site Files window, as shown in Figure 6-14.

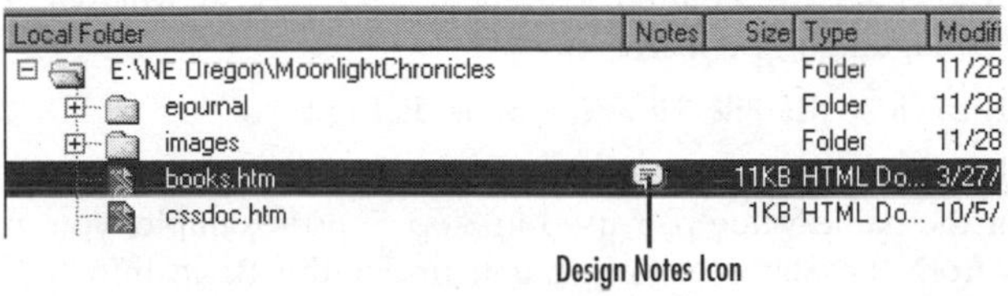

Local Folder	Notes	Size	Type	Modifi
⊟ 📁 E:\NE Oregon\MoonlightChronicles			Folder	11/28
⊞ 📁 ejournal			Folder	11/28
⊞ 📁 images			Folder	11/28
📄 books.htm	💬	11KB	HTML Do...	3/27/
📄 cssdoc.htm		1KB	HTML Do...	10/5/

Design Notes Icon

Figure 6-14: A Design Note associated with a document

There are many ways to view some or all of the information within your Design Notes. To view the contents of a design note associated with a document use any of these methods:

- Double-click a file's Design Notes icon in the Site Files window, as seen in Figure 6-14.

- Select a file and choose File → Design Notes.

- Choose Design Notes from the contextual menu in the Local Files pane or Site Map pane.

- If the Show When File is Opened option is enabled in the Design Notes dialog box, the Design Note will open automatically when you open the document with which it is associated.

The contents of your Design Notes can be retrieved and displayed in the Local Files and Remote Files panes of the Site Files window.

Here's how it works:

1. Use View → File View Columns in the Site window (Windows) or Site → Site Files View → File View Columns (Macintosh) to open the File View Columns category of the Site Definition dialog box (see Figure 6-6).

2. The Notes item in the Column List merely displays a balloon indicator in the Site Files window next to documents with associated Design Notes (see Figure 6-14). Enable this column by selecting Notes from the Column List and checking the Show checkbox. To add a custom column that displays the actual contents of notes, continue with Step 3.

3. Use the plus (+) button to add a new column.

4. Specify a Column Name of your choice, such as Status. (Although using a name that matches the property specified in Step 5 is advisable, you can use any name you like for the column heading.)

5. In the Associate with Design Note field, specify the Name portion of the name/value pair you want to display in this column. You can pick a predefined name (Assigned, Due, Status, or Priority) from the pop-up menu, or enter a custom name (which should match a name/value pair used commonly across all your Design Notes, not the name of a specific document). Pick Status to extract the **status** field from the Basic Info tab of the Design Notes. To display the full text of the Notes field, enter **notes** (it isn't one of the pop-up menu options, but it corresponds to the comments entered into Design Notes).

6. Enable the Show checkbox for this item.

7. You can also set the column alignment and choose whether to share the column configuration publicly.

8. Click OK to close the File View Columns dialog box.

9. In the Design Notes dialog box associated with each document, provide a value for the name/value pair used in Step 5. For example, you might choose a status from the Status pop-up menu under the Basic Info tab or assign a value to a custom name/value pair under the All Info tab. See the previous section for details.

The columns you create in the File View Columns category of the Site Definition dialog box are shown in the Site Files window. You can sort files in the Local Files pane of the Site Files window by clicking on the column headings. For example, you can sort files according to which have Design Notes or according to their status or priority fields (if you've created appropriate custom columns for these). If you've enabled the Upload Design Notes for Sharing option, Design Notes is uploaded to the server and made available in the Remote Files pane of the Site Files window.

Design Notes can also be sorted and searched using the Design Notes Report, explained in the section "Site Reports" later in this chapter.

Removing Design Notes

Design Notes are stored in *.mno* files (which are just XML files). Dreamweaver stores *.mno* files in *_notes* folders (one for each folder of your site, including its local root folder). Of course, Dreamweaver handles the housekeeping for you, so you usually don't have to worry about this issue.

You can delete unwanted Design Notes in several ways:

- To delete a Design Note attached to an individual file, use File → Design Notes to open the Design Notes dialog box. Click on the All Info tab in this dialog box and then use the minus (-) button to delete all properties listed in the Info field. Once you've deleted all the contents, click OK and Dreamweaver will delete the entire *.mno* file.

- To delete Design Notes associated with files that no longer exist, use the Clean Up button in the Design Notes category of the Site Definition dialog box.

- To delete Design Notes en masse, delete one or more *.mno* files in the *_notes* folders scattered throughout your site's local folder and its subfolders. The Site → Define Sites → Remove command, which deletes a site definition, also deletes Design Notes for the site but leaves behind the empty *_notes* folders. (You'll have to use the Windows File Explorer or the Macintosh Finder to delete the folders.)

Preparing an Existing Site for Use

How do you use Dreamweaver to manage an existing site? Whether you've created an entire site with another site-management tool such as FrontPage or simply created some HTML files in another program, it's easy to "import" an existing site into Dreamweaver. Dreamweaver 4 also reads site definition files from earlier versions of Dreamweaver.

You don't literally import your existing site files into Dreamweaver. Instead, you tell Dreamweaver about your existing site by creating a *site definition*. The next section ensures that you have your web site prepared for use within Dreamweaver so you can benefit from the later advice on checking and fixing broken links. See the Macromedia TechNote 14031 "How to convert an existing site into a Dreamweaver site" for additional details, including how to convert from FrontPage. The TechNote can be found at *http://www.macromedia.com/support/dreamweaver/ ts/documents/existing_site.htm*.

Refer to "Cleaning Up Your HTML Code" in Chapter 7, especially when using HTML files from another program.

Importing an Existing Site

If you already have a local copy of your web site on your hard drive, you can create a site definition for it, as described in the section "Defining a Site" earlier in this chapter. (If you modify a file without having defined the site, relative links will be changed to absolute *file:///* links.) If you don't have a copy of your site on your local drive already, you can use Dreamweaver to download an entire site from a remote server. To download a site with Dreamweaver, you must have authorized access to the FTP site or network drive on which the site is stored; Dreamweaver will not download someone else's site via HTTP (although other utilities will). If you already have your local and remote sites set up in Dreamweaver but want to make sure they're synchronized before continuing, see the section "Synchronizing Files" later in this chapter.

To download a remote site using Dreamweaver:

1. Create a new site definition using Site → Define Site, as described earlier.

2. In the Local Info category of the Site Definition dialog box (see Figure 6-2), specify the local folder to which you want to download the site.

3. Provide the information necessary to access the site, such as its FTP address, in the Remote Info category of the Site Definition dialog box (see Figure 6-3). Click OK to save your site definition.

4. Open the Site window using Window → Site Files.

5. Choose Site → Refresh Remote in the Site window (Windows) or Site → Site Files → Refresh Remote (Macintosh). Dreamweaver downloads the directory structure of the remote site, but not all the files within it. If you click the plus (+) button to display a folder's contents in the Remote Files pane, Dreamweaver downloads the folder listing as needed.

6. Click once in the Remote Files pane to make it active, and then choose Site → Synchronize. Instead, you can select the root folder in the Remote Files pane and use Site → Get. However, Site → Synchronize has several advantages over Get: it lets you preview the list of files to be transferred, allows you to deselect individual files, gives you an ongoing progress bar, and outputs a report when finished.

7. In the Synchronize Files dialog box (see Figure 6-16), you can choose to synchronize the Entire Site or Selected Remote Files Only (if the latter option is not available, you forgot to click in the Remote Files pane, as directed in

Step 6). For the Direction, select Get Newer Files from Remote and then click the Preview button. It may take Dreamweaver a few minutes to read the directory structure of a large site. Dreamweaver will show you the size of remote files in the Remote Files pane; if not, make sure that the Size column isn't hidden under View → File View Columns in the Site window (Windows) or Site → Site Files View → File View Columns (Macintosh).

8. In the Synchronization Preview dialog box (see Figure 6-17), Dreamweaver will show a list of files to be downloaded. Uncheck the checkbox in the Action column next to files that you don't want to download. Click OK to proceed with the download.

Downloading a large site can take a long time (several hours), even over a fast connection. Dreamweaver shows the size of each file as it downloads, plus an overall progress bar. The progress bar shows the percentage of the total number of files downloaded; it doesn't consider differences in file sizes. During an FTP download, you can't use Dreamweaver for anything else (although you can use other programs during this time). To interrupt the download, click the Stop Current Tasks icon in the Synchronize Preview dialog box.

As files are downloaded, their Status changes to Updated in the Synchronize Preview dialog box. If a file can't be downloaded from the remote server, Dreamweaver displays an error. You must click OK in response to the error to download the remaining files. After the transfer completes (or is aborted), save the Log file for further inspection. (The Log file is simply a text file and can be opened in any text reader.) The problematic file's status will be shown as Not Updated and be listed in the Log file under, "Files Not Updated Due To User Interaction."

Dreamweaver should preserve the remote server's file dates in the Local Files and Remote Files panes and also in the Windows File Explorer or Macintosh Finder. In practice, Dreamweaver sometimes assign today's date to local files during synchronization; such files may be reuploaded unnecessarily during the next synchronize operation. Use Site → Get to download selected files from the server; it doesn't seem to suffer from the same file date problem.

 Dreamweaver may write a zero-length file or a corrupted file if the transfer of a specific file fails. If you don't delete this incomplete file and redownload the correct version from the remote server, Dreamweaver won't remember that it is corrupted. Worse yet, if Dreamweaver has mistakenly assigned today's date to the corrupted file, it will think that it is more recent than the server version. Therefore, the corrupted file may be uploaded to the server during the next synchronization. Again, check the file log and file dates and sizes carefully to avoid problems.

Dreamweaver doesn't compare file sizes to determine which files need to be transferred, only file dates. If a file is corrupted, use the Site → Get command to download a file from the remote server manually, or use Site → Put to manually upload a file to the server.

Cleaning Up a Site

Dreamweaver can check for broken links and orphaned files on a file-by-file basis or for the entire site. It also warns you about external links, which can be verified manually or using the External Link Checker extension discussed in Chapter 22.

To check your complete site for broken links, use Site → Check Links Sitewide, Ctrl+F8 (Windows), or Cmd+F8 (Macintosh). This opens the Link Checker dialog box, shown in Figure 6-15, giving you a list of the Broken Links, External Links, and Orphaned Files that were found within the site.

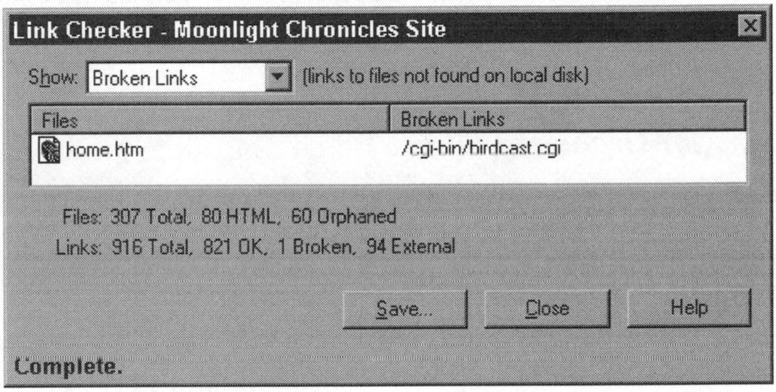

Figure 6-15: The Link Checker dialog box

The broken links that occur when developing a site can be repaired easily from this dialog box.

Clicking the Save button in the Link Checker dialog box saves the Link Check Results. It does not save or resave the selected files. When fixing broken links, the corrected files are saved automatically.

Broken Links

Broken links are links that point to a file that can't be found. To display broken links, select Broken Links from the Show drop-down list in the Link Checker dialog box. Double-clicking a filename in the files list opens that document, which helps determine exactly which link is broken.

To fix a broken link, select the bad URL from the Broken Link column in the Link Checker dialog box. You can hand-edit the link or browse to a new file using the folder icon that appears next to it. (If you can't see the folder icon, widen the column by dragging the vertical line that separates the columns.)

After fixing a broken link, press the Tab key or the Enter Key (Windows) or Return key (Macintosh) to proceed to the next link. Dreamweaver asks you whether it should update the link everywhere it was used within your site. If you answer No, Dreamweaver corrects only the single bad link. If you answer Yes, Dreamweaver attempts to automatically update occurrences of the bad link throughout your site. If File Check In/Check Out is enabled, it attempts to check out files before performing the update and check them back in afterwards.

 Broken links may or may not represent a true problem. For example, links to external programs, such as CGI scripts, may be flagged as broken links, but need not necessarily be fixed. Use the Site → Change Links Sitewide option (in the Site window under Windows or the main menu bar on the Macintosh) to replace links sitewide, whether broken or not.

Searching for Orphaned Files

Orphaned files are those files that are not used anywhere within the site; they may link to other files, but no other files link to them (i.e., there are no incoming links to this file). To display orphaned files, select Orphaned Files from the Show drop-down list in the Link Checker dialog box.

There is no automated way to remedy orphaned files. For each orphaned file you may opt to manually:

- Create a link to it from another document, if it is a needed file.

- Remove it from your site and delete it from server during the next synchronization to keep the server clean and save space.

- Create a separate folder for orphaned files in case you need them later.

If you synchronize all files on a site, Dreamweaver will upload orphaned files as well, so it is best to remove them from your local site folder before synchronization.

Checking External Links

External links are links that refer to resources outside your web site, including other web sites, such as *http://www.amazon.com*, and email links, such as *mailto:wish-dreamweaver@macromedia.com*. To see a list of external links (including email links), select External Links from the Show drop-down list in the Link Checker dialog box. Links that begin with the address specified in the HTTP Address field (under the Local Info category in the Site Definition dialog box) are considered local links.

By default, Dreamweaver doesn't verify external links. You have a number of options for verifying external links:

- Download and install the External Link Checker utility from the Dreamweaver Exchange. This extension can check external links in a single document or an entire site. See Chapter 22 for details.

- You can check external links manually by copying and pasting them into the address line of a browser.

- If you save the list of external links using the Save button in the Link Checker dialog box, you can use another program to check the links. For example, if you open a list of links in Eudora, all the links will become "hot" and you can click on each one to test it. Instead, you might import the list of links into a program that can automatically verify external links, such as Adobe SiteMill.

Updating Your Site

Dreamweaver has several options for synchronizing the local and remote versions of your site (both uploading to and downloading from the remote server). The Remote Files pane in the Site window shows the remote version of your site and the Local Files pane shows the local version. Files can be transferred manually in either direction or synchronized automatically based on the file dates.

The first time you upload your site, be sure to upload all documents, images, and scripts used to create the web pages. After that, you need to upload only the documents that have changed.

When you Get (download) or Put (upload) files, Dreamweaver ordinarily asks if it should include all dependent files (such as GIFs and JPEGs). If you enable the Don't Ask Me Again checkbox and click Yes, Dreamweaver always copies the dependent files between the local folder and remote server. This copying slows uploads and downloads dramatically.

To force the Dependent Files request dialog to reappear, hold down the Alt key (Windows) or Opt key (Macintosh) when you transfer a file. Under Edit → Preferences → Site → Dependent Files, configure the Prompt on Get/Check Out and Prompt on Put/Check In options to change this setting permanently.

To upload your file to a remote site, you must connect to the server specified under the Remote Info category of the Site Definition dialog box (as described earlier in this chapter). Configure the server options, often an FTP server, before proceeding. Test your connection using the Connect to Remote Host button in the Site window toolbar, as seen in Figure 6-11. (You can practice using the Remote Files pane even without FTP access. Simply choose Local/Network access and set up a folder on your *local* drive to act as a dummy *remote* site.)

Dreamweaver automatically disconnects from a remote site after 30 minutes of inactivity. You can change this timeout setting under Edit → Preferences → Site → Minutes Idle (some web servers may disconnect you before the specified time). In my experience, Dreamweaver may have difficulty reconnecting to a server after disconnecting due to inactivity (the problem doesn't occur when using the Disconnect button manually).

If Dreamweaver has trouble connecting to the remote server and transferring files at the expected speed, restart Dreamweaver and try again.

Earlier in this chapter, in the section "Importing an Existing Site," we learned how to download an entire remote site. But that one-time operation is unusual; more typically, you'll either download or upload selected files only. The next few sections explain the different ways to transfer files between the local folder and remote site. FTP operations tie up Dreamweaver, which prevents you from using it during large files transfers. Click the Stop Current Tasks icon in the lower-right corner of the Site Window to interrupt a transfer.

There are so many ways to sling files around in Dreamweaver's Site window that it is easy to get confused, especially when using the File Check In/Check Out feature.

 If File Check In/Check Out is enabled, use Check Out to download files for editing; use Get to download files that you don't intend to edit. Use Check In to upload revised files (use Site → Undo Check Out to relinquish control over a file without editing it); don't use Put to upload files when File Check In/Check Out is enabled. When File Check In/Check Out is disabled, use Get to download files and Put to upload files. Avoid manually dragging files between the Remote Files and Local Files panes.

Get, Download, and Check Out

Here are some ways that you can download files from the server (i.e., copy files from the Remote Files pane to the Local Files pane):

Drag files from the Remote Files pane to the Local Files pane
> This method isn't recommended. For one thing, you can easily drag and drop files into the wrong folder, leading to duplicated files or overwriting another file of the same name. Furthermore, it doesn't check out the file for editing even when File Check In/Check Out is enabled. The reference (oldest) copy of a file always resides on the server. Therefore, if you try to copy an older file from the server over a new version on the local folder, Dreamweaver asks, "Do you wish to overwrite your local copy of index.html?" (This message would be better if it emphasized that you may overwrite a newer file in the local folder.)

Select files in either the Remote Files or Local Files pane and use Get
> There are numerous ways to execute the Get command. In Windows you can choose Site → Get in the Site window or Ctrl+Shift+D. On the Macintosh you can choose Site → Site Files View → Get or Cmd+Shift+D. On either platform you can use the Get button in the Site window toolbar or the Get command in the pop-up contextual menu.

The Get command always downloads files from the remote site to the local site, even if you selected files in the Local Files pane. Get doesn't check out files even if File Check In/Check Out is enabled. Use Get to download files when File Check In/Check Out is disabled or when you want to download a file without editing it.

Select files in either the Remote Files or Local Files pane and use Check Out
This option is available only if File Check In/Check Out is enabled. There are numerous ways to check out files, such as using the Check Out button in the Site window toolbar or the Check Out command in the pop-up contextual menu. Using Check Out automatically downloads files from the remote site to the local site, even if you selected files in the Local Files pane. Use Check Out instead of Get if File Check In/Check Out is enabled and you want to edit a file.

If the Check Out Files when Opening option is enabled (see Figure 6-3), opening a locked file will check it out for editing.

 After downloading files, be sure that you are seeing the latest version by using Shift+F5 to refresh the Local Files pane.

Put, Upload, and Check In

You can also upload files to the server (i.e., copy files from the Local Files pane to the Remote Files pane) in several different ways, including:

Dragging files from the Locate Files pane to the Remote Files pane
This method isn't recommended. For one thing, you can easily drag and drop files into the wrong folder, leading to duplicated files or overwriting another file of the same name. Furthermore, it doesn't check in the file even when File Check In/Check Out is enabled. The reference (oldest) copy of a file always resides on the server. Therefore, if you try to copy an older file from the local folder over a newer version on the remote site, Dreamweaver asks, "Index.html is newer on the remote server. Do you wish to overwrite it?"

Selecting files in either the Remote Files or Local Files pane and using Put
There are numerous ways to execute the Put command. In Windows you can choose Site → Put in the Site window or Ctrl+Shift+U. On the Macintosh you can choose Site → Site Files View → Put or Cmd+Shift+U. On either platform you can use the Put button in the Site window toolbar or the Put command in the pop-up contextual menu.

The Put command always uploads files from the local site to the remote site, even if you selected files in the Remote Files pane. Put doesn't check in files even if File Check In/Check Out is enabled, so it is useful to submit updates while retaining owenership of a checked-out file. Use Put to upload files when File Check In/Check Out is disabled.

Selecting files in either the Remote Files or Local Files pane and using Check In
This option is available only if File Check In/Check Out is enabled. There are numerous ways to check in files, such as using the Check In button in the Site window toolbar or the Check In command in the pop-up contextual menu. Using Check In automatically uploads files from the local site to the remote site, even if you selected files in the Remote Files pane. Use Check In instead of Put when File Check In/Check Out is enabled if you want to submit revisions and relinquish control of a file.

 After uploading files, be sure that you are seeing the latest version by using Alt+F5 (Windows) or Opt+F5 (Macintosh) to refresh the Remote Files pane. After uploading files, test the entire site thoroughly and fix any broken links or missing files.

Finding, Selecting, and Transferring Files

There are several ways to find and select files in the Remote Files and Local Files panes. Earlier, we saw ways to select files manually. The following methods rely on Dreamweaver to select the files for us based on some criterion:

- Select a file in the Local Files pane and choose Locate in Remote Site from the contextual menu or the Edit menu in the Site window.

- Select a file in the Remote Files pane and choose Locate in Local Site from the contextual menu or the Edit menu in the Site window.

- When using Windows, use the Select Newer Local, Select Newer Remote, or Select Checked Out Files options under the Edit menu in the Site window. On the Macintosh these options appear under the Site → Site Files View menu. (When you select files in the Site Map pane, Windows also offers the Edit → Invert Selection option in the Site window.)

You can transfer the selected files between the Remote Files and Local Files panes using the methods described in the preceding sections. For example, to upload an entire web site, you could click on the local root folder in the Local Files pane of the Site window and then use the Put button to *post* (upload) the files to the server.

Synchronizing Files

Dreamweaver can automatically select revised files to be uploaded. Chose Edit →
Select Newer Local in the Site window (Windows) or Site → Site Files View →
Select Newer Local (Macintosh) and Dreamweaver will automatically compare the
file dates and times between the local and remote server, selecting only the files
that are newer on the local computer. Once the selections are made, click the
Check In button to upload files (if File Check In/Check Out is disabled, use the
Put button to upload files instead).

Conversely, sometimes you want to make sure you have the latest files from the
remote server when working on your local copy of the site. Chose Edit → Select
Newer Remote in the Site window (Windows) or Site → Site Files View → Select
Newer Remote (Macintosh) and Dreamweaver will dutifully select only the files
that are newer on the remote server. Click the Get button to download the newer
files to your computer (if the File Check In/Check Out feature is enabled and you
want to edit the files, use the Check Out option instead). The Select Newer
Remote option is useful for downloading files that were updated by an automated
server-side application or by other developers in your workgroup.

You can also automatically synchronize the remote and local sites to ensure that
they both have the latest files. To open the Synchronize Files dialog box shown in
Figure 6-16, select Site → Synchronize.

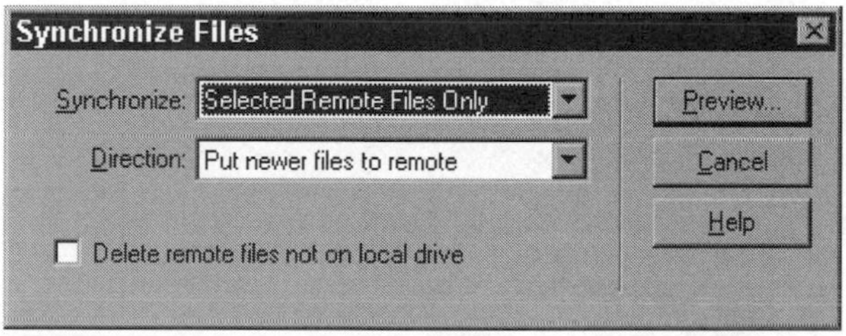

Figure 6-16: The Synchronize Files dialog box

The values available for the Synchronize option in this dialog box are:

Entire Site
> Synchronizes all files (including orphaned files), whether selected or not

Selected Local Files Only
> Synchronizes the files selected in the Local Files pane only (available only
> when the Local Files pane is active)

Selected Remote Files Only
> Synchronizes the files selected in the Remote Files pane only (available only
> when the Remote Files pane is active)

The values available for the Direction option in this dialog box are:

Put newer files to remote
Uploads files that are newer on the local machine to the remote server. It does not download any files from the remote server to the local machine.

Get newer files from remote
Downloads files that are newer on the remote server to the local machine. It does not upload any files from the local machine to the remote server.

Get and put newer files
Downloads newer files from the remote server and uploads newer files to the remote server so that both the remote and local machines have the latest version of all specified files.

 If you have a server-side script or application that generates pages automatically, do not check the Delete Remote Files Not On Local Drive option; it removes any files on the remote server for which there is no corresponding file on the local machine.

Once these selections have been made, click Preview to get a list of the pages that will be affected by the synchronization process. The Synchronize Preview dialog box, shown in Figure 6-17, displays the files to be synchronized.

Synchronize		
Unchecked files will not be processed.		
Action	**File**	**Status**
☑ Put	ejournal\12a.jpg	
☑ Put	ejournal\45sm.jpg	
☑ Put	ejournal\46.jpg	
☑ Put	ejournal\46sm.jpg	
☑ Put	ejournal\closure.gif	
☑ Put	ejournal\emailtemplate.htm	

Files: 132 will be updated

OK   Cancel   Help

Unchecked files will not be processed.

Figure 6-17: The Synchronize Preview dialog box

Files to be uploaded are indicated by a Put checkbox in the Action column. Files to be downloaded are indicated by a Get checkbox in the same column. You can uncheck the checkboxes to selectively omit files from the transfer. Click OK to initiate the file transfer. You can interrupt the file transfer using the Stop Current Task button that appears in the dialog box while Dreamweaver synchronizes files. When the file transfer is complete, click the Save Log button that appears to save a

Log file detailing the files transferred. See the section "Importing an Existing Site" earlier in this chapter for important details on the Synchronization option.

If you are having trouble with FTP transfers, you can view the FTP log file by using Window → Site FTP Log in the Site window (Windows) or Site → FTP Log (Macintosh). The log file error messages may be somewhat cryptic. For example, if you've exceeded your disk space quota on the remote server, the log may display a generic failure message, such as "Cannot Put File," indicating that the upload failed but not giving the specific reason.

Site Reports

Dreamweaver 4 implements a new system of site reporting. You can open the Site Reports dialog box, shown in Figure 6-18, by selecting Site → Reports.

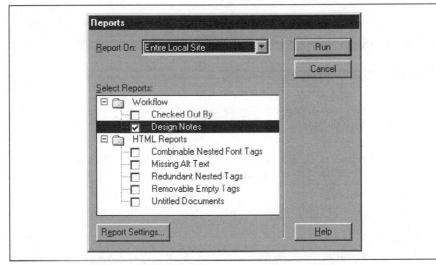

Figure 6-18: The Reports dialog box

Reports can be generated for the Current Document, Entire Local Site, Selected Files in Site, or a specified Folder. Each of these scopes can have any or all of the following reports generated for it.

Two Workflow Reports are available:

Checked Out By
Creates a report listing files that have been checked out but not yet checked back in. The Report Settings button in the dialog box allows you to limit the report to files checked out by a particular user.

Design Notes
Creates a report containing Design Notes that meet the specified criteria. The Report Settings button in the dialog box leads to the Design Notes Report Options dialog box, shown in Figure 6-19, where you can limit the search. In

the left-most column, specify a property name from the name/value pairs you've used in your Design Notes. Figure 6-19 shows how to search for Design Notes with a status of "needs attention." You can also search for notes that contain a particular string. You can search using several matching schemes, including regular expressions (see Table 7-1).

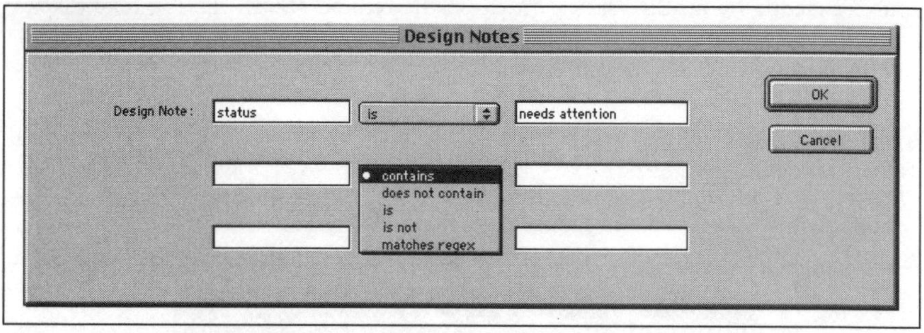

Figure 6-19: Design Notes Report Options dialog box

There are five available HTML Reports:

Combinable Nested Font Tags
> Creates a report of all nested <font> elements within the scope of the report that should be merged

Missing Alt Text
> Creates a report of all missing alt attributes associated with <img> elements or other objects that require an alt attribute for compatibility with HTML 4

Redundant Nested Tags
> Creates a report of all redundant nested tags that should be merged, such as:
> <small><small>my text</small></small>

Removable Empty Tags
> Creates a report of all empty elements that should be removed, such as <div> elements with no content

Untitled Documents
> Creates a report of all documents that have empty <title> elements or whose <title> element is set to "Untitled Document"

A sample Reports Results dialog box is shown in Figure 6-20.

The Reports Result dialog box shows problematic files and the line number on which the problem exists. You can open a document that needs adjusting by double-clicking its name. To help find the problematic line in Code view, turn on line numbering using View → Code View Options → Line Numbers. You can then make the necessary repairs in either Code view or Design view. To remove redundant tags, use the Cleanup HTML command, shown in Figure 7-1.

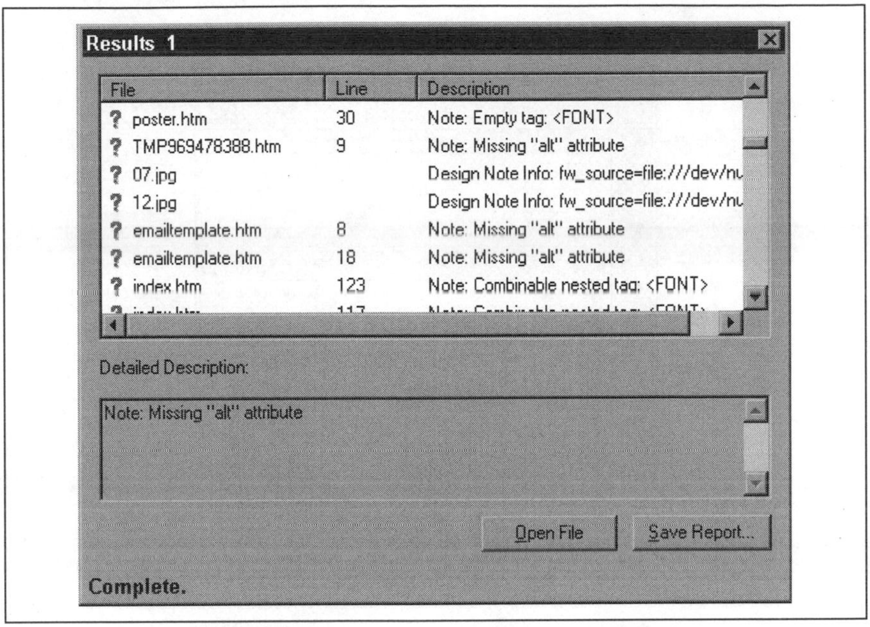

Figure 6-20: Reports Results dialog box

Assets Panel

The Assets panel provides a central repository for nine asset categories (Images, Colors, URLs, Flash, Shockwave, Movies (QuickTime), Scripts, Templates, and Library items) that are used within your site. With the Assets panel, you can easily incorporate frequently used items within multiple pages. Open the Assets panel, shown in Figure 6-21, using Window → Assets or F11.

The Window → Templates command opens the Templates category of the Assets panel (a.k.a. the Templates panel). The Window → Library command opens the Library category of the Assets panel (a.k.a., the Library panel). The Templates panel is discussed in Chapter 8, and the Library panel is discussed in Chapter 9. Except for the Templates and Library categories, each category of the Assets panel includes a Site list and a Favorites list. You can choose between the Site list and Favorites list using the radio buttons near the top of the Assets panel (see Figure 6-21).

The upper pane of the Assets panel shows a preview of the item selected in the lower pane. For the Flash, Shockwave, and Movie categories, a Play button (a green triangle) appears in the preview area's upper-right corner. The context menu and pop-up arrow menu in the Assets panel's upper right corner differ for each category and also depending on whether the Site list or Favorites list is active.

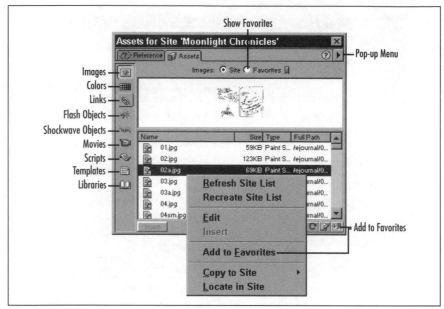

Figure 6-21: The Assets panel

The Site List

The Site list of each category in the Assets panel is a list of items used within the site. You can drag and drop items from the Assets panel into the Document window (or use the Insert button in the lower-left corner of the Assets panel). For example, dragging a library item into a document inserts the contents of that library item into the document. When the URLs, Colors, or Templates categories of the Assets panel are active, the Insert button changes to an Apply button. For example, dragging a color into a document applies a `<font color>` tag; dragging a template onto a document applies a template to the document.

 Assets within your site are automatically added to the Site list of the Assets panel if you have enabled the site cache. For example, click the Images icon (and select the Site list radio button) to list all images in the site.

After adding or removing assets within the site, refresh to Site list to ensure that it reflects the latest assets. To refresh the Site list within the Assets panel:

- Click the Refresh Site List button at the bottom of the Assets panel.

- Choose Refresh Site List from the contextual menu or the pop-up arrow menu in the Assets panel's upper-right corner.

If you add or remove assets outside of Dreamweaver, you should recreate the Site list from scratch. To recreate the Site list:

- Ctrl-click (Windows) or Cmd-click (Macintosh) the Refresh Site List button at the bottom of the Assets panel.

- Choose Recreate Site List from the contextual menu or the pop-up arrow menu in the Assets panel's upper-right corner.

The Assets panel uses site-root-relative paths for the location of assets so that they can be found from anywhere within the site structure. To speed up the Assets panel, activate the Enable Cache checkbox under the Local Info category of the Site Definition dialog box by using Site → Define Sites → Edit → Local Info.

The Favorites List

Because a site can contain a large number of assets, the Assets panel allows you to add your most frequently used assets to a second pane called the Favorites list. The Favorites list for each category is empty until you add assets to it. To add an item to the Favorites list, select an asset in the Site list and click the Favorites icon in the lower-right corner of the panel. Alternatively, you can right-click (Windows) or Ctrl-click (Macintosh) on the item in question and select Add to Favorites from the contextual pop-up menu. To view your Favorite assets, use the Favorites radio button at the top of the Assets panel.

We've learned a tremendous amount about Dreamweaver site management in this chapter. In the next chapter, we cover ways to keep your HTML code tidy and how to use find and replace to update multiple documents.

CHAPTER 7

Managing HTML Documents

In the preceding chapter, we discussed ways to manage your entire site, including links between documents. Let's focus now on managing individual HTML documents. Although Dreamweaver automatically creates HTML for you, you can edit the HTML manually to add attributes not directly supported by Dreamweaver and to gain precise control over your document. Dreamweaver can automatically clean up your HTML code by removing empty tags, redundant tags, and nonstandard HTML.

This chapter covers HTML document management, including the following topics:

- Cleaning up sloppy HTML
- Using the History panel to review changes and record commands
- Using Find and Replace, the Quick Tag Editor, and spell checker
- Checking browser compatibility

Cleaning Up Your HTML Code

Clean HTML code is one sign of a conscientious HTML developer. No matter which tools you used to create your original HTML document, Dreamweaver can be used to clean it up and ensure compliance with HTML 4 standards. Although Dreamweaver features so-called Roundtrip HTML, it will rewrite HTML code when opening documents according to the settings under Edit → Preferences → Code Rewriting. You can hand-edit your HTML in the Document window's Code pane (View → Code) or in the Code inspector (Window → Code Inspector or F10).

Clean Up HTML

Although Dreamweaver's visual paradigm makes it easy to edit your page, it can also lead to duplicate tags and empty tags. Thankfully, Dreamweaver can automatically find and fix these and other problems in your HTML code. Use Commands → Clean Up HTML to open the Clean Up HTML dialog box, shown in Figure 7-1.

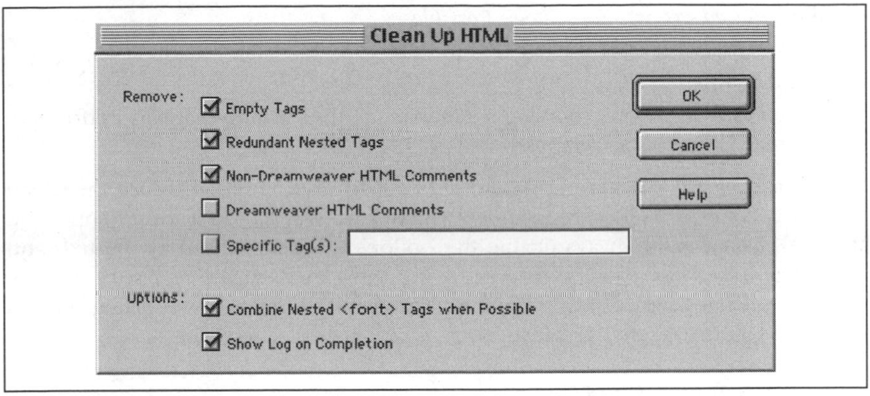

Figure 7-1: The Clean Up HTML dialog box

The options in this dialog box control how Dreamweaver decides which HTML tags to remove, merge, or ignore.

The following checkboxes determine which tags Dreamweaver removes:

Empty Tags
Removes tags containing no content, such as `<a></a>` or `<b></b>`.

Redundant Nested Tags
Removes redundant tags, such as `<b><b>content</b></b>`, resulting in `<b>content</b>`.

Non-Dreamweaver HTML Comments
Removes all comments not added by Dreamweaver, which may also remove scripts and stylesheets that have been included in comment markers (`<!-- -->`) to support older browsers. Use with caution.

Dreamweaver HTML Comments
Removes Dreamweaver HTML features that rely on comments. Use with caution.

Removing Non-Dreamweaver HTML Comments removes any comments you've added, plus comments added by other programs. Consider using Design Notes instead of comments if you intend to strip out comments to optimize your HTML. Removing Dreamweaver HTML Comments turns template-based documents and library items into normal HTML code. It also removes tracing images, but does not remove comments inserted using Insert → Invisible Tags → Comments or SSIs inserted using Insert → Server-Side Include.

Specific Tag(s)
Removes the listed HTML tag. For multiple tags, specify a comma-separated list such as `font, b, div`. The Find and Replace option is easier to use to remove tags across multiple documents.

Managing HTML Docs

Combine Nested <font> Tags When Possible
> Combines nested <font> tags into a single <font> tag.

Show Log on Completion
> Displays a dialog box showing a summary of the cleanup that was performed, such as "1 empty tag removed."

You should create a custom keyboard shortcut to make it easier to use the Clean Up HTML command on each document (there's no way to run it for an entire site at once). You should always enable the options that remove empty, nested, and redundant tags, but exercise caution with the other options (and Undo any mistaken changes before saving the file). The default options in the dialog box, as shown in Figure 7-1, are the safest.

Clean Up Word HTML

Dreamweaver can clean up HTML documents created in Microsoft Word. It works well when cleaning up documents created in Word 97 and 98, but less so when the documents were created in Word 2000 and XP, which use CSS extensively. (You can take advantage of MS Word's CSS features as discussed in Chapter 10.) Use Commands → Clean Up Word HTML to open the Clean Up Word HTML dialog box shown in Figure 7-2. (The dialog box also appears when using File → Import → Import Word HTML.)

The following options are available on the Basic tab of the dialog box:

Remove Word-specific markup
> Deletes HTML tags that work only in Word. See the Detailed tab for more options.

Clean Up CSS
> Removes CSS tags added by Microsoft Word. See the Detailed tab for more options.

Clean up <font> tags
> Removes redundantly nested <font> tags.

Fix invalidly nested tags
> Cleans up improperly nested tags so that <font>...</font> becomes <font>...</font>.

Set background color
> Used to add a background color because Word doesn't set one.

Apply source formatting
> Formats the HTML code for readability according to your Dreamweaver preferences.

Show log on completion
> Displays results when the cleanup process is complete.

The Detailed tab of this dialog box varies depending on whether you are importing a Word 97/98 document or a Word 2000 document (see Figure 7-2). When importing a Word 2000 document, the Detailed tab allows greater control over the Remove All Word-specific Markup and Clean Up CSS options.

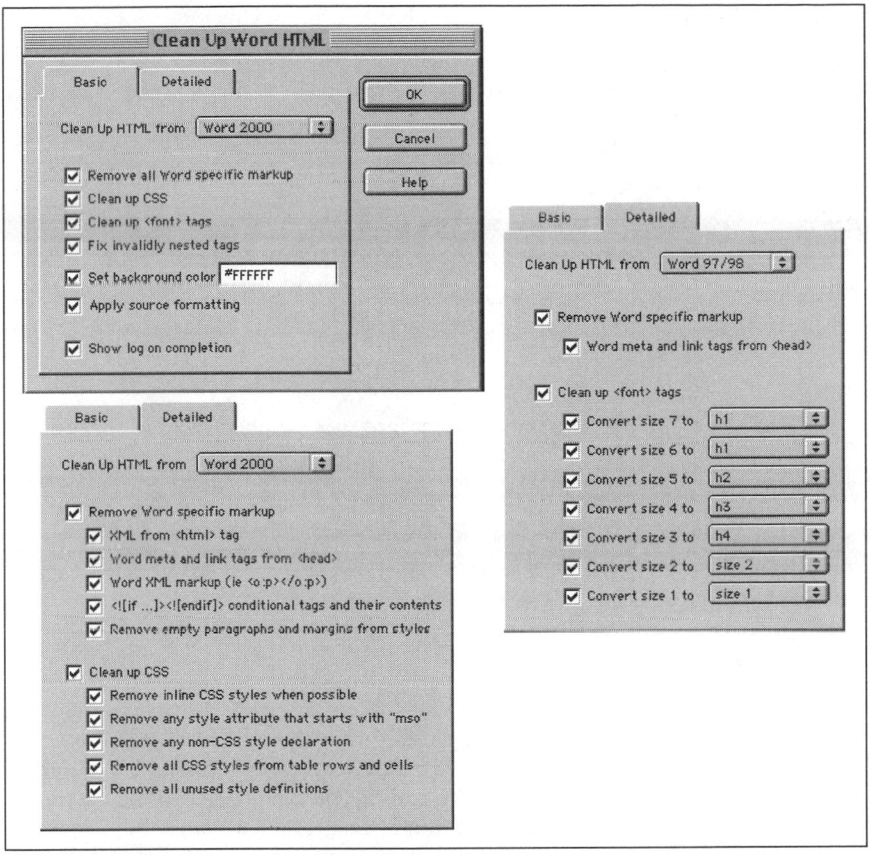

Figure 7-2: The Basic and Detailed tabs of the Clean Up Word HTML dialog box

The Remove Word-specific Markup checkbox enables the following five settings:

XML from <html> tag
Removes Word's XML elements from within the <html> tag.

Word meta and link tags from <head>
Removes Word-specific <meta> and <link> tags within the <head> tag (also applies to Word 97/98).

Word XML markup (i.e., <o:p> </o:p>)
Removes all XML-based markup added by Word.

<![if ...]><![endif]> conditional tags and their contents
Removes Word-specific conditional tags and their contents, which aren't supported in normal HTML or JavaScript-enabled documents.

Remove empty paragraphs and margins from styles
Removes all empty <p> elements and document margin measurements from style attributes.

The Clean Up CSS checkbox enables the following five settings:

Remove Inline CSS styles when possible
Removes `style` attributes and makes them part of the `<style>` tag when possible.

Remove any style attribute that starts with "mso"
Removes Word-specific style attributes.

Remove any non-CSS style declaration
Removes CSS attributes that do not conform to the W3C specification.

Remove all CSS styles from table rows and cells
Removes `style` attributes from `<tr>`, `<th>`, and `<td>` elements and converts CSS tables to HTML tables, if necessary.

Remove all unused style definitions
Removes stylesheet declarations that are not applied within the current documents.

You should generally leave all the options checked. Once the cleanup process completes, Dreamweaver will optionally display the results.

When cleaning up Word 97/98 HTML, Dreamweaver converts `<font>` tags to heading tags based on the font size, as seen in Figure 7-2.

Clean Up FrontPage HTML

As with Word, Microsoft FrontPage creates nonstandard HTML code. You can clean up your FrontPage documents by using the Cleanup FrontPage HTML Site-wide extension available from Dreamweaver Exchange (see Chapter 22). It can be can run on individual pages or an entire site. If you have installed the extension, you can use Commands → Clean Up FrontPage HTML to open the Clean Up FrontPage HTML dialog box shown in Figure 7-3.

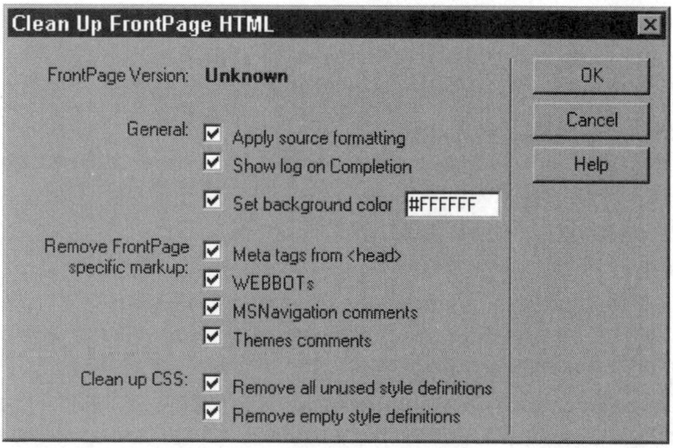

Figure 7-3: The Clean Up FrontPage HTML dialog box

You should generally leave all the options checked. Once the cleanup process completes, Dreamweaver optionally displays the results. Most of the settings in this dialog box are self-explanatory or similar to the cleanup options described earlier. The following three options remove FrontPage-specific markup elements:

WEBBOTs
> Removes server extensions indicated by `<!-- webbots -->`.

MSNavigation comments
> Removes navigation controls indicated by `<!-- MSNavigation -->`.

Themes comments
> Removes the themes information indicated by `<!-- themes -->`.

The three items shown here could also be removed by using Dreamweaver's Clean Up HTML command to remove Non-Dreamweaver comments, but the Cleanup FrontPage HTML extension allows you to do it for the entire site at once.

Find and Replace

You can clean up your HTML manually by using Find and Replace to delete or change text or HTML tags. You can open the Find and Replace dialog box, shown in Figure 7-4, using Edit → Find and Replace, or Ctrl+F (Windows), or Cmd+F (Macintosh). Figure 7-4 shows the simplest version of the Find and Replace dialog box (for Source Code and Text searches).

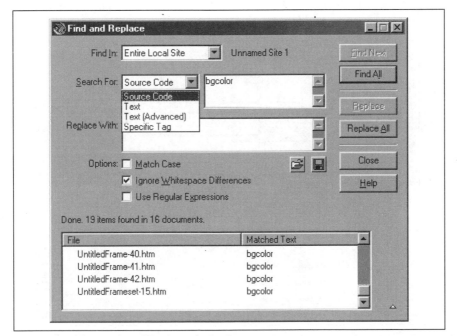

Figure 7-4: The Find and Replace dialog box

You can configure numerous options, including where to search and what to look for:

Find In

> Use this option to specify whether to search the Current Document, Entire Local Site, Selected Files in Site, or Folder (in the last case, a field appears that allows you to specify or browse to the folder to be searched).

Search For

> Use this option to specify whether to search the Source Code, Text, Text (Advanced), or Specific Tag.

Find All

> Using the Find All button automatically expands the dialog box to show a list containing all occurrences of the text. You can also use the arrow in the dialog box's lower-right corner to expand or collapse the bottom portion.

When using the Search For Source Code option, Dreamweaver searches for the precise text in your HTML code. For example, if you search for "<font>," it won't find <font color="990099" size="+2"> or </font>. Search for "font" (without the angled brackets) instead.

When using the Search For Text option, Dreamweaver searches the text visible in the Design pane and ignores any HTML tags that might interrupt your search string. For example, searching for "Dreamweaver book" would find the text resulting from HTML, such as Dreamweaver book.

Using the Search For Text (Advanced) option, as shown in Figure 7-5, allows you to refine your search considerably.

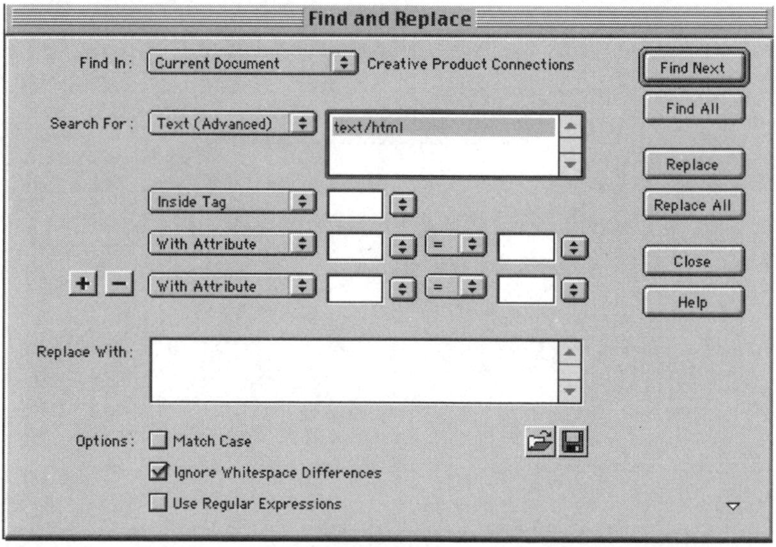

Figure 7-5: The Find and Replace Text (Advanced) dialog box

You can limit your search to a specific tag (and search for text either inside or outside that tag). You can refine the search further by clicking the plus (+) button and making additional selections. You can limit the search to tags that contain or don't contain a specific attribute (and even set constraints on the attribute's value). You can also control whether the matched text must contain or not contain a string or tag, and whether the matched text must occur within or without another tag. In other words, you have an incredible amount of control. For example, you can easily find all the `<p>` elements with an `align="left"` attribute, or all the `<p>` elements not aligned left but with the word "holiday" in their contents.

The most advanced choice is the Search For Specific Tag option, as shown in Figure 7-6.

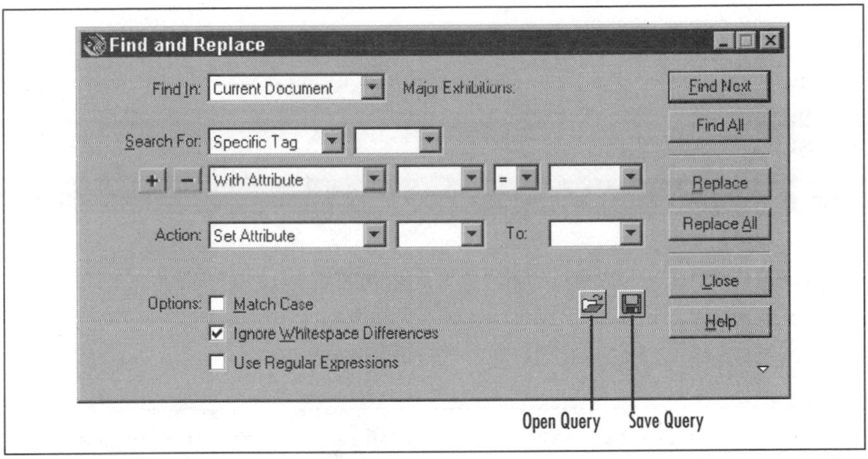

Figure 7-6: The Find and Replace dialog box

This dialog box lets you search for a tag with one or more attributes (use the plus (+) button to specify additional attributes), and then choose an Action from the following list:

> Replace Tag and Content
> Replace Content
> Remove Tag and Content
> Strip Tag
> Change Tag
> Set Attribute
> Remove Attribute
> Add Before Start Tag
> Add After End Tag
> Add After Start Tag
> Add Before End Tag

You can use the Search For Specific Tag option to add text, elements, or attributes to all the pages in a site. For example, to add `alt` attributes to all image elements, search the entire local site for `img` tags with a specified `src` attribute. Then set the Action option to Set Attribute to set your `alt` attribute's value. You can also use the Add Before End action to add a copyright notice within the `<body>` of all pages.

The Find and Replace dialog box also offers the following options (the Open Query and Save Query buttons are indicated in Figure 7-6):

Match Case

> Limit matches to text of the exact letter case. For example, searching for "Dreamweaver" would not find "dreamweaver" or "DreamWeaver."

Ignore Whitespace Differences

> Ignores whitespace (spaces, tabs, and newline characters) when determining matches. For example, searching for "Dreamweaver" would find both "Dream weaver" and "dr eamweaver."

Use Regular Expressions

> Causes specific characters (such as ?, *, \w, and \b) in your search string to be interpreted as regular expression operators. See Table 7-1.

Open Query button

> Opens a saved Dreamweaver Find and Replace query operation.

Save Query button

> Saves the current Find and Replace query operation.

The Replace All button searches for and replaces the string in one or more files specified in the Find In field. You can't Undo the operation unless the scope is limited to the current document. Although you may be able to correct the problem with a new, carefully crafted search, make a backup copy before using Replace All throughout the entire site.

Searching with regular expressions

If you have enabled the Use Regular Expressions option in the Find and Replace dialog box, you can use the *regular expressions* listed in Table 7-1 in your Search For field. Regular expressions are useful in performing *wildcard searches*, which are more flexible than searching for exact strings. See *Mastering Regular Expressions* by Jeffrey E. Friedl (O'Reilly) for extensive practice with regular expressions.

Table 7-1: Regular expressions

Expression	Matches	Example
?	The preceding character zero or one time (i.e., preceding character is optional)	ta?k finds tak or tk, but not tik or taak
*	The preceding character zero or more times	w*k finds wok, ok, or kwanza, but not walla
+	The preceding character one or more times	aw+l finds crawl or awwl, but not wake
. (period)	Any one character except a newline	.ow finds cow or crow, but not ow
^	The specified string at the beginning of a line	^w finds wok or wrap, but not kiwi
$	The specified string at the end of a line	$w finds cow or crow, but not wok
x|y	Either statement	ow|aw finds crawl or cow, but not wake
[abc]	Any of the characters in the brackets	[aei] finds crawl or ale, but not concho
[a-z]	Any characters in range	[0-9] matches all numeric digits
[^abc]	Any character other than those listed	[^aeu] finds concho or silo, but not wake
[^a-z]	Any characters not in range	[^0-9] matches all non-numeric characters
{n}	Exactly *n* occurrences of the preceding character	e{2} finds creel or creep, but not crepe or creeep
{n,m}	At least *n* but no more than *m* instances of the preceding letter	e{2,3} finds creel or creeep, but not screeeech
\b	The letter at the beginning of a word	\bq finds queen, but not Iraq
\B	The letter not at the beginning of a word	\Bq finds Iraq, but not queen
\d	Any numeric digit; same as [0–9]	\d finds R2D2, but not Boba Fett
\D	Any nondigit character; same as [^0–9]	\D finds Boba Fett, but not R2D2
\f	A form feed	\f finds form feeds
\n	A line feed (newline)	\n finds newline characters (ASCII 10)
\r	A carriage return	\r finds carriage returns (ASCII 13)
\s	A single whitespace character (space, tab, line feed, or form feed)	\s finds the space in King Tut
\S	A single nonwhitespace character	\STut finds KingTut, but not King Tut
\t	A tab character	\t finds tab characters (ASCII 9)
\w	Any alphanumeric character; same as [A–Za–z0–9]	q\w finds quest, but not q%est
\W	Any non-alphanumeric character	\Wq finds &q, but not iq
\x	Escaped characters (non-metacharacters)	\/ finds slashes; \(finds parentheses, etc.

To search for a Return character without using regular expressions, deselect the Ignore Whitespace Differences option and use Ctrl+Enter or Shift+Enter (Windows) or Ctrl+Return, Shift+Return, or Cmd+Return (Macintosh) as the search text. (When using regular expressions, you can search for \r.) Return characters appear as spaces, not as line breaks, in the Design pane of the Document window. Searching for the Return character does not find `<br>` and `<p>` tags.

Regular expressions operators can be combined. For example, the regular expression \d+\/\d+\/\d+ finds dates of the form xx/xx/xx.

Parentheses are used to "remember" strings in the regular expression to be used later. For each expression in parentheses, you can use the matching text by substituting $n as a placeholder in the replacement string. For example, you can convert between U.S.- and European-style dates by searching for (\d+)\/(\d+)\/(\d+) and replacing it with $2/$1/$3. Try it!

Tag Selector

The Tag Selector is located in the Status bar at the bottom of the Document window and is shown in Figure 7-7. It displays the HTML tags related to the selected object. You can select a tag by clicking its name in the Tag Selector. You can adjust the selected object by right-clicking (Windows) or Ctrl-clicking (Macintosh) on its tag and selecting from the contextual menu shown in Figure 7-7.

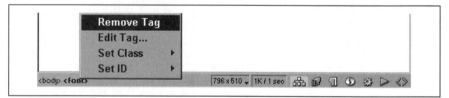

Figure 7-7: Tag Selector pop-up menu options

Remove Tag
> Deletes the selected HTML tag but not any tags nested within it. You can't delete certain tags, such as `<body>`, `<table>`, `<tr>`, and `<td>` tags using this menu option.

Edit Tag
> Opens the Quick Tag Editor (discussed next).

Set Class
> Applies or removes a CSS class selector style to format the selected tag (as described in Chapter 10 and shown in Figure 10-16).

Set ID
> Applies or removes a CSS ID selector style to format the selected tag (as described in Chapter 10 and shown in Figure 10-6).

Use Edit → Select Parent Tag and Edit → Select Child to select another tag.

Quick Tag Editor

The Quick Tag Editor (QTE) gives you direct control over a single HTML tag without having to open the Code view or Code inspector. The QTE has several modes, as seen in Figure 7-8, and you can open it in several ways.

To open the QTE in Edit Tag mode (to edit an existing tag), select only one element, and then:

- Right-click (Windows) or Ctrl-click (Macintosh) on the Tag Selector in the status bar and choose Edit Tag from the contextual menu.

- Use Modify → Quick Tag Editor, Ctrl+T (Windows), or Cmd+T (Macintosh).

- Right-click (Windows) or Ctrl-click (Macintosh) on an element in the Document window and choose Edit Tag from the contextual menu.

- Click the Quick Tag Editor icon at the right edge of the Property inspector (see Figure 1-5).

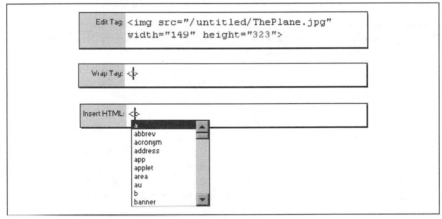

Figure 7-8: The three modes of the Quick Tag Editor

You may want to wrap a tag within a <span> tag to allow you to add a hyperlink to tags that don't ordinarily support hyperlinks. To open the QTE in Wrap Tag mode (to wrap a new tag around two or more existing tags), select two or more elements and then:

- Right-click (Windows) or Ctrl-click (Macintosh) and choose Wrap Tag from the contextual menu.

- Use any method that opens the QTE (when more than one element is selected, the QTE defaults to the Wrap Tag mode instead of the Edit Tag mode).

To open the QTE in Insert HTML mode (to insert a new tag), ensure that no elements are selected and then:

- Right-click (Windows) or Ctrl-click (Macintosh) on an unoccupied space in the Document window and choose Insert HTML from the contextual menu.

- Use any of the methods that open the QTE (when no elements are selected, the QTE defaults to the Insert HTML mode instead of the Edit Tag mode).

The simple QTE pop-up window lets you insert or edit a single tag. You can change the tag attributes directly without the constraints of the Property inspector. The QTE also lets you select attributes to add from the Tag Hints drop-down list, as seen in Figure 7-8.

Table 7-2 lists some common QTE shortcuts.

Table 7-2: Quick Tag Editor options

Shortcut	Operation
Tab	Selects the next attribute.
Shift-Tab	Selects the previous attribute.
Ctrl+T (Windows) or Cmd+T (Macintosh)	Opens the Quick Tag Editor and cycles through its three modes.
Show drop-down Tag Hints	Open a drop-down list by typing a space after the closing quotes of any attribute; the delay can be adjusted or tag hints can be disabled under Edit → Preferences → Quick Tag Editor.
Navigate Tag Hints list	Type the first few letters of an attribute name or use the arrow keys. Press Enter (Windows) or Return (Macintosh) to select an item.

To apply changes made in the QTE, click in any other area of the document (or press the Tab key if the Apply Changes Immediately While Editing option is enabled under Edit → Preferences → Quick Tag Editor). If you made a visible change to your document, such as changing the font color or the size of an image, it is reflected immediately in the Document window.

Copy and Paste HTML

In addition to standard copying, cutting, and pasting, Dreamweaver allows you to copy and paste HTML code directly. This feature allows you to copy and paste information from one portion of your document to another with or without including the HTML code. Table 7-3 shows the effect of various combinations of cut and paste.

Table 7-3: Copy and Paste from Design View

Copy operation	Paste operation	Results
Edit → Copy	Edit → Paste	Copies an exact duplicate, including HTML code, to the new location.
Edit → Copy HTML	Edit → Paste	Pastes the HTML code into the document's Design view.
Edit → Copy	Edit → Paste HTML	Pastes the text of the selection without HTML code included.
Edit → Copy HTML	Edit → Paste HTML	Copies an exact duplicate, including HTML code, to the new location.

The Edit → Copy command cannot be used to copy steps from the History panel; use the Copy Steps button in the History panel instead (see Figure 7-9). Use Edit → Paste HTML to see the JavaScript that underlies the steps copied from the History panel.

Apply Source Formatting

Dreamweaver can format your HTML to make it more legible without affecting its underlying meaning. Source formatting is applied by using Commands → Apply Source Formatting. For example, this command changes this code from its current eclectic and illegible state:

```
<ul><li><font face="Copperplate Gothic Bold" size="4"><a href="http://
berry-basket.com">Berry Basket</a></font></li> <li><font
face="Copperplate Gothic Bold" size="4"><a href="http://bettys-kitchen.
com">Betty's Kitchen</a></font></li>
```

into this:

```
<ul>
    <li><font face="Copperplate Gothic Bold" size="4"><a href="http://
berry-basket.com">Berry
        Basket</a></font></li>
    <li><font face="Copperplate Gothic Bold" size="4"><a href="http://
bettys-kitchen.com">Betty's
        Kitchen</a></font></li>
</ul>
```

Source formatting is controlled by the Code Format and Code Color categories under Edit → Preferences and the *SourceFormat.txt* file discussed in Chapter 18.

You can specify an external code editor, such as BBEdit or HomeSite, by using Edit → Preferences → File Types / Editors → External Code Editor. To open an HTML file in the external editor, use Edit → Edit With *ApplicationName*, Ctrl+E (Windows), or Cmd+E (Macintosh).

Checking Spelling

Dreamweaver offers customizable dictionaries for spellchecking. Start the spellchecker using Text → Check Spelling or Shift+F7. The spellchecker checks the selected text and provides suggestions for misspelled or unrecognized words. If no text is selected, it starts checking at the cursor location and will optionally "wrap around" until the entire document has been checked.

Dictionaries are stored in the *Dreamweaver 4/Configuration/Dictionaries* folder. The English version of Dreamweaver ships with U.S. English and U.K. English dictionaries. Dictionaries in additional languages can be downloaded from Macromedia's site and should be placed in the same folder. The spelling dictionary can be chosen under Edit → Preferences → General → Spelling Dictionary. You can add to your custom dictionary, stored in the *Personal.dat* file in the *Dictionaries* folder, using the Add to Personal button in the Check Spelling dialog box. Your personal dictionary is simply a text file that can be edited in a word-processor to add, correct, or remove words in the dictionary.

The spellchecker always checks the visible text in the Design pane of the current Document window. It can't check spelling in the Code pane, nor can it check spelling for the entire site all at once.

History Panel

The History panel tracks all your actions in the Document window, such as menu options you have selected and characters you have typed. You can use it to undo, redo, and automate one or more commands, but it doesn't track your actions in the Site window and it isn't available when in Code view. To open the History panel, shown in Figure 7-9, use Window → History or Shift+F10.

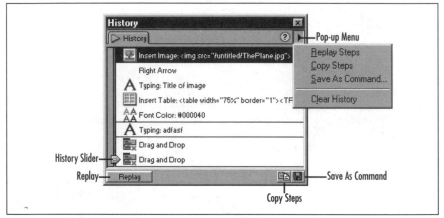

Figure 7-9: The History panel

The vertical slider on the left side can be used to undo and redo steps in the History panel. You can also click to the left of a step to undo to that point. Use Edit → Undo, or Ctrl+Z (Windows), or Cmd+Z (Macintosh) to undo a single step. Use Edit → Redo, or Ctrl+Y (Windows), or Cmd+Y (Macintosh) to redo a single step. Set the maximum levels of Undo using Edit → Preferences → General → Maximum Numbers of History Steps (large numbers may consume excessive memory and slow performance).

The history is kept separately for each open document and disappears when you close a document. Unlike most other programs, however, you can undo steps even after saving a document (as long as you haven't closed it). You can clear the History panel, using the Clear History command in the pop-up menu, to conserve memory, but doing so prevents you from using undo.

If you undo several steps and then start a new action, the undone actions are discarded (i.e., those steps can't be recovered).

Replaying Steps

The History panel allows you to repeat a step or series of steps that have been performed. Select the step(s) that you wish to repeat and click the Replay button (indicated in Figure 7-9) or choose Replay Steps from the pop-up menu.

You can't edit steps or modify their order in the History panel, but you can skip steps. To do so, select a step and then use Ctrl-click (Windows) or Cmd-click (Macintosh) to select additional steps (they need not be contiguous). For example, you can select the first, third, and fifth steps in a process, but skip the second and fourth steps. When you click the Replay button, only the selected steps are repeated.

The History panel shows the history for the current window only (although it maintains a history for all open documents). To copy a series of steps into another document:

1. Select the desired steps in the History panel.

2. Copy the steps to the clipboard by using the Copy to Clipboard button (see Figure 7-9) or the Copy Steps command from the pop-up menu; the Edit → Copy command won't work for this purpose.

3. Switch documents or open a new document.

4. Paste the steps into the new document using Edit → Paste, Ctrl+V (Windows), or Cmd+V (Macintosh). The copied steps will be executed.

Commands can be applied to individual elements, but not to groups of elements. For example, you can resize three images separately, but not as a group. See "Applying Steps to Multiple Objects" in the Dreamweaver Help for details on applying steps to multiple elements (the trick is to select the next element using the Shift and arrow keys, not the mouse).

 Use the Copy Steps button in the History panel to copy one or more selected commands; then use Edit → Paste as HTML to see the underlying JavaScript. This is a good way to learn or edit the JavaScript behind any Dreamweaver function.

Creating Custom Commands

Creating custom commands from the History panel allows you to repeat a task multiple times. To create a command from steps that have already been performed, highlight the steps in the History panel and click the Save As Command button (see Figure 7-9). This button opens the Save As Command dialog box, which allows you to name your command. Custom commands appear on your Commands menu and can be used in any Dreamweaver file, not just the original document. Good uses for custom commands include Copyright or Designed By statements, privacy policies, or anything that's used across multiple pages or multiple sites.

 Dreamweaver can't record mouse movements, but it can record all of your keyboard shortcuts. If you wish to record a series of intricate menu options, use your keyboard to open and select the options, or use the shortcut keys.

Commands that can't be played back, such as mouse movements, are indicated by a black line or a red X in the History panel. Performing actions without the mouse may take some practice. See Edit → Keyboard Shortcuts (especially the Code Editing and Document Editing commands) for lists of keyboard commands. Remember that you can use the Tab key and arrow keys to navigate in dialog boxes and file lists, and any Windows menu command can be accessed using the Alt key.

Editing the Commands menu

To edit the name of a custom command or delete it at a later time, use Commands → Edit Command List. You can't edit the actual commands—only their names; to change a command's operation, you must delete and recreate it.

Commands are shown in the order they were created. To change the order, edit the *menu.xml* file, which controls Dreamweaver's menus, directly. See Chapter 19 for details.

Use Commands → Get More Commands to download additional commands, (i.e., Extensions) from the Dreamweaver Exchange. These commands are discussed in Chapter 22.

Recording a command

If you know you'll want to play back the steps you are about to take, record them using Commands → Start Recording, Ctrl+Shift+X (Windows), or Cmd+Shift+X (Macintosh). This command records all of your keystrokes and object insertions until you select Commands → Stop Recording or press Ctrl+Shift+X (Windows) or Cmd+Shift+X (Macintosh) again. While recording, the cursor looks like a cassette tape. Recorded commands aren't stored in the Commands menu but can be played back using Commands → Play Recorded Command, Ctrl+P (Windows), or Cmd+P (Macintosh).

Working with Browsers

Dreamweaver can help you preview your HTML pages in different browsers and check browser compatibility. Here are some URLs from which you can download the major browsers:

- Internet Explorer (*http://www.microsoft.com/windows/ie*)
- Netscape Navigator (*http://home.netscape.com/netscape*)
- America Online (*http://www.aol.com*)
- Opera (*http://www.opera.com*)
- iCab (*http://www.icab.com*)
- Lynx (*http://www.lynx.org*)

Preview in Browser

Dreamweaver allows you to set up two web browsers with hot-key access. In most cases one browser will be a version of Internet Explorer and one will be a version of Netscape Navigator. To preview your document in your primary web browser, use File → Preview in Browser → *browser1* (F12); to preview your document in your secondary browser use File → Preview in Browser → *browser2*, Ctrl+F12 (Windows), or Cmd+F12 (Macintosh). Set up browsers with which to preview your documents by selecting Edit → Preferences → Preview in Browser or File → Preview in Browser → Edit Browser List.

 Your primary browser is also used to display Dreamweaver's Help files. If the keyboard shortcuts don't work on the Macintosh, turn off the Hot Function Key option in the Keyboard Control Panel.

To debug a document in the primary browser, use File → Debug in Browser → *browser1*, Alt+F12 (Windows), or Opt+F12 (Macintosh).

To debug a document in the secondary browser use File → Debug in Browser → *browser2*, Ctrl+Alt+F12 (Windows), or Cmd+Opt+F12 (Macintosh).

Browser Compatibility Checking

To check your document's browser compatibility, use File → Check Target Browsers to open the Check Target Browsers dialog box shown in Figure 7-10.

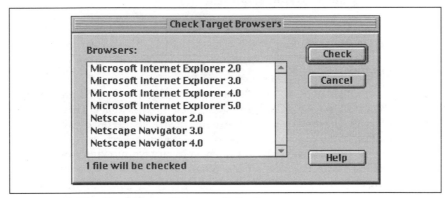

Figure 7-10: The Check Target Browsers dialog box

In this dialog box, you can check for element and attribute compatibility for all web browsers from IE2 to IE5 and from NN2 to NN4. The DW4.01 updater includes compatibility checking for Netscape Navigator 6. Once you have selected the applicable browsers, Dreamweaver provides a report similar to the one shown in Figure 7-11. The browser compatibility check does not check whether scripts work in a particular browser. Table 12-1 and 12-3 address JavaScript compatibility.

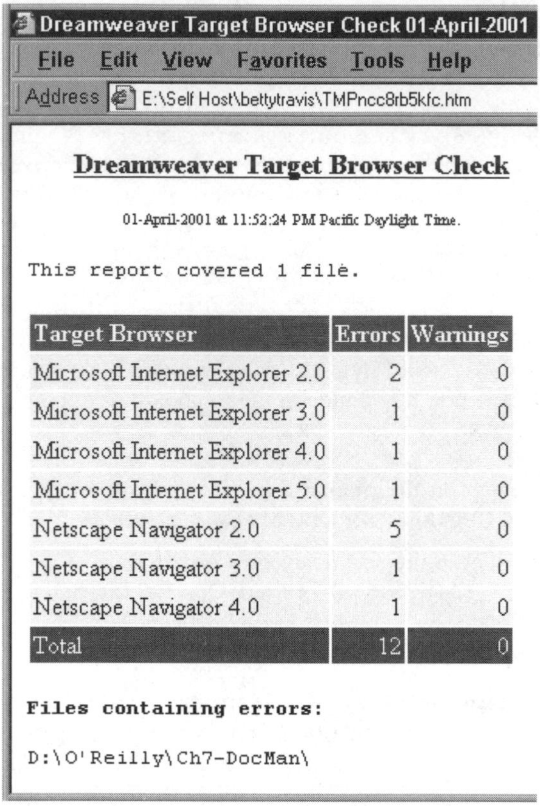

Figure 7-11: The Target Browser Check report

Browser profiles

The browser profiles used by the Check Target Browser command are text files stored in the *Dreamweaver 4/Configuration/BrowserProfiles* folder. These text files can be edited in Dreamweaver or an external text editor. You can create new browser profiles or download additional browser profiles, such as for NN6, from the Macromedia Dreamweaver site. If you create your own browser profile, follow the format requirements described under "About browser-profile formatting" under Help → Using Dreamweaver (F1).

This chapter aimed to give you the skills to manage an individual HTML document more efficiently. In the next chapter we'll explore Dreamweaver's template features, which are used to standardize multiple HTML pages.

CHAPTER 8

Templates

Dreamweaver templates can increase your efficiency significantly. If you use the same or similar layout across a series of pages, a template allows you to quickly redesign or update multiple pages at once. Templates are also great for workgroups; they let you standardize page layouts while preventing developers from accidentally deleting or changing locked elements. Let's see how templates can enhance standardization and reduce development time. (If your site is heavily data-driven, consider using Dreamweaver UltraDev.)

Creating a Template

A template is similar to other HTML documents except that certain areas are locked. In fact, the entire template (except the page title) is locked by default; only the editable regions that you create within the template can be changed.

When designing templates, remember:

- Information that should appear on all pages should be noneditable (part of the template).
- Create editable regions to hold any page-specific information that will vary in pages that use the template.
- Test your template before creating dozens of pages based on it. Although you can automatically update all pages based on a template, it is easiest when the changes are minor. Major changes to a template may require you to manually update the pages based on the template. For example, deleting an editable region from a template will delete the content in that region on each page, unless you move the content to another region (see Figure 8-8).

Documents created using the File → New command are based on the default document template, *default.html*, which can be customized as described in Chapter 20.

Starting a Template

Create a template from scratch using File → New to open a blank document, or base a template on an existing file by using File → Open. Any content you add appears on the pages derived from this template.

Use File → Save as Template to save the template. This command opens the Save As Template dialog box, where you should specify the name for the template. You can also specify the site to which the template applies. Dreamweaver gives the template a *.dwt* extension and saves it in the *Templates* folder within the specified site's root folder (which is why you specify a filename only and not a folder). The window title bar of a template file contains the word <<Template>>. Saved templates appear in the Templates panel (Window → Templates).

Using Images in Templates

If you own Fireworks, you can use it to lay out your template, *slice* it up (divide it into smaller pieces for optimization), and export it as an HTML table for use in Dreamweaver. (If you don't own Fireworks, I strongly recommend you buy a copy. You can download a trial version from Macromedia's site.) Procedure 3 explains how to create such a table in Fireworks. Refer also to the Help → Lessons → Creating Slices tutorial accessible from Fireworks' Help menu.

Procedure 3

1. Open your source image, typically a *.png* file, in Fireworks.

2. In Fireworks, select an element or region to be sliced and use the Insert → Slice command or the Slice tool to create a slice. Repeat for as many regions as you'd like to slice.

3. In Fireworks, use File → Export Preview → Options → Format to choose JPEG or GIF format (BMP and TIFF files are not web-compatible formats).

4. In Fireworks' Export Preview dialog box click the Export button to open the Export dialog box. (File → Export is another way to open the Export dialog box if you've already closed the Export Preview dialog box.) In the Export dialog box, set the Save as Type option to HTML and Images; set the HTML option to Export HTML File; set the Slices option to Export Slices. Because Fireworks exports a separate image for each slice, enable the Put Images In Subfolder checkbox to keep the exported images in a tidy folder. Use the Include Areas Without Slices checkbox to also export images for areas that are not sliced.

5. In Fireworks, while still in the Export dialog box, choose a filename for your HTML file and click the Save button. Fireworks will export the images

according to your choices in Step 4 and create an HTML page containing a table that uses the sliced images. By default, the sliced images' filenames are based on the saved file's name plus the row and column number, such as *myfile_r2_c3.gif*. The naming convention for exported slices can be configured using the Document Specific tab of Fireworks' HTML Setup dialog box (opened by using either File → HTML Setup or the Options button in the Export dialog box).

6. If you want to use this table as the basis for your entire page, open the HTML page that you just exported from Fireworks in Dreamweaver's Document window using File → Open. If you want to insert the table into an existing Dreamweaver document, choose Insert → Interactive Images → Fireworks HTML instead.

7. When you select the table and open the Property inspector, you'll see that Dreamweaver identifies it as a Fireworks Table (if you are in Standard view and not Layout view).

8. In Dreamweaver, use File → Save as Template.

Figure 8-1 shows an example Fireworks Table and the Property inspector.

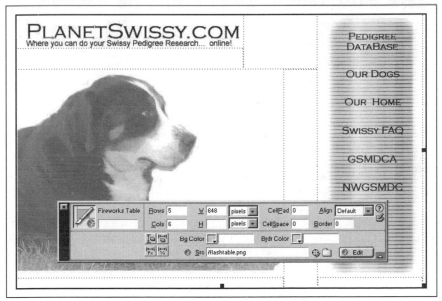

Figure 8-1: Fireworks Table imported into Dreamweaver

Although this layout might look good for a single page, it won't work as well if the content on the page varies. Any information that exceeds the dimensions of the original table may distort the layout and ruin the page's composition. To make this layout usable for the addition of text and other images, you'll probably want to remove the image of the dog from the table itself and use it as a background image (using the CSS `background-image` property described in Table 10-4). You'll also want to merge the remaining cells and remove any white images occupying them. Leave the menu bar and the title graphic alone; they'll become permanent parts of the template. Figure 8-2 shows what the document might look like after you've made these changes. Resave the file as a template using File → Save as Template when you're done.

Creating Links in a Template

Links can be added to images or text within templates just as they would be in a standard HTML document. Templates can also use client-side or server-side image maps. Figure 8-2 shows an image map being added to a template.

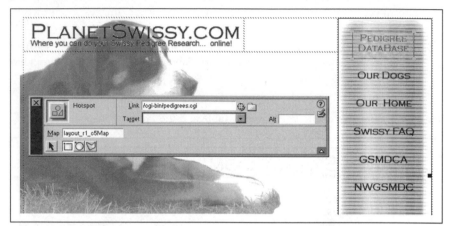

Figure 8-2: Creating an image map on a template

 When creating links within templates, avoid errors by using the file browser to select files. Your links should be relative to the Site Root and should start with a slash (/).

If you've enabled the Edit → Preferences → Invisible Elements → Client-Side Image Maps checkbox, you'll see a small icon representing the <map> tag for any image maps you create. Move this icon somewhere unobtrusive, such as the bottom of the page, so that it doesn't distract people using the template.

Adding Template Fields

A template's *editable regions* are areas that allow pages derived from the template to be customized. To add an editable region, highlight an element and use Modify → Templates → New Editable Region, Ctrl+Alt+V (Windows), or Cmd+Opt+V (Macintosh). In the New Editable Region dialog box, shown in Figure 8-3, provide a Name for the editable region (i.e., *template field*) and click OK. Dreamweaver won't allow two regions in a single template to have the same name. The new template field is surrounded by a light blue outline and has a blue tab displaying its name. Repeat this process for each new template field.

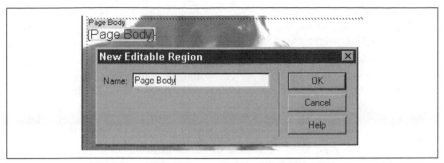

Figure 8-3: The New Editable Region dialog box and an editable region highlighted in a document

You can also make an image into an editable region (in which case it is displayed in dark gray). You can highlight existing text and use Modify ‣ Templates ‣ New Editable Region to make it editable (in DW3, this option was named Mark Selection as Editable). HTML formatting styles applied to a template field serve as the default style for elements inserted in its place, but styles can be modified using HTML (not CSS) during page development.

Editable regions are enclosed in comment tags as seen here:

```
<!-- #BeginEditable "regionName" -->editable content<!-- #EndEditable -->
```

Anything between the comments is editable; anything outside the comments is not. In the preceding example, only the text is editable, not the tags that surround it. Note how the following example includes the `<p></p>` tags within the editable region:

```
<!-- #BeginEditable "editableParagraph" -->
<p>This is a paragraph</p>
<!-- #EndEditable -->
```

You can add new paragraphs within an editable region if the template field encompasses a block-level tag, such as `<p></p>`. To prevent new paragraphs from being added, ensure that the template field doesn't encompass a block-level tag (tweak the HTML in Code view, if necessary). To allow a user to place an image but not text, ensure that the `src` attribute, but not the `<img>` tag itself, is within an editable template area.

When working with a template that uses a table for page layout, you'll probably want to make one or more cells editable regions. To do so, select a `<td>` tag from the Tag selector and use Modify → Templates ‣ New Editable Region.

Exporting and importing XML content

Templates are similar to XML documents in that they define the structure of a document separate from its contents. A template's editable regions are analogous to XML name/value pairs (the region's name corresponds to the XML attribute's name, and the region's content corresponds to the XML attribute's value). Therefore, Dreamweaver can export data from a template to an XML file and can import data from an XML source into a template.

To export data from a file based on a template to an XML file, use the File → Export → Export Editable Regions As XML command. Dreamweaver creates a new HTML document that references the original template but contains the contents of the editable regions. (This command is active only when editing a file based on a template. It is not available when editing an ordinary HTML file or when editing a template itself.) You can choose to export the file using standard Dreamweaver XML tags or using the editable region names as XML tags. An example of the former style might look as follows:

```
<?xml version="1.0"?>
<templateItems template="/Templates/Untitled-4.dwt">
    <item name="doctitle"><![CDATA[
<title>Untitled Document</title>
]]></item>
    <item name="region1"><![CDATA[
<p>This is some text</p>
]]></item>
</templateItems>
```

To import data from an XML source, use the File → Import → Import XML Into Template command. Dreamweaver creates a new HTML document based on the template specified by the XML file and fills in the editable regions with the data in the XML file. This operation is analogous to choosing File → New From Template in that it creates a new HTML document based on a template (the difference being that it also fills in the editable fields). To ensure that the XML file follows the correct format, you can first export a dummy file as described in the preceding paragraph and use it as a basis for other XML files.

Saving a Template

Whenever you change a template, you should resave it and update all the documents that use the template. When you resave the template using File → Save, Dreamweaver displays a list of pages derived from the current template and asks you whether to update them. Choosing to update the pages opens the Update Pages dialog box shown in Figure 8-4.

This dialog box can be confusing. When you save a template and choose to update the pages based on it, this dialog box opens automatically and shows the results of the update. You can change the Look In pop-up menu to update an entire site. However, if you close the dialog box and reopen it via Modify → Templates → Update Pages (or even Modify → Library → Update Pages), you can choose to update files that use any template (or library item, as seen in Figure 9-4 in the next chapter). Use the dialog box's Start button to commence the update, or simply use the Close button to dismiss it.

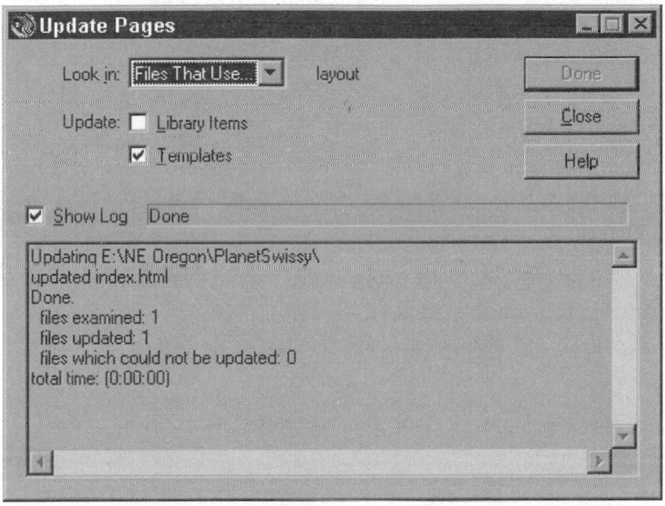

Figure 8-4: The Update Pages dialog box

Using Your Template

To create a new document based upon a template, use File → New From Template and select a template to use from the Select Template dialog box shown in Figure 8-5. (You can also create a new document by choosing the New From Template option from the arrow pop-up menu in the Templates panel discussed in the next section.) Documents derived from a template file are indicated by an asterisk in the Document window's title bar.

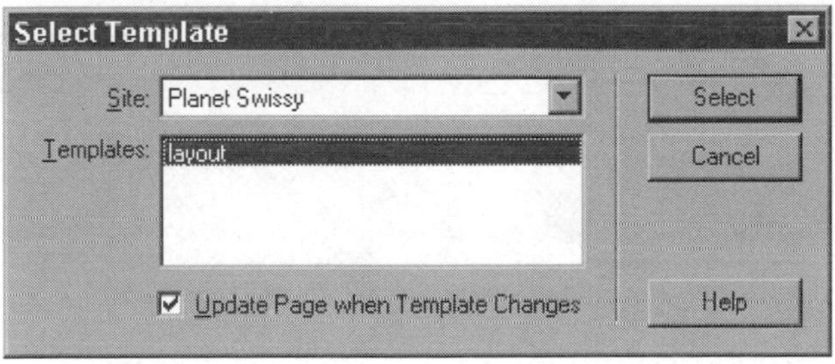

Figure 8-5: The Select Template dialog box

From the Select Template dialog box, you have access to all templates that have been saved as a part of any web site. You can also enable the Update Page When Template Changes checkbox to ensure that the page always uses the latest version of the template.

New documents based on a template automatically include any contents stored as part of the template. Pages based on a template include comment tags within the <html> tag of the document, such as the following:

```
<html><!-- #BeginTemplate "/Templates/mytemplate.dwt" -->
<!-- #EndTemplate --></html>
```

Only the editable regions can be modified. (Placeholder content from the template may appear in the editable region, but can be replaced.)

You can add text, insert images, or do anything allowed by the template. To add content to a region, select it first using one of these methods:

- Click anywhere inside an editable region.

- Click the blue tab in the upper-left corner of the region (it contains the region's name).

- Choose Editable Regions from the contextual menu and choose the region's name.

- Choose the region's name from the Modify → Templates menu.

 Use replaceable text to provide a hint about the content expected in an editable region. For example, you might use placeholder text that says, "Put your name here."

Figure 8-6 shows a document based on a template. The editable areas are indicated by the blue outlines. Dreamweaver prevents you from editing other areas (the cursor changes to a circle with a slash through it when you try to edit things that aren't editable.)

Figure 8-6: Editable regions in a document based on a template

You cannot add CSS styles or a behavior to a template-based document unless the style or behavior is in an external file referenced by the template. By default, only the <title> tag is editable in the head of a template-based document. Dreamweaver creates an editable region named doctitle by default.

```
<!-- #BeginEditable "doctitle" -->
<title>document title is editable</title>
<!-- #EndEditable -->
```

To insert additional tags allowed within the head of a document, enter Code view, place the cursor after the closing </title> tag, and use Dreamweaver's typical tools to insert head content (including JavaScript tags).

If you use another editor such as HomeSite to edit non-editable regions of a document based upon a template, you will have problems updating that document in the future.

To insert a layer in an editable region, use the Insert → Layer menu option (using the Draw Layer tool in the Objects panel won't work because it tries to add the tag in an uneditable portion of the document). Avoid inserting layers into table cells because NN4 doesn't support layers within tables.

Template Operations in the Assets Panel

The Templates category of the Assets panel (a.k.a. the Templates panel) allows you to delete, rename, duplicate, and apply templates to documents. As shown in Figure 8-7, the Templates panel lists all the templates available for the current site (any templates defined for the site are added to the Templates panel automatically). It also shows a preview of the selected template. To open the Templates panel, select Window → Templates or click on the Templates icon in the Assets panel.

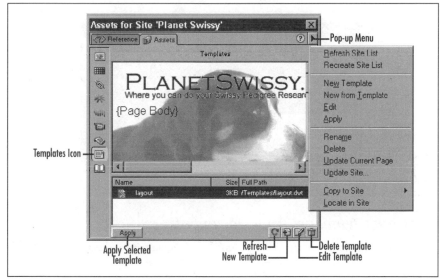

Figure 8-7: The Templates category of the Assets panel

You can change the template associated with a document by dragging a template from the Templates panel and dropping it onto the current document. You can perform other manipulations using the pop-up menu or icons in the Templates panel (see Figure 8-7).

Modifying the Template

To edit a template, open it using File → Open. Select Files of Type: Template files (*.dwt*) from the drop-down list and pick a template from the *Templates* folder.

(Double-clicking the name of a template in the Templates panel is another, much simpler way to open it.)

When editing a template, you can add new editable regions or make any other changes that you could make to a normal HTML document. Use File → Save to save your changes (you'll be prompted to update documents based on the template).

To remove an editable region, use Modify → Templates → Remove Editable Region and choose the region's name from the list of regions in the template. Remember that when you delete an editable region, you risk deleting content on pages derived from the template. Dreamweaver gives you the option of deleting such content or moving it to a different editable region as seen in Figure 8-8.

Linking Templates to Documents

To change the template associated with a file, drag the new template from the Templates panel and drop it onto the document, or select Modify → Templates → Apply Template to Page. If the page contains content that does not fit into the fields of the new template, Dreamweaver displays the dialog box shown in Figure 8-8. You can either merge the content into an existing field or delete the content.

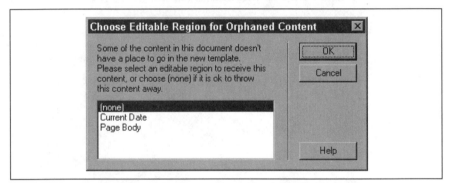

Figure 8-8: The Choose Editable Region for Orphaned Content dialog box

Detaching Templates from Documents

Templates sometimes constrain document development in undesirable ways. You can't add <meta> tags, CSS styles, behaviors, or timelines to a document based on a template because these elements insert information in the head section of a document (the head section of a document based on a template is locked, except for the document's title). Therefore, add these elements directly to the template, not to the document based on the template.

To allow greater freedom, you can remove the template's influence over the document using Modify → Templates → Detach from Template. Once detached from the template, the document editing is no longer constrained to editable regions, and updates made to the template do not affect the current document.

The Commands → Clean Up HTML → Remove Dreamweaver HTML Comments option also detaches the template from a template-based file (it strips out the comment tag used to track templates in Dreamweaver).

Reapplying a template to a document is best avoided. It will generally create duplicate template graphics, links, and text.

Template Operation Summary

Table 8-1 summarizes the template operations.

Table 8-1: Template operations

Operation	Commands
Open Templates panel	Window → Templates
Edit an existing template[a]	File → Open (Files of Type Template files) or double-click the name in Templates panel
Create a new template[a]	File → New, followed by File → Save as Template
Create new document based on a template[a]	File → New from Template
Apply a template to an existing file[a]	Modify → Templates → Apply Template to Page
Delete a template[a]	Select a template in Templates panel and press the Delete key
Refresh the template list[a]	Use the Refresh icon in Templates panel
Update the current page based on revised templates[a]	Modify → Templates → Update Current Page
Update files sitewide based on the revised template[a]	Modify → Templates → Update Pages
Detach a template from a file	Modify → Templates → Detach from Template
Define an editable region[b]	Modify → Templates → New Editable Region Ctrl+Alt+V (Windows) Cmd+Opt+V (Macintosh)
Remove an editable region[b]	Modify → Templates → Remove Editable Region
Copy templates between sites[b]	Use the Copy to Site option in the Templates panel
Select a region[b]	Modify → Templates → *name*
Change the highlighted color of editable regions	Edit → Preferences → Highlighting → Editable Regions and Locked Regions

[a] Also available from the Templates panel using either an icon or the pop-up menu (see Figure 8-7).
[b] Available from the contextual menu using right-click (Windows) or Ctrl-click (Macintosh).

In this chapter, we've seen how to save development time through the use of templates. In the next chapter, we'll cover another great timesaver—the Dreamweaver Library.

Templates

CHAPTER 9

The Library

Dreamweaver's Library allows you to insert frequently needed HTML items quickly. Better still, Dreamweaver maintains a link to the original library asset so copies can be updated automatically throughout the site whenever the original changes. This feature makes library items an ideal alternative to frames when you need a navigation bar, header, or footer on multiple pages—or even to replace a phone number or email address throughout your site.

Creating a Library Item

The Assets panel can hold many types of assets, such as images, colors, and URLs. But the Library category of the Assets panel can hold complex HTML that the other categories cannot. For convenience, we'll refer to the Library category of the Assets panel as the Library panel, even though it isn't a separate panel. To open the Library panel, use Window → Library or click on the Library icon in the Assets panel. To create a library entry, simply drag and drop an item from the Document window into the Library panel. You can add graphics, text, and even email addresses to the Library. Provide a name for the new library item when you add it to the Library. The Library panel shows a small preview of the item, as seen in Figure 9-1.

You can also add selected items to the Library using Modify → Library → Add Object to Library, Ctrl+Shift+B (Windows), or Cmd+Shift+B (Macintosh). You can also use the New Item button in lower-right corner of the Library panel to add an item to the Library (the Insert button inserts items from the Library into the current document, not vice versa). You can also choose New Library Item from the pop-up arrow menu in the upper-right corner of the Library panel. This menu also contains other options, described in Table 9-1.

A library item must include matching opening and closing tags, so be sure to select the entire tag before adding it to the Library.

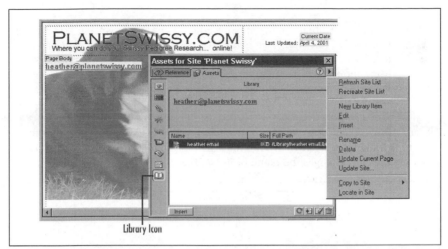

Library Icon

Figure 9-1: The Library category of the Assets panel (Library panel)

 Library items cannot contain head content; they can contain only items allowed within the `<body>` tag. Behaviors, stylesheets, and timelines can't be placed in a library item.

Using a Library Item

To insert a library item into your document, select the item in the Library panel and click the Insert button at the bottom of the Library panel. You can also simply drag and drop an item from the Library panel to the Document window to insert it. Insert any library item as many times in as many documents as you wish.

When you insert a library item, it creates an *instance* of the original library item. Dreamweaver inserts the HTML code of the original item, plus comments that allow it to reference the original. Dreamweaver updates the library item instance if the original library item changes. The inserted code is similar to Example 9-1. Note that a comment identifies the beginning of the library item and the name of the file containing it.

Example 9-1: HTML code for a library item instance

```
<!-- #BeginLibraryItem "/Library/heather email.lbi" -->
<b>
  <font size="2"><a href="mailto:heather@planetswissy.com">
  heather@planetswissy.com
  </a></font>
</b>
<!-- #EndLibraryItem -->
```

Instances of library items are not editable and do not have editable regions the way that documents based on templates do. If you need to edit an instance of a library item, detach it from the original first using the Detach from Original button in the Property inspector (see Figure 9-3).

Library items are saved as *.lbi* files in the *Library* folder within the site's root folder (Figure 9-2 shows this folder in the Site window). Renaming a library item in the Library panel also changes the name of its *.lbi* file.

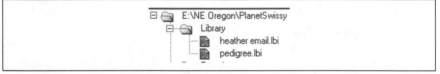

Figure 9-2: Library items stored in the Library folder

You can copy library items between sites using the Copy To Site option in the pop-up menu shown in Figure 9-1. To copy library items between computers copy the *.lbi* files manually and place them in the appropriate folder.

Creating a Library Item Using a Behavior

In earlier chapters, we covered some Dreamweaver objects, such as navigation bars, rollover images, and jump menus, that use behaviors. (If you are not familiar with JavaScript behaviors you should revisit this section after reading Part III, which describes them.) The JavaScript code for a behavior is stored in the <head> portion of an HTML document and therefore a behavior cannot be stored in a library item. To work around the limitation, save a *function call* to the behavior in the library item instead. Dreamweaver inserts the appropriate JavaScript function into the <head> section of your document.

To edit a library item that includes a behavior:

1. Detach the library item instance from the original library entry using the Detach from Original button in the Property inspector, as shown in Figure 9-3.

2. Adjust the behavior parameters as you would for any other behavior.

3. Select all the elements and objects for this particular library item and then choose Modify → Library → Add Object to Library.

4. Give the new library item the same name as the original item, using exactly the same spelling and capitalization (if you want the change to be reflected in other documents that use the original library item).

5. Select Modify → Library → Update Pages in the Update Pages dialog box shown in Figure 9-4 to update the documents that use the library item.

6. Use the Look In field to select files that use the updated library item.

7. Click the Start button. Dreamweaver creates a log of the matches found.

See "Editing a behavior in a library item" under Help → Using Dreamweaver (F1) for more information.

Figure 9-3: The Property inspector for a library item

Modifying Library Items

Library items can be edited, renamed, and deleted. When an original library item changes, you can update any instances of the item within the current document or across the entire site. To update the library items in the current document, use Modify → Library → Update Current Page; to update the library items in the entire site, use Modify → Library → Update Pages (these options work in Design view but not Code view). Dreamweaver uses the Update Pages dialog box, as seen in Figure 9-4, when updating pages sitewide.

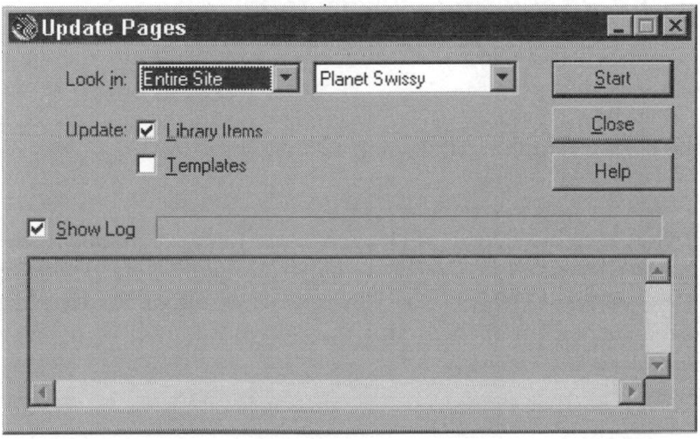

Figure 9-4: The Update Pages dialog box

Editing Library Items

Library items are stored in .lbi files in the Library folder within the site's root folder. These files contain plain text and can be edited like any typical HTML document. To edit a library item, double-click its name in the Library panel, or select it and then click the Open button in the Property inspector (see Figure 9-3). Either gesture opens the Library item as a separate HTML window, as shown in Figure 9-5 (note the words <<Library Item>> in the Document window's title bar).

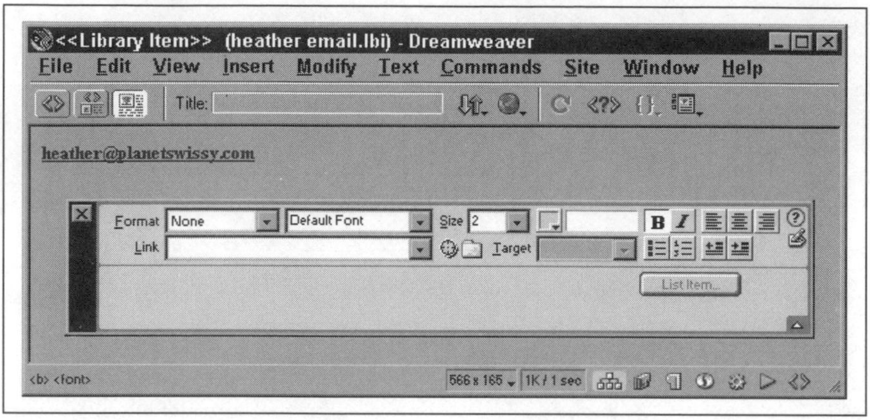

Figure 9-5: Editing a library item as an HTML document

You can modify the Library item in the same way as any other HTML document, provided you don't add any head content, such as CSS styles or behaviors. Doing so will add <style> tags outside of the <head> tag, which is not HTML 4.0-compliant (although IE5.5, NN6, and Opera 5 seem to tolerate such transgressions).

Deleting and Re-creating Library Items

To delete a library item, select it in the Library panel and use the Delete icon in the lower-right corner of the window. Deleting a library item does not remove instances of it from existing pages where it was used; instead, it essentially detaches the library item from all documents that use it.

 If you have accidentally deleted a library item, you can re-create it from an instance of the item. Select the entire item, including the <!-- #BeginLibraryItem --> and <!-- #EndLibraryItem --> comment tags, and then click the Recreate button in the Property inspector (see Figure 9-3).

You can't re-create a library item from a detached instance. Instead, you'll need to save the library item again by using Modify → Library → Add Object to Library and giving it the same name as the original.

Library Operation Summary

Table 9-1 summarizes the Library operations.

Table 9-1: Library operations

Operation	Commands
Open Library panel	Window → Library or click Library icon in Assets panel.
Edit existing library item[a]	Double-click filename in Library panel, or use File → Open (Files of Type Library files).

Table 9-1: Library operations (continued)

Operation	Commands
Create a new library item[a]	Modify → Library → Add Object to Library; Ctrl+Shift+B (Windows); Cmd+Shift+B (Macintosh).
Insert library item into document[a]	Click Insert icon in Library panel or drag and drop from Library panel into Document window.
Delete library item[a]	Select item in Library panel and press Delete key.
Rename library item[a]	Select item in Library panel and choose Rename from pop up arrow menu.
Refresh library item list[a]	Use Refresh icon in Library panel.
Update library items on current page[a]	Modify → Library → Update Current Page.
Update library items sitewide[a]	Modify → Library → Update Pages.
Detach item instance from original library item[b]	Click Detach from Original button in the Property inspector.
Recreate library item[b]	Click the Recreate button in the Property inspector.
Copy library files between sites[b]	Choose Copy to Site from the pop-up arrow menu in the Library panel.
Find all files that use a library item	Choose Locate in Site from the pop-up arrow menu in the Library panel.
Change highlighted color of library items	Edit → Preferences → Highlighting → Library Items.

[a] Also available from the Library panel either from an icon or from the pop-up menu (see Figure 9-1).
[b] Available from the contextual menu using right-click (Windows) or Ctrl-click (Macintosh).

In the next chapter, you'll cover Dreamweaver's use of Cascading Style Sheets. Topics include associating a stylesheet with your document, using a stylesheet with a template, adding stylesheet objects to your elements, and creating external stylesheets.

CHAPTER 10

Cascading Style Sheets

Cascading Style Sheets (CSS) are one of the greatest features to come out of the World Wide Web Consortium (W3C). CSS simplifies repetitive formatting tasks, such as indenting the first line of every paragraph, by defining styles to be applied within a page. Attaching the same CSS stylesheet to multiple pages (or to the template on which multiple pages are based) makes it easy to redefine styles globally throughout your site. CSS can be used to set page attributes (such as margins and background images), provide rollover states for hyperlinks, align images, and format tables.

An exhaustive discussion of CSS is beyond the scope of this book, but this chapter will give you a good overview and cover its use in Dreamweaver. For full details on CSS, see *Cascading Style Sheets: The Definitive Guide* by Eric A. Meyer (O'Reilly). For quick-reference information including browser, CSS1, and CSS2 support, choose O'Reilly CSS Reference from the Book pop-up menu in the Reference panel (Window → Reference).

CSS Overview

Conceptually, CSS is pretty simple—you define styles that can be applied easily over one or more pages. But the details can get confusing unless you're familiar with the terminology (especially because Dreamweaver's terminology varies slightly from that used elsewhere). We'll start with the big picture and work our way towards the details.

CSS Versus HTML Styles

First let's compare CSS to so-called HTML styles (discussed in Chapter 11).

CSS stylesheets:

- Are managed using the CSS Styles panel (see Figure 10-15), the Edit Style Sheet dialog box, the New Style dialog box, and the Style Definition dialog box. The CSS Styles panel shows only the styles available in the current document.

- Require browsers supporting CSS1 (or later). Therefore, CSS generally works only in 4.0 browsers or later (see Table 10-1). CSS code is not HTML, but can be stored in an HTML page within `<style>` tags or within `style=""` attributes associated with other elements.

- Offer advanced and precise control over all aspects of page formatting, including paragraph formatting, image alignment, margins, spacing, borders, element positioning, and special effects.

- Offer automatic updating; if a CSS style changes, all content that uses the style will be updated automatically.

- Use a compact and efficient notation. Multiple HTML pages can use a single stylesheet. CSS defines rules for the application of conflicting styles.

- Doesn't distinguish between character and paragraph formatting.

- Are based on a W3C standard.

HTML styles:

- Are managed using the HTML Styles panel (see Chapter 11). The styles in the HTML Styles panel are accessible to all pages on a site.

- Offer compatibility with older browsers (IE3, NN3, and earlier) that do not support CSS. HTML styles are a convenience offered in Dreamweaver, but they use basic HTML tags that don't require special browser features.

- Offer imprecise control over fonts and little control over many page-formatting options.

- Must be manually reapplied if a style changes (i.e., no automatic updating).

- Suffer from verbose notation; multiple pages cannot share common styles.

- Distinguish between character and paragraph formatting, similar to MS Word.

- Are an invented convenience offered by Macromedia.

CSS and Browsers

Table 10-1 shows the level of CSS support in the major browsers. Although you'll need Version 4 or later for CSS1 support, even 4.x browsers don't necessarily implement all the CSS1 rules. Notable exceptions are highlighted where applicable. See the compatibility matrix of CSS property support at *http://www.webreview.com/style/css1/charts/mastergrid.shtml*.

Table 10-1: CSS support in major browsers

CSS Support	Browsers
None	IE2 and earlier; NN 3 and earlier
Partial CSS1 support	IE3
CSS1	IE4 or later; NN4 (has some bugs); Opera 4 and later
CSS1 and CSS2	IE5.5 or later; NN6 or later; Opera 5

CSS Roadmap

You need to understand several important concepts when using CSS styles in Dreamweaver, and they can't all be covered immediately. For example, I intentionally defer discussing how to apply CSS styles because the method depends on the type of CSS styles you've defined. Once you understand the nuances of CSS styles, you'll know how to apply them and why. Figure 10-1 gives you a roadmap to this chapter so you can decide in which order you'll read the sections. Buckle up! It's a long ride, but worth the trip.

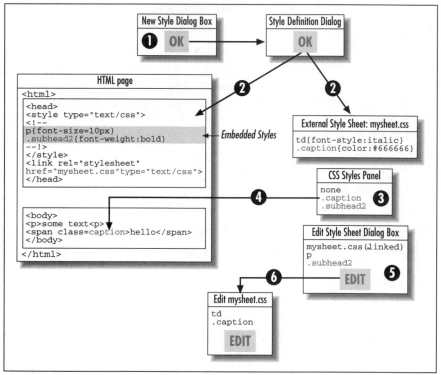

Figure 10-1: CSS styles roadmap

As you can see, there is a lot going on in Figure 10-1, so let's take a closer look at the life cycle of a CSS style (creation, storage, and application):

1. New styles are created using the New Style dialog box as seen in Figure 10-5 (Text → CSS Styles › New Style), which leads to the Style Definition dialog box (Figures 10-7 through 10-14).

2. Styles defined in the Style Definition dialog box are deposited either in the HTML document or an external file. Embedded styles are stored within the HTML file itself; external stylesheets are separate *.css* files.

3. Custom CSS styles, known as *class selectors* (such as .caption and .subhead2) are shown in the CSS Styles panel (Figure 10-15); *type selectors* that redefine existing HTML tags, such as p, are not.

4. Both embedded styles and styles from external stylesheets can be used to format the HTML document's body content.

5. The Edit Style Sheet dialog box (Figure 10-2) lists *embedded styles* individually (including ones that don't show up in the CSS Styles panel), but lists only the *filenames* of external stylesheets—not the styles within them.

6. Highlighting an external stylesheet's filename in the Edit Style Sheet dialog box and clicking the Edit button opens another dialog box that lists all the styles in an external stylesheet (see Figure 10-4). To actually edit a style, click the Edit button to go back to the Style Definition dialog box (see Step 2 of this list).

We'll cover these topics in the following sections:

- "CSS Operations" summarizes such operations as defining, applying, and editing styles and stylesheets.

- "Stylesheets" explains where styles are stored—namely embedded in the HTML document or in external stylesheets (in a separate external *.css* file).

- "Styles" covers details on the syntax of styles themselves and describes the different kinds of styles you're likely to use (custom classes, styles that redefine an HTML tag, and CSS selectors). We'll explain how to define new styles and store them in the embedded stylesheet or in a new or existing external stylesheet.

- "Defining a Style" covers the eight different panes in the Style Definition dialog box that can be used to set the properties for your style.

- "CSS Styles Panel" covers how the CSS Styles panel is used to manage and apply styles.

- "Editing CSS Styles and Stylesheets" revisits some dialog boxes and explains how to revise existing styles and stylesheets.

- "Cascading and Inheritance" talks about precedence of styles and resolving potentially conflicting styles.

- "CSS Element Selection Patterns" and "Downloading Fonts with CSS2" cover some advanced topics.

CSS Operations

Table 10-2 gives a quick overview of using CSS Styles in Dreamweaver. The remainder of the chapter covers these operations in detail.

Table 10-2: CSS operation summary

Operation	Shortcut
Open the CSS Styles panel	Window → CSS Styles, Shift+F11, or the CSS Styles icon in the Launcher bar
Add a style to an internal or embedded stylesheet	Text → CSS Styles → New Style
Attach an external stylesheet using the `<link>` tag[a]	Text → CSS Styles → Attach Style Sheet
Attach an external stylesheet using the `@import` directive	Text → CSS Styles → Edit Style Sheet → Link → Import
Detach an external stylesheet	Text → CSS Styles → Edit Style Sheet → Remove
View a list of external stylesheets and embedded styles	Text → CSS Styles → Edit Style Sheet; Ctrl+Shift+E (Windows); Cmd+Shift+E (Macintosh)
Export embedded styles to an external *.css* file	Text → CSS Styles → Export CSS Styles
Convert CSS styles to HTML styles	File → Convert → 3.0 Browser Compatible
Apply a class selector[a]	Text → CSS Styles → *stylename* or use Set Class in the Tag Selector's contextual menu
Apply an ID selector	Use Set ID in Tag Selector's contextual menu
Duplicate an embedded style	Text → CSS Styles → Edit Style Sheet → Duplicate
Duplicate an external style	Text → CSS Styles → Edit Style Sheet → Edit → Duplicate
Delete an embedded style[a]	Text → CSS Styles → Edit Style Sheet → Remove
Delete an external style from an external stylesheet	Text → CSS Styles → Edit Style Sheet → Edit → Remove
View a list of styles in an external stylesheet	Double-click *.css* file in Site window; Ctrl-click (Windows) or Opt-click (Macintosh) the Edit Style Sheet button in the CSS Styles panel
Remove a style attached to a single element (clear styling)[a]	Text → CSS Styles → None

[a] Also available as an option in the CSS Styles panel.

We'll continue our top-down tour of CSS styles in sequential order. We'll cover the different places where CSS styles can be stored and then cover the different types of CSS styles.

Stylesheets

A *stylesheet* is simply a collection of CSS styles (formatting rules). Stylesheets do *not* appear in the CSS Styles panel, but some styles defined within them do. Stylesheets are accessed using the Edit Style Sheet dialog box, shown in Figure 10-2, and accessed via Text → CSS Styles → Edit Style Sheet.

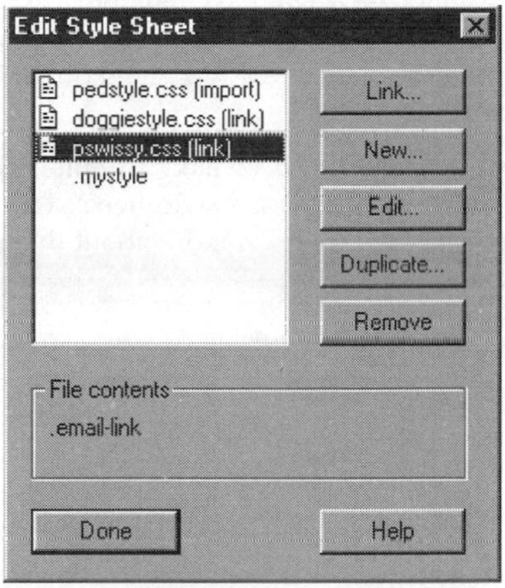

Figure 10-2: The Edit Style Sheet dialog box

The Edit Style Sheet dialog box can be confusing; it displays the internal styles defined in the embedded stylesheet but displays only the names of external stylesheets (not the styles within them). External stylesheets are indicated in the dialog box by the word "(link)" or "(import)" after their names. If you highlight the name of an external stylesheet in the list, however, the lower portion of the dialog box shows the styles defined within it.

Let's look at both embedded and external stylesheets to avoid confusing stylesheets with the styles that they contain.

Embedded Stylesheets

An *embedded stylesheet* (a.k.a. *document stylesheet*) is merely a collection of styles included in a `<style>` tag within the head portion of an HTML document (Example 10-3 and Example 10-5 both illustrate embedded stylesheets). For now, just recognize that any CSS styles stored within an HTML document are collectively referred to as an embedded stylesheet. The name is really a misnomer; there is no separate "sheet," just an HTML document with extra stuff in it (obviously, there can be only one embedded stylesheet per HTML document).

We'll see how to add a new style to a document's embedded stylesheet later. Because the embedded stylesheet doesn't have a separate name (remember, it's contained in the same *.html* file as your HTML code) Dreamweaver displays its individual styles in the Edit Style Sheet dialog box.

Sometimes you'll import HTML documents that already contain CSS styles. Microsoft Word 2000 and XP convert Word document styles to CSS styles when using Word's File → Save As HTML option. If you import such a document into Dreamweaver using File → Import → Import Word HTML, you will be prompted to clean up the HTML using the Clean Up Word HTML dialog box. Use the Detailed tab of this dialog box to control the way in which Dreamweaver modifies Word's CSS styles. (HTML documents exported from Word 97/98 don't use CSS styles.)

Embedded stylesheets cannot be shared by multiple documents. Therefore, use external stylesheets to hold styles that you expect to use with multiple web pages. To create an external stylesheet from existing embedded styles, use Text → CSS Styles → Export CSS Styles.

Also note that an HTML document can contain an embedded stylesheet and also include links to one or more external stylesheets (as seen in Figure 10-1). Speaking of external stylesheets, let's learn more about them.

External Stylesheets

An *external stylesheet* is a collection of CSS styles stored in a separate external *.css* file (not an HTML file).

> External stylesheets allow you to use the same stylesheet for multiple web pages, making it easy to apply design changes across a site.

You can link to an existing external stylesheet using the Link button in the Edit Style Sheet dialog box (see Figure 10-2). This button opens the Link External Style Sheet dialog box shown in Figure 10-3.

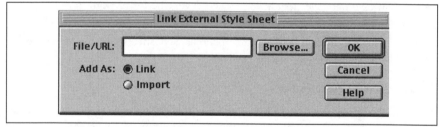

Figure 10-3: The Link External Style Sheet dialog box

You'll notice that there are two ways to link to an external stylesheet using this dialog box's Add As option. Selecting the Link radio button causes Dreamweaver to use a `<link>` tag to point to the external stylesheet you've chosen, such as:

```
<link rel="stylesheet" href="pswissy.css" type="text/css">
```

Surprisingly, selecting the Import radio button does not copy the external sheet's styles to your embedded stylesheet; instead, it causes Dreamweaver to use the `@import` directive instead of the `<link>` tag to reference your external stylesheet. The two variants are shown in Example 10-1. (You would not ordinarily mix the two methods of linking to external stylesheets; we do so for comparison purposes only. Notice that both variants are stored within the head of the HTML document. Furthermore, notice that the `@import` directive is within the `<style>` tag, whereas the `<link>` tag is not.)

Example 10-1: References to imported and linked external stylesheets appearing in the HTML document

```
<head>
<title>My Document</title>
<meta http-equiv="Content-Type" content="text/html; charset=iso-8859-1">
<style type="text/css">
<!--
@import url(stylesheet1.css);
-->
</style>
<link rel="stylesheet" href="stylesheet2.css" type="text/css">
</head>
```

You will ordinarily use the `<link>` alternative. In fact, using Text → CSS Styles → Attach Style Sheet bypasses the Link External Style Sheet dialog box entirely and assumes you want to use `<link>` instead of `@import`.

> The `@import` CSS2 directive is supported in IE4+ and Opera 3+, but will be ignored by NN4. CSS stylesheets (*.css* files) can themselves contain `@import` directives linking to other *.css* files.

You can insert a `<link>` tag manually by using Insert → Head Tags → Link and specifying **stylesheet** for the Rel field; Dreamweaver will automatically set the Type field to `text/css`. To edit an existing `<link>` tag's properties, double-click the corresponding Link icon in the Document window's Head Content bar (View → Head Content).

If you try to open a *.css* file in Dreamweaver, Dreamweaver presents a dialog box similar to the one shown in Figure 10-4. The dialog box's title indicates the name of the stylesheet being edited (in this case Dreamweaver's *help.css* stylesheet). This dialog box can also be accessed by holding down the Ctrl key (Windows) or Cmd key (Macintosh) when clicking the Edit Style Sheet icon in the CSS Style panel.

There are many ways to create external stylesheets, including:

- Using File → Export → Export CSS Styles (or Text → CSS Styles → Export CSS Styles) to export a new external stylesheet. Dreamweaver exports the styles defined within the `<style>` tag (it exports the CSS styles, but not the HTML tags). Existing `@import` directives, which are stored within the `<style>` tag, are exported as well. Any `<link>` tags, which reside outside the `<style>` tag (see Example 10-1), are not exported.

- Creating a new style using the New Style dialog box (see Figure 10-5) and choosing Define In: (New Style Sheet File). Dreamweaver creates a new external stylesheet and automatically links it to the current document.

- Creating a *.css* file by hand in any text editor. Don't include any HTML tags, just the style rules, as shown in Example 10-2.

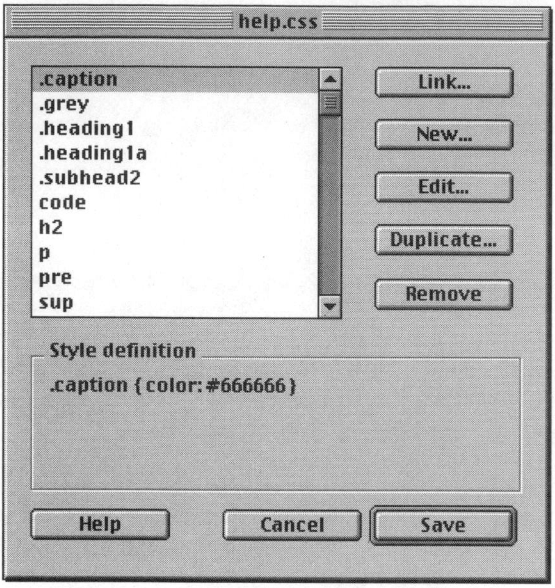

Figure 10-4: Listing styles in an external stylesheet

Example 10-2: An excerpt from the Dreamweaver 4\Help\UsingDreamweaver\htm\ help.css external stylesheet

```
p { font-family: Verdana, Arial, Helvetica, sans-serif; font-size: 11px}
td { font-family: Verdana, Arial, Helvetica, sans-serif; font-size: 11px}
pre { font-family: "Courier New", Courier, mono; font-size: 11px}
.subhead2 { font-family: Verdana, Arial, Helvetica, sans-serif; font-size:
12px; font-weight: bold; line-height: 14px}
.grey { color: #666666 }
.caption { color: #666666 }
```

You should store *.css* files closest to where they'll be needed. If used in a limited section of your site, you may store them in a subfolder near the related *.html* pages. If used for your entire site, consider storing them in a folder named *CSS* within the site's root folder.

Styles

Now that we've seen where styles are stored, let's look at styles themselves in more detail. A *style* is a formatting *rule* that can be applied to an item, such as text, an image, or a table. For example, you can define a style that uses 14-pt, blue, Helvetica text and apply it to all your subheadings. As usual, Dreamweaver provides a friendly UI for defining styles. You can open the New Style dialog box, where you'll begin the process of adding a new style, by using Text → CSS Styles → New Style. You will need to make your Type selection in this dialog box first because it affects the dialog box's other fields. Figure 10-5 shows three variations of the New Style dialog box—Make Custom Style (class), Redefine HTML Tag, and Use CSS selector—based on the Type radio button selection.

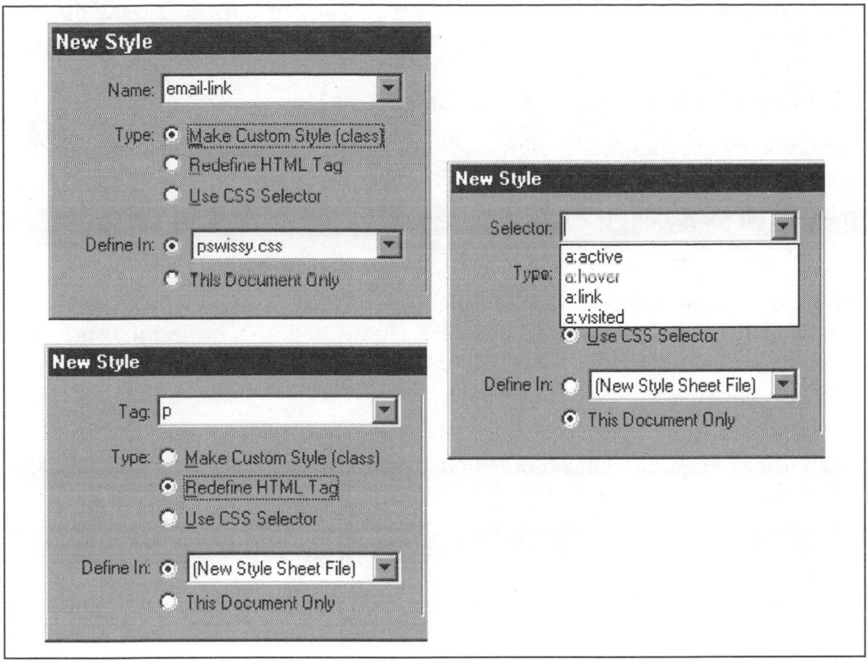

Figure 10-5: Using the New Style dialog box

All possible CSS style types can be stored in both embedded and external stylesheets. Use the This Document Only radio button (see Figure 10-5) to add a style to the embedded stylesheet; otherwise, pick a new or existing external stylesheet to hold the new style you'll be defining.

Only custom styles created using the Make Custom Style (class) option appear in the CSS Styles panel (see Figure 10-15). These styles are called *class selectors* and also appear under the Text → CSS Styles menu. The styles that redefine HTML tags and other CSS Selectors appear elsewhere (see Figure 10-2 and Figure 10-4).

Though Dreamweaver writes the CSS style code for you, it helps to know what the rules look like if you want to edit them by hand.

A style or rule is comprised of a *selector* followed by one or more declarations separated by semicolons and enclosed in curly braces. Each declaration is comprised of a property/value pair. Thus, each style looks something like this:

```
selector {property1: value1; property2: value2}
```

CSS selectors are not directly related to the Tag Selector in Dreamweaver's status bar; the latter is just a name that Macromedia picked for one of its UI features.

Now let's look at the three variants of CSS styles that you can create using the New Style dialog box.

Making Custom Styles (Class Selectors)

Custom styles (also known as *class selectors*) are convenient for defining your own custom formatting when HTML tags don't suffice.

The general form looks like this:

```
.classSelector {property1: value1; property2: value2}
```

To create a class selector rule, use the Type: Make Custom Style (Class) radio button in the New Style dialog box (see Figure 10-5). The selector name must begin with a period followed by a letter (Dreamweaver adds the period for you). After the initial letter, you can include other letters or numbers, but not spaces (avoid underscores as well).

Then, using the Style Definition dialog box's options, you might define the following style to be applied to subheadings. (Dreamweaver writes the code for you.)

```
.subhead2 { font-family: Verdana, Arial, Helvetica, sans-serif;
           font-size: 12px; font-weight: bold; line-height: 14px}
```

By definition, any selector starting with a period (.) is a class selector. When you define a class selector, its name appears in the Set Class submenu within the contextual menu associated with the Tag Selector, as seen in Figure 10-16. Class selectors also appear in, and can be applied using, the CSS Styles panel, the Text → CSS Styles submenu, and the pop-up contextual menu (see Figure 10-17). When a class selector is applied to an element, Dreamweaver adds a `class` attribute to the HTML tag like this (hence the name "class selector"):

```
<p class="subhead2">Hello my honey</p>
```

When a class selector is applied to a span of text where no block tag exists, Dreamweaver adds a `<span>` tag, like this:

```
Hello my <span class="subhead2">baby</span>
```

Class selectors are only one type of CSS style rule that Dreamweaver helps you to define. Let's examine some others.

Redefining HTML Tags (Type Selectors)

CSS allows you to redefine the attributes of existing HTML tags using a *type selector* rule of the following form:

```
typeSelector {property1: value1; property2: value2}
```

Type selectors are sometimes known as *element selectors*, but I'm going to call them type selectors throughout this chapter. Note that unlike class selectors, a type selector must match the name of an existing HTML tag and no period precedes it. To create a type selector rule, use the Type: Redefine HTML Tag radio button in the New Style dialog box and then select an HTML tag to redefine from the Tag field (see Figure 10-5).

Again, use the Style Definition dialog box's option to set the style's properties. The following type selector rule sets the text style to be used within <p> tags.

```
p { font-family: Arial, Helvetica, sans-serif;
    font-size: 10px; font-variant: small-caps; color: #00FFFF}
```

 Type selectors do not appear in the CSS Styles panel and are not applied to HTML elements manually. Type selectors are applied to appropriate tags on the page automatically. When placed in an external stylesheet used by all your pages, a type selector can redefine a tag across the entire site.

Type selectors stored in the embedded stylesheet, like all embedded styles, can be edited in Code view and are listed in the Edit Style Sheet dialog box. Type selectors stored in external stylesheets, like all external styles, are accessed by selecting their parent stylesheet in the Edit Style Sheet dialog box and clicking the Edit button.

Using CSS Selectors

CSS allows extraordinary specificity and flexibility in the application of custom styles. First, we'll discuss a type of CSS selector, readily accessible via Dreamweaver's UI, known as *pseudo-class selectors*. We'll cover *ID selectors* after that.

Pseudo-class selectors

We can use so-called *pseudo-class selectors* to change the appearance of hyperlinks created with the <a> tag. These selectors are different from other selectors we've seen so far because they are dynamic. They can be used to create rollover effects in browsers that support them.

To customize the appearance of hyperlinks, use the Type: Use CSS Selector radio button in the New Style dialog box (see Figure 10-5) and then select one of the following four options from the Selector pop-up menu in the dialog box. If you want to define more than one of these pseudo-class selectors, you should do so in the order a:link, a:visited, a:hover, a:active. I list them in that order here, although they are listed alphabetically in the dialog box itself.

a:link
: Defines the style to be applied to unvisited links

a:visited
: Defines the style to be applied to visited links

a:hover
: Defines the style to be applied when the mouse rolls over a hyperlink (new in CSS2)

a:active
: Defines the style to be applied when a hyperlink is being clicked

When you finish defining your style in the Style Definition dialog box, Dreamweaver dutifully creates a pseudo-class selector of the form:

a:*action* {*property1*: *value1*; *property2*: *value2*}

where *action* is either link, visited, hover, or active.

As with the type selectors that we saw earlier, pseudo-class selectors automatically affect all hyperlinks created with the <a> tag. Example 10-3 attempts to change the color of hyperlinks in various states.

Example 10-3: Changing the color of hyperlinks

```
<html><head><style type="text/css">
<!--
a:link { color: #FF0000 }
a:visited { color: #0000FF }
-->
</style></head>
<body bgcolor="#FFFFFF" text="#000000">
  <a href="dummylink.html">This text uses a CSS selector.</a>
</body></html>
```

Example 10-3 instructs the browser to use red for unvisited hyperlinks and blue for visited links (which works in most browsers, including IE5 and NN4.7 on Windows). But don't go overboard, as support for the active and hover states is less consistent and can adversely affect the display of the visited and unvisited states. Consider the following set of styles:

```
a:link { color: #FF0000 }
a:visited { color: #0000FF }
a:hover { color: #00FFFF }
a:active { color: #00FF00 }
```

These styles theoretically instruct the browser to use red for unvisited hyperlinks, blue for visited links, cyan for rollovers, and green for links being clicked. Unfortunately, practice diverges considerably from theory. Although IE5 displays unvisited links in red, rollovers in cyan, and visited links in blue (so far so good!), it doesn't consistently display clicked links in green, and sometimes displays visited links in green instead of blue. Furthermore, depending on the styles defined in the pages you link to, visited links occasionally don't respond to rollovers. NN4.7 properly displays unvisited links in red and visited links in blue, but ignores the active and hover states.

 Be sure to test your styles in all target browsers. To test unvisited links, you need to clear your link history and refresh the page in your browser.

To clear the link history in IE5, use Tools → Internet Options → General → Clear History; in NN4.7 use Edit → Preferences → Navigator → Clear History.

We can construct several other CSS selectors, including ID selectors.

ID selectors

So far, we've seen class selectors, type selectors, and pseudo-class selectors. Another commonly used CSS style is the *ID selector*. An ID selector starts with a pound sign (#) and is used to format tags with a matching id attribute (just as class selectors format tags with a matching class attribute).

The general form looks like this:

```
#idSelector {property1: value1; property2: value2}
```

To create an ID selector rule, use the Type: Use CSS Selector radio button in the New Style dialog box (see Figure 10-5). Instead of choosing a spoon-fed pseudo-class selector from the Selector pop-up menu, specify an ID selector beginning with a pound sign (#) and a letter. After the initial letter, you can include other letters or numbers, but not spaces (avoid underscores as well). Your ID selector rule may look like this:

```
#crucial {font-size: 48px; font-weight: bold; color:red}
```

By definition, any selector starting with a pound sign (#) is an ID selector. When you define one, its name will appear in the Set ID submenu within the contextual menu associated with the Tag Selector, as seen in Figure 10-6.

Figure 10-6: Setting the ID with the Tag Selector

When an ID selector is applied to an element, Dreamweaver adds an id attribute to the HTML tag like this (hence the name "ID selector"):

```
<p id="crucial">Help me please!</p>
```

Here's a dirty little secret. You can create *any* type of selector using the Type: Use CSS Selector radio button in the New Style dialog box simply by entering an appropriate selector in the Selector field. For example, you can create a class selector by beginning your selector name with a period; you can create a type selector by entering the name of a valid HTML tag. (The radio buttons that Dreamweaver provides for making custom styles and redefining HTML tags are just a convenience.) Likewise, you can enter a pseudo-class selector such as a:link by hand instead of using the pop-up menu.

A full discussion of the possible types of selectors is beyond the scope of this book. Consult the section "CSS Element Selection Patterns" later in this chapter for a brief overview of the otherwise gory details. You'll see that class, type, ID, and pseudo-class selectors are only four of the CSS selectors you can employ.

Defining a Style

Finally, we come to defining a style. By now, hopefully you understand the context in which you define and apply CSS styles. In the New Style dialog box (see Figure 10-5), click the OK button after choosing the type of CSS style to create and deciding where to store it. This step opens the Style Definition dialog box. Figure 10-7 shows one of the eight panes of this dialog box. Its title becomes "Style definition for *stylename*" if you edit a style that is stored internally; it becomes "Style definition for *stylename* in *stylesheet.css*" if you edit a style stored in an external stylesheet.

The Style Definition Dialog Box

Let's see how to set the attributes for a new style that you are defining. To define a new style, use Text → CSS Styles → New Style (or the New Style button in the CSS Styles panel) to open the New Style dialog box. Once you've made your selections in that dialog box (see Figure 10-5), click the OK button to reach the Style Definition dialog box discussed here. Double-clicking an existing style also brings you directly here (allowing you to edit an existing style's attributes).

The Style Definition dialog box contains 8 categories through which you can customize roughly 60 attributes for a style. You'll probably use only a small fraction for any single style rule. When you're done defining the style's properties, click the OK button to save your style (the choice of where to save it and what to call it was made earlier in the New Style dialog box). The Style Definition dialog box doesn't include support for all CSS2 attributes. See the section "Editing Styles in External Stylesheets" later in this chapter for information on adding attributes by hand.

Defining (creating) a style is not the same as applying (using) it. Although we've already alluded to how styles are applied, we'll cover it in more detail later.

Dreamweaver can't display many of the properties that it lets you set for a style (these properties are indicated by an asterisk in the various panes of the Style Definition dialog box). Use the Preview in Browser option (F12) to test your pages. Each of the eight categories is discussed in the following sections.

Default values are shown in constant-width bold. Italicized values, such as *length*, are placeholders. Recognized units are px, pts, cm, mm, in, em, ex, and %, such as 10px, 12pt, 1cm, 10mm, 2em, 0.5in, or 10%.

Options for which you can select one of multiple choices are shown separated by a vertical bar (|) and enclosed in square brackets ([ ]). Double vertical bars (| |) indicate a non-exclusive choice. Remember that not all browsers support all properties; some browsers may support a property but not support all attribute values specified in the CSS standard. Dreamweaver shows you only a subset of the attributes available in the CSS1 and CSS2 standards. Other CSS1 and CSS2 attributes can be entered by hand.

CSS Type properties category

The properties in the Type category of the Style Definition dialog box affect text appearance. The options are shown in Figure 10-7 and summarized in Table 10-3, where the defaults are shown in bold.

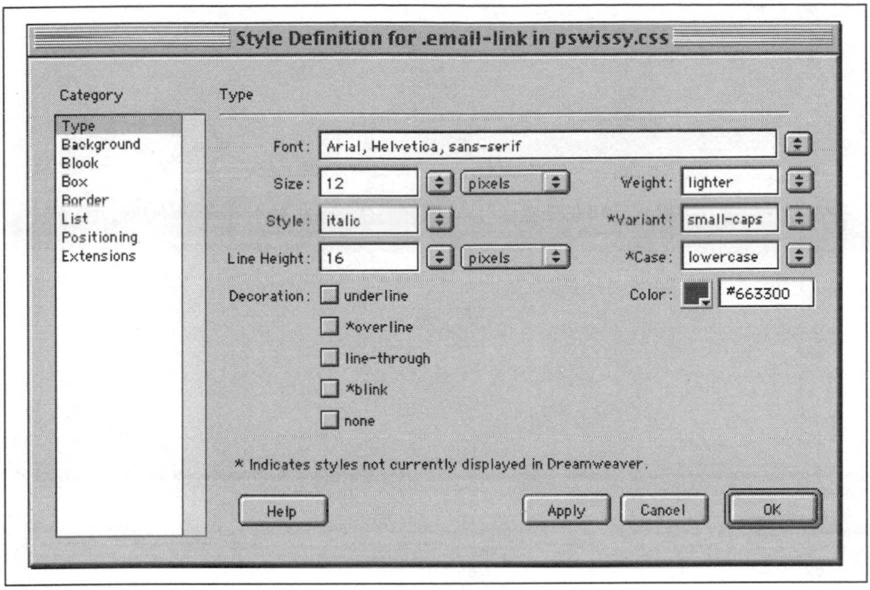

Figure 10-7: Style Definition: Type properties

Table 10-3: CSS Type properties

Property	CSS code
Font	font: [*font-family*]	caption	icon	menu	messagebox	small-caption	statusbar	window	document	workspace	desktop	info	dialog	button	pull-down-menu	list	field	**inherit**]
Size	font-size: [9	10	12	14	16	18	24	36	xx-small	x-small	small	medium	large	x-large	xx-large	smaller	larger	*length*	*percentage*	**inherit**]
Style	font-style: [**normal**	italic	oblique	inherit]
Line Height	line-height: [**normal**	number	length	percentage	inherit]
Weight	font-weight: [**normal**	bold	bolder	lighter	100	200	300	400	500	600	700	800	900	inherit]
Variant	font-variant: [**normal**	small-caps	inherit]
Case	text-transform: [capitalize	uppercase	lowercase	**none**	inherit]
Color	color: [*rgbvalue*	*colorname*]
Decoration	text-decoration: [**none**	[underline		overline		line-through		blink]	inherit]

See the section "Downloading Fonts with CSS2" later in this chapter for details on using the @font-face directive to ensure that a font is available on the user's system.

CSS Background properties category

The properties in the Background category of the Style Definition dialog box affect the appearance of the background of HTML objects, including the document itself, text, images, layers, and tables. The options are shown in Figure 10-8 and summarized in Table 10-4.

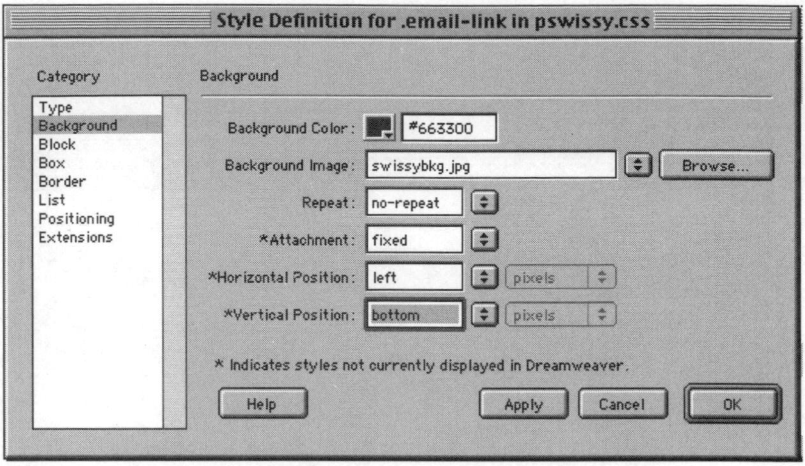

Figure 10-8: Style Definition: Background properties

Table 10-4: CSS Background properties

Property	CSS code
Background Color	background-color: [*rgbvalue* | *colorname*]
Background Image	background-image: [*url* | **none**]
Repeat	background-repeat: [no-repeat | repeat-x | repeat-y | **repeat**]
Attachment	background-attachment: [fixed | **scroll**]
Horizontal and Vertical Position	background-position: [*percentage* | *length*] | [**top** | center | bottom] | | [**left** | center | right] | inherit]

Example 10-4 defines a style that sets the background image of the page and prevents it from scrolling when the page content scrolls (although the background-attachment property doesn't work in NN4). It also prevents the image from being tiled and gives much greater control than the background attribute of HTML <body> tag (the latter can be set under Modify → Page Properties).

Example 10-4: Type selector defining Background properties

```
body { background-attachment: fixed;
       background-color: #FFFFFF;
       background-image: url(layout_r3_c1.gif);
       background-repeat: no-repeat;
       background-position: left bottom}
```

CSS Block properties category

The properties in the Block category of the Style Definition dialog box affect the appearance of block objects, such as images, tables, div elements, and paragraph text. The options are shown in Figure 10-9 and summarized in Table 10-5.

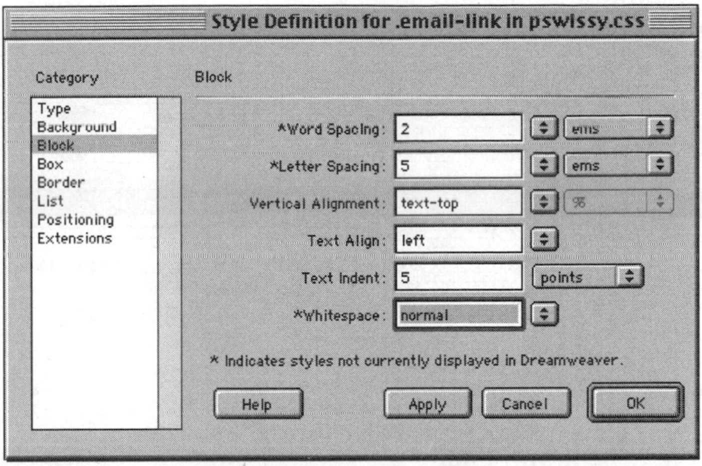

Figure 10-9: Style Definition: Block properties

Table 10-5: CSS Block properties

Property	CSS code
Word Spacing	word-spacing: [**normal** I *length* I inherit]
Letter Spacing (kerning)	letter-spacing: [**normal** I *length* I *percentage* I inherit]
Vertical Alignment	vertical-align: [baseline I sub I super I top I text-top I **middle** I bottom I text-bottom I *percentage* I *length* I inherit]
Text Align	text-align: [**left** I right I center I justify I *string* I inherit]
Text Indent	text-indent: [*length* I *percentage* I inherit]
Whitespace	white-space: [**normal** I pre I nowrap I inherit]

Many browsers do not support letter spacing, and Internet Explorer ignores the `whitespace` attribute. When using the sub and super options for the `vertical-align` attribute, reduce the font size in the Type properties pane of this dialog box.

CSS Box properties category

The properties in the Box category of the Style Definition dialog box affect the margins and padding of block objects. The options are shown in Figure 10-10 and summarized in Table 10-6.

The margin properties define the spacing between the borders of two adjacent objects, such as an image on a page. The padding properties define the spacing immediately surrounding an object, such as a table cell. The border options, set in the Border properties pane, define the spacing between an object and its own borders, such as the borders of a table. The default padding is zero for most objects, but margins should be set explicitly to zero if desired because the default margins are usually nonzero. However, most spacing options don't show up in Dreamweaver, so be sure to preview your changes in a browser.

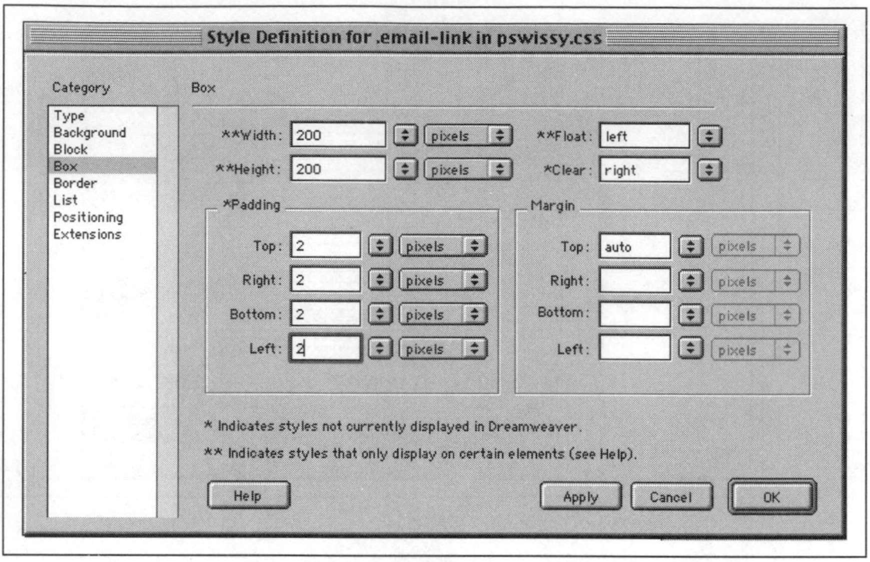

Figure 10-10: Style Definition: Box properties

Table 10-6: CSS Box properties

Property	CSS code
Width	width: [*length* | *percentage* | **auto** | inherit]
Height	height: [*length* | *percentage* | **auto** | inherit]
Float	float: [left | right | **none** | inherit]
Clear	clear: [**none** | left | right | both | inherit]
Padding: Top	padding-top: [*width* | inherit]
Padding: Right	padding-right: [*width* | inherit]
Padding: Bottom	padding-bottom: [*width* | inherit]
Padding: Left	padding-left: [*width* | inherit]
Margin: Top	margin-top: [*width* | inherit]
Margin: Right	margin-right: [*width* | inherit]
Margin: Bottom	margin-bottom: [*width* | inherit]
Margin: Left	margin-left: [*width* | inherit]

CSS Border properties category

The properties in the Border category of the Style Definition dialog box affect the border color and spacing of objects such as images, tables, paragraphs, and layers. The options are shown in Figure 10-11 and summarized in Table 10-7.

The default border spacing is 1 for most objects. The margin and padding spacing are set in the Box properties pane.

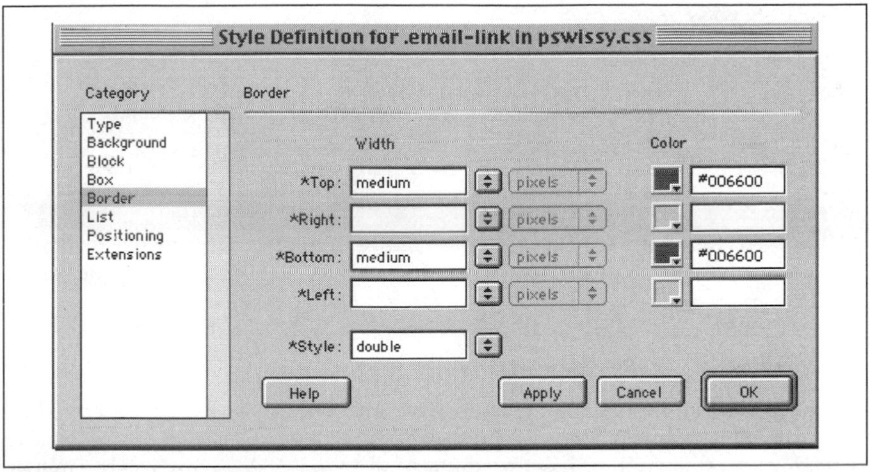

Figure 10-11: Style Definition: Border properties

Table 10-7: CSS Border properties

Property	CSS code
Top Width	Border-top-width: [medium I thin I thick I *length*]
Right Width	Border-right-width: [medium I thin I thick I *length*]
Bottom Width	Border-bottom-width: [medium I thin I thick I *length*]
Left Width	Border-left-width: [medium I thin I thick I *length*]
Color	Border-color: [*color* I transparent I inherit]
Style	Border-style: [none I hidden I dotted I dashed I **solid** I double I grooved I ridge I inset I outset I inherit]

CSS List properties category

The properties in the List category of the Style Definition dialog box affect the appearance of formatted lists, including bullet placement and appearance. The options are shown in Figure 10-12 and summarized in Table 10-8.

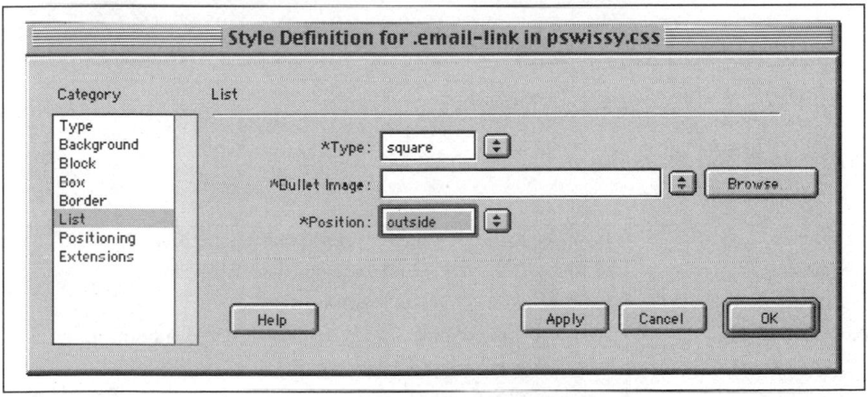

Figure 10-12: Style Definition: List properties

Table 10-8: CSS List properties

Property	CSS code
Type	list-style-type: [disc I circle I square I decimal I lower-roman I upper-roman I lower-alpha I upper-alpha I none I inherit]
Bullet Image	list-style-image: [url I none I inherit]
Position	list-style-position: [inside I outside I inherit]

NN4 doesn't support the `list-style-image` attribute. Dreamweaver doesn't display the full spectrum of values (there are about 50!) available for the `list-style-type` property in CSS2.

CSS Positioning properties category

The properties in the Positioning category of the Style Definition dialog box affect the positioning, visibility, and overflow settings of objects. The options are shown in Figure 10-13 and summarized in Table 10-9. These options are a very cumbersome way of defining layers. You're better off using Dreamweaver's visual tools for this purpose, as discussed in Chapter 4.

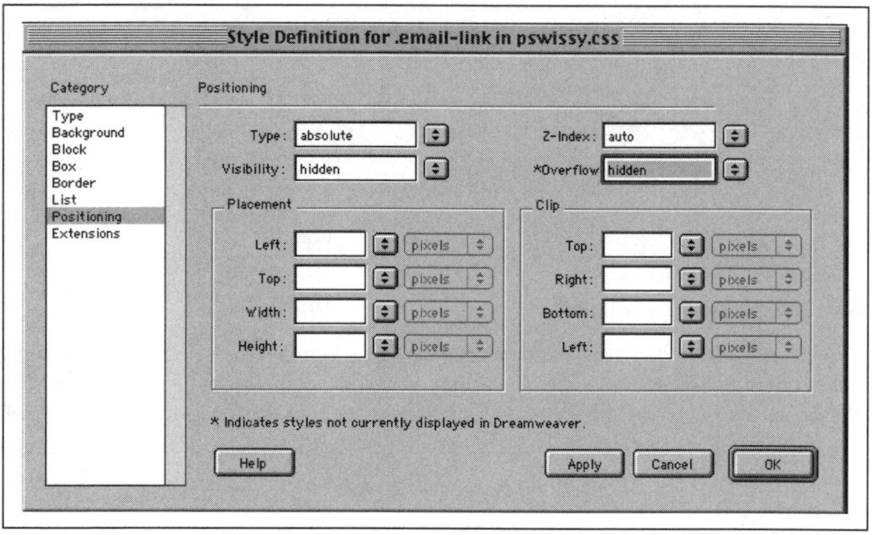

Figure 10-13: Style Definition: Positioning properties

Table 10-9: CSS Positioning properties

Property	CSS code
Type	position: [static I relative I **absolute** I inherit]
Visibility	visibility: [inherit I **visible** I collapse I hidden]
Z-Index	z-index: [auto I integer I **inherit**]
Overflow	overflow: [**visible** I hidden I scroll I auto I inherit]
Placement: Left	left: [length I percentage]
Placement: Top	top: [length I percentage]

Table 10-9: CSS Positioning properties (continued)

Property	CSS code
Placement: Width	width: [*length*	*percentage*]
Placement: Height	height: [*length*	*percentage*]
Clip: Top	Right	Bottom	Left	clip: [rect (*t*, *r*, *b*, *l*)	auto	inherit]

CSS supports `fixed` as another possible value for the `position` attribute, but that value is not available in this dialog box.

CSS Extensions properties category

The properties in the Extensions category of the Style Definition dialog box affect the way a document appears within a browser. The options are shown in Figure 10-14 and summarized in Table 10-10.

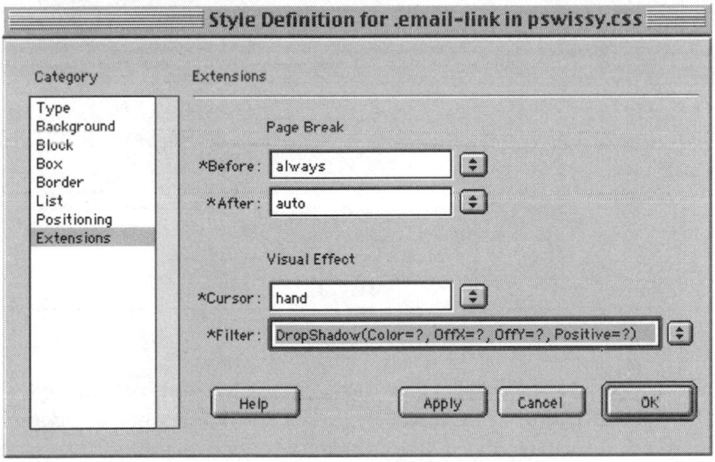

Figure 10-14: Style Definition: Extensions properties

Table 10-10: CSS Extensions properties

Property	CSS code
Page Break: Before	page-break-before: [**auto**	always	avoid	left	right	inherit]
Page Break: After	page-break-after: [**auto**	always	avoid	left	right	inherit]
Cursor	cursor: [**auto**	crosshair	default	default	e-resize	ne-resize	nw-resize	n-resize	se-resize	sw-resize	s-resize	e-resize	w-resize	text	wait	help	inherit]
Filter	filter: [alpha	blendtrans	blur	chroma	dropshadow	fliph	flipv	glow	gray	invert	light	mask	revealtrans	shadow	wave	xray]

The `page-break-before` and `page-break-after` properties affect page breaking when a web page is printed, but no current browser supports either property. The `filter` property is supported by IE for Windows only. The `cursor` property is supported in NN6, IE5, and Opera 5 (and later versions).

CSS Styles Panel

Now that we've covered how and where to define styles, we can get down to the business of using them. The CSS Styles panel, shown in Figure 10-15, allows you to create new styles, apply existing styles, or attach new stylesheets. Open the CSS Styles panel using Window → CSS Styles, Shift+F11, or the CSS Styles icon in the Launcher bar.

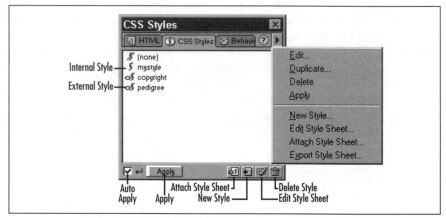

Figure 10-15: The CSS Styles panel

The CSS Styles panel shows styles from both embedded and external stylesheets (it shows the names of the styles themselves, not the names of the stylesheets). It shows only class selector styles (those that start with a period). Type selectors (those that redefine HTML tags), pseudo-class selectors (such as `a:link`), and ID selectors (those starting with #) appear in the Edit Style Sheet dialog box instead.

The options available within the CSS Styles panel include:

Auto Apply checkbox
Applies the style you click on in the CSS Styles panel to the currently selected element in your document. If this checkbox is unchecked, you must click the Apply button manually to apply a style, which can be tedious.

Apply button
Applies the currently selected style to the selected element in your document.

Attach Style Sheet
Attaches an external stylesheet to the current document making the styles it contains available within the current document.

New Style
Creates a new style that can be stored in either an external stylesheet or within the current document.

Edit Style Sheet

Opens the Edit Style Sheet dialog box, as seen in Figure 10-2, where you can choose the stylesheet to edit, create new styles, etc.

Delete Style

Deletes the selected style from either the external stylesheet file or from within the current HTML document.

Applying and Clearing CSS Styles

We've learned about the different CSS styles (selectors), how they are created, and where they are stored. The good news is that styles are applied in the same way whether they are stored internally or externally. However, the CSS Styles panel is used to apply class selector styles only. Let's take a closer look at applying these and other selectors (styles).

Applying and clearing class selector styles

Here are some ways to apply class selector styles to the selected text or object:

- Click the Apply button in the CSS Styles panel.

- Pick the style name from the menu using Text → CSS Styles → *stylename*.

- Assign a **class** attribute by hand (or using the Quick Tag Editor) to an existing HTML tag. If you assign it a value of a matching a class selector, then the custom style will be applied.

- Right-click (Windows) or Ctrl-click (Macintosh) on the Tag Selector to open the contextual menu and choose the style name from the Set Class submenu (see Figure 10-16). Select None from the pop-up submenu to clear a previously applied style.

- Select CSS Styles → *stylename* from the contextual menu in the Document window, as shown in Figure 10-17.

Figure 10-16 shows how to apply a class selector using the Tag Selector.

Figure 10-16: Using the Tag Selector to apply a class selector

Figure 10-17 shows how to use the contextual menu to apply a class selector.

If you apply a class selector style to a selection not contained in a block element, Dreamweaver automatically inserts a **<span>** tag to contain the **class** attribute, as shown in the following code:

```
<p>But this <span class="pgraph">text</span> isn't!</p>
```

P̲aragraph Format ▸	
L̲ist ▸	
Ali̲gn ▸	
Fo̲nt ▸	
S̲tyle ▸	
HTML St̲yles ▸	
C̲SS Styles ▸	✓ **N̲one**
Si̲ze ▸	**copyright**
	email-link
Open Attached Template	**pedigree**
Edita̲ble Regions ▸	
	N̲ew Style...
Insert H̲TML...	**E̲dit Style Sheet...**
E̲dit Tag <body>...	**A̲ttach Style Sheet...**
Make L̲ink	*Export Style Sheet...*
Remove Link	

Figure 10-17: Using the contextual menu to apply a class selector

If you apply a style to a document containing a single line of text that is not
contained by an element other than the **<body>** element, the class is applied to
the entire **<body>** element.

 To remove a class selector, click anywhere inside text with that style
applied and then select Text → CSS Styles → None or click the
(none) style in the CSS Styles panel.

When clearing the style from a selection, the **class** property is removed from the
tag. If the style is applied to a **<span>** tag, then the **<span>** tag is also removed.
Clearing a style from a single object is not the same thing as deleting the style
entirely.

Applying and clearing type selector and pseudo-selector styles

Recall that type selector styles redefine HTML tags. Therefore, they are not applied
explicitly. Any type selector style you define is applied to all matching HTML tags.

Similarly, the pseudo-class selectors (**a:link**, **a:visited**, etc.) are automatically
applied to any **<a>** tags containing an **href** attribute.

Because these selectors are applied automatically, the only way to eliminate their
influence (i.e., clear them) is to delete the selectors themselves. The affected tags
will refresh automatically.

Applying and clearing ID selector styles

The last type of CSS style we examined was the ID selector style.

Here's how to apply and clear an ID selector:

- Assign an id attribute by hand (or by using the Quick Tag Editor) to an existing HTML tag. If you assign it a value of a matching ID selector, then the custom style will be applied. If you delete the id attribute, the style is effectively cleared.

- Right-click (Windows) or Ctrl-click (Macintosh) on the Tag Selector to open the contextual menu and choose the style name to apply from the Set ID submenu (refer to Figure 10-6). Select None from this pop-up submenu to clear a previously applied style.

Editing CSS Styles and Stylesheets

Because stylesheets are merely collections of styles, editing a stylesheet means to add, remove, or edit the styles within it. Perform these operations in the Edit Style Sheet dialog box (see Figure 10-2).

Here are several ways to open the Edit Style Sheet dialog box:

- Click the Edit Style Sheet button in the CSS Styles panel.

- Use Text → CSS Styles → Edit Style Sheet, Ctrl+Shift+E (Windows), or Cmd+Shift+E (Macintosh).

- Select CSS Styles → Edit Style Sheet from the contextual menu in the Document window.

- Click the CSS Styles icon in the Head Content bar to open the Property inspector, and click the Edit Style Sheet button in the Property inspector.

The Edit Style Sheet dialog box shows both embedded styles and external stylesheets.

Editing Embedded Styles

To edit an embedded style, double-click its name in the Edit Style Sheet dialog box. This action opens the Style Definition dialog box, where you can modify a style using Dreamweaver's friendly UI. Embedded styles can also be edited by hand using Code view. (Although <style> tags belong within the <head> portion of a document, a <style> tag within the <body> portion of a document is indicated by a shield icon as shown in Figure 18-1. The placeholder icon is visible only if the Edit → Preferences → Invisible Elements → Embedded Styles and View → Visual Aids → Invisible Elements options are enabled.)

You can also edit an embedded class selector style by double-clicking its name in the CSS Styles panel. To edit other types of style rules (type selectors and ID selectors) use the Edit Style Sheet dialog box, or hand-edit them in Code view.

Editing Styles in External Stylesheets

Editing a style that has been stored in an external stylesheet is similar to editing an embedded style, but there are some important differences. You can double-click the name of an external style in the CSS Styles panel, but as with embedded styles, this panel shows class selector styles only.

To edit the other types of style rules (type selectors and ID selectors) open the Edit Style Sheet dialog box (see Figure 10-2). This dialog box shows the name of external stylesheets, not their individual styles. Double-click an external stylesheet to open another dialog box (see Figure 10-4) that lists all styles found within that external stylesheet. From this dialog box, you can Link to a new stylesheet file, create a new style, edit an existing style, duplicate an existing style, or remove a style from your document.

To edit the CSS code in an external stylesheet directly, edit the .css file in an external text editor (restart Dreamweaver to force it to recognize changes to external .css files). If you try to open a .css file in Dreamweaver, Dreamweaver presents a dialog box similar to the one shown in Figure 10-4.

Further CSS Topics

In the following sections, we've collected some important topics that provide advanced information for interested readers.

Cascading and Inheritance

Cascading stylesheets allow you to establish a hierarchy of styles. Styles are inherited from surrounding tags. For example, if you apply a CSS style using a body type selector, the style affects everything within the <body> tag of the document. If you then apply separate styles to, say, <p> tags within the body, they'll be formatted using a combination of the specified styles.

Consider Example 10-5. It shows an embedded stylesheet that defines type selectors for the <body> and <p> tags and a class selector (.pgraph). Note that the pgraph style is applied to a <p> element in the HTML document.

Example 10-5: An embedded stylesheet defining stylized text within an HTML document

```
<html><head><style type="text/css">
<!--
body { font-family: Arial, Helvetica, sans-serif;
       color: #0000FF}
p { font-size: 10pt}
.pgraph { font-family: "Times New Roman", Times, serif;
          font-size: 12pt; font-style: italic}
a:link { background-color: #003399}
-->
</style></head>
<body bgcolor="#FFFFFF">
<p class="pgraph">This is pgraph text</p>
<p>But this text isn't!</p>
</body></html>
```

In Example 10-5, what format will be used for the text, "But this text isn't!" enclosed in <p> tags? It will be 10pt, blue, Arial because it inherits the font and color from the body style rule and uses the point size defined in the p style rule.

What about the format of the text, "This is pgraph text"? It will be 12pt, italic, blue, Times New Roman. The font-family and font-size declarations in the .pgraph style rule override those in the body and p style rules, and the italic style is added on top. Because the .pgraph rule doesn't define its own color, it inherits the text color defined in the body rule.

This example illustrates two important principles and gives us a chance to explain a few more:

- Formatting styles are inherited as described in the preceding scenario.

- When attributes do not conflict, they are all applied.

- When attributes do conflict, the innermost tag's attributes have *precedence*. Conflicting properties are not "averaged" together. For example, if there are two color attributes, the innermost overrides the other—the two colors are not combined or blended.

- Type selectors (such as body and p) redefine the attributes of all tags in the page (or for all pages that use the shared external stylesheet) automatically.

- Properties defined in class selectors (i.e., CSS styles such as .pgraph) always override matching (conflicting) properties defined in type selectors. This hierarchy allows type selectors to be applied universally but permits the use of class selectors for exceptions.

- If two style rules have the same precedence, the last one applied wins. For example, if two stylesheets define conflicting rules, the last applied stylesheet overrides earlier stylesheets. Styles within the embedded stylesheet take precedence over styles in external stylesheets.

- HTML formatting applied using, for example, the Text → Size menu or the Property inspector trumps CSS styles. The HTML font size specified here would override the CSS property of a similar name:

```
<p class="pgraph">This is <font size="7">pgraph</font> text</p>
```

I've glossed over some intricacies such as using inline styles and the !important modifier, but this overview should help you considerably.

Remember, you can attach multiple external stylesheets to a single HMTL document using multiple <link> statements.

```
<link rel="stylesheet" href="mysheet1.css" type="text/css">
<link rel="stylesheet" href="mysheet2.css" type="text/css">
```

Using the @import directive, an external stylesheet can even refer to a different external stylesheet (see the section "External Stylesheets" earlier in the chapter for details on the difference between <link> and @import).

Dreamweaver tries to prohibit you from creating conflicting style rules, although you can do so by attaching pre-existing external stylesheets. If you use multiple stylesheets in the same document, try to avoid defining redundant or conflicting styles. Otherwise, the styles of the last loaded external stylesheet take precedence over those from earlier external stylesheets (and the embedded styles take precedence over external styles).

CSS Element Selection Patterns

You can use the Use CSS Selector option in the New Style dialog box (see Figure 10-5) to enter the CSS selectors shown in Table 10-11.

These selectors allow you to define styles that are applied to a tag only when it appears inside another tag, or styles that are applied only when a certain attribute is set within a tag.

Unless otherwise stated, these selectors are supported in NN4, NN6, IE4, and IE5.x on both Macintosh and Windows.

Table 10-11: CSS element selector patterns

Pattern	Selector	Matches	Example
*	Universal	Any element.	`* {color: red}`
elem	Type or Element	Elements named *elem.*	`p {color: red}`
.classname	Class	Any element with a class equal to *classname.*.	`.pgraph {color : red}`
#idname	ID	Any element with an id equal to *idname.* Buggy in NN4 and IE4/5.x.	`#pgraph {color : red}`
parent descend	Descendant	Elements named *descend* within elements named *parent.*	`div p {color: red}`
parent > child	Child	Elements named *child* that are direct children of elements named *parent.*	`div>p {color: red}`
first + second	Adjacent	Elements named *second* immediately preceded by elements named *first* .	`div + p {color: red}`
elem[attrib]	Attribute	Elements named *elem* containing the attribute *attrib.*	`div[align] {color: red}`
elem[attrib =value]	Attribute value	Elements named *elem* containing *attrib* set to precisely *value.*	`div[align="left"] {color:red}`
elem[attrib ~=value]	Attribute single value	Elements named *elem* containing *attrib* set to a space-separated list of values containing word *value.*	`img[alt~="Fig"] {margin:5px}`
elem[attrib |=value]	Attribute hyphenated value	Elements named *elem* containing *attrib* set to hyphenated words starting with *value.* First supported in NN6 and IE5.	`img[alt|="Fig"] {margin:5px}`

In addition to the prefab pseudo-classes, discussed earlier under "Pseudo-class selectors," you can use the Use CSS Selector option in the New Style dialog box (see Figure 10-5) to enter the CSS pseudo-classes shown in Table 10-12.

Table 10-12: CSS element pseudo-classes

Pattern	Pseudo-class	Matches	Example
elem:first-child	`:first-child`	*elem* (when it is the first child element of its parent)	`div:p {color: red}`
elem:link *elem*:visited	Link	*elem* (if it is the source of a visited or unvisited hyperlink)	`a:link {color: red}` `a:visited {color: red}`

elem:active
elem:hover
elem:focus
	Dynamic	*elem* (when the user clicks a link, rolls over a link, or gives focus to an element)	`a:active {color: red}`
			`a:hover {color: red}`
			`a:focus {color: red}`

elem:lang(*x*)	`:lang()`	*elem* (if it is in the human language specified by *x*)	`div:lang(en)`

Downloading Fonts with CSS2

To enforce the use of the same font for all operating systems, you can use the @font-face CSS rule. The **src** attribute can be used to download fonts. (Such a technique may be overkill for small amounts of text. You can also use Flash Text for fancy fonts, which Flash can embed seamlessly. However, Flash is impractical for large amounts of text and Flash text is not automatically indexed by search engines.)

Example 10-6 shows a sample stylesheet that uses two @font-face rules.

Example 10-6: Downloading a font using a stylesheet

```
<style type="text/css" media="screen, print">
    @font-face { font-family: "comic sans";
                 src: url(http://mysite.com/fonts/comicsans)}
    @font-face { font-family: "jester";
                 font-weight: bold;
                 font-style: italic}
    h1 {font-family: "comic sans"}
    h2 {font-family: "jester", serif}
</style>
```

When a browser encounters a stylesheet, it processes the rules that control the rendering of each heading. In Example 10-6, the h1 and h2 type selectors set <h1> elements to the Comic Sans font and set <h2> elements to Jester.

Web browsers supporting CSS2 (IE5.5, NN6, or later) examine the @font-face rules to find the closest matching font. In Example 10-6, a CSS2-compatible browser downloads Comic Sans from the specified URL if the font isn't already installed locally. On the other hand, if Jester isn't installed, the browser uses the rules to find the closest available font or uses synthesis to create a similar font from the provided descriptors. CSS2 allows agents to ignore any font-descriptor that is not recognized or to add custom descriptors to improve font substitution, matching, or synthesis.

Although the @font-face rule requires a CSS2-compatible browser, earlier browsers (prior to IE5.5 and NN6) are not affected adversely. A CSS1-capable browser uses the default sans serif font if Comic Sans is not installed, and it uses the default serif font if Jester is not installed.

That concludes the discussion of CSS in Dreamweaver. I hope you enjoyed the ride. The next chapter covers Dreamweaver's HTML styles, which are thankfully much simpler than CSS.

CHAPTER 11

HTML Styles

HTML styles provide an easy way to apply character and paragraph formatting with a single click. You can create and store HTML-based styles to quickly format text items such as headings, paragraphs, and copyright notices. Let's see how to use this convenient timesaver.

As mentioned in the preceding chapter, HTML styles are an authoring-time convenience that apply basic HTML tags that work with any version of any browser. HTML styles don't offer "live updating" like Cascading Style Sheets or Dreamweaver's Template and Library features. An HTML style must be reapplied manually if you want to update formatting. HTML styles apply HTML formatting tags and therefore take precedence over globally applied CSS styles.

Creating HTML Styles

HTML styles are applied and managed by using the HTML Styles panel, shown in Figure 11-1. Open it using Window → HTML Styles, the HTML Styles icon in the Launcher bar, Ctrl+F11 (Windows), or Cmd+F11 (Macintosh).

Unlike styles that appear in the CSS Styles panel, which are specific to the current document, styles stored in the HTML Styles panel are available to all documents in your site. This feature makes HTML styles easier to apply locally, whereas CSS styles are easier to manage globally.

HTML styles cannot contain text or other content—they are used strictly for formatting. To insert, for example, a formatted copyright notice, you can use the History panel to record a "macro" command. You can also use the Assets panel to store favorite images, colors, and other assets. Although there is no text category in the Assets panel, you can use the Library category to hold commonly needed chunks of HTML (which can include text). Library assets have the advantage of being linked so that, unlike HTML styles, all instances of a library item update if the original item changes.

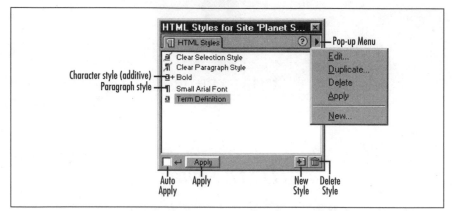

Figure 11-1: The HTML Styles panel

Character Formatting Versus Paragraph Formatting

Two default "styles"—Clear Selection Style and Clear Paragraph Style—always appear at the top of the HTML Styles panel. These pseudo-styles are used to remove existing formatting from either a character span or an entire paragraph. Character formatting can be applied to any span of characters; paragraph formatting affects an entire paragraph.

For example, bold formatting can be applied on a character-by-character basis—a single word or even a single character could be bolded while leaving the rest of a paragraph unbolded. But certain attributes, such as alignment, make sense only when applied to an entire paragraph (i.e., the same paragraph can't have text that is both centered and left-aligned; all the text must share the same alignment).

Because HTML defines both character-level tags (such as `<i>` and `<b>`) and paragraph-level tags (such as `<p>` and `<h1>`), Dreamweaver supports both character-level and paragraph-level HTML styles.

Defining an HTML Style's Attributes

Create a new HTML style by clicking the New Style icon in the HTML Styles panel, as indicated in Figure 11-1. Clicking this icon opens the Define HTML Style dialog box, shown in Figure 11-2, where you'll assign the text formatting for the style.

Table 11-1 explains the Define HTML Styles dialog box options.

Table 11-1: The Define HTML Style dialog box options

Property	Description
Name	A unique name for your style. Unlike CSS styles, you can use spaces in the name. Styles are alphabetized in the HTML Styles panel (but the two default styles are always shown at the top).
Apply To: Selection	Creates a character style, which is applied to the selected text span only. Character styles are indicated by a small "a" symbol next to their names in the HTML Styles panel.

Table 11-1: The Define HTML Style dialog box options (continued)

Property	Description
Apply To: Paragraph	Creates a paragraph style, which is applied to an entire block of text, such as that between the `<p>` and `</p>` tags. Paragraph styles are indicated by a small paragraph symbol next to their names in the HTML Styles panel.
Add to Existing Style	When a style is applied, this option adds the newly applied style's formatting on top of existing formatting. Use it to add a bold style without undoing existing italic formatting. Additive styles are indicated by a plus (+) sign next to their names in the HTML Styles panel.
Clear Existing Style	Deletes any existing formatting from the affected character selection or paragraph before applying the new HTML style. Enable this radio button to "clear and reformat" in one step.
Font	Specifies the font to be applied by this style. To clear existing `font face` attributes, specify Default Font for the Font and enable the Clear Existing Style option.
Size	Sets either the absolute or relative font size. To clear existing `font size` attributes, specify None for the Size and enable the Clear Existing Style option.
Color	Sets the text color to be applied. To clear existing `font color` attributes, use a blank value (not all zeros) for the Color and enable the Clear Existing Style option.
Style	Character styles to be applied. Use the Bold and Italic toggle buttons or the Options menu (Underline, Strikethrough, Teletype, Emphasis, Strong, Code, Variable, Sample, Keyboard, Citation, and Definition). Multiple selections are allowed.
Format	Sets the block style to be applied (Heading 1 though Heading 6, paragraph, or preformatted). Applies to paragraph styles only.
Alignment	Sets alignment to be applied (left, center, right). Applies to paragraph styles only.

Because styles are sorted alphabetically in the HTML Styles panel, you can group styles in the list by naming them appropriately.

Use a space at the beginning of a style's name to force it to appear at the top of the HTML Styles panel (after the two built-in styles). You can group character styles separately from paragraph styles by using an underscore to begin their names.

There are several other ways to open the Define HTML Style dialog box:

- Choose Text → HTML Styles → New Style.

- Right-click (Windows) or Ctrl-click (Macintosh) on the selection in the Document window and choose HTML Styles → New Style from the contextual menu.

- Double-click the name of an existing style in the HTML Styles panel.

When creating a new style, attributes of the currently selected text are used to fill in the attributes in the Define HTML Style dialog box. You can use the Clear button in this dialog box to reset the style attributes to their default values.

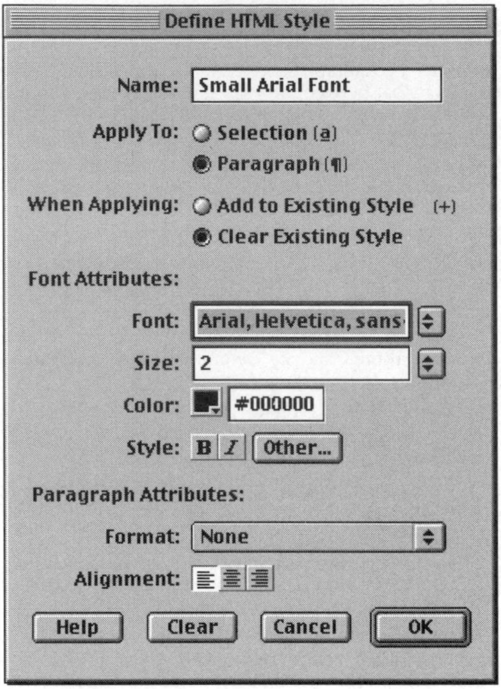

Figure 11-2: The Define HTML Style dialog box

Applying HTML Styles

Once you have created your HTML styles, you can apply them as follows:

Select the text to which you want to apply the style (if applying a paragraph format, click anywhere in the paragraph—you don't need to select the entire paragraph). Then:

- Select a style in the HTML Styles panel and click the Apply button (see Figure 11-1). If the Auto Apply checkbox is enabled, you don't need to click the Apply button.

- Select Text → HTML Styles → *styleName*.

- Right-click (Windows) or Ctrl-click (Macintosh) on the selection in the Document window and choose HTML Styles → *styleName* from the contextual menu.

For example, if you applied a left-aligned paragraph style that uses Size 2, black, Arial text to the following text:

This site is still under construction. Please check back soon.

The result would be:

```
<p align="left">
  <font face="Arial, Helvetica, sans-serif" size="2" color="#000000">
    This site is still under construction. Please check back soon.
  </font>
</p>
```

If you applied a character style that uses Size 2, black, italicized Book Antiqua text instead, the result might be:

```
This site is still under <i><font face="Book Antiqua, Times New Roman"
size="2" color="#000000">construction</font></i>. Please check back soon.
```

Editing HTML Styles

To edit an existing HTML style, simply double-click its name in the HTML Styles panel (disable the Auto Apply option to prevent the style you're editing from being applied to the current selection). You cannot edit the styles that come built into the HTML Styles panel (i.e., Clear Selection Style and Clear Paragraph Style).

Once inside the Define HTML Styles dialog box, make any desired changes to the style definition. If you modify an HTML style, the changes are not propagated to text to which the style was previously applied. You must reapply the style manually to any text you wish to update.

 Enable the When Applying: Clear Existing Style option so when you reapply your modified style, it also eliminates formatting left behind by the previous version of the style.

Styles are stored in the *styles.xml* file inside the *Library* folder within your site's root folder. The file's contents look something like this:

```
<mm:style name="Add Bold" type="char" apply="add" bold />
<mm:style name="green" type="char" apply="replace" color="#00CC99" bold
italic />
```

The *styles.xml* file can be edited in any text editor and even copied to another site's *Library* folder if you want to copy your favorite styles to a new site.

Part III covers Dreamweaver's use of JavaScript behaviors.

PART III

Behaviors and Interactive Elements

Part III covers the use of JavaScript behaviors to add interactivity and animation to your pages.

CHAPTER 12

Behaviors and JavaScript

Dreamweaver provides numerous preprogrammed *behaviors* that add interactivity, check the browser version, control window layout, and perform animation. If Dreamweaver doesn't have a built-in behavior for the job, you can download more behaviors from the Dreamweaver Exchange or write your own in JavaScript (JS).

For more on JavaScript, see the O'Reilly JavaScript Reference in the Reference panel (Window → Reference) or see *JavaScript: The Definitive Guide* by David Flanagan (O'Reilly). Note that JavaScript (which was called LiveScript until Netscape renamed it) has no direct relation to Sun's Java language; people in this industry just drink too much coffee. Macromedia Flash's ActionScript language uses the same syntax as JavaScript and implements some identical object classes (both are derivatives of the ECMA-262 standard).

Even if you don't know JavaScript, Dreamweaver makes it easy to use JavaScript via its built-in behaviors. In fact, we've already used some behaviors earlier in the book. The rollover image, navigation bar, and jump menu objects are implemented using built-in behaviors.

Browser JavaScript Support

Dreamweaver's behaviors are implemented in JavaScript and therefore require a JavaScript-capable browser. Table 12-1 lists the JavaScript versions supported by the major browsers. (Microsoft's implementation of JavaScript is called JScript. Although JScript is very similar to JavaScript, it is not identical. If you create your own behaviors, test them in both Internet Explorer and Netscape.) Note that Dreamweaver's JavaScript debugger works with NN4.5+ (Macintosh and Windows) and IE4+ on Windows, but not earlier browsers, IE for Macintosh, NN6, or Opera.

Table 12-1: Scripting support in major browsers

Scripting language	Browser support
None	IE3 (Macintosh only) or any browser in which user has disabled JavaScript
JavaScript 1.0 (JScript 1.0)	IE3 (Windows only), NN2
JavaScript 1.1	NN3, Opera 3
JavaScript 1.2 (JScript 1.2)	IE4, NN4, Opera 4
JavaScript 1.3	IE5, IE5.5, NN4.0.7+, Opera 5
JavaScript 1.4	IE6, NN6
VBScript	IE3+ (Windows), IE5+ (Macintosh)

JavaScript support doesn't always correspond with a particular version, such as 1.2, 1.3, or 1.4. For example, some JavaScript 1.2 features were missing from Internet Explorer until IE5.5, and IE5.5 also supports some JavaScript 1.4 features. For a matrix of browser support for each JavaScript command see *http://www.dwian.com/addenda/js_matrix.html*.

Browser Compatibility

You can safely assume that most visitors have a JavaScript-capable browser. If not, yours won't be the only site they have trouble accessing.

 You should install the free Dreamweaver 4.01 update as it fixes some behaviors for use with NN6. Over 95 percent of web visitors use Version 4 or newer browsers. Supporting older browsers probably isn't worthwhile, except on your gateway (home) page to direct them to another page.

Macromedia has written robust behaviors, but not all work on all browsers and platforms. Whereas some behaviors work with 3.0 browsers, almost all work with 4.0+ browsers (see Table 12-3 for details). Use File → Check Target Browsers to find potential problems (mainly browsers that don't support particular events), but don't expect it to detect all incompatibilities. The File → Convert → 3.0 Browser Compatible command converts layers and CSS styles only. It does nothing to detect behavior incompatibility with 3.0 browsers nor does it modify a document's JavaScript code.

Ironically, the underpowered browsers you want to guard against are the same ones that don't allow accurate version checking or plugin checking. Furthermore, browser-to-plugin communication is not supported on IE for Macintosh (which is why you can't detect plugins or use the Dreamweaver debugger in that configuration). Conversely, automatic detection sometimes fails when new versions of plugins or browsers are released. (There is nothing so frustrating as being admonished to download a plugin that you have already installed.) Therefore, it is often better to let the user choose which version of a site to view rather than try to autodetect the browser's settings.

Using Behaviors

Using behaviors is an easy three-step process:

1. Decide what action you want to take (such as whether to validate the user's data entry or pop up a new window).

2. Decide when you want to take the action (such as when the user selects an item from a menu).

3. Decide where you want to look for the event (i.e., to which element you want to attach the behavior).

The *action* that you want to take dictates which behavior you'll use. You'll often want to react to user activities, such as mouseclicks, keyboard entry, or resizing the browser. These and other *events* can be used to trigger actions; the browser will run the chosen behavior automatically when the designated event occurs.

You must decide where to apply a behavior in order to limit its scope to the events you are interested in. For example, you might take some action when the user clicks on a button, but you might ignore mouseclicks elsewhere. Therefore, you'll attach your behaviors to HTML elements, such as images, buttons, text, or the body tag. Sometimes a behavior applied to one tag influences another HTML element. For example, a behavior applied to a checkbox could be used to change the properties of another element or to update the contents of a frame.

You'll typically configure a behavior's *parameters* using Dreamweaver's friendly UI. For example, when using the Open Browser Window behavior you'll specify parameters for the window's height and width (see Figure 12-11).

There you have it! Just attach a behavior (action) to an HTML element, tell Dreamweaver what event to use as a trigger, and provide parameters to customize the behavior for your particular needs. Let's see how.

The Behaviors Panel

The Behaviors panel, shown in Figure 12-1, provides access to the installed behaviors. Open it using Window → Behaviors, Shift+F3, or the Behaviors icon in the Launcher bar.

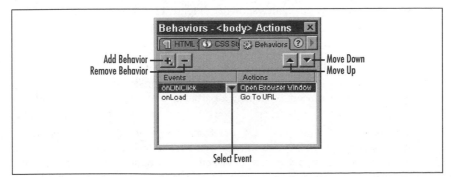

Figure 12-1: The Behaviors panel

Behaviors are generally applied to objects within your page, although they can be applied to the <body> tag as well. For example, you might apply a behavior to an image to make it act as a button with a rollover effect. Select the desired object in the Document window and add behavior(s) using the Behaviors panel.

 The Behaviors panel shows behaviors associated with the currently selected object, not all behaviors used in the current document. Available behaviors are listed under the Add Behavior pop-up menu (the plus (+) button).

Table 12-2 describes the controls found on the Behaviors panel.

Table 12-2: The Behaviors panel

Control	Description
Add Behavior [+]	Adds a behavior to the currently selected object.
Remove Behavior [-]	Deletes the selected behavior from the list of applied behaviors.
Move Up arrow	Moves the selected behavior up in the event-processing order (relevant only if multiple behaviors are applied).
Move Down arrow	Moves the selected behavior down in the order event-processing order.
Events column	Lists the events that trigger the actions in the Actions column. Change events using the Select Event button (see Figure 12-1). Double-click an event name to edit the behavior's parameters.
Select Event	Select the event to trigger this behavior from the pop-up menu. The available events vary based on the behavior, the object to which it's attached, and the targeted browser(s).
Actions column	Lists behaviors that have been applied to the currently selected object. Double-click an action's name to edit the behavior's parameters. You can't change a behavior's intrinsic action (it's inherent in its JavaScript code). To change an action, delete the existing action and add a different behavior instead.

Built-in Behaviors (Actions)

The Add Behavior pop-up menu, shown in Figure 12-2, lists the *actions* (behaviors) available in the Behaviors panel.

Here are some important things to note:

- The menu is used to apply many different types of behaviors to unrelated elements. Although Dreamweaver dims the menu choices that you can't use, it may leave you confused about why a particular action is unavailable and how to make it active.

- The contents of this menu are determined by the *.js* files stored under *Dreamweaver 4/Configuration/Behaviors/Actions*. (The comments in these files also explain the behavior's requirements and limitations.) You can delete the ones you never use, edit them, or add your own. You can also link to copies of these *.js* files for increased efficiency when using the same behavior on multiple web pages. Using external *.js* files prevents Dreamweaver from updating the JavaScript, so keep your *.js* files up to date when installing Dreamweaver updates.

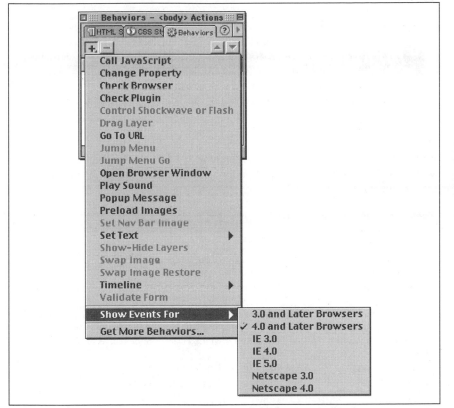

Figure 12-2: Actions available in the Behaviors panel

- Use the Get More Behaviors option to download additional behaviors from the Dreamweaver Exchange.

- The Show Events For option is somewhat confusing. It does not affect which options are available in this menu; instead, it limits the available *events* (not actions) to trigger an action. It does nothing to prevent you from adding unsupported actions in the first place. See Table 12-3 instead.

- Behaviors cannot be applied to a document based upon a template. Apply behaviors to the template instead (see Chapter 8) and place those behaviors in a linked external *.js* file.

Behavior Summary

The built-in behaviors shown in Figure 12-2 are summarized in Table 12-3. Remember that some menu choices will be inactive depending on what object you have selected in your HTML document. Other behaviors are active only when certain HTML elements have been inserted. For example, the Show-Hide Layers behavior is active only if the page contains one or more layers. When we discuss each behavior, we'll tell you what is necessary to make it active in the Add Behavior menu.

 Behaviors typically require that an element have an id attribute by which it can be referenced, but some behaviors reference elements by their name attribute. For example, NN6 requires that a layer's name attribute be set before using it with behaviors that manipulate layers. Download the free DW 4.01 updater to ensure that behaviors work with NN6.

All behaviors listed in Table 12-3 fail silently in IE3 for the Mac, but work in IE3 for Windows, NN3+ (Macintosh and Windows), and IE4+ (Macintosh and Windows) unless otherwise noted.

Table 12-3: Dreamweaver's default behaviors

Behavior	Descriptions
Call JavaScript	Inserts a call to another JavaScript function.
Change Property	Changes the specified property of the specified tag.
Check Browser	Optionally branches to different URLs based on the browser's brand and/or version.
Check Plugin	Optionally branches to different URLs based on the presence/absence of a plugin (fails in IE3/IE4 on Macintosh).
Control Shockwave or Flash[a]	Plays, stops, and rewinds Flash or Shockwave movies.
Drag Layer	Allows the user to drag layers.
Go To URL	Opens a document in a specified location.
Jump Menu[a]	Creates a jump menu.
Jump Menu Go[a]	Adds a Go button to an existing jump menu.
Open Browser Window	Opens the specified document with the specified window attributes in a new browser window.
Play Sound[a]	Plays audio files.
Popup Message	Creates a pop-up alert message box.
Preload Images[a]	Preloads images for rollovers and image swaps.
Set Nav Bar Image[a]	Creates a navigation bar.
Set Text of Frame	Sets the text content of a frame.
Set Text of Layer[b]	Sets the text content of a layer.
Set Text of Status Bar	Sets the text content of the browser's status bar.
Set Text of Text Field	Sets the text content of a text field within a form.
Show-Hide Layers[b]	Shows or hides one or more layers.
Swap Image[a]	Swaps an existing image for another image (see Figure 13-2).
Swap Image Restore[a]	Restores a swapped image (see Figure 13-3).
Go To Timeline Frame[c]	Goes to a keyframe in a timeline.
Play Timeline[c]	Plays the specified timeline.

Table 12-3: Dreamweaver's default behaviors (continued)

Behavior	Descriptions
Stop Timeline[ac]	Stops the specified timeline.
Validate Form	Validates the format of text entry fields (see Table 16-2).
Show Events For	Indicates which browsers you intend to support. Dreamweaver limits the events for a given action based on the target browser.
Get More Behaviors	Accesses the Dreamweaver Exchange where you can download additional behaviors.

[a] Fails silently in IE3 on both Macintosh and Windows.
[b] Fails in all Version 3 browsers (requires CSS support).
[c] In NN3 (both Macintosh and Windows) the image source animation and behavior invocation work, but the layer animation fails silently.

Events (Triggers)

Once you apply an action (behavior) to an element, Dreamweaver assumes the default events as shown in Table 12-4. To trigger the action using a different event, pick one from the Select Event pop-up menu (using the arrow that appears next to the currently selected action, as seen in Figure 12-3).

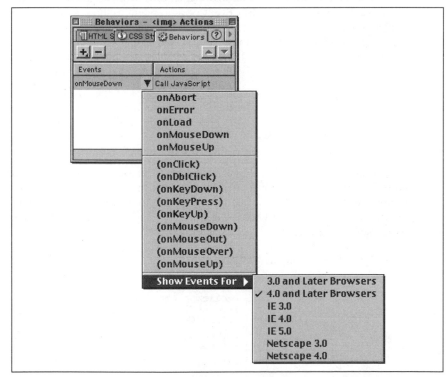

Figure 12-3: Picking an event to trigger an action

The Select Event menu lists different events, depending on the HTML object to which the behavior is applied and the setting under the Show Events For submenu.

Event names appearing in parentheses can be applied to <a> tags only. If you choose such an event, Dreamweaver automatically wraps a null link (with href="javascript:;") around the selected element and applies the behavior to the <a> tag instead. See the section "Call JavaScript behavior" later in this chapter for an example.

 To execute timer-based actions, apply a behavior to the Behaviors channel of a timeline, and trigger it with an onFrame event. See Chapter 17 for details on timelines.

The Show Events For submenu

The Show Events For submenu (which appears in both the Add Behavior and Select Event pop-up menus) lets you choose which browsers you intend to target. It limits the events shown on the Select Event pop-up menu to those supported by the specified browser(s). The older browsers support very few events; if you choose 4.0 and Later Browsers from the menu, it shows only the events that work in all 4.0 browsers. On the other hand, picking an individual browser, especially a recent version of IE, often displays a huge number of events to choose from.

Table 12-4 lists the events that are available for each type of tag when choosing the 4.0 and Later Browsers option from the Show Events For menu. If you select a different option, the available tags and events may differ substantially from those shown in the table. Search for "About Events" under Help → Using Dreamweaver (F1) for a list of events and the browsers that support them.

Although several events can often trigger an action, Dreamweaver uses the most common event as the default, as indicated by the entry in a bold font in the right-hand column. For example, if you attach a behavior to a <body> tag, the triggering event defaults to onLoad (the action is triggered when the page loads unless you change the event).

Table 12-4: Events for 4.0 and later browsers

Objects	Tag	4.0 browser events
Link	<a>	**onClick**, onDblClick, onKeyDown, onKey-Press, onKeyUp, onMouseDown, onMouseOut, onMouseOver, onMouseUp
Image map area	<area>	onClick, onDblClick, onMouseOut, **onMouseOver**
Body	<body>	onBlur, onError, onFocus, **onLoad**, onResize, onUnload
Form	<form>	onReset, **onSubmit**
Frameset	<frameset>	onBlur, onFocus, **onLoad**, onResize, onUnload
Image	<img>	onAbort, onError, onLoad, **onMouseDown**, onMouseUp

Table 12-4: Events for 4.0 and later browsers (continued)

Objects	Tag	4.0 browser events
Form: Button	`<input type= "button">`	onBlur, **onClick**, onFocus, onMouseDown, onMouseUp
Form: Checkbox	`<input type= "checkbox">`	onBlur, **onClick**, onFocus, onMouseDown, onMouseUp
Form: File selection	`<input type= "file">`	onBlur, **onChange**, onFocus, onKeyDown, onKeyPress, onKeyUp
Form: Password	`<input type= "password">`	onBlur, **onChange**, onFocus, onKeyDown, onKeyPress, onKeyUp
Form: Radio button	`<input type= "radio">`	onBlur, **onClick**, onFocus, onMouseDown, onMouseUp
Form: Reset button	`<input type= "reset">`	onBlur, **onClick**, onFocus, onMouseDown, onMouseUp
Form: Submit button	`<input type= "submit">`	onBlur, **onClick**, onFocus, onMouseDown, onMouseUp
Form: Text	`<input type= "text">`	**onBlur**, onChange, onFocus, onKeyDown, onKeyPress, onKeyUp, onSelect
Text Area	`<textarea>`	onBlur, **onChange**, onFocus, onKeyDown, onKeyPress, onKeyUp, onSelect
Select	`<select>`	onBlur, **onChange**, onFocus

Table 12-4 does not show many of the tags to which you can apply behaviors when targeting newer browsers (for example, IE4 or IE5 allow you to attach behaviors to dozens of tags, many of which aren't supported in other browsers). Conversely, if you target 3.0 browsers, many fewer events and tags are available. To see precisely what events are available for which tags in other browsers, you can inspect the *.htm* files in the following folder: *Dreamweaver 4/Configuration/ Behaviors/Events*.

You can download additional browser profiles from the Dreamweaver support site. For example, the Netscape 6 Pack, featuring updated behaviors, is available separately and as part of the Dreamweaver 4.01 update (see *http://www. macromedia.com/support/dreamweaver/downloads/*).

JavaScript

Dreamweaver works with JavaScript in a variety of ways. In addition to using JavaScript behaviors, you can link to scripts in external *.js* files, edit *.js* files directly, and debug JavaScript code.

Adding Scripts to Documents

When you apply behaviors using the Behaviors panel, Dreamweaver adds the JavaScript to the `<script>` tag within the `<head>` tag. (All scripts used throughout a site are listed in the Scripts category of the Assets panel.) If you apply the same behavior twice within the same document, Dreamweaver is smart enough not to duplicate the JavaScript code within the `<script>` tag. You can even modify the JavaScript functions by hand in Code view, provided you don't change a function's name, Dreamweaver won't overwrite your changes even if you reapply the same behavior.

The Insert Script dialog box

The Insert → Invisible Tags → Scripts menu command opens the Insert Script dialog box where you can enter scripts by hand. The Script button in the Objects panel's Invisibles category opens the same dialog box. See the "Script Tag" section in Chapter 2 for more details.

Call JavaScript behavior

The Call JavaScript behavior is used to execute a line of JavaScript code. That line can include a call to a custom function or a built-in function such as *window. close()*. Figure 12-4 shows the exceedingly simple dialog box that lets you enter your parameters for the Call JavaScript behavior.

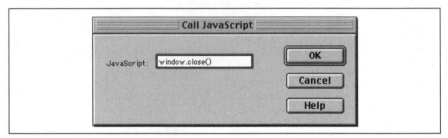

Figure 12-4: The Call JavaScript parameters dialog box

Other behaviors have more complex parameters, but Dreamweaver always writes the HTML code for you. If you apply the Call JavaScript behavior to an image, the resulting HTML code might be:

```
<img src="mybutton.jpg"  onMouseDown="MM_callJS('window.close()')">
```

However, if you choose the onClick event, which cannot be applied to an <img> tag, instead of the onMouseDown event, Dreamweaver automatically wraps the <img> tag in a null link, such as in:

```
<a href="javascript:;" onClick="MM_callJS('window.close()')">
  <img src="mybutton.jpg"></a>
```

 Similarly, to apply a behavior to text, you must first wrap the text of interest in an <a> tag with a null link (href="javascript:;"). Using a null link prevents the document from changing when the link is clicked (using # for your link causes some browsers to jump to the top of the current document).

Using External JavaScripts

Applying a behavior in Dreamweaver adds the JS code directly to your HTML document, which can be inefficient. Although Dreamweaver is smart enough not to duplicate JS code within a single document, it duplicates the code if you use the same behavior on more than one page. To add scripts to a web page based on a template, place scripts in an external *.js* file and link to it from the template.

> Instead, you can link to external JavaScript (*.js*) files, which are downloaded only once and subsequently read from the browser cache thereafter. This technique avoids duplication and makes it easy to update your scripts across your entire site. You should set your server's MIME type for *.js* files to `application/x-javascript` (ask your webmaster for help setting MIME types).

To insert a reference to an external JavaScript (*.js*) file:

1. Write your JS code, or simply copy the code inserted by Dreamweaver's behaviors into a new *.js* file (copy the JS code between the `<script>` tags, but exclude the tags themselves).

2. Save your *.js* file to a folder within your site (you might create a folder called *javascript* within your root folder for this purpose).

3. Use Insert → Invisible Tags → Script to create a `<script>` tag. Dreamweaver inserts it within the `<body>` tag by default, which is also legal. You can use Code view to insert scripts within the `<head>` tag instead.

4. A gold shield icon in the Document window represents a script in the document (use View → Visual Aids → Invisible Elements to ensure that the icon is visible). If you place your script in the document head instead, a script icon appears in the Head Content bar (View → Head Content).

5. To open the Property inspector, double-click the script icon in either the Document window or Head Content bar.

6. Change the `src` attribute in the Property inspector to point to your *.js* file. Use a Site Root Relative path. The result may look like this:

```
<script language="JavaScript" src="/javascript/jump_menu_go.js"></script>
```

Editing JavaScript

Dreamweaver allows you to edit JavaScript that is embedded in your HTML document or stored in an external *.js* file.

Editing embedded JavaScript in the Script Properties dialog box

First, let's talk about scripts embedded within your document's HTML code. To open the Property inspector, double-click the script icon in either the Document window or the Head Content bar (as described in the preceding section). Click the Edit button in the Property inspector to open the Script Properties dialog box, shown in Figure 12-5.

This dialog box allows you to edit scripts directly. You should generally leave the script's Type set to Client-Side (server-side JavaScript is something else entirely). Unfortunately, this dialog box doesn't let you set the version of JavaScript for the `language` attribute, as you can with Insert → Invisible Tags → Scripts. Its only options are JavaScript and VBScript, but at least it won't alter an existing `language` attribute set to JavaScript1.1 or JavaScript1.2.

Script Properties

Language: JavaScript   Type: Client-side   OK

Source: _____   Browse...   Cancel

Help

Script:
```
<!--
function MM_callJS(jsStr) { //v2.0
   return eval(jsStr)
}
//-->
```

Figure 12-5: The Script Properties dialog box

The `language` attribute has been deprecated in HTML 4.0, and may not be recognized by future browsers. Use `type="text/Javascript"` within your `<script>` tag to comply with HTML 4.0 and XHTML standards.

After editing your script, save your changes by clicking the OK button or discard changes using the Cancel button. Of course, you can also hand-edit your scripts in Code view or the Code Inspector; the Script Properties dialog box is just a convenient way to edit the `<script>` tag in isolation.

Editing external JS files in the Code view editor

Suppose your script tag contains a link to an external JavaScript (*.js*) or VBScript (*.vbs*) file, as set by the `src` attribute, such as:

```
<script language="JavaScript" src="checksize.js"> </script>
```

External code cannot be edited in the Script Properties dialog box; however, click the Edit button in the Property inspector to edit it in the Code view window, as seen in Figure 12-6.

The Edit button in the Property inspector opens Code view only if there are no embedded scripts within the HTML file. If you've used both linked and embedded scripts in the same HTML file, use the File → Open command to open the *.js* or *.vbs* file instead.

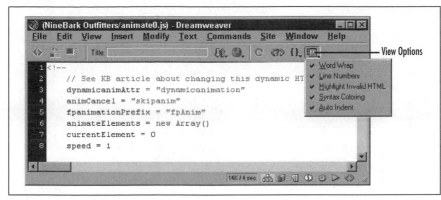

Figure 12-6: Code view for external scripts

When using Code view to edit an external script, many of Dreamweaver's menu options are disabled. The options available in this mode are listed in Table 12-5.

Table 12-5: Menu options for manipulating JavaScript files

Menu option	Windows	Macintosh
File → New	Ctrl+N	Cmd+N
File → New From Template	Alt+F, W	N/A
File → Open	Ctrl+O	Cmd+O
File → Save	Ctrl+S	Cmd+S
File → Save As	Ctrl+Shift+S	Cmd+Shift+S
File → Design Notes	Alt+F, G	N/A
File → Exit	Ctrl+Q	Cmd+Q
Edit → Undo	Ctrl+Z	Cmd+Z
Edit → Redo	Ctrl+Y	Cmd+Y
Edit → Cut	Ctrl+X	Cmd+X
Edit → Copy	Ctrl+C	Cmd+C
Edit → Paste	Ctrl+V	Cmd+V
Edit → Select All	Ctrl+A	Cmd+A
Edit → Find and Replace	Ctrl+F	Cmd+F
Edit → Find Next	F3	F3
Edit → Indent Code	Ctrl+]	Cmd+]
Edit → Outdent Code	Ctrl+[	Cmd+[
Edit → Balance Braces	Ctrl+^	Cmd+^
Edit → Set Breakpoint	Ctrl+Alt+B	Cmd+Opt+B
Edit → Remove All Breakpoints	Alt+E, V	N/A
Edit → Edit with External Editor	Ctrl+E	Cmd+E
Edit → Preferences	Ctrl+U	Cmd+U
View → Code	Alt+V, C	N/A
View → Code View Options → Word Wrap	Alt+V, O, W	N/A
View → Code View Options → Line Numbers	Alt+V, O, L	N/A

Table 12-5: Menu options for manipulating JavaScript files (continued)

Menu option	Windows	Macintosh
View → Code View Options → Highlight Invalid HTML	Alt+V, O, H	N/A
View → Code View Options → Syntax Coloring	Alt+V, O, S	N/A
View → Code View Options → Auto Indent	Alt+V, O, A	N/A
View → Show/Hide Panels	F4	F4
Text → Indent	Ctrl+Alt+]	Cmd+Opt+]
Text → Outdent	Ctrl+Alt+[	Cmd+Opt+[

JavaScript Debugger

Dreamweaver 4 includes a JavaScript debugger that allows you to debug JS code, but there are some caveats.

The debugger:

- Requires NN4.5+ (Macintosh and Windows, but excluding NN6) or IE4+ (Windows only).

- Requires that both Java and JavaScript be enabled in your browser's preferences.

- Will debug JS code embedded in HTML documents or stored in external *.js* files.

- Will not work in any version of IE on the Mac, in any version of NN6 on either platform, or in Opera.

- Will not debug JS code when you use frames. You must debug each framed HTML page separately.

- Will not debug JS code in templates or documents attached to templates. You must detach a document from its template before debugging it.

- May not work on the Macintosh if TCP/IP access is set to AppleTalk or PPP. The workaround, as described in Macromedia TechNote 15020, is to change the TCP/IP setting to connect via a different method.

- May hinder system performance or interfere with other operations such as viewing the Help files in the browser. Close the debugger when it is no longer needed.

Running the Debugger

To run the debugger you must brave a slew of dialog boxes:

1. Open the HTML document you want to debug (you can't start the debugger while editing as *.js* file). Save any recent changes to the file.

2. With your HTML document open, select File → Debug in Browser → *browser*.

3. Dreamweaver checks your code for syntax errors and reports errors in the JavaScript Syntax Errors dialog box shown in Figure 12-7.

4. If there are no syntax errors, Dreamweaver launches the debugger for the chosen browser. If asked whether to start debugging, click OK.

5. Because the debugger itself is a Java applet, the browser displays an ominous warning about potential security risks of network access (the debugger connects with the browser but does not make any network connections).

6. If using Internet Explorer, Click the Yes button in Internet Explorer's Security Warning dialog box (not shown). You can accept the Macromedia Security Certificate by clicking the Macromedia Dreamweaver name in this dialog box and then clicking the Install Certificate option. If asked whether to start debugging, click OK.

7. If using Netscape, click the Grant button in Netscape's Java Security dialog box (not shown). Click the Remember This Decision checkbox in that dialog box to avoid being asked again next time.

8. Finally, the JavaScript Debugger opens (see Figure 12-8).

Let's looks a little more carefully at some of the debugging tools.

The JavaScript Syntax Errors dialog box

The JavaScript Syntax Errors dialog box, shown in Figure 12-7, provides the file-name, line number, error type, and description for each error. When you select an error from the list, the bottom of the dialog provides a detailed description of the usual cause of such errors. Use the Go To Line button (or simply double-click one of the errors in the list) to find the corresponding line in the script where you should fix the error.

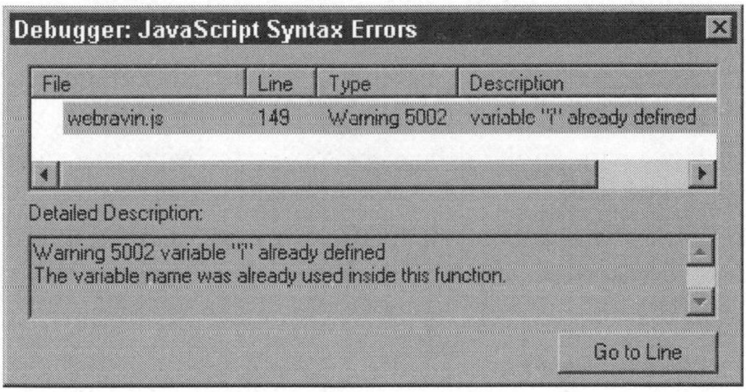

Figure 12-7: The JavaScript Syntax Errors dialog box

The JavaScript Debugger window

Dreamweaver's debugger offers the typical features needed to find and fix errors, such as the ability to set breakpoints, watch variables, and step through your code. See "Debugging JavaScript Code" in the online Help for a quick overview, especially if you've never use a debugger before. The JavaScript Debugger is shown in Figure 12-8. The lower pane (the Watcher) is used to examine variables and change their values.

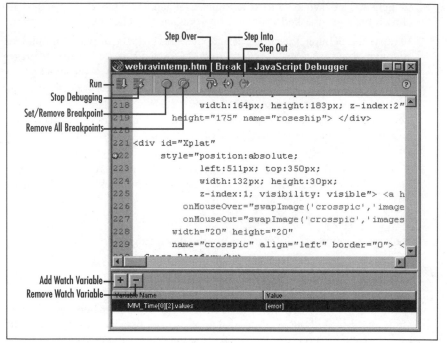

Figure 12-8: The JavaScript Debugger

Here are some quick hints regarding the debugger:

- Before starting a debugging session, you can set breakpoints in your embedded scripts (those within your HTML file) or in external scripts (those in *.js* files). You'll be warned if you haven't set at least one breakpoint before running the debugger.

- Use the Run button in the debugger's toolbar to begin execution or to continue execution until the next breakpoint is reached.

- You'll often need to interact with the browser to trigger a script. For example, if testing a rollover effect, you should roll the mouse over the button of interest in the browser. Be sure to place breakpoints where they'll actually be reached (setting a breakpoint in a function that is never called won't help). When a breakpoint is reached, the Debugger window should come to the front.

- The debugger may hinder system performance and prevent you from viewing the online Help. Stop the debugger when it is no longer needed.

- If your browser doesn't respond, the debugger may be paused. Use the Run button (F8) to resume execution. If nothing seems to work, try quitting your browser and restarting the debugger.

- Type **javascript:** on the Netscape browser's command line to open its JavaScript console where you can see error messages or test JS code. This console helps to solve problems not apparent in Dreamweaver's debugger, such as when the browser can't find a particular function in your JS code.

Table 12-6 summarizes the debugging operations. To set a breakpoint, click the line in your script at which to add the breakpoint, and then click the Add/Remove Breakpoint icon.

 In Code view, you can use the Code Navigation menu (see Figure 12-6) to set breakpoints in a JS function or on the line containing the HTML tag that calls the function. In the latter case, once the breakpoint is reached, click the Step Into icon to debug your JS function (you may need to click it more than once). Breakpoints can also be set in the debugger itself.

To monitor a variable's value, highlight its name in the debugger window and click the plus (+) button (see Figure 12-8). This adds the variable to the watch list. You can also click the plus (+) button and type in the name of a variable. You can change a variable's value in the Value column of the watcher pane.

Table 12-6: Debugger command summary

Operation	Menu option or icon	Windows	Macintosh
Debug in primary browser	File → Debug in Browser → *browser1*	Alt+F12	Opt+F12
Debug in secondary browser	File → Debug in Browser → *browser2*	Ctrl+Alt+F12	Cmd+Opt+F12
Run (continue to next breakpoint)	Run icon	F8	F8
Close debugger	Stop Debugging icon	Alt+F4	Close box
Add/Remove breakpoint	Edit → Set/Remove Breakpoint or icon	F7 or Ctrl+Alt+B	F7 or Cmd+Opt+B
Clear all breakpoints	Edit → Remove All Breakpoints or icon	Alt+E, V	N/A
Step over a function	Step Over icon	F9	F9
Step into a function	Step Into icon	F10	F10
Step out of a function	Step Out icon	F11	F11
Watch variable	Plus (+) button in lower pane	N/A	N/A
Remove watched variable	Minus (−) button in lower pane	N/A	N/A

Browser Configuration Behaviors

Earlier, we saw the Call JavaScript behavior in action. Let's explore three more DW behaviors, which, like all behaviors, are applied via the Behaviors panel. We'll examine other behaviors in subsequent chapters.

Check Browser

The Check Browser behavior sends the user to different pages based on the browser's brand and version. Applying the Check Browser behavior (typically to the <body> tag) opens the dialog box shown in Figure 12-9, where you can set its parameters.

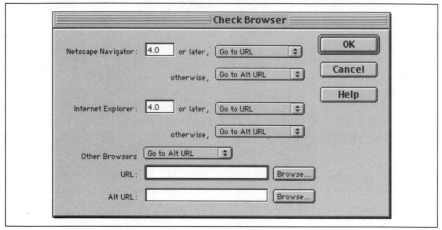

Figure 12-9: Check Browser behavior parameters

This behavior splits visitors into three groups depending on whether you select the Stay On This Page, Go To URL, or Go To Alt URL option. You can change the version number used to discriminate between browsers (i.e., you don't have to leave it at Version 4.0 for either brand, and it doesn't need to be the same for both brands). You can use this behavior to separate users by brand, rather than by version, by sending all Netscape users to one URL and all Internet Explorer users to the Alt URL. You can apply the same behavior (with different parameters) to subsequent pages to discriminate even further.

Note that this behavior works with Version 3+ browsers, except for IE on the Macintosh, which requires Version 4 or later. Therefore IE3 on the Macintosh, like all browsers that don't support JavaScript, will stay on the current page. You should set the Other Browsers pop-up menu option to Stay On This Page, which handles browsers whose brand the behavior can't determine.

Some browsers provide false header information when they identify themselves to your server. They aren't being deceptive intentionally, but rather stating that they should be treated as if they were one of the major browsers. As alluded to at the beginning of the chapter, no browser detection script works flawlessly with all browsers, so test carefully or let the user manually choose which version of your site to visit.

Check Plugin

The Check Plugin behavior sends the user to different pages based on whether the visitor's browser has a particular plugin installed. Applying the Check Plugin behavior (typically to a button or to the `<body>` tag) opens the dialog box shown in Figure 12-10, where you can set its parameters.

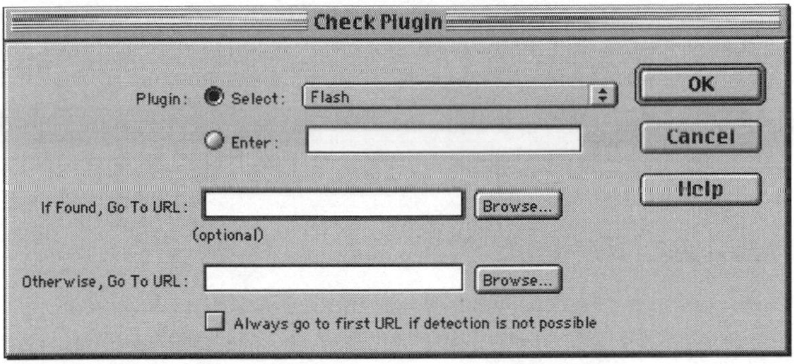

Figure 12-10: Check Plugin behavior parameters

Select the name of the plugin from the existing list (Flash, Shockwave, LiveAudio, Netscape Media Player, or QuickTime) or enter its name manually. The specified name must match the plugin name found under Netscape's About Plug-ins command (which is under the Netscape Help menu on Windows or the Apple menu on the Mac).

Specify the URLs of the pages to load if the plugin is (or is not) detected. Checking for plugins isn't always reliable; IE3 and IE4 on the Mac can't detect plugins, and sometimes automated detection fails when new browsers are released. Furthermore, this behavior doesn't distinguish between different versions of a plugin (such as the Flash 4 Player versus the Flash 5 Player).

To detect the Flash plugin's presence and version number, see the Moock Flash Player Inspector at *http://www.moock.org/webdesign/flash/detection/moockfpi/*.

Although IE doesn't support the use of JavaScript to test for Netscape-style plugins, if an ActiveX version of the plugin is available, IE for Windows downloads it automatically if needed. See Chapter 5 for details. If running on IE5 or later on the Mac, this behavior inserts a VBScript function that tests for the plugin.

Therefore, you should either ask users to tell you if they have the plugin installed, or enable the "Always Go to First URL if Detection is not Possible" checkbox. The latter assumes that visitors have the plugin if its presence can't be determined (this applies primarily to Internet Explorer because Netscape can always detect plugins). Sending the user to a page containing content that requires a plugin will often cause the browser to prompt the user to download the plugin.

Always give your visitors the option to tell you that they have the right plugin or an easy way to download it if they don't. Some plugins, such as QuickTime and Shockwave for Director, can be installed using off-line installers licensed from the software publisher.

When using plugins, ensure that the server MIME types are set correctly for the media file types being served. If the user can't view the content, it may be because of a server MIME configuration problem or the user may truly lack the plugin. The MIME type for each plugin is listed under Netscape's About Plug-ins command (which is under the Netscape Help menu on Windows or the Apple menu on the Macintosh).

Open Browser Window

The Open Browser Window behavior is used to load a document in a new window. The behavior's parameters are set in the dialog box shown in Figure 12-11.

Open Browser Window

URL to Display: [   ] [Browse...]   [OK]
                                                       [Cancel]
Window Width: [   ]   Window Height: [   ]   [Help]

Attributes: ☐ Navigation Toolbar   ☐ Menu Bar

             ☐ Location Toolbar   ☐ Scrollbars as
                                         Needed

             ☐ Status Bar   ☐ Resize Handles

Window Name: [   ]

Figure 12-11: Open Browser Window behavior parameters

Uncheck the window Attributes shown in Figure 12-11 to eliminate window embellishments such as toolbars. Specify a Window Name if the window is targeted by hyperlinks or controlled via JavaScript (the Window Name must not contain spaces or special characters).

This **MM_openBrWindow** function inserted by the Open Browser Window behavior simply calls the JavaScript **window.open()**, as shown here:

```
function MM_openBrWindow(theURL,winName,features) { //v2.0
  window.open(theURL,winName,features);
}
```

By default, it is triggered by the **onLoad** event of the **<body>** element, as shown here:

```
onLoad="MM_openBrWindow('url.htm','newWindow','status=yes,
  scrollbars=yes,width=400,height=600')"
```

To use this function with the Check Browser or Check Plugin behavior, you will need to modify the JS of those behaviors. For example, this statement in the Check Plugin behavior loads the specified URL into the current window:

```
if (theURL) window.location=theURL;
```

To use the **MM_openBrWindow** function to direct the contents to a new window, you can replace the **window.location=theURL** statement with the function call to **MM_openBrWindow**:

```
if (theURL) MM_openBrWindow('url.htm','newWindow','status=yes,
    scrollbars=yes,width=400,height=600')"
```

To close a window, use the Call JavaScript behavior (as described earlier) to execute the **window.close()** JavaScript function. Avoid using the **onUnload** event to open another window when a user closes a browser window (it is really annoying).

The next chapter covers Dreamweaver behaviors that affect images in your HTML documents.

CHAPTER 13

Image Behaviors and Fireworks

Earlier, we saw how Dreamweaver can create complex layouts using tables and layers. We also saw how to create rollover effects and navigation bars without hand-coding. Let's revisit these topics in the context of what we've learned about Dreamweaver behaviors and the Behaviors panel. Later in the chapter, we discuss how to create effects in Fireworks and import them into Dreamweaver.

Rollover Images

Recall that rollover images can be inserted using Insert → Interactive Images → Rollover Image (see Figure 2-11). When you insert a rollover image, Dreamweaver inserts the same JavaScript used by the Preload Images, Swap Image, and Swap Image Restore behaviors. (Note that these behaviors have no effect in IE3 on either Macintosh or Windows.)

Preload Images

The Preload Images behavior ensures smooth rollovers by downloading assets to the cache for quicker access when they are needed. Applying the Preload Images behavior opens the dialog box shown in Figure 13-1, where you can specify one or more image files to preload.

Use the plus (+) button to add an item to the list and use the Browse button to select a new file or change an existing file. You can add as many files to this list as you wish, including files that aren't images. However, excessive preloading can increase your document's load time dramatically (and preloaded images aren't reflected in the download time estimate shown in the Document window's status bar).

To preload images when an HTML page loads, attach the Preload Images behavior to the <body> tag and trigger it with the onLoad event. Dreamweaver applies this behavior automatically if you enable the Preload Images checkbox when applying the Swap Image behavior (discussed next).

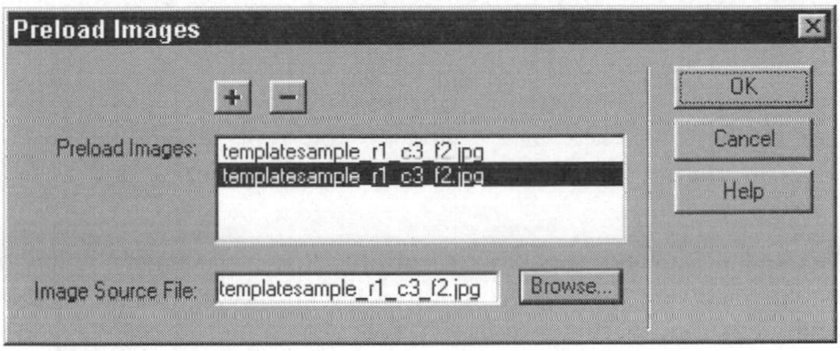

Figure 13-1: Preload Images behavior parameters

To use the Preload Images behavior with files derived from a template, add the Preload Images behavior to the template file.

Swapping and Restoring Images

The Swap Image and Swap Image Restore behaviors combine to create a rollover effect. Applying the Swap Image behavior opens the dialog box shown in Figure 13-2.

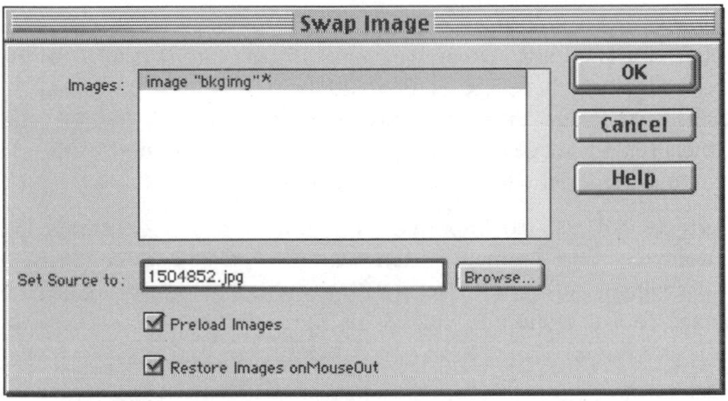

Figure 13-2: Swap Image behavior parameters

The Images list in this dialog box shows the names of images in the current document, including images in other frames. This behavior can't be applied unless the document or frameset contains at least one image.

An <img> tag's name attribute must be set to manipulate the image via JavaScript. Use the Property inspector to assign a unique name to each image on a page.

You'll typically apply the Swap Image behavior to an image acting as a button, but it can also be used to create a so-called *disjoint rollover* in which rolling over one image changes another image, even an image in another frame. Select the image to be replaced from the Images list (images within frames are listed as "Image *imageName* in Frame *frameName*"). Specify the replacement image in the Set Source To field; the replacement image is scaled to the same size as the original image, if necessary.

Enable the Preload Images checkbox to preload the replacement image automatically. Enable the Restore Images onMouseOut checkbox to restore the original image when the mouse cursor rolls off the object. Because NN4 can't process events for images directly, Dreamweaver adds the behaviors to the <a> tag encompassing the image, as shown in Example 13-1.

Example 13-1: Wrapping an image in a null link to apply a behavior

```
<a href="javascript:;"
   onMouseOut="MM_swapImgRestore()"
   onMouseOver="MM_swapImage('mybutton','','rollover.jpg',1)">
  <img src="starting.jpg"
       width="300" height="110"
       name="mybutton" border="0">
</a>
```

If the image acts as a link, the <a> tag's href attribute can be set to any URL. If the <a> tag doesn't exist, Dreamweaver adds it automatically. If the Restore Images onMouseOut checkbox is enabled, the onMouseOut event is used to trigger the Swap Image Restore behavior. If the Preload Images checkbox is enabled, the Preload Images behavior is automatically attached to the document's <body> tag and triggered with the onLoad event..

Rollover effects can also be imported from Fireworks, as described later in this chapter. Rollovers and animation can also be created by changing the src attribute of an image using the Change Property behavior. To create a slideshow, add an image to a timeline and change its src attribute in successive keyframes, as discussed in Chapter 17.

Swap Image Restore

The Swap Image Restore behavior restores the most recently swapped image to its original state. This behavior is typically applied automatically when using the Swap Image behavior by enabling the Restore Images onMouseOut checkbox. If you apply the Swap Image Restore behavior manually, apply it to the same element that the Swap Image behavior is attached to. Together these behaviors create the rollover effect seen in Figure 13-3, in which a bullet appears next to the Info menu option when the cursor rolls over it.

Navigation Bars

Typically, navigation bars are placed within a frameset, and the buttons on the bar are used to switch the content of the main frame. Consider a simple case in which the left-hand frame contains a navigation bar with three buttons. The three buttons display three different pages of information in the main window. (Navigation bars require NN3+ or IE4+ on both Macintosh and Windows.)

Figure 13-3: Button with rollover behavior

Although you can create a navigation bar by applying the Set Nav Bar Image behavior manually, creating one by using Insert → Interactive Images → Navigation Bar is easier (see Figure 2-13). You can modify an existing navigation bar by using Modify → Navigation Bar.

Creating a navigation bar inserts three Set Nav Bar Image actions, each triggered by a different event (onClick, onMouseOver, or onMouseOut), as shown in Figure 13-4. These three actions are attached to each button in the navigation bar and the buttons work in concert. Clicking any button in a navigation bar displays its Down image and causes the other buttons to revert to their Up images.

Figure 13-4: Three actions implementing the Set Nav Bar Image behavior in the Behaviors panel

Select one of the buttons in the navigation bar and then double-click one of the actions in the Behaviors panel to open the Set Nav Bar Image behavior parameters dialog box. The Basic tab of this dialog box, shown in Figure 13-5, is similar to the one that appears when creating a navigation bar using the Insert → Interactive Images → Navigation Bar option.

The Advanced tab of the Set Nav Bar Image dialog box is shown in Figure 13-6. This dialog box's options allow you to override or augment the default action taken when a button in the navigation bar is clicked. For example, you might alter the appearance of another image. Images besides the current button are listed in the Also Set Image field of this dialog box. Select an image from this list and specify the replacement image in the To Image File field (images swapped in this manner are indicated by an asterisk, as shown in Figure 13-6).

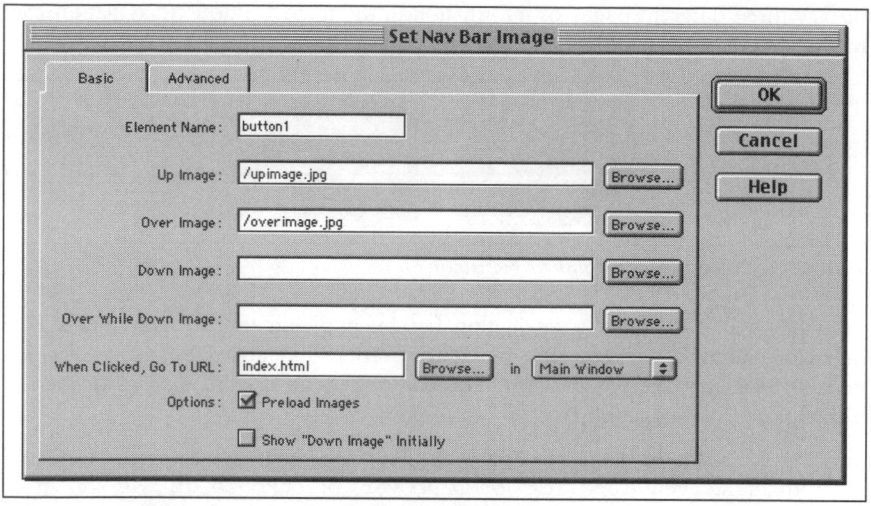

Figure 13-5: The Basic tab of the Set Nav Bar Image dialog box

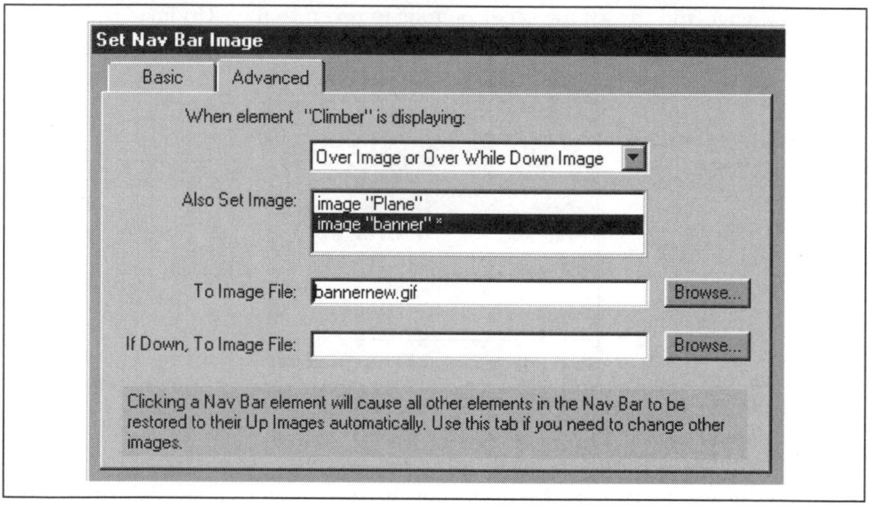

Figure 13-6: The Advanced tab of the Set Nav Bar Image dialog box

Use the "When Element is Displaying: Over Image or Over While Down Image" option to affect another image while the mouse pointer is over the button. (You can choose two display states—one if the button is Up and another if it is Down.) Use the "When Element is Displaying: Down Image" option to change the display of another image after the user clicks a button.

Fireworks

Fireworks 4 (FW4) is bundled with DW4 in the Dreamweaver 4 Fireworks 4 Studio. This section covers integration between FW4 and DW4 (earlier versions of Fireworks offer more limited integration).

Fireworks isn't just a bitmap and vector graphics editing program—it can create interactivity, sliced image tables, links, and image maps. See Fireworks' Help → Welcome option for tutorials and lessons on creating animations, rollover effects, and pop-up menus in Fireworks. Also see Macromedia's *Using Fireworks* manual and Chapter 12 in Macromedia's *Using Dreamweaver* manual.

Creating Tables in Fireworks

Layout tables can create an interface that defies the grid pattern typically associated with tables. Using Fireworks' slice feature, you can optimize each area of your page separately and then export it as a layout table. You can combine GIFs and JPEGs in the same table, or use animated GIFs for some slices while applying rollover effects to others.

When slicing your table, start with the complete image. Segment it into as simple a grid as possible, and block out the areas that will become rollover images and animated GIFs. To slice the image in Fireworks, use the Slice tool to draw the slice area on the image. (You can also select an object with Fireworks' pointer tool or select an area with its marquee tool, and then choose Insert → Slice.)

Figure 13-7 shows what a sliced image might look like in Fireworks. For more tips on using slices to create tables and optimize images, choose Help → Lessons → Creating Slices from Fireworks' Help menu.

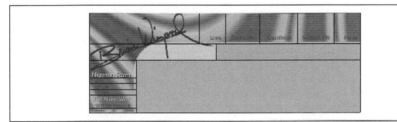

Figure 13-7: A sliced Fireworks image

Export the sliced table from Fireworks using File → Export Preview (see Procedure 3 in Chapter 8), and insert it into Dreamweaver using Insert → Interactive Images ▸ Fireworks HTML or the Insert Fireworks HTML button in the Objects panel's Common category (see Chapter 5). Changes made to the layout table in Dreamweaver are automatically reflected inside Fireworks (and vice versa). Figure 13-8 shows what the table might look like after being imported into Dreamweaver and turned into a template.

If you are not using Fireworks, manually cut the image and save each slice as a separate file. Create a table within Dreamweaver and use Insert → Image to place each slice in a table cell. Resize the cells, if necessary, and set the border, cell padding, and cell spacing attributes to zero to create a seamless layout. Furthermore, you should ensure that images are aligned in the top-left corner of the cells using the horizontal and vertical alignment attributes. Place transparent spacer images at the right and bottom of the table to prevent columns containing text from expanding without limits.

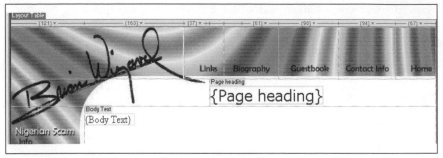

Figure 13-8: A sliced table with editable template regions

Creating Rollovers Using Fireworks

You can create rollover effects in Fireworks and then import them into Dreamweaver as outlined in Procedure 4.

Procedure 4

1. Launch the Fireworks 4 application.

2. In Fireworks, choose Help → Lessons → Creating Rollovers with Drag-and-drop Behaviors.

3. The Fireworks lesson walks you through creating two kinds of rollovers. First you'll create a rollover effect that replaces the image being rolled over. Then you'll create a disjoint rollover, in which rolling over one image causes a text label to appear elsewhere (similar to a tool tip). When you finish the tutorial lesson, continue with Step 4.

4. In Fireworks, set the export format to JPEG (or GIF) under File → Export Preview → Options. Using rollover effects with animated GIFs isn't advisable because browsers get confused about which frame of the animated GIF to display.

5. Use Fireworks' Export dialog box (accessible via the Export button in the Export Preview dialog box or using File → Export) to export your work. Set the Save As Type option to HTML and Images; set the HTML option to Export HTML File; set the Slices option to Export Slices; enable the Put Images In Subfolder option (new in Fireworks 4) to export the slice files to the chosen folder.

6. In Fireworks, while still in the Export dialog box, choose a filename for your HTML file and click the Save button to export the table and images (see Procedure 3 in Chapter 8 for details).

7. Open the exported table in Dreamweaver's by using File → Open, or insert it into an existing document by using Insert → Interactive Images → Fireworks HTML or the Insert Fireworks HTML button in the Objects panel's Common category.

8. All necessary behaviors and assets are transferred to your Dreamweaver document, and your rollover effect can be previewed in a browser (F12).

Dreamweaver and Fireworks Integration

We've seen how to import HTML tables and rollover effects from Fireworks into Dreamweaver. Similarly, you can create a pop-up menu in Fireworks and import it into Dreamweaver. (In Fireworks, choose Help → Lessons → Creating a Pop-up Menu for details.)

Dreamweaver and Fireworks use Design Notes to ensure that changes made in one program are accessible in the other. Table 13-1 lists the commands in Dreamweaver that require or enable integration with Fireworks.

Table 13-1: Fireworks-related operations in Dreamweaver

Description	Dreamweaver operation
Insert *.png, .gif,* and *.jpg* files created in Fireworks (or another program).	Insert → Image
Edit the original source image (*.png* file) used by Fireworks and recreate the *.gif* or *.jpg* file.	Double-click the image in Dreamweaver's Document window
Optimize the web palette and format of an image.	Commands → Optimize Image in Fireworks
Create a web photo album from a folder of images.	Commands → Web Photo Album
Reload an image in Dreamweaver when it is modified in Fireworks.	Edit → Preferences → File Types / Editors → Reload Modified Files
Save changes to the Dreamweaver HTML file when launching Fireworks.	Edit → Preferences → File Types / Editors → Save on Launch
Configure Fireworks as the primary graphics editor for *.png, .gif,* and *.jpg* files.	Edit → Preferences → File Types / Editors → Editors
Import tables, rollover effects, image maps, and pop-up menus created in Fireworks into Dreamweaver.	Insert → Interactive Images → Fireworks HTML (or use the Insert Fireworks HTML button in the Objects panel)
Paste HTML from the clipboard.	Edit → Paste HTML
Activate Design Notes to enable integration between Dreamweaver and Fireworks.	Site → Define Sites → Edit → Design Notes → Maintain Design Notes

There are several ways to launch Fireworks from within Dreamweaver to edit an image, assuming that Fireworks is set as the primary graphics editor. In most cases, editing a *.gif* or *.jpg* image will open the original *.png* file if the image was created in Fireworks:

- Double-click the image in Dreamweaver's Document window. (If you double-click a *.gif* or *.jpg* file in the Site window, it opens the *.gif* or *.jpg* file in Fireworks, but does not open the original *.png* file.)

- Select the image in the Document window and click the Edit button in the Property inspector.

- Right-click (Windows) or Ctrl-click (Macintosh) on the image in the Document window or the image's filename in the Site window and choose Edit With Fireworks 4 from the contextual menu.

Table 13-2 lists options in Fireworks (not Dreamweaver) that impact on the integration of the two programs.

Table 13-2: Relevant operations in Fireworks

Description	Fireworks operation
Introduction to Fireworks.	Help → Welcome
Create sliced tables in Fireworks.	Help → Lessons → Creating Slices Insert → Slice
Create rollover effects in Fireworks.	Help → Lessons → Creating Rollovers with Drag-and-drop Behaviors
Create pop-up menus in Fireworks.	Help → Lessons → Creating a Pop-up Menu; Insert → Pop-up Menu
Create a link in Fireworks.	Highlight text, then use Insert → Slice. Add URL using Object panel (Window → Object)
Create an image map in Fireworks and set its properties.	Use the Insert → Hotspot command to create an image map. Use the Object panel (Window → Object) to enhance it and add URLs
Apply Behaviors in Fireworks.	Window → Behaviors
Configure the HTML export style, file extension, and format.	File → HTML Setup → General
Configure table export settings.	File → HTML Setup → Table
Configure slice export settings.	File → HTML Setup → Document Specific
Set the file export format, such as GIF, JPEG, or animated GIF.	File → Export Preview → Options → Format
Export HTML links, tables, rollover effects, pop-up menus, or image maps.	File → Export → Save As Type: HTML and Images
Export in Dreamweaver Library format.	File → Export → Save As Type: Dreamweaver Library (*.lbi*)
Export CSS Layers.	File → Export → Save As Type: CSS Layers (*.htm*)
Use PNG format when launching Fireworks from an external application.	Edit → Preferences → Launch and Edit
Copy HTML code to clipboard.	Edit → Copy HTML Code
Update HTML code even when Dreamweaver is not running.	File → Update HTML

The next chapter covers Dreamweaver behaviors that use layers to create animation and other effects.

CHAPTER 14

Layer Behaviors

Layers provide a third dimension to your web documents—they can be stacked like glass plates so their contents overlap. Layers also offer absolute positioning of elements in a document. You can create visual effects by modifying a layer's visibility, contents, and position over time.

Layer Size and Position

Layers require 4.0+ versions of the major browsers. For maximum compatibility with Netscape Navigator and Internet Explorer, create layers using the `<div>` tag. For example, a layer implemented with a `<div>` tag using absolute positioning might look like this:

```
<div id="Layer1"
   style="position:absolute; visibility:visible;
      left:67px; top:39px; width:161px; height:172px;
      z-index:1; overflow:scroll">
</div>
```

Avoid `<span>` tags, which work in IE only, and avoid `<layer>` and `<ilayer>` tags, which work in NN4.x only. For more details, see the "Layers" section in Chapter 4.

Layers are controlled using the attributes discussed in Table 4-5. These attributes can be set in the Property inspector, as shown in Figure 4-7. A script can reference a layer's id (in this case, `Layer1`) to modify its properties. By default, when you add a layer to your document, Dreamweaver adds the `MM_reloadPage` behavior to ensure that layers are properly updated when resizing the Netscape browser window. If your site does not support Netscape browsers, you can shut this option off under Edit → Preferences → Layers → Netscape 4 Compatibility. You can add or remove this JavaScript manually in a document using Commands → Add/Remove Netscape Resize Fix.

Dragging and Dropping Layers

The Drag Layer behavior creates a moveable layer that the user can drag and drop. Use this behavior to create games or other interesting interfaces. For example, you might let a user move cards in a game of solitaire or drop a coin in a jukebox.

To apply the Drag Layer behavior in the Behaviors panel, the document must contain a layer object. However, the behavior cannot be applied to the layer itself. Instead, you'll typically attach the behavior to the document's <body> tag, where it will be triggered by the onLoad event. To prevent a layer from being immediately draggable when the document loads, attach the Drag Layer behavior to an image and trigger it using the onMouseDown event; the layer won't be draggable until the user clicks on the image.

Adding the Drag Layer behavior opens the Basic tab of the Drag Layer dialog box, shown in Figure 14-1.

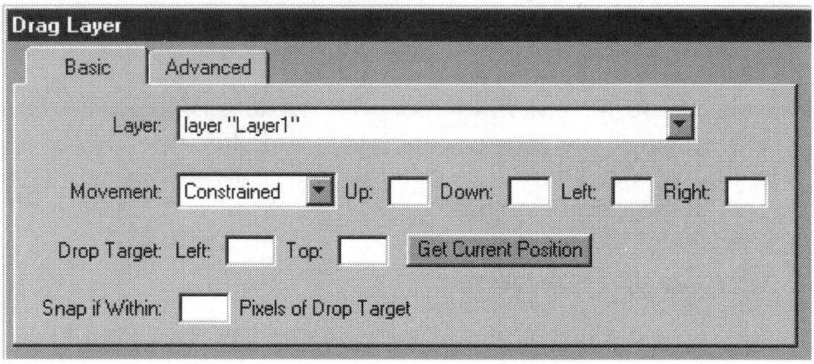

Figure 14-1: Basic Drag Layer behavior parameters

The Basic tab's contents differ slightly, depending on the value chosen for the Movement option.

Layer
> The Layer option specifies the id of the layer that the user can drag and drop. To make multiple layers draggable, apply the behavior multiple times (nested layers move with their parent but aren't well supported in NN4.)

Movement
> When Movement is set to Constrained, the Up, Down, Left, and Right fields are used to constrain movement. When Movement is Unconstrained, the user can drag the layer anywhere within the browser window.

Up, Down, Left, and Right
> These coordinates limit the movement of the layer when Movement is set to Constrained. Set Up and Down to the same number to constrain the layer to horizontal movement only. Set Left and Right to the same number to constrain the layer to vertical movement only.

Drop Target, Left, Top, and Get Current Position

If Drop Target coordinates are not specified, the layer is dropped only when the user releases the mouse. If the Left and Top Drop Target coordinates are specified, the layer is dropped automatically when its upper-left corner is within range of the Drop Target position (as specified by the Snap if Within option). The Drop Target option is typically used for jigsaw puzzles or similar elements that must be dragged to a particular location. Click the Get Current Position button to automatically fill in the Left and Top fields with the layer's current position.

Snap if Within

This option specifies the tolerance within which the layer is snapped to the Drop Target coordinates. A typical value is 50 pixels (about half an inch).

The Advanced tab of the Drag Layer dialog box, shown in Figure 14-2, provides finer control over draggable layers.

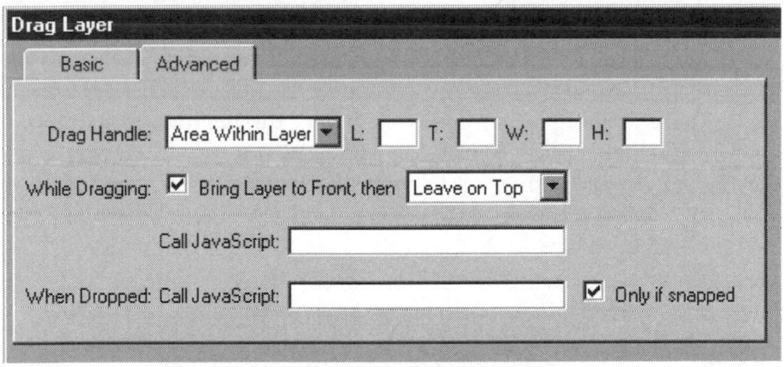

Figure 14-2: Advanced Drag Layer behavior parameters

The Advanced tab's contents differ slightly, depending on the value chosen for the Drag Handle option.

Drag Handle

This option determines where the user must click to initiate the drag action (the entire layer is always dragged in unison). If this option is set to Entire Layer, the user can click anywhere within the layer's bounding box to begin dragging it. If this option is set to Area Within Layer (as seen in Figure 14-2), the L (left), T (top), W (width), and H (height) fields define a hotspot area within which the user must click. For example, you might require a user to click on the handle of a coffee mug to drag it. The coordinates are relative to the upper-left corner of the layer itself.

While Dragging: Bring Layer to Front

Enabling this checkbox causes the selected layer to come to the foreground while being dragged. Bringing a layer to the foreground prevents it from disappearing behind other items while the user drags it.

Bring Layer to Front, then...
This option controls whether the dragged layer reverts to its original stacking order (Restore Z-Index) or remains in front of other layers (Leave on Top) once it is dropped. This option is relevant only if the Bring Layer To Front option is enabled.

Call JavaScript
This field specifies the JavaScript command or function call to execute when the drag operation begins. Use it to trigger an action when the user clicks on the draggable item.

When Dropped: Call JavaScript
The field specifies the JavaScript command or function call to execute when the layer is dropped. If you enable the Only If Snapped checkbox, the JavaScript executes only when the layer is dropped at the correct location (as specified by the Drop Target coordinates on the Basic tab of the same dialog box). You might use this option to display a message when the user drags the layer to the correct location.

Resizing Layers

You can use the Change Property behavior to alter the height and width of a layer. The behavior can be applied to another element, but not to the layer itself. To allow the user to change a layer's size, attach this behavior to a button and trigger it with an `onClick` event. Applying the behavior opens the Change Property dialog box, shown in Figure 14-3.

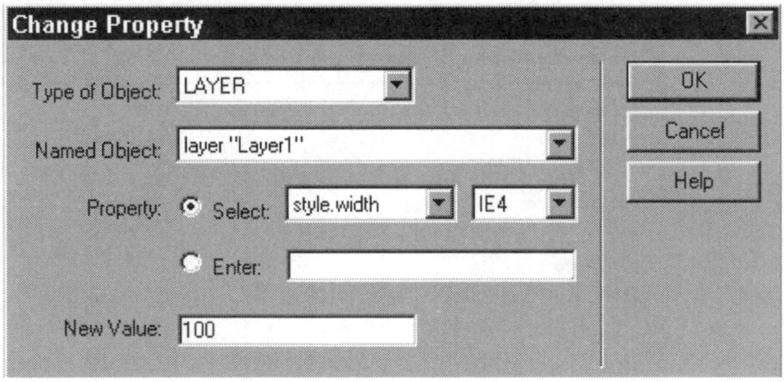

Figure 14-3: Changing a layer's width in Internet Explorer

Procedure 5 adjusts the height or width of a layer in Internet Explorer.

Procedure 5

1. Add a layer object using Insert → Layer.

2. Apply the Change Property behavior to an image that will act as a button. Applying the behavior opens the dialog box shown in Figure 14-3.

3. In the dialog box, select LAYER from the Type of Object pop-up list.

4. Pick the name of a layer from the Named Object pop-up list.

5. Enable the Property Select radio button and choose IE4 from the browser version pop-up list on the far right.

6. Choose style.width from the Property Select pop-up list.

7. Specify a measurement, such as 50px or 75%, in the New Value field.

8. To change the layer's height, repeat Steps 2 through 7, but choose style.height from the pop-up list in Step 5.

 To change the height and width of a layer dynamically in NN4, use the Resize Layer behavior by Massimo Foti, available from the Dreamweaver Exchange.

See Table 16-1 for details on the properties that can be changed with the Change Property behavior. See Chapter 17 for details on animating layers using timelines.

Altering Layers Dynamically

You can alter the content of a layer dynamically to update a page in response to a visitor's choices. You can change a layer's content by using the Set Text of Layer behavior or by changing its innerHTML or innerText properties with the Change Property behavior.

Updating HTML Within a Layer

The Set Text of Layer behavior alters text, including HTML, within a layer element. To apply this behavior, choose Set Text → Set Text of Layer from the Add Behavior (+) pop-up menu in the Behaviors panel. This behavior requires Version 4.0+ browsers. The behavior requires that at least one layer exist on the page, but the behavior cannot be applied to a layer element. Applying the behavior to a button, for example, opens the Set Text of Layer dialog box, shown in Figure 14-4.

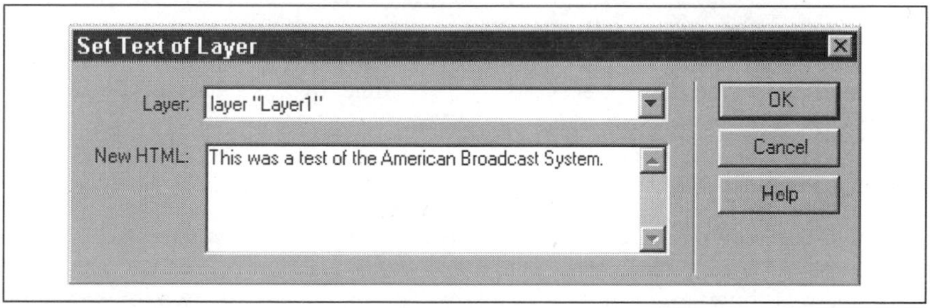

Set Text of Layer	✕
Layer:	layer "Layer1" ▾	OK
New HTML:	This was a test of the American Broadcast System.	Cancel
		Help

Figure 14-4: Set Text of Layer behavior parameters

In this dialog box, select the layer to modify and specify the replacement text or HTML. (You can create your text using the Document window and then copy the resulting HTML to this dialog box.) When triggered, the behavior overwrites the layer's content with the specified HTML. You can use an onMouseOver event to trigger the change and use an onMouseOut event to restore the layer's original contents. (There is no simple way to remember the layer's previous contents, but you can restore them manually with a second instance of the behavior.)

Changing Layer Properties

You can also use the Change Property behavior to change the content of a layer by altering the innerHTML or innerText properties (These properties apply to IE4+ and NN6 only; neither property works in NN4.)

The procedure is similar to Procedure 5, except that you set the Type of Object field to DIV and pick either innerHTML or innerText from the pop-up Property Select menu in the Change Property dialog box. In the New Value field, specify the replacement HTML or replacement text for the layer.

As with the Set Text of Layer behavior, you can use a mouse event to change the property of the layer and then use another event to change it back.

Changing Layer Visibility

You can change the visibility of different layers, rather than change the content of a single layer, to create pseudo-animations or alter the browser window's contents in response to user actions. You can change the visibility of a layer using the Show-Hide Layer behavior or the Change Property behavior.

Show-Hide Layers behavior

The Show-Hide Layers behavior changes one or more layers' visibility property. Whereas the Change Property behavior must be applied separately for Netscape and Internet Explorer, the Show-Hide Layers behavior works with both browsers automatically. Furthermore, you can change the visibility of multiple layers each time the behavior is applied. You can attach the behavior to a button to show or hide layers based on user actions. Create a tooltip-style rollover by applying the behavior twice (trigger it once with an onMouseOver event to show the layer; trigger it again with an onMouseOut event to hide the layer). Chapter 17 explains how to change layer visibility over time by applying the Show-Hide Layers behavior to a timeline (see Figure 17-6).

Change Property Behavior

Although the Show-Hide Layers behavior is a much easier to use, let's see how to change layer visibility using the Change Property behavior. This serves as a good illustration of how to change a property that differs in the two browsers by applying the Change Property behavior twice—once for Internet Explorer (using style.visibility) and once for Netscape (using visibility).

To set the layer visibility using the Change Property behavior for Internet Explorer browsers:

1. Follow Steps 1 through 5 in Procedure 5.

2. Choose `style.visibility` from the Property Select pop-up list.

3. Specify a value for the `visibility` property (`visible`, `hidden`, `default`, or `inherit`) in the New Value field.

To set the layer visibility using the Change Property behavior for Netscape browsers:

1. Follow Steps 1 through 4 in Procedure 5.

2. Enable the Property Select radio button and choose NS4 from the browser version pop-up list on the far right.

3. Choose `visibility` from the Property Select pop-up list.

4. Specify a New Value for the `visibility` property (`visible`, `hidden`, `default`, or `inherit`).

You can trigger the visibility change using an event such as `onClick`.

Chapter 17 has more detailed information on using timelines to modify layers and their attributes over time. The next chapter covers behaviors that alter text in your document and in the browser's status bar.

CHAPTER 15

Text Behaviors

This chapter covers Dreamweaver's text behaviors, which can specify text for layers, frames, text fields, alert boxes, and the browser status bar.

Altering Text

Dreamweaver's text behaviors, such as the Set Text of Layer behavior covered in the previous chapter, can update plain text (and sometimes HTML code) in the target element.

Generating Dynamic Text via JavaScript

When setting text using Dreamweaver's Set Text behaviors, text contained within curly braces is treated as a JavaScript expression.

For example, the following text would display today's date:

```
Today's date is {new Date()}
```

To display a document's modification date, you can use Dreamweaver's Insert → Date command (discussed in Chapter 2) or JavaScript of the form:

```
Document last modified on {document.lastModified}
```

To display an actual curly brace in the text, precede it with a backslash, such as in:

```
This is how you display a curly brace \{
```

Altering Text and HTML in Frames

Use the Set Text of Frame behavior to update the text, including HTML, in a frame without reloading the entire document. Naturally, to use this behavior, the document must contain one or more frames (Chapter 4 explains how to add frames). To apply this behavior, choose Set Text → Set Text of Frame from the Add Behavior (+) pop-up menu in the Behaviors panel. This behavior is typically applied to an image acting as a button. Applying the behavior opens the Set Text of Frame dialog box, shown in Figure 15-1.

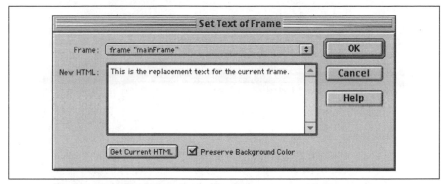

Figure 15-1: Set Text of Frame behavior parameters

In this dialog box, select the frame to modify and specify the replacement HTML text in the New HTML field. When triggered, the behavior overwrites the content of the layer with the specified HTML.

 The New HTML field's content replaces the frame's body content, but you can't change a frame's head content with this behavior. Do not include the <html>, <head>, and <body> tags in the New HTML field.

Use the Get Current HTML button to retrieve the frame's initial HTML code. The current HTML is useful as the basis for modifying the frame's content or if you want to restore the original contents with a second instance of the behavior. Enable the Preserve Background Color checkbox to avoid changing the frame's existing background color.

Altering Text in Text Fields

The Set Text of Text Field behavior alters the text in a text field contained within a form. Therefore, to use this behavior, the document must contain at least one form with at least one text field (Chapter 3 explains how to add forms and text fields to a document). This behavior is often used to update the content of a text field based on earlier selections in the form. Therefore, this behavior is typically applied to other form objects, such as radio buttons and menus, that impact the text field in some way. For example, suppose a form includes a radio button that asks the user to indicate whether he works for a corporation or an educational institution. If the user selects the Educational radio button and the form also asks about the number of employees, you might update the Number of Employees text field to read, "Does not apply to educational institutions."

To apply this behavior, choose Set Text → Set Text of Text Field from the Add Behavior (+) pop-up menu in the Behaviors panel. Applying the behavior opens the Set Text of Text Field dialog box, shown in Figure 15-2.

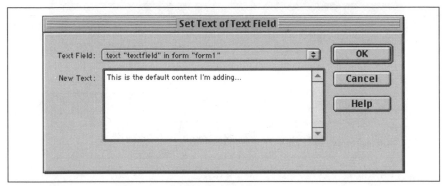

Figure 15-2: Set Text of Text Field behavior parameters

In this dialog box, select the desired form text field from the Text Field pop-up list. Enter the replacement text in the New Text field. The New Text field cannot include HTML code, but it can include JavaScript.

For example, suppose that every page of your site contains a link to a form used to submit errata for the web site. The form should include a URL field where the user can indicate the problematic page's address. You might apply the Set Text of Text Field behavior to the <body> tag of the errata submission page to fill in the referring URL automatically, by specifying New Text of the form:

```
{document.referrer}
```

For advanced form management, including dynamic text fields, consider using a server-side solution such as Dreamweaver UltraDev and ColdFusion.

Adding a Message to the Status Bar

The browser's status bar typically displays a link's destination when the mouse rolls over a link. But the Set Text of Status Bar behavior can be applied to a link to provide help text more unobtrusively than using an alert dialog box or a rollover graphic.

To apply this behavior, choose Set Text → Set Text of Status Bar from the Add Behavior (+) pop-up menu in the Behaviors panel. Applying the behavior opens the Set Text of Status Bar dialog box, shown in Figure 15-3. In the Message field of this dialog box, specify the text to appear in the visitor's browser status bar (keep it under 50 characters to fit on the browser status line).

You'll typically attach the Set Text of Status Bar behavior to a link and trigger it with the onMouseOver event. When the behavior is triggered, it overwrites any other information on the status bar by setting the window.status JavaScript property. When the user rolls off the link, the status bar continues to display the custom status until something else changes it, such as a link without a custom behavior applied (which displays its destination on the status bar). However, if the `window.defaultStatus` JavaScript property (which sets the default status bar text) is defined, the status bar displays the default text when the mouse rolls off a link.

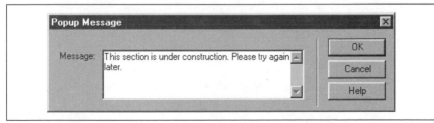

Figure 15-3: Set Text of Status Bar dialog box

The Set Text of Status Bar behavior can't set the `window.defaultStatus` property, so use the Call JavaScript behavior to do so. Apply the Call JavaScript behavior (see Figure 12-4) to the document's `<body>` tag and enter the following JavaScript (note the capitalization of the property name):

```
window.defaultStatus="Default Status Text"
```

To clear the status bar explicitly, use another instance of the Set Text of Status Bar behavior to set the Message to a blank space, and trigger it with the `onMouseOut` event.

The Set Text of Status Bar behavior's Message field cannot contain HTML code, but it can contain JavaScript. For example, to create a custom status message that incorporates the default status bar text, set the Message field to something like:

```
{"Custom Text:" + window.defaultStatus}
```

Creating Pop-up Messages

Use the Popup Message behavior to create an alert box that displays a message to the user. Applying the Popup Message behavior in the Behaviors panel opens the Popup Message dialog box, shown in Figure 15-4.

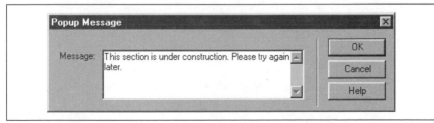

Figure 15-4: The Popup Message dialog box

In the Popup Message dialog box's Message field, enter the text for the alert box. The resulting alert box, shown in Figure 15-5, includes an OK button. Alert boxes prevent users from continuing until they click the OK button, so use the Popup Message behavior sparingly.

Figure 15-5: An alert box as displayed to the user

You can incorporate JavaScript in the message text, but the dialog box's appearance is not customizable. To simulate a multibutton dialog box, display an HTML form designed to look like a dialog box by using the Open Browser Window behavior.

The next chapter covers miscellaneous behaviors that don't fit within the previously discussed categories.

CHAPTER 16

Miscellaneous Behaviors

This chapter covers the Dreamweaver behaviors that don't fit within the categories discussed in other chapters.

Changing Object Properties

The Change Property behavior can set various object properties, as we saw in Procedure 5 in Chapter 14. Applying the Change Property behavior in the Behaviors panel opens the Change Property dialog box shown in Figure 16-1.

Change Property	
Type of Object: DIV	OK
Named Object: div "Layer1"	Cancel
Property: ● Select: style.fontFamily IE4	Help
○ Enter: style.top	
New Value: 14	

Figure 16-1: Change Property behavior parameters

The dialog box options are as follows (see Table 16-1 for details):

Type of Object
Select an object type from the pop-up list. Each object type corresponds to a single HTML tag, except for the LAYER option, which matches all HTML tags that can be used to display layers.

Named Object

Select one of the HTML entities matching the chosen Type of Object. For example, if Type of Object is IMG, the Named Object pop-up menu lists all `<img>` tags in the current document.

Property

Select either a predefined property or enter a custom one using the following options:

Select

Enable the Select radio button to choose from a pop-up list of attributes supported by the current browser for the current object.

Browser pop-up list

Choose the browser you are supporting (NS3, IE3, NS4, or IE4). The chosen browser determines which properties appear in the Select pop-up list for each object type.

Enter

Enable the Enter radio button to enter a property manually in the adjacent field. Consult the O'Reilly HTML Reference information in the Reference panel for tag properties.

New Value

Specify the updated value for the property.

Table 16-1 lists the object properties that can be set in Netscape Navigator and Internet Explorer. Use the LAYER object type to change the properties of a layer, even if the layer is implemented using a `<div>` tag. To change layer properties, which are referenced differently in Internet Explorer and Netscape, you must apply the Change Property behavior twice (once for each browser), as seen in the "Changing Layer Visibility" section in Chapter 14.

Table 16-1: Object properties that can be changed by the Change Property behavior

Object type	HTML tag	Object properties
LAYER	`<layer>`, `<ilayer>`, `<div>`, and `<span>`	NN4+: `top`, `left`, `zIndex`, `clip`, `visibility`, `document.bgColor`, `document.background`. Internet Explorer: `style.top`, `style.left`, `style.width`, `style.height`, `style.zIndex`, `style.clip`, `style.visibility`, `style.backgroundColor`, `style.backgroundImage`, `style.filter`.
DIV	`<div>` tags only	Select the DIV object type only when setting attributes of a `<div>` tag that is not used to implement a layer; otherwise, select objects of type LAYER to set layer attributes. If DIV is selected, the settable attributes are same as for SPAN.

Table 16-1: Object properties that can be changed by the Change Property behavior (continued)

Object type	HTML tag	Object properties
SPAN	`<span>` tags only	Select the SPAN object type only when setting attributes of a `<span>` tag that is not used to implement a layer; otherwise, select objects of type LAYER to set layer attributes. You can set the following attributes for SPAN objects: IE4+: `style.fontFamily`, `style.fontStyle`, `style.fontWeight`, `style.fontSize`, `style.borderStyle`, `style.borderWidth`, `style.borderColor`, `style.backgroundColor`, `style.backgroundImage`, `style.filter`. IE4+ and NN6: `innerHTML` and `innerText`.
IMG	`<img>`	`src` (not supported in IE3)
FORM	`<form>`	`action`
INPUT/ CHECKBOX	`<input type= "checkbox">`	`checked`
INPUT/ RADIO	`<input type= "radio">`	`checked`
INPUT/TEXT	`<input type= "text">`	`value`
INPUT/ PASSWORD	`<input type= "password">`	`value`
TEXTAREA	`<textarea>`	`value`
SELECT	`<select>`	`selectedIndex`

As with other behaviors, to use the Change Property behavior with a template-based document, you must apply it to the template itself.

Multimedia Controls

Dreamweaver offers behaviors for controlling sounds and multimedia assets (Shockwave and Flash).

Playing Sound

You can use the Play Sound behavior to add sound to your web site. To play a simple beep, you could attach the behavior to a button and trigger it using the `onMouseDown` event. To play background music, you could attach the behavior to the `<body>` tag and trigger it using the `onLoad` event.

Applying the Play Sound behavior opens the Play Sound dialog box (not shown), with which you can specify the sound file to play. Web delivery typically requires compressed formats such as *.mid* (MIDI), *.mp3* (MPEG-3), *.mod* (Amiga MOD format used by WinAmp), or *.ra* (RealAudio). Other formats include *.wav* (WAVE), *.au* (Sun's sound format), and *.aif* (AIFF).

Another common format is *.swa* (Shockwave audio), which is similar to *.mp3* and typically played back using either the Flash or Shockwave plugin instead of the Play Sound behavior. In fact, all audio playback requires a browser plugin and can be notoriously inconsistent across platforms and browsers. Generally, Flash is your best bet for simple audio playback, although Shockwave offers more advanced control at the expense of a larger, less-popular plugin. If you use the Play Sound behavior, set the server MIME type for the sound file's type, and test your web page thoroughly in all target browsers on all platforms.

The Play Sound behavior adds code in several places. Like all behaviors, it adds a function call to the object used to trigger the event. For example, the onClick event, which triggers the MM_controlSound function, might be added to a button as follows:

```
onClick="MM_controlSound('play','document.CS991467446390',
    '/images/paws.wav')"
```

Dreamweaver also adds the MM_controlSound function to the document's head content.

The selected sound file is embedded in your HTML page as follows:

```
<embed name='CS991467446390'
        src='/images/paws.wav', loop=false, autostart=false
        mastersound, hidden=true width=0 true=0>
</embed>
```

Use the Property inspector's Play button to preview the sound. Use the Property inspector's Parameters button (or hand-edit the HTML) to set loop to true (which causes the sound to loop indefinitely). There is no need to change the autostart property because the chosen event triggers the sound. If you don't want to wait for a sound to stop of its own accord, create your own JavaScript function to pause or stop a sound (use the MM_controlSound function inserted by the Play Sound behavior as a starting point).

Dreamweaver automatically assigns a cryptic name (CS991467446390 in this case) for the name attribute of the <embed> tag. This name is used in the function call to find the embedded sound object. If you change the name, update it in both places.

Control Shockwave or Flash

The Control Shockwave or Flash behavior can play, stop, rewind, or go to a specified frame in a Shockwave or Flash movie. Shockwave or Flash frames are used for animation and are not directly related to HTML frames. To apply the behavior, at least one Shockwave or Flash asset must be present in the document (see Chapter 5). The behavior is typically applied to an image acting as a play or stop button. To use this behavior:

1. Insert a Shockwave or Flash asset using Insert → Media → Flash or Insert → Media → Shockwave (or the Insert Flash and Insert Shockwave buttons in the Objects panel's Common category).

2. Use the Property inspector to assign a meaningful name to the Shockwave or Flash asset.

3. Select the element, such as an image, to act as the button used to trigger the event.

4. Apply the behavior by choosing Control Shockwave or Flash from the Add Behavior (+) pop-up menu in the Behaviors panel.

5. Applying the Control Shockwave or Flash behavior opens the Control Shockwave or Flash dialog box, shown in Figure 16-2. Choose the name of the Shockwave or Flash asset, as set in Step 2, from the Movie pop-up list. (The menu lists the names of <embed> tags whose src attribute specifies a file with a *.dcr*, *.dir*, *.swf*, or *.spl* extension. It also lists the names of <object> tags whose classid attribute signifies a Shockwave or Flash asset. You need only apply the behavior once, as both the <embed> and <object> tags ordinarily have the same name.)

6. Select an Action—Play, Stop, Rewind, or Go To Frame. If applicable, specify the Shockwave or Flash frame number to go to (specifying a frame name is not allowed).

Figure 16-2 shows the Control Shockwave or Flash dialog box.

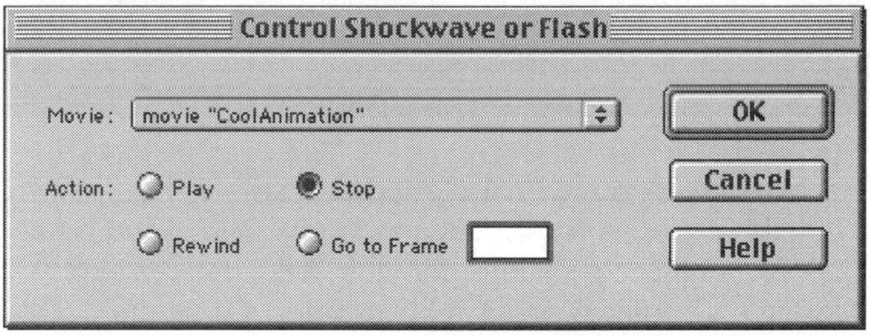

Figure 16-2: Control Shockwave or Flash behavior parameters

To go to a named frame in a Shockwave movie, append #*frameName* to the Shockwave URL (i.e., the src attribute of the <embed> tag and the movie attribute in the <object> tag), such as:

> *http://www.dwian.com/samples/demo.dcr#intro*

Naturally, Flash and Shockwave provide commands to control the playback of movies; the Control Shockwave or Flash behavior is simply an alternative way to control a movie via JavaScript from the browser. For finer control, you may prefer to use ActionScript (for Flash) or Lingo (for Shockwave) instead. The ActionScript or Lingo would be applied to buttons within the Flash or Shockwave movie. For example, play and stop buttons could be embedded within the Flash or Shockwave movie rather than appear as separate elements in the browser window.

Using Form Controls

The Validate Form, Jump Menu, and Jump Menu Go behaviors are used with forms, as first discussed in Chapter 3.

Form Validation

The Validate Form behavior validates the type of data entered in form text fields (to use this behavior, the document must contain at least one form with at least one text field). Typically, you'll attach the behavior to the form's Submit button and trigger it using the `onClick` event (which is the same as attaching it to the Form itself and triggering it with the `onSubmit` action).

Applying the behavior in the Behaviors panel opens the Validate Form dialog box, shown in Figure 16-3.

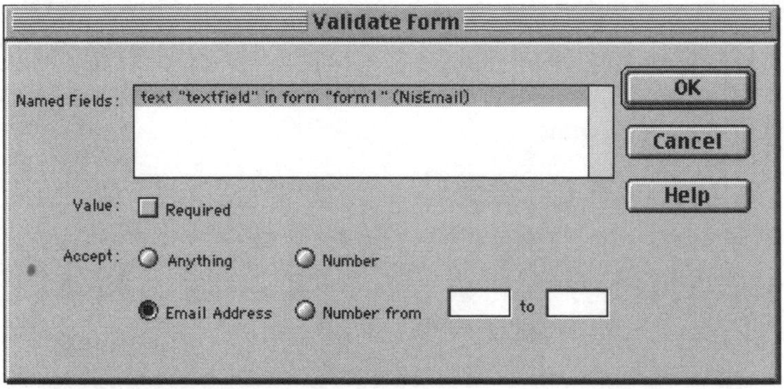

Figure 16-3: Validate Form behavior parameters

Table 16-2 explains the options in the Validate Form dialog box. The Notation column lists the abbreviations shown after each text field in the Named Fields list, which indicate the validation settings for that field. For example, the notation (`RisMail`) indicates a required email address and (`NinRange3:10`) indicates an optional number between 3 and 10.

Table 16-2: Validate Form options

Control	Definition	Notation
Named Fields	This field displays a scrolling list of text fields in the form. Highlight a text field from the list and set the remaining options. You can validate multiple text fields with one instance of the behavior.	N/A
Required	Enable this checkbox to force the user to enter a value for the text field. The space character alone is sufficient to meet this requirement.	R = required; N = not required
Anything	This option allows any type of input.	N/A
Email Address	This option requires the field to include an @ character preceded and followed by at least one other character. It does not check for a valid email address.	isEmail
Number	This option limits user input to valid numbers. Permitted characters include 0–9, plus (+), minus (–), decimal point (.), parentheses (), and percentage (%). Leading and trailing spaces are allowed. A plus (+) or minus (–) is allowed as the first character only. Commas are not allowed. For example, "+123.456", "5%", "(15)" and "–987" are allowed, but "123–456–7890", "6.5.4" and "123,456" are not.	isNum

Table 16-2: Validate Form options (continued)

Control	Definition	Notation
Number from...to...	This option is similar to the Number option, but also requires that the field contain a numeric value within the specified range (inclusive). Negative and floating-point numbers are allowed. The first number must be less than the second number (specify a negative range as –5 to –1, not –1 to –5).	`inRangeMin:Max`

If an error is found during validation, the browser displays an error message indicating the name of the text field and the nature of the problem.

> Give your text fields meaningful names because the text field name is displayed in the error message. Set the text field names before applying the behavior because the behavior won't update automatically if you change the text field names.

You'll typically validate all text fields at once by applying the behavior to the Submit button. If the text fields are not validated successfully, the form's contents are not submitted to the server. (The user can remedy the situation and resubmit the form, however.)

If you prefer to validate individual fields as the user enters data into the form, apply the Validate Form behavior to a text field and trigger it with the `onBlur` event. However, this method is not entirely reliable. If the validation fails, the browser does not force focus back onto the problematic field, and thus allows the user to continue with the rest of the form, even if a field is invalid. Therefore, you should validate the form data again when the Submit button is clicked.

Validating other types of form objects, such as radio buttons, is usually unnecessary because most objects constrain user input by nature. But Dreamweaver doesn't offer a built-in way to require, for example, that a user select an option from a pop-up menu. For this and other more advanced forms of text field validation, such as limiting the number of characters in a text field, search the Dreamweaver Exchange for the keyword "validate." At the Exchange you'll find behaviors that do such things as validate phone numbers. Server-side scripts can also perform form validation and return an error message to the browser, if necessary.

Jump Menus

In Chapter 3, we saw how to insert a jump menu by using Insert → Form Objects → Jump Menu (or by using the Jump Menu tool in the Objects panel's Forms category). With our new understanding of behaviors, we can see that when you insert a jump menu, Dreamweaver inserts a List/Menu object and attaches the Jump Menu behavior to it. If you enable the Insert Go Button After Menu option in the Insert Jump Menu dialog box (see Figure 3-18), Dreamweaver also inserts a button form object and attaches the Jump Menu Go behavior to it.

Understanding jump menus in this way allows us to create them by hand and edit existing ones. You can convert any List/Menu object into a Jump Menu by applying the Jump Menu behavior to it manually. (The Jump Menu behavior is available in the Behaviors panel only when a List/Menu object is selected.)

When you apply or edit the Jump Menu behavior, Dreamweaver opens the Jump Menu dialog box, shown in Figure 16-4. Although it is very similar to the Insert Jump Menu dialog box seen in Figure 3-18, it lacks the Menu Name field and the Insert Go Button After Menu checkbox.

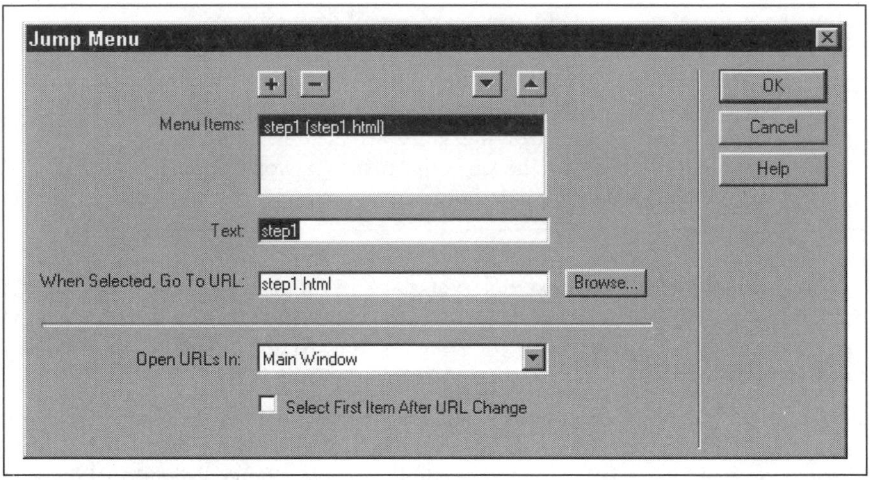

Figure 16-4: Jump Menu behavior parameters

Use this dialog box to modify the attributes of an existing Jump Menu (double-click an existing Jump Menu action in the Behaviors panel to edit its attributes). You can change a Jump Menu's name by selecting the corresponding List/Menu object and editing its name in the Property inspector (this name is used to associate a Go button with the menu). You can also edit the list values in a Jump Menu by clicking the List Values button in the Property inspector, as seen in Figure 16-5. List values can also be accessed by right-clicking (Windows) or Ctrl-clicking (Macintosh) on a List/Menu element and choosing the List Values option from the contextual menu.

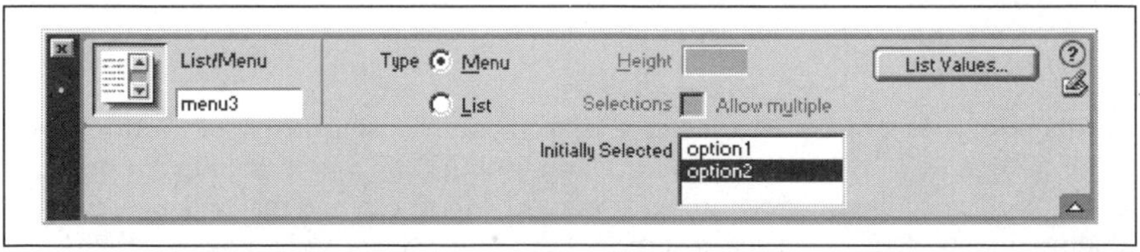

Figure 16-5: The Property inspector for List/Menu objects (jump menus)

You can add a Go button to an existing menu by attaching the Jump Menu Go behavior to a button object. Actually, the Jump Menu Go behavior can be applied to any object, provided that a jump menu already exists within the document. To avoid confusion, you should apply the Jump Menu Go behavior to a button near the List/Menu that acts as the jump menu.

To add a Go button to an existing jump menu that lacks a Go button:

1. Ensure that a jump menu (i.e., a List/Menu object with the Jump Menu behavior attached) exists.

2. Insert a form button by using Insert → Form Objects → Button (or by using the Button tool in the Objects panel's Forms category). By default, Dreamweaver creates a Submit button.

3. Select the newly created Submit button and open the Property inspector, as shown in Figure 16-6. In the Property inspector, set the Action to None and change the Label to "Go" or "Do It!" You can also edit an existing Go button in this way to change its label. Be sure to use a meaningful label.

4. Using the Add Behavior (+) pop-up menu in the Behaviors panel, apply the Jump Menu Go behavior to the button.

5. In the Jump Menu Go dialog box, shown in Figure 16-7, select the Jump Menu's name from the Choose Jump Menu pop-up list (which shows only List/Menus with the Jump Menu behavior applied).

Figure 16-6 shows the Property inspector as it appears when a Go button is selected.

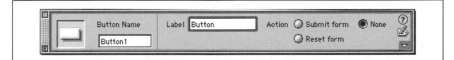

Figure 16-6: The Property inspector for button objects

Figure 16-7 shows the Jump Menu Go dialog box, which appears when the Jump Menu Go behavior is added or edited.

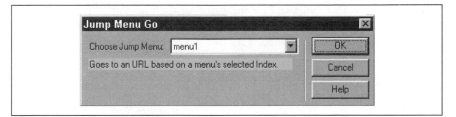

Figure 16-7: The Jump Menu Go dialog box

A web page (or a form) can contain more than one jump menu and more than one Go button.

Using Go To URL

Hyperlinks typically load a new document into the browser window (or a frame) when the user clicks the link. The Go To URL behavior offers additional flexibility because it can load new documents into two or more frames with a single click. It can also load a new document when triggered by any event, such as a rollover. It can be triggered from a timeline to load a document without user interaction.

Applying the Go To URL behavior in the Behaviors panel opens the Go To URL dialog box, shown in Figure 16-8.

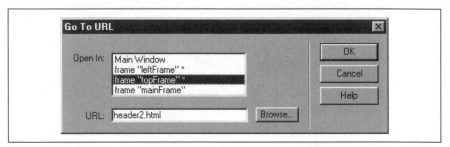

Figure 16-8: The Go To URL dialog box

As seen in Figure 16-8, Dreamweaver displays all frames plus the Main window in the Open In list of the dialog box. (You can attach the Go To URL behavior to any element, but if you attach it to a `<frameset>` tag or if no frames exist, only the Main Window is listed.)

Select a frame in the Open In list and specify the URL of the document to load. An asterisk after the frame's name in the Open In list marks frames for which links have been set. If you set a URL for the Main Window, it replaces the entire frameset, and any URLs that have been specified for frames are moot. If desired, change the triggering event for the action in the Behaviors panel.

Calling a Behavior from a Link

As seen earlier, you can use an event associated with an object to execute a behavior. You can also call the function directly from a hyperlink using the `javascript:` protocol followed by the name of the function to execute and its associated parameters. An example of this technique is shown in Figure 16-9.

Figure 16-9: Calling JavaScript directly via a hyperlink

Note that the link field in Figure 16-9 (which corresponds to the `href` attribute) contains:

```
javascript:MM_goToURL('parent','testing.html');
```

This statement instructs the browser to execute the `MM_goToURL` function using the supplied parameters. The effect is similar to triggering the Go To URL behavior with the `onClick` event.

An alternative technique for attaching a behavior to a text span is discussed under "About behaviors and text" under Help → Using Dreamweaver.

The next chapter covers timelines and behaviors associated with them.

CHAPTER 17

Timelines

In Chapter 14, we examined the behaviors used to manipulate layers. Timelines also allow us to manipulate layers (and images) over time. Timelines are a Dreamweaver convenience used to generate *dynamic HTML* (DHTML), as the combination of JavaScript, HTML, and CSS is often known. Timelines depend heavily on layers and therefore require Version 4.0+ browsers, and some features work only in Internet Explorer. However, over 95 percent of web site visitors use 4.0+ browsers, and most of those use IE4+ browsers.

Timelines Panel

Each *frame* of a timeline represents a moment in time, akin to a frame in a video; timeline frames have no relation to the HTML frames and framesets discussed in Chapter 4.

Timelines are manipulated in the Timelines panel, shown in Figure 17-1. To open the Timelines panel, use Window → Timelines (Shift+F9).

A single HTML document can contain multiple timelines (use the Timelines pop-up menu in the Timelines panel to switch between them). The time axis runs from left to right; higher frame numbers represent later points in time. The *playback head*, shown in Figure 17-1 as a red rectangle and vertical line, indicates the current animation frame.

You can animate objects over time by adding them to the *animation channels* in a timeline. The duration of each object animation is indicated by an *animation bar*, which is a subportion of an animation channel. Each animation bar contains an object plus instructions to change its properties, such as its position, over time. Because an animation bar might not span all frames of a timeline, an animation channel can contain more than one animation bar in series.

Use the Rewind button (see Figure 17-1) to return to Frame 1 of the timeline. Use the Back and Play buttons to step through the animation. Click and hold the

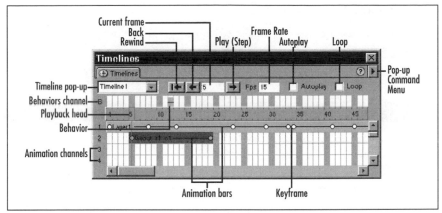

Figure 17-1: The Timelines panel

mouse down on these buttons to run the animation forward or backward. A pop-up command menu is also accessible by clicking the arrow at the upper-right corner of the Timelines panel.

Comparison with Director Score and Flash Timelines

Although Dreamweaver timelines are similar to Macromedia Director's Score and Macromedia Flash's Timeline, there are some important differences.

A single object cannot occupy two animation channels in the same frame. To display two copies of an object simultaneously, duplicate the object in your document and add the two instances to separate animation channels.

If layers overlap, the one with the highest zIndex is drawn in front of other layers. Layers are always rendered in front of other page content, including images added directly to timelines. To change an image's rendering order, insert it into a layer and adjust the layer's zIndex using the Property inspector or the Layers panel.

 A layer's rendering order is independent of its animation channel number. Layers are rendered according to their zIndex property regardless of whether they are present in a timeline. Elements not in a timeline are not animated, but they are rendered along with timeline content.

When an animation completes, the object retains the attributes set in the last keyframe of its animation bar (it doesn't disappear automatically as it would in Director). To erase an object in Flash, create a blank keyframe; to hide a layer in Dreamweaver, set its visibility attribute manually or use the Show-Hide Layers behavior to do so.

Adding Objects to Timelines

Layers and images are the only object types that can be added to timelines. You can add an image or layer to a timeline in several ways:

- Select an image or layer and choose Modify → Timeline → Add Object to Timeline.

- Select an image or layer and press Ctrl+Alt+Shift+T (Windows) or Cmd+Opt+Shift+T (Macintosh).

- Drag and drop an image or layer from the Document window to the Timelines panel.

- Select a layer (not the contents within it) and then right-click (Windows) or Ctrl-click (Macintosh) and choose Add to Timeline from the contextual menu.

- Select a layer and then choose the Add Object option from the pop-up arrow menu in the upper-right corner of the Timelines panel.

To add an element that is not an image or layer to a timeline, insert the element into a layer and then add the layer to the timeline instead. Even though images can be added directly to a timeline, placing them within a layer offers greater control. If you add an independent image to a timeline and later wrap that image in a layer, the image's original animation bar will disappear from the timeline. Simply add the layer containing the image to the timeline instead.

You cannot add objects to a timeline in a document based on a template. Add the objects to the timeline in the template instead.

Keyframes

A *keyframe* is a frame in which one or more object properties, such as a layer's position, are set explicitly (keyframes are indicated by white circles within an animation bar, as seen in Figure 17-1). The browser interpolates between keyframes to create so-called *tween* frames (short for "in-between" frames).

By adding a series of keyframes and setting the position of the layer at each one, you can create an animation path, as shown in Figure 17-2. (The Modify → Timeline → Record Path of Layer command, discussed later, adds keyframes automatically.)

Adding an object to a timeline automatically creates a beginning and ending keyframe, which cannot be removed. To add more keyframes, select an animation bar, and then:

- Choose Modify → Timeline → Add Keyframe, or press the F6 key.

- Hold down the Ctrl key (Windows) or Cmd key (Macintosh) and click any frame in an animation bar.

- Right-click (Windows) or Ctrl-click (Macintosh) and choose Add Keyframe from the contextual menu.

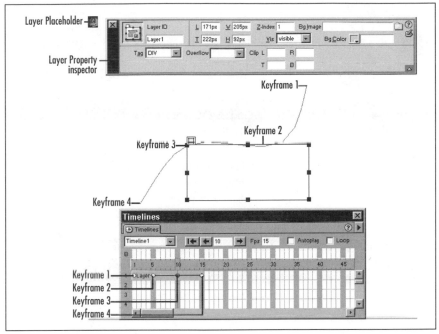

Figure 17-2: Animation path over time

You can't add keyframes if more than one animation bar is selected. Keyframes are always added at the current position of the playback head (which automatically moves to the frame in which you clicked). To move a keyframe to a different frame (to change the time at which it occurs), drag it along the animation bar.

Manipulating Animation Bars

An animation bar represents both an object and its attribute changes over time. You can change the object used in an animation sequence by selecting an animation bar and then:

- Using the Modify → Timeline → Change Object command
- Selecting the Change Object option from the contextual menu
- Selecting the Change Object option from the pop-up arrow menu in the Timelines panel

To change the duration of an animation bar:

- Drag the beginning or ending keyframe of the animation bar. Hold down the Ctrl key (Windows) or Cmd key (Macintosh) while dragging to prevent other keyframes from moving proportionally.
- Insert a frame using Modify → Timeline → Add Frame.
- Delete a frame using Modify → Timeline → Remove Frame.

Timelines

A layer object doesn't disappear from the document window when its animation bar ends. Hide the layer by moving it off-screen or setting its visibility to hidden.

To select multiple animation bars, use Shift-click. If the Timelines panel is active, you can use Ctrl+A (Windows) or Cmd+A (Macintosh) to select all animation bars in a timeline. (File → Select All selects all elements in the Document window, not the Timelines panel.)

You can even copy and paste timelines between documents. Dreamweaver will copy the animation sequence and the objects that it refers to unless an object of the same name already exists in the destination document. After copying an animation to a new document, you can use the Modify → Timeline → Change Object command to change the object associated with an animation.

To shift an animation in time, drag the entire animation bar forward or back (right or left) in the timeline. Remember that an object can't occupy two animation bars in the same frame simultaneously; Dreamweaver prevents you from dragging the animation bar if doing so would violate this constraint.

Altering Object Properties

Timelines can modify the `width`, `height`, `top`, `left`, `z-index`, and `visibility` attributes of layers, but width and height changes work in Internet Explorer only (they are ignored by NN4 and Opera). Timelines can also modify the `src` attribute of images to create a slideshow. To change other image attributes, such as to animate its position, place the image within a layer (likewise for other HTML elements) and then alter the layer attributes.

 Select a keyframe before modifying an object's properties. You can modify one or more properties at each keyframe using the Property inspector (or by moving or resizing a layer in the Document window).

Table 17-1 explains how to set the attributes of layers and images. The `src` attribute applies to images only; the remaining properties apply to layers only.

Table 17-1: Setting properties of layers

Property	Select a keyframe and then change property
src	Change the Src field in the Property inspector (applies to images only).
visibility	Change the Vis field in the Property inspector. Layers appear on the page even after their animation terminates, unless the visibility is set to hidden. Also see the Show-Hide Layers behavior.
width	Change the W field in the Property inspector or use the resize handles to resize the layer in the Document window. (Supported by IE4+ only; has no effect in Netscape.)

Table 17-1: Setting properties of layers (continued)

Property	Select a keyframe and then change property
height	Change the H field in the Property inspector or use the resize handles to resize the layer in the Document window. (Supported by IE4+ only; has no effect in Netscape.)
z-Index	Change the zIndex field in the Property inspector or change the Z column value in the Layers panel.
top	Change the T field in the Property inspector or move the layer in the Document window (drag the tab in the layer's upper-left corner).
left	Change the L field in the Property inspector or move the layer in the Document window (drag the tab in the layer's upper-left corner).

Animating Layer Position

Procedure 6 shows how to change a layer's position over time.

Procedure 6

1. Create a layer using the Draw Layer tool in the Objects panel's Common category (see Chapter 4 for details).

2. Add the layer to the timeline using Modify → Timeline → Add Object to Timeline.

3. Click on a keyframe, such as the ending keyframe, in the Timelines panel (avoid double-clicking it, which selects an entire animation bar).

4. In the Document window, select the layer and drag it to a new location (use the tab in the layer's upper-left corner to drag it).

5. A thin gray line marks the animation path for the layer. The layer will animate between the two keyframes over time.

6. To create a more complex animation path, add one or more keyframes and repeat Steps 3 and 4 for each intermediate keyframe.

If an animation bar contains two keyframes, the animation path is a straight line. When using additional keyframes, the animation path is a Bézier curve as seen in Figure 17-2. To alter the path, change the position of the layer in a keyframe, adding keyframes as necessary. To create straight line paths, create a series of separate animation bars, each with beginning and ending keyframes only.

Recording an animation path

You can record an animation path directly by selecting a layer and choosing Modify → Timeline → Record Path of Layer (or by choosing Record Path from the contextual menu). When you select Record Path, the Timelines panel opens. Drag the layer by the tab in its upper-left corner using the left mouse button. Drag it around the Document window along the desired path to create an animation, as shown in Figure 17-3. (Dreamweaver creates keyframes as needed to approximate the intended path.)

Timelines

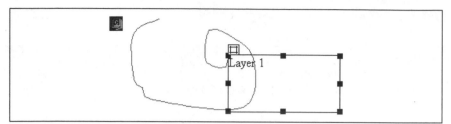

Figure 17-3: Layer with recorded path

Changing Properties with the Properties Panel

You can also alter properties by selecting a keyframe and then setting the new value in the Property inspector. Figure 17-4 shows how to set the Left and Top coordinates for two keyframes of an animation using the Property inspector.

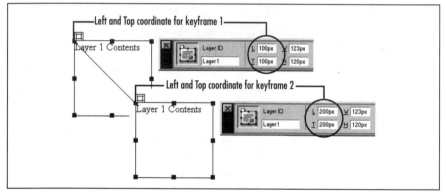

Figure 17-4: Layer at positions (100, 100) and (200, 200)

> Property changes made when a keyframe is selected affect that keyframe only (although it causes tween frames to be recalculated). Select a keyframe or create one, if needed, before changing an object's properties. Property changes made when a tween frame is selected affect the entire animation bar.

Changing the layer position while a tween frame is selected shifts the entire path without altering its shape. For example, if you select a tween frame and increase the Left coordinate by 50 pixels, the entire animation path shifts 50 pixels to the right. Likewise, changing a property without first selecting a keyframe changes the property's setting for the entire timeline (the life span of the document).

Working with Images

You can alter an image's `src` attribute over time, which changes the picture displayed by changing the graphic file associated with the `<img>` tag. Select a keyframe before changing the `src` attribute in the Property inspector. Changing the `src` attribute outside of a keyframe changes it for the entire document's lifespan. All image files should be the same size (if not, they will all be scaled to the size of the image indicated in the Property inspector).

To move an image over time, place it in a layer and animate the layer in a timeline. To create the effect of images appearing and disappearing, insert the images into layers and then change the layer visibility over time. This technique is often more effective than changing a single image's `src` attribute. Likewise, you can simulate a change in both an image's graphic and position by animating two different images in two different layers as follows:

1. Create a layer and insert the first image into it.

2. Animate the first layer's position using a timeline as described in Procedure 6.

3. In the last frame of the animation, hide the layer by using the Property inspector to set its Vis property to hidden (or by using the Show-Hide Layers behavior as described later).

4. Create a second layer and insert the second image into it.

5. Animate the second layer's position so it begins where the previous layer's animation ended.

6. Set the layer's visibility to hidden until reaching the frame in which you want it to appear.

Animation Rate

A timeline's *frame rate* controls animation playback speed and can be changed in the Fps field of the Timelines panel. The default frame rate is 15 frames per second (fps). Lowering the frame rate below 6 or 8 fps may result in jerky animation. Because animation is processor-intensive, higher frame rates may not be achievable on lower-end machines. The target frame rate is the maximum speed at which the animation will occur; achieving the rate is not guaranteed. Each time line can have a different frame rate.

 Browsers are not optimized for animation. For serious animation, especially when using audio and interactivity, consider using Flash, Shockwave, or Synchronized Multimedia Integration Language (SMIL).

Keep animations simple and don't expect a high frame rate. If you must use browser animation, consider these tips:

- Keep animated elements as small as possible.

- Don't animate more than a few elements at a time.

- Preload images using the Preload Images behavior.

- Use the Show-Hide Layers behavior and the Set Text of Layer behavior to create pseudo-animations. Likewise, change the layer background color using the Change Property behavior.

- Allow users to move layers using the Drag Layer behavior.

Adding Behaviors to Timelines

In Chapter 14, we covered the behaviors that manipulate layers (namely Drag Layer and Set Text of Layer). You can add other behaviors to a timeline, such as the Set Text of Status Bar behavior, which displays a message in the browser status bar, or the Show-Hide Layers behavior, which (surprise!) shows and hides layers.

Behaviors are added in the Timelines panel's *Behaviors channel*, indicated by the letter B in Figure 17-5.

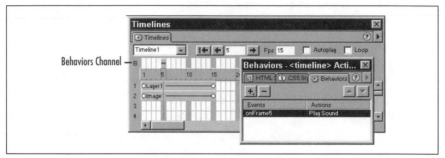

Figure 17-5: A behavior in the Timelines panel

To add a behavior to a timeline, click a frame in the Behaviors channel of the Timelines panel and choose a behavior from the Behaviors panel's Add Behavior (+) pop-up menu. (You can also use Modify → Timeline → Add Behavior to Timeline, which opens the Behaviors panel for you). Timeline behaviors can be added in any frame of the timeline (in either keyframes or tween frames).

 You can associate multiple behaviors with the same frame of a timeline. Behaviors are applied in the Timelines panel's Behaviors channel, not to the animation channels. They can be used to trigger actions at specific times without user interaction, even if you're not performing animations.

Attaching a behavior to a timeline adds the same JavaScript code that is added when attaching the behavior to other objects. The primary difference is that timeline events are always triggered when a particular frame is reached (for example, the event might be onFrame15). If you place a behavior in the wrong frame, simply drag it to a different frame of the Behaviors channel.

 You must deselect the Behaviors channel in the timeline before you can apply a behavior to another element on the page. Click a timeline animation channel to deselect the Behaviors channel.

To delete all behaviors attached to a frame, click the frame in the Behaviors channel of the Timelines panel and choose Modify → Timeline → Remove Behavior. To delete a single behavior when more than one is attached to the same frame, use the Remove Behavior (-) button in the Behaviors panel.

Show-Hide Layers Behavior

The most common behavior you'll use in a timeline is, not surprisingly, one that controls layer visibility. Applying the Show-Hide Layers behavior, using the Add Behavior (+) pop-up menu in the Behaviors panel, opens the Show-Hide Layers dialog box shown in Figure 17-6.

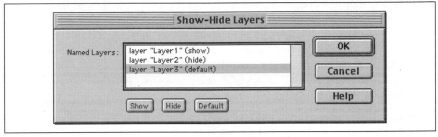

Figure 17-6: The Show-Hide Layers dialog box

The Show-Hide Layers dialog box lists all layers in the current document, not just those added to a timeline. The dialog box does not list images. To hide an image, insert it into a layer and then hide the layer. As seen in Figure 17-6, use the Show and Hide buttons to show or hide each layer. You can also leave layers at their default (current) setting. Add this behavior in the Behaviors channel of a timeline in the frame you want the change to occur. This same behavior can be attached to an HTML element, such as an image acting as a button, to show or hide layers under user control. It can be applied to the <body> tag to show or hide layers when the document loads.

Controlling Timelines

Dreamweaver provides behaviors to start, stop, and loop timelines. Each timeline can be started and stopped independently, and they can each have different frame rates (set using the Fps field in the Timelines panel).

Starting a Timeline

You can start a timeline automatically using autoplay or trigger it with another event, such as a button click.

Playing a timeline with autoplay

To start a timeline when the document loads, enable the Autoplay checkbox (see Figure 17-1) in the Timelines panel (if using multiple timelines, the autoplay mode can be set separately for each timeline). When you set a timeline to autoplay, Dreamweaver automatically attaches the Play Timeline action to the document's <body> tag and triggers it with the onLoad event.

Starting and stopping a timeline with an event

To play a timeline, apply the Timeline → Play Timeline behavior using the Add Behavior (+) pop-up menu in the Behaviors panel. This behavior is typically applied to an image acting as a "Play" button and triggered by the onMouseDown event. Applying it opens the Play Timeline dialog box (not shown) from which you can choose the timeline to play. Apply one instance of the behavior for each timeline you wish to play. You can even apply this behavior in the Behaviors channel of one timeline to start another timeline.

By default, a timeline plays once and then stops. To stop a timeline prematurely, apply the Timeline → Stop Timeline behavior using the Add Behavior (+) pop-up menu in the Behaviors panel. This behavior is typically applied to an image acting as a "Stop" button and triggered by the onMouseDown event. Applying it opens the Stop Timeline dialog box (not shown) from which you can choose to stop all timelines or a specific timeline. Again, you can apply this behavior in the Behaviors channel of one timeline to stop another timeline.

Looping a Timeline

Timelines can be played once (the default), played a limited number of times, or looped indefinitely. If you enable the Loop checkbox in the Timelines panel (see Figure 17-1), Dreamweaver adds the Go To Timeline Frame behavior to the frame following the last occupied frame of the timeline. The behavior causes the timeline to loop back to the beginning when it reaches its end.

By default, the Go To Timeline Frame behavior causes the timeline to loop indefinitely. To edit the behavior's parameters, select the frame containing the behavior in the Behaviors channel of the Timelines panel. Then, open the Behaviors panel and double-click the Go To Timeline Frame action. This gesture opens the Go To Timeline Frame dialog box, shown in Figure 17-7, which lets you set the starting frame of the loop and specify how many times to repeat the loop. If the Loop field is left blank, the timeline will loop indefinitely.

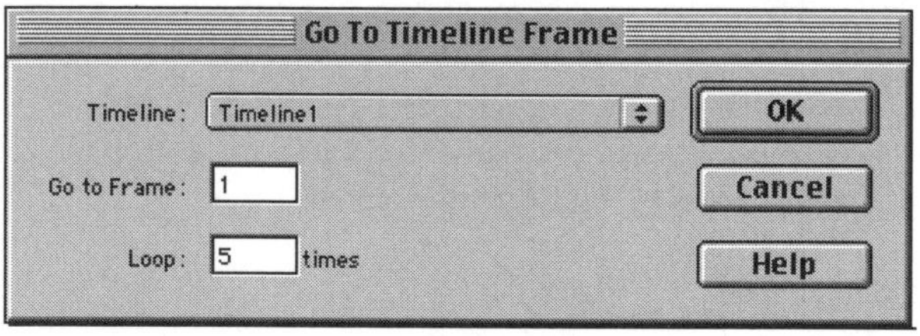

Figure 17-7: Go To Timeline Frame behavior parameters

To change the loop's ending frame, move the behavior to a different frame of the Behaviors channel in the Timelines panel. Test your animation to ensure that it loops seamlessly (the animation doesn't stutter or jump when the timeline loops).

The Go To Timeline Frame behavior can also be applied manually by choosing Timeline → Go To Timeline Frame from the Add Behavior (+) pop-up menu in the Behaviors panel. This behavior could be applied to an image acting as a "Rewind" button and triggered by the onMouseDown event. If this behavior is applied outside of the Timelines panel, it ignores the Loop field setting and stops the timeline after reaching the destination frame. To play the timeline once it arrives at the new frame, attach the Play Timeline behavior to the same HTML tag used for the Go To Timeline Frame action; trigger the Play Timeline action with the same event, but make sure it appears last in the Behaviors panel.

Timeline Operation Summary

Table 17-2 summarizes the timeline-related commands.

Table 17-2: Timeline operations

Operation	Command
Open the Timelines panel	Window → Timelines (Shift+F9)
Add a keyframe	Modify → Timeline → Add Keyframe (F6)
Remove a keyframe	Modify → Timeline → Remove Keyframe (Shift+F6)
Delete a frame	Modify → Timeline → Remove Frame
Add a frame	Modify → Timeline → Add Frame
Add a behavior	Modify → Timeline → Add Behavior to Timeline
Record animation in real time	Modify → Timeline → Record Path of Layer
Add an object to a timeline	Modify → Timeline → Add Object to Timeline
Use a different object with an animation sequence	Modify → Timeline → Change Object
Delete an object (animation bar)	Modify → Timeline → Remove Object
Delete an animation channel from a timeline	Select it in the Timelines panel and press the Delete key
Change a timeline's frame rate	Use the Fps field in the Timelines panel
Switch between timelines	Use the Timelines pop-up menu in the Timelines panel
Create a new timeline	Modify → Timeline → Add Timeline
Delete an entire timeline	Modify → Timeline → Remove Timeline
Rename a timeline	Modify → Timeline → Rename Timeline
Delete frame behaviors in the Behaviors channel	Modify → Timeline → Remove Behavior
Play a timeline	Enable the Autoplay checkbox or apply the Timeline → Play Timeline behavior
Stop a timeline	Apply Timeline → Stop Timeline behavior
Jump to a specific frame in a timeline	Apply Timeline → Go To Timeline behavior (also see the Loop checkbox)
Preview an animation in Dreamweaver	Use the Rewind, Back, and Play buttons in the Timelines panel
Preview an animation in browser	File → Preview in Browser (F12)

This part of the book covered how to apply and use behaviors to add dynamic features and interactivity to your web pages. The next part discusses how to extend Dreamweaver by adding new behaviors, altering menus and shortcut keys, and adjusting Dreamweaver's preferences.

PART IV

Configuring and Extending
Dreamweaver

Part IV covers ways to configure, customize, and extend Dreamweaver to enhance your productivity.

CHAPTER 18

Dreamweaver Preferences

This chapter covers the 16 category panes of the Dreamweaver Preferences dialog box. Open the Preferences dialog box (see Figure 18-1) by using Edit → Preferences, Ctrl+U (Windows), or Cmd+U (Macintosh). Some Site window preferences are set in the Site Definition dialog box (Site → Define Sites → Edit) as discussed in Chapter 6.

General Preferences

The Preferences dialog box's General category configures the following preferences:

Show Only Site Window on Startup
> Determines whether Dreamweaver opens the Site window or a Document window on startup.

Open Files in New Window
> Determines whether the File → Open command replaces the current document or creates a new Document window. The File → New command always creates a new Document window. This option is available under Windows only; on the Macintosh, Dreamweaver always opens a new Document window.

Warn when Opening Read-Only Files
> If enabled, Dreamweaver provides an alert box if you open a read-only (locked) file. Use the Site → Check Out command to unlock a file for editing.

Add Extension when Saving
> You can specify the file extension to use when saving HTML files—typically *.htm* or *.html*. The Commands → Create Web Photo Album command uses the preference setting in Fireworks' File → HTML Setup → General dialog box when creating HTML files.

Update Links when Moving Files
> Determines whether to update links when you move, delete, or rename documents through Dreamweaver's Site window. Available options are:

Prompt
> Ask the user whether to update links.

Never
> Don't update links (and don't prompt the user).

Always
> Update links without prompting the user.

Show Dialog when Inserting Objects
> Allows you to insert placeholders for certain object types without being prompted for more information. If enabled, Dreamweaver prompts the user to specify additional information when inserting the following object types in the Objects panel: Image, Table, Email, Server-Side Includes, Flash, Shockwave, Generator, Anchor, Script, Comment, Applet, and Plugin. If this option is disabled, use the Property inspector to set object properties. Even when this preference is enabled, holding down the Ctrl key (Windows) or Cmd key (Macintosh) overrides the preference and inserts placeholder objects. Many other object types are not affected by this preference. The Other Character, Rollover Image, Tabular Data, Navigation Bar, Date, Fireworks HTML, Flash Button, Flash Text, and Jump Menu objects always open a dialog box when inserted. The Layer, Horizontal Rule, ActiveX, and Forms objects (other than Images and Jump Menus) never display a dialog box when inserted.

Faster Table Editing (Deferred Update)
> If enabled, table cells sizes are not adjusted until you click outside the table or press Ctrl+Space (Windows) or Cmd+Space (Macintosh).

Rename Form Items when Pasting
> If enabled, when a form object is pasted into a document, it is automatically given a unique name. Leave this option enabled.

Enable Double-Byte Inline Input
> If enabled, Dreamweaver allows double-byte characters, as is required for double-byte languages such as Japanese and Chinese.

Maximum Number of History Steps
> Specifies the number of history steps to be tracked in the History panel. Defaults to 50. Larger numbers may consume excessive memory and disk space.

Object Panel
> Determines whether the Objects panel displays object names, icons, or both.

Spelling Dictionary
> You can select which dictionary to use with the Text → Check Spelling (Shift+F7) command. See Chapter 7.

Code Colors Preferences

The Preferences dialog box's Code Colors category sets the colors used for HTML code shown in Code view (View → Code View) and the Code Inspector. Table 18-1 lists the default colors. These colors are applied as you edit HTML code and can be applied to documents created outside Dreamweaver using the Commands → Apply Source Formatting menu command. They do not affect Design view.

Table 18-1: Code Colors defaults

Option	Default	Used for
Background	#FFFFFF (white)	Background of Code pane and Code Inspector.
Text	#000000 (black)	Tag contents, such as text within <body> tags and JavaScript elements that are not keywords or strings.
Comments	#808080 (gray)	Items within <!-- and --> tags.
Tag Default	#000080 (dark blue)	Tags and attributes for which a Tag Specific color has not been set.
Script Reserved Keywords	#0000FF (blue)	Reserved JavaScript keywords, such as var.
Script Other Keywords	#800000 (brick red)	JavaScript functions names such as close and eval.
Script Strings	#008000 (green)	Literal strings within quotes, such as "Hello world".

To set the color used for a specific HTML tag, highlight a tag name in the Tag column of the Tag Specific list, and configure the following options:

Tag Specific color
> Select the Default color (the Tag Default color) or a custom color. The Tag Specific color is used to display the tag and the attributes within it.

Apply Color to Tag Contents
> If enabled, applies the Tag Specific color to the contents; otherwise, tag contents use the Text color. For example, this option sets the color of text within <p> and </p> tags in Code view (but does not affect Design view).

Code Format Preferences

The Preferences dialog box's Code Format category sets the code formatting options for the HTML code visible in Code view (View → Code View) and the Code Inspector. The preferences determine the formatting applied to new documents and additions to existing documents. Existing documents, including documents created outside Dreamweaver, can be reformatted by using the Commands → Apply Source Formatting menu command. Beyond the options available in the Dreamweaver preferences, HTML source formatting is controlled by the *SourceFormat.txt* file in the *Dreameaver 4/Configuration* folder as described in the next section.

The following preferences can be set in the Code Format preferences:

Indent

The Indent option turns on indentation for tags with the `indent` attribute in the *SourceFormat.txt* file.

> *Use*
>
> Select whether to indent code segments using Spaces or Tabs.

> *Table Rows and Columns*
>
> Indents `<table>`, `<td>`, `<th>`, and `<td>` tags.

> *Frames and Framesets*
>
> Indents `<frame>` and `<frameset>` tags.

Indent Size

Sets the number of spaces (if Use is set to Spaces) or tabs (if Use is set to Tabs) to indent text with the Text → Indent command.

Tab Size

Sets the width of tab stops (defaults to four characters). Tab stops are used when pressing the Tab key or when indenting code automatically (if Use is set to Tabs).

Automatic Wrapping...After Column

If enabled, inserts a hard carriage return if a line of HTML code reaches the specified width.

Line Breaks

Specifies the line break format: CR LF (Windows), CR (Macintosh), or LF (Unix). Choose the platform that matches your web server. If using an external HTML editor, such as NotePad, on Windows, set this option to CR LF. If using an external HTML editor, such as SimpleText, on the Macintosh, set this to CR. Files uploaded via FTP in ASCII mode ignore this setting (they always use CR LF). When downloading file via FTP in ASCII mode, Dreamweaver determines the appropriate line break character for your operating system automatically.

Case for Tags

Specifies whether to use `<UPPERCASE>` or `<lowercase>` format for HTML tags. You should use lowercase format for XHTML compliance.

Case for Attributes

Specifies whether to use the `UPPERCASE="value"` or `lowercase="value"` format for attributes within HTML tags. You should use lowercase format for XHTML compliance.

Override Case Of: Tags or Attributes

If enabled, Dreamweaver changes the case of HTML tags and attributes of any document opened in Dreamweaver. It also overrides the case used when hand-editing your HTML. If disabled, Dreamweaver leaves existing HTML alone.

Centering: Use DIV Tag or Use CENTER Tag

Select the Use DIV Tag radio button to center objects using the DIV tag, which is appropriate for Version 4+ browsers. Select the Use CENTER Tag radio button to support older Version 3 browsers. You should use the DIV option for XHTML compliance, because the `<center>` tag is deprecated.

The SourceFormat.txt File

The *SourceFormat.txt* file, found in the *Dreameaver 4/Configuration* folder, offers more control over HTML source code formatting than Dreamweaver's preferences afford. You can edit this file in a text editor, but you must restart Dreamweaver for the changes to take effect.

There are three sections to the *SourceFormat.txt* file as indicated by the <?options>, <?elements>, and <?attributes> tags (the <?end> tag terminates the file).

<?options>

The <?options> section corresponds roughly to the options available in the Code Format preferences dialog box.

The indentation settings are as follows (note that the tag is spelled "indention," not "indentation"):

```
<indention enable indent="2" tabs="4" use="spaces" active="1,2">
```

The <indention> tag's enable, indent, tabs, and use attributes correspond to the Indent, Indent Size, Tab Size, and Use fields respectively in the Code Format preferences. The active attribute defines the groups of tags to be indented. Indentation group numbers are specified by assigning a value to the igroup attribute, such igroup="1" or igroup="2". Two predefined groups correspond to the Table Rows and Columns (group 1) and the Frames and Framesets (group 2) options in the Code Format preferences.

The <?options> section configures other options as follows:

```
<lines autowrap column="76" break="CRLF">
<omit options="0">
<element case="lower">
<attribute case="lower">
<colors text="0x00000000" tag="0x00000000" unknowntag="0x00000000"
comment="0x00000000" invalid="0x00000000" object="0x00000000">
<directives break="1,0,0,1">
<directives delimiter="%3C%25=" break="0,0,0,0">
```

The <lines> tag's autowrap, column, and break attributes correspond to the Automatic Wrapping, After Column, and Line Break preferences. The <omit> tag is reserved for future use. The case attribute of the <element> and <attribute> tags corresponds to the Case for Tags and Case for Attributes preferences. The <colors> tag corresponds to the Code Color preferences cited in Table 18-1. The <directives> tag controls the formatting of third-party tags.

<?elements> and <?attributes>

The <?elements> section of the *SourceFormat.txt* file defines formatting preferences for individual tags. For example, this line defines the formatting attributes of the <p> tag.

```
<p break="1,0,0,1" indent>
```

The four numbers following the **break** attribute indicate the number of line breaks to insert before the opening tag, after the opening tag, before the closing tag, and after the closing tag. The **indent** attribute tells Dreamweaver to indent this tag according to the settings in the **<?options>** section.

These two lines assign the **<td>** and **<frameset>** tags to indention groups 1 and 2 using the **igroup** attribute:

```
<td break="1,0,0,1" indent igroup="1">
<frameset break="1,0,0,1" indent igroup="2">
```

The **noformat** attribute prevents Dreamweaver from changing the format of the tag contents, as is the case with the **<pre>** tag:

```
<pre break="1,0,0,1" noformat>
```

The **<?attributes>** section of the *SourceFormat.txt* file defines custom capitalization for the specified HTML attributes.

The **namecase** attribute specifies the exact case to use for this particular element, which is important because JavaScript is case-sensitive. The following line ensures the correct case for **onMouseOver**:

```
<onMouseOver namecase="onMouseOver">
```

The **sameCase** attribute forces the value of an attribute to be capitalized in the same way as the attribute name:

```
<align samecase>
```

The **sameCase** attribute is also used for Boolean attributes, which don't have values, and should not be removed.

```
<checked samecase>
```

See the comments within the *SourceFormat.txt* file itself for more information about its format. Search for "Changing default HTML formatting" under Help → Using Dreamweaver (F1) for more information.

Code Rewriting Preferences

The Preferences dialog box's Code Rewriting category controls whether and how HTML code is modified when Dreamweaver opens a document. It can be used to clean up HTML or leave it alone. Also see Chapter 7.

Fix Invalidly Nested and Unclosed Tags
    If enabled, Dreamweaver corrects improperly nested HTML tags. For example, **<p><b>text</p></b>** is rewritten as **<p><b>text</b></p>**.

Remove Extra Closing Tags
    If enabled, Dreamweaver corrects closing tags with no corresponding opening tag. For example, if it finds a **</p>** element without a corresponding **<p>** element, it adds the **<p>** element to preserve spacing, but it deletes a **</b>** element if no matching **<b>** element is found.

The following two options are active only if at least one of the preceding two options is enabled:

Warn when Fixing or Removing Tags
> If enabled, Dreamweaver summarizes the fixes it made when opening the document. It doesn't let you confirm the changes, it just informs you of the changes it made. If you want to abort the changes, don't save the document.

Never Rewrite Code in Files with Extensions...
> Use this option to prevent Dreamweaver from changing HTML code within the listed types of files (defaults to *.asp*, *.cfm*, *.cfml*, *.ihtml*, *.js*, *.jsp*, *.php*, and *.php3*). For example, add the *.php4* extension to prevent Dreamweaver from rewriting PHP code.

Encode Special Characters in URLs Using %
> Encodes special characters in URLs using their hexadecimal ASCII values to ensure that web servers recognize them properly. For example, the space character, whose ASCII code is 32 is encoded as %20, because 20 in hexadecimal is equivalent to 32 in decimal. Leave this option enabled for maximum compatibility.

Encode <, >, &, and " in Attribute Values Using &
> Encodes the <, >, &, and " characters as `&gt;`, `&lt;`, `&amp;`, and `&quot;` within attributes values to ensure that web browsers recognize them properly. Leave this option enabled for maximum compatibility and XHTML compliance, unless it conflicts with third-party tags (to avoid corrupting attributes in server-side scripts, use the "Never Rewrite Code in Files with Extensions" option).

CSS Styles Preferences

The Preferences dialog box's CSS Styles category controls how Dreamweaver creates and edits CSS Styles. Also see Chapter 10.

When Creating CSS Styles: Use Shorthand For
> Create CSS Styles using the shorthand notation for Font, Background, Margin and Padding, Border and Border Width, and List-Style attributes. For example, when this preference is enabled, Dreamweaver creates font settings as properties of the `font` tag instead of individual CSS attributes such as `font-style`, `font-width`, and `font-variant`.

When Editing CSS Styles: Use Shorthand
> Determines whether and how Dreamweaver updates CSS Styles when editing an existing document.

> *If Original Used Shorthand*
>> If the original document did not use shorthand properties, Dreamweaver doesn't convert them to shorthand properties.

> *According to Settings Above*
>> Dreamweaver overwrites existing CSS properties according to the settings for the "When Creating CSS Styles: Use Shorthand For" preferences.

File Types / Editors Preferences

The Preferences dialog box's File Types / Editors category defines which external applications to use for various file extensions.

Open in Code View

> Specifies the file types to be opened in Dreamweaver's Code view (defaults to *.js*, *.txt*, and *.asa*).

External Code Editor

> Specifies the external text editor optionally used to edit HTML and other code, typically HomeSite (Windows) or BBEdit (Macintosh), which ship with Dreamweaver on their respective platforms. The application chosen here appears in the Edit → Edit With... menu command and is accessible using Ctrl+E (Windows) or Cmd+E (Macintosh).

Reload Modified Files

> Determines whether to reload a document that has been modified outside of Dreamweaver, usually an image edited in Fireworks or a *.swf* file edited in Flash. Available options are:

Prompt

> Ask the user whether to reload modified files.

Never

> Don't reload modified files (and don't prompt the user).

Always

> Reload modified files without prompting the user.

Save on Launch

> Determines whether to resave a document when an external editor (such as Fireworks, BBEdit, or HomeSite) is launched to manipulate it. Available options are:

Prompt

> Ask the user whether to reload modified files.

Never

> Don't reload modified files (and don't prompt the user).

Always

> Reload modified files without prompting the user.

Extensions list

> A list of file types for which to set external editors. Select a file type from the list to set the corresponding external editor in the Editors column. Use the plus (+) and minus (–) buttons to add or remove file types. The most important ones to set are the *.png*, *.gif*, *.jpg*, *.jpe*, and *.jpeg* file types, typically edited with Fireworks.

Editors list

> A list of external editors for each file extension listed in the Extensions list. Use the plus (+) and minus (–) buttons to add or remove editors from the list. Multiple editors can be specified and the primary editor can be designated by clicking the Make Primary button. The primary and secondary editors appear

in the contextual menu. For example, you can right-click (Windows) or Ctrl-click (Macintosh) on a *.gif* image in the Document window and choose Edit With Fireworks 4 from the contextual menu.

Fonts / Encoding Preferences

The Preferences dialog box's Fonts / Encoding category configures the default display fonts.

Default Encoding

This preference specifies the character-encoding scheme, which sets the `charset` attribute of the `<meta>` tag (see Chapter 2). English and Western European languages should use the Western (Latin1) option.

Font Settings

This preference lets you choose an encoding scheme from the list to set its default font and point size for the proportional font, fixed font, and Code Inspector font. These settings do not affect the text displayed in the visitor's browser. Use the Text → Font and Text → Size commands, or the Property inspector, to adjust the font and point size that web site visitors see.

Proportional Font and Size

This setting determines the default font and point size for proportional text in Design view.

Fixed Font and Size

This setting determines the default font and point size for fixed-width text in Design view, such as preformatted text.

Code Inspector

This setting determines the default font and point size for text in Code view and the Code Inspector.

Highlighting Preferences

The Preferences dialog box's Highlighting category controls the highlight color when various elements are displayed in the Design pane. Table 18-2 lists the default colors.

Table 18-2: Highlighting colors

Option	Default	Controls the border of:
Editable Regions	#CCFFFF (light blue)	Editable regions of a template-based document
Locked Regions	#FFFFCC (light yellow)	Noneditable regions of a template-based document
Library Items	#FFFFCC (light yellow)	Instances of library items
Third-Party Tags	#CCFFFF (light blue)	Elements added by third-party tags

Invisible Elements Preferences

The Preferences dialog box's Invisible Elements category, seen in Figure 18-1, determines whether hidden elements are displayed in the Design pane.

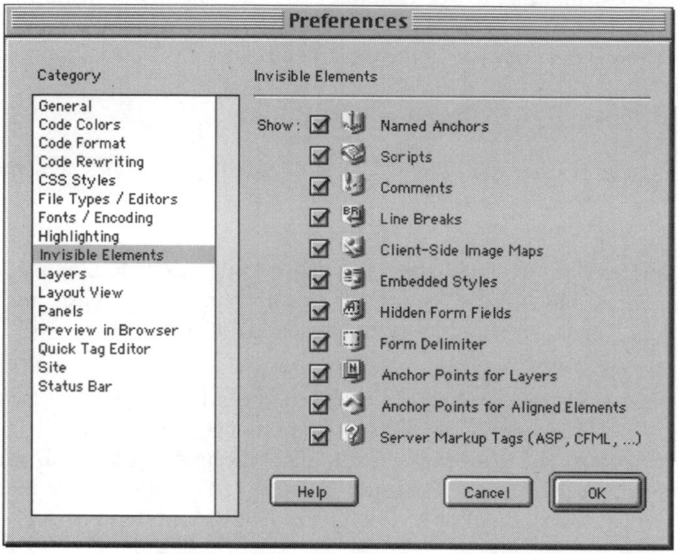

Figure 18-1: Invisible Elements icons

Table 18-3 lists the icon types for each invisible element. Also see the View →
Visual Aids → Invisible Elements menu command.

Table 18-3: Invisible Elements placeholders

Option	Displays a placeholder representing:
Named Anchors	Anchors of the form `<a name=" ">`.
Scripts	JavaScript or VBScript code embedded with `<script>` tags.
Comments	Comments indicated by `<!-- -->`.
Line Breaks	Line breaks created with ` ` tags.
Client-Side Image Maps	Client-side image maps (`<map>` tags).
Embedded Styles	Stylesheets (`<style>` tags) within the `<body>` tag. (Stylesheets within the `<head>` tag appear as a CSS Styles icon in the Head Content bar. See Chapter 10.)
Hidden Form Fields	Elements of type `<input type="hidden">`.
Form Delimiter	Elements of type `<form>` (Form delimiters are indicated by a dashed red line surrounding form elements, not by the icon shown in Figure 18-1.)
Anchor Points for Layers	Layers (`<div>`, and `<span>` tags). Layers implemented with `<layer>`, `<ilayer>` display a similar icon with an N instead of a C. See the Preferences dialog box's Layers category.
Anchor Points for Aligned Elements	Aligned elements, such as `<img align="left">`.
Server Markup Tags (ASP, CFML, …)	Third-party tags that have been inserted. See Chapter 20.

Layers Preferences

The Preferences dialog box's Layers category controls the default settings for newly created layers. See Chapter 4 for details on these options, which can be changed in the Property inspector when a layer is selected.

Tag
> Specifies the HTML tag—SPAN, DIV, LAYER, ILAYER—used to create layers. Use DIV (the default).

Visibility
> Specifies the visibility—default, inherit, visible, or hidden—of newly created layers. Use visible (the default) in most cases.

Width
> Sets the width of your layers created using Insert → Layer (ignored if you draw the layer using the Draw Layer tool in the Objects panel's Common category).

Height
> Sets the height of the layers created using Insert → Layer (ignored if you draw the layer using the Draw Layer tool in the Objects panel's Common category).

Background Color
> Sets the default background color for layers.

Background Image
> Sets the default background image for layers.

Nest when Created Within a Layer
> Allows the creation of nested layers (which are not well-supported in Netscape), such as `<layer><layer></layer></layer>`.

Netscape 4 Compatibility: Add Resize Fix when Inserting Layer
> Automatically inserts the `MM_reloadPage` function when a layer is added to a document. This function resizes layers in NN4 when the document window is resized. Also see Commands → Add/Remove Netscape Resize Fix.

Layout View Preferences

The Preferences dialog box's Layout View category configures the Table Layout view (View ▸ Table View ▸ Layout View) for editing layout tables. See Chapter 3 for details on layout tables.

Autoinsert Spacers
> Select the When Making Autostretch Tables radio button to use spacer images when creating tables that stretch to fit the user's browser window. The Never option causes columns to collapse if they are empty when an autostretch column is added.

Spacer Image
> Create or select a spacer image and specify the web site in which it will be used. Spacer images must use Site Root-Relative paths to work properly when uploaded to a server.

Table 18-4 lists the default color for various visual aids related to layout tables.

Table 18-4: Layer Color defaults

Option	Description	Default color
Cell Outline	Outline color of unselected cells	#0099FF (blue)
Cell Highlight	Outline color of a selected cell	#FF0000 (red)
Table Outline	Outline of a layout table	#009900 (greed)
Table Background	Color of unoccupied (empty) areas in a layout table	#DDDDDD (gray)

Panels Preferences

The Preferences dialog box's Panels category controls the stacking order of panels and the icons that appear in the Launcher bar (and Mini-Launcher).

Always on Top

A list of panels that should appear in front of the Document window. By default, all panels are selected (Assets, Behaviors, Code Inspector, CSS Styles, Frames, History, HTML Styles, Launcher, Layers, Objects, Properties, Reference, Timelines, and All Other Panels).

Show in Launcher

This preference specifies the icons to be shown in the Launcher bar (also shown in the Mini-launcher in the Document window's status bar if the Edit → Preferences → Status Bar → Show Launcher in Status Bar option is active). Use the plus (+) and minus (–) buttons to add or delete items and use the arrow buttons to change their order. By default, the list contains Site, Assets, HTML Styles, CSS Styles, Behaviors, History, and Code Inspector.

Preview in Browser Preferences

The Preferences dialog box's Preview in Browser category configures the list of web browsers available to preview and debug your Dreamweaver documents.

Browsers list

A list of the browsers configured to preview documents. The default browser, usually Internet Explorer or Netscape, is included in the list if it is present when Dreamweaver is installed. Use the plus (+) and minus (–) buttons to add and remove browsers from the list. Use the Edit button to specify the application path to a browser. You can specify more than two browsers, although only two are accessible via keyboard shortcuts.

Primary Browser

Enable this checkbox for the browser you wish to be your primary browser. Preview a web page in this browser by using File → Preview in Browser → *primary* (F12). Debug a web page's JavaScript in this browser by using File → Debug in Browser → *primary*, Alt+F12 (Windows), or Opt+F12 (Macintosh). The primary browser is also used to access Dreamweaver Help files under Help → Using Dreamweaver (F1).

Secondary Browser

Enable this checkbox for the browser you wish to be your secondary browser. Preview a web page in this browser by using File → Preview in Browser, Alt+F12 (Windows), or Opt+F12 (Macintosh). Debug in this browser by using File → Debug in Browser → *secondary*, Ctrl+Alt+F12 (Windows), or Cmd+Opt+F12 (Macintosh).

Preview Using Local Server (Windows Only)

This option allows you to use your locally running web server to preview your documents. Using a local server allows you to preview documents with server-side scripts and elements included.

Quick Tag Editor Preferences

The Preferences dialog box's Quick Tag Editor category configures the Quick Tag Editor (see Chapter 7).

Apply Changes Immediately While Editing

If enabled, this option applies changes you have made to your document with the Quick Tag Editor when using the Tab key to cycle between elements.

Enable Tag Hints

If enabled, a pop-up list of attributes for the current HTML tag appears when you type a space after the closing " of any attribute. To select from this list, double-click on the available option.

Tag Hints Delay

When Enable Tag Hints is enabled, this slider controls the delay before the Quick Tag Editor appears.

Site Preferences

The Preferences dialog box's Site category sets preferences that configure your site definition and Site window. See the Site → Define Sites → Edit option and Chapter 6 for many more site configuration options.

Always Show Local/Remote Files on the Left/Right

Specifies whether the Local Files or Remote Files pane should always be displayed in the Site window, and on which side (left or right). The preference defaults to display Local Files on the Right.

Dependent Files: Prompt on Get/Check Out

Optionally prompts you to download dependent files (images, scripts, stylesheets, etc.) used by the selected document when it is downloaded from the web server.

Dependent Files: Prompt on Put/Check In

Optionally prompts you to upload dependent files used by the selected document when it is uploaded to the server.

FTP Connection: Disconnect After...Minutes Idle

Determines the number of minutes after which an FTP connection is disconnected if there is no activity. The preference defaults to 30 Minutes, but a web server may disconnect inactive connections before then.

FTP Time Out...Seconds

Determines the period during which Dreamweaver attempts to make a connection to the specified FTP server. Dreamweaver gives up if the connection cannot be established in the allotted time. The default is 60 seconds.

Firewall Host

Use this preference to specify the proxy server name used to get through a firewall to upload information to your FTP server. Ask your webmaster for help.

Firewall Port

Provides the firewall port number (the default is 21) used to make an FTP connection. Ask your webmaster for help.

Save Files Before Putting

If enabled, this option saves all files before posting them to the remote site.

Define Sites

Click this button to go to the Define Sites dialog box, where you can configure existing sites or add new ones.

Status Bar Preferences

The Preferences dialog box's Status Bar category configures the Document window's status bar. (Select Edit Sizes from the Window Size Selector pop-up menu in the status bar to quickly access these preferences.)

Window Sizes

A list of available window sizes, useful for checking your page's appearance at various screen resolutions. Add to this list by using the Tab and Enter keys to create additional lines. The list appears in the Window Size Selector pop-up menu in the status bar, as discussed in Chapter 1.

Connection Speed

Specifies the connection speed used to calculate the estimated download time for a page, visible in the Document window's status bar. The options range from 14.4 Kbps (very slow) to 1500 Kbps (very fast DSL or T1 speeds). The default is 28.8 Kbps, but most users have at least 56 Kbps connections. The 64 and 128 Kbps settings represent single-channel and dual-channel ISDN connections, respectively.

 Bear in mind that 56 Kbps (kilobits per second) is equivalent to 7 KB/sec (kilobytes per second) and the effective throughput is often half the theoretical speed. Therefore, set the Connection Speed to 28.8 or 33.6 Kbps to approximate the realistic download time for 56 Kbps modems.

Show Launcher in Status Bar

If enabled, the icons for the panels shown in the Launcher are also shown in the Mini-launcher at the right of the status bar. Contents of the Mini-launcher can be set under Edit → Preferences → Panels → Show in Launcher.

The next chapter shows how to modify the Objects panels, Dreamweaver menus, and keyboard shortcuts.

CHAPTER 19

Customizing the Interface

Dreamweaver 4 offers greater extensibility and customization than its predecessors and competitors. Beyond the preferences covered in the previous chapter, you can customize Dreamweaver's menus, keyboard shortcuts, and Objects panel (downloadable extensions, described in Chapter 22, often modify these UI elements to give developers access to enhanced functionality).

Customizing Menus

Dreamweaver menus are defined in an XML-like syntax and stored in the *Dreamweaver 4/Configuration/Menus/menus.xml* file. To customize the menus, exit Dreamweaver and modify the *menus.xml* file in a text editor, such as WordPad (Windows) or BBEdit (Macintosh).

Do not edit the *menus.xml* file in an XML-savvy editor, as it is not a true XML file. It contains ampersands (&) that generate errors when the XML is parsed. Also, don't edit *menus.xml* in Dreamweaver. Don't change the existing id attributes within the file. If you make a mistake, restore *menus.xml* from the backup copy, *menus.bak*, provided by Macromedia in the same folder.

The *menus.xml* file defines menu bars, menus, and menu items. Example 19-1 shows an excerpt of the code that defines Dreamweaver's Edit menu.

Example 19-1: An excerpt of the Edit menu definition

```
<menu name="_Edit" id="DWMenu_MainSite_Edit">
   <menuitem name="Cu_t"     key="Cmd+X"   enabled="dw.canClipCut()"
           command="dw.clipCut()"   id="DWMenu_MainSite_Edit_Cut" />
```

Example 19-1: An excerpt of the Edit menu definition (continued)

```
<menuitem name="_Copy"    key="Cmd+C"  enabled="dw.canClipCopy()"
         command="dw.clipCopy()"  id="DWMenu_MainSite_Edit_Copy" />
<menuitem name="_Paste"  key="Cmd+V"  enabled="dw.canClipPaste()"
         command="dw.clipPaste()" id="DWMenu_MainSite_Edit_Paste" />
<separator />
<menuitem name="Select _All" key="Cmd+A"
         enabled="site.getCurrentSite() != ''"
         command="site.selectAll()"
         id="DWMenu_MainSite_Edit_SelectAll" />
</menu>
```

Although you can edit the *menus.xml* file directly, the Commands menu can be modified indirectly as described in the "Creating Custom Commands" of Chapter 7.

Let's see how to modify Dreamweaver's menus via the *menus.xml* file directly. After saving your changes to the *menus.xml* file, restart Dreamweaver to access your new menu commands.

Modifying Menus and Menu Items

As you can see from Example 19-1, the *menus.xml* file's tags are very similar to HTML tags. Note, for example, that <menu> and </menu> tags appear in pairs and <menuitem> tags are self-contained. You can move and add menus and menu items using these XML-like tags. See the section "About menus.xml tag syntax" under Help → Extending Dreamweaver for more information about the format and contents of this file.

Moving menus and menu items

To change the order of menus, select an entire menu object from its opening <menu> tag to its closing </menu> tag and all <menuitem> tags in between. Then use your text editor's cut and paste options to reorder menus as desired.

To move a menu item within a menu or to move a menu item to a new menu, select and cut the entire <menuitem> element, and then paste it into its new location.

Adding a menu item

To add a menu item to a menu, add a <menuitem> tag, which has the following attributes:

name (required)
   Specifies the name of the menu as it should appear in the menu. An underscore in the name indicates that the following letter can be used to access the menu item with the Alt key under Windows (the underscore is ignored on the Macintosh). For example, if the menu item name is C_ut and the menu name is _Edit, the item can be accessed using Alt+E, U under Windows in addition to any shortcut defined by the key attribute.

id (required)

The required menu item `id` must identify each menu item uniquely. If you add a menu item, ensure that its `id` doesn't match the `id` of existing menu items. Do not change the `id`s of built-in menu items, as doing so would make those items inaccessible to other areas of the program.

key

Specifies the keyboard shortcut for this menu item, including any combination of the following modifiers and special keys. (It is usually easier to modify keyboard commands using Edit → Keyboard Shortcuts.) Use a plus (+) sign to separate modifier keys. For example, Cmd+Opt+A indicates that the menu item's command should be executed when the user presses Ctrl+Alt+A (Windows) or Cmd+Opt+A (Macintosh). Dreamweaver automatically accommodates the differences between modifier keys on the two platforms:

Cmd

Indicates the Control key (Windows) or Command key (Macintosh)

Alt or Opt

Indicates the Alt key (Windows) or Option key (Macintosh)

Shift

Indicates the Shift key on both platforms

Ctrl

Specifies the Control key or Ctrl key on both platforms

Special keys

F1 through F12, PgDn, PgUp, Home, End, Ins, Del, Tab, Esc, BkSp, and Space

enabled

Specifies a JavaScript function that returns `true` if the menu item should be active. As seen in Example 19-1, the `dw.canClipCut()` function determines whether the Edit → Cut menu item should be active. Presumably, this function checks whether something is selected in the Document window. If not, there is nothing to cut, and the menu choice is inactivated.

checked

Specifies a JavaScript function that returns `true` if the menu item should have a checkmark appearing next to it, as seen in the View → Visual Aids submenu.

dynamic

Indicates a menu item that is configured dynamically by an HTML file. If you include the `dynamic` attribute, you must also supply a `file` attribute.

command

Specifies a JavaScript command that is executed when a user selects this menu item. A menu item must include either a `file` or `command` attribute.

file

Specifies an HTML file that controls the function of the menu item. For example, selecting Insert → Table opens the document *Dreamweaver 4/ Configuration/Commands/Format Table.htm*. That document may display a dialog box asking for additional input and run an appropriate JavaScript function. The `file` attribute overrides the `command`, `enabled`, and `checked` attributes. A menu item must include either a `file` or `command` attribute.

arguments

Provides a comma-separated list of arguments passed to the file specified by the `file` attribute. Enclose string arguments within single quotes (') inside the double quotes used to delimit the attribute's value, such as `arguments="'right', false"` (see Example 19-2).

domrequired

Indicates whether the Design view and Code view should be synchronized before executing the code associated with this menu item. If the value is `false`, the changes made to the document do not require synchronization before execution.

app

Specifies whether to show this menu item in `dreamweaver` (Dreamweaver) or `ultradev` (UltraDev) only. If this attribute is omitted, the menu item is shown in both applications.

platform

Specifies whether to show this menu item on either `mac` (Macintosh) or `win` (Windows) only. If this attribute is omitted, the menu item is shown on both platforms.

Adding a separator

You can add a horizontal separator to a menu by adding a `<separator />` element. Separators can appear between any two `<menuitem>` elements, but not between `<menu>` elements.

The `<separator />` element has one optional attribute, `app`, which can be set to `dreamweaver` or `ultradev` as described previously.

Adding a Menu

To create a new menu or submenu, add a `<menu>` element to the *menus.xml* file. The `<menu>` element has the following attributes:

name (required)

Specifies the name of the menu that appears in Dreamweaver's menu bar. An underscore in the name indicates that the following letter can be used to access the menu with the Alt key under Windows (the underscore is ignored on the Macintosh). For example, if the menu name is _Edit, it can be accessed using Alt+E under Windows.

id (required)

The required menu `id` must identify each menu uniquely. If you add a menu, ensure that its `id` doesn't match the `id` of existing menus. Do not change the `id`s of built-in menus, as it makes those items inaccessible to other areas of the program.

app

Specifies whether to show this menu in dreamweaver (Dreamweaver) or ultradev (UltraDev) only. If this attribute is omitted, the menu is shown in both applications.

platform

Specifies whether to show this menu on either mac (Macintosh) or win (Windows) only. If this attribute is omitted, the menu is shown on both platforms.

A <menu> element can contain one or more <menuitem> tags, as well as multiple <separator/> elements, and must be terminated with a </menu> tag. To create a submenu, nest a <menu> element within another <menu> element. The outermost <menu> element must be contained within a pair of <menubar> </menubar> tags.

Menu Bars

The *menus.xml* file defines a number of menu bars for Dreamweaver using the <menubar> tag. Many menu bars are used for contextual pop-up menus, although *menus.xml* also defines the main menu bar for the Macintosh and the Document window and Site window menu bars under Windows. The <menubar> attributes are explained here for developers writing third-party extensions (see Chapter 22) that define their own menu bars.

name (required)

The *menus.xml* file defines menu bars named "Main Window" and "Site Window," but menu bars are identified by id, not name. The menu bar name is required but can be set to "" (blank), such as for contextual menus.

id (required)

The required menu bar id must identify each menu bar uniquely. Do not change the ids of built-in menu bars, as it prevents them from being displayed in the program.

app

Specifies whether to show this menu bar in dreamweaver (Dreamweaver) or ultradev (UltraDev) only. If this attribute is omitted, the menu bar is shown in both applications.

platform

Specifies whether to show this menu bar on either mac (Macintosh) or win (Windows) only. For example, the Site window menu bar is defined for Windows only, as explained in Chapter 6. If this attribute is omitted, the menu item is shown on both platforms.

A <menubar> element must contain one or more <menu> tags and be terminated with a </menubar> tag. All <menu> elements must be contained within <menubar> elements.

Customizing Keyboard Shortcuts

You can modify Dreamweaver keyboard shortcuts by editing the *menus.xml* file, but it is easier to assign shortcuts via the Keyboard Shortcuts dialog box. Keyboard shortcuts are summarized in Appendix A. Some shortcuts may not work on some computers, particularly laptops, which intercept some function keys. If a shortcut does not work on the Macintosh, turn off the Hot Function Key option in the Keyboard Control Panel.

The Keyboard Shortcuts Dialog Box

Use the Edit → Keyboard Shortcuts command to open the Keyboard Shortcuts dialog box shown in Figure 19-1.

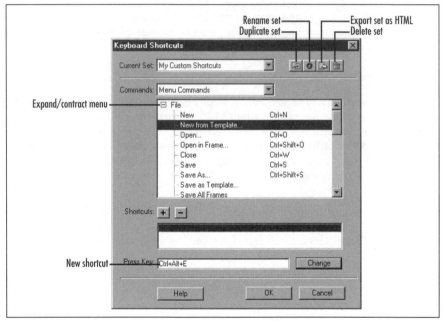

Figure 19-1: The Keyboard Shortcuts dialog box

This dialog box includes options to customize and manage keyboard shortcut *sets* (i.e., a collection of keyboard shortcuts):

Current Set
> Choose from one of the factory sets—BBEdit, Dreamweaver 3, or HomeSite—that emulate the keyboard shortcuts of other programs, or select Macromedia Standard (the default DW4 shortcuts). Custom sets that you define also appear in this pop-up list.

Commands
> After selecting a custom set from the Current Set pop-up list, select which menu bar to modify from the Commands pop-up list. The available options differ slightly between Windows and the Macintosh.

> *Menu Commands*
>> Dreamweaver's main menu bar commands (positioned at the top of the Macintosh monitor or appearing in the Document window under Windows).

Site Menu Commands (Windows only)

Site window menu bar commands. There is no separate Site window menu bar on the Macintosh. See Chapter 6 for details.

Code Editing

Commands that work in the Document window's Code view (also apply to the Code Inspector).

Document Editing

Commands that work in the Document window's Design view.

Site Window (Windows only)

Additional shortcut keys that work when the Site window is active but don't rely on the Site window menu bar. These shortcuts are included in the Document Editing category on the Macintosh.

Menu list

Use the plus (+) icons (Windows) or triangles (Macintosh) next to the menu names, to expand a menu and display the items within it. Select the menu item that you want to modify.

Shortcuts

This field lists the current shortcut for the selected menu item. Click the plus (+) button to add multiple keyboard shortcuts for the same menu command. Use the minus (-) button to remove keyboard shortcuts.

Press Key

Once you've selected the menu item to modify, click in the Press Key field to make it active. Press one or more keys to be used for the keyboard shortcut, such as the function keys or Ctrl+Shift+Q. Dreamweaver fills in the mnemonic codes in the Press Key field for you (don't attempt to type C-t-r-l to specify the Ctrl key, just press the Ctrl key). Click the Change button to replace the currently selected line in the Shortcuts field with the new shortcut specified in the Press Key field (if the Press Key field is blank, Dreamweaver erases the current keyboard shortcut).

Define a keyboard shortcut for each menu option as desired. Click the OK button to save your changes or the Cancel button to abort them.

 You cannot modify the keyboard shortcuts in a built-in (factory) set. Duplicate a set using the Duplicate Set icon, and then make changes to the duplicate set.

Managing Custom Keyboard Shortcuts

When you enter a keyboard shortcut in the Press Key field of the Keyboard Shortcuts dialog box, Dreamweaver tells you whether the shortcut is already in use. Although the Press Key field is a convenient way to check if a keyboard shortcut is available, it isn't completely reliable. It reports keyboard shortcuts used on either Windows or Macintosh, even if they aren't active on the current platform.

To use a keyboard shortcut already assigned to a <menuitem> tag, remove the key="*shortcut*" attribute from that tag in the *menus.xml* file. The same keyboard shortcut can be used for different purposes on different platforms (Macintosh or Windows) using the <menuitem> tag's platform attribute. The same keyboard shortcut can be used for different applications (Dreamweaver or UltraDev) using the <menuitem> tag's app attribute. Avoid reassigning the Ctrl+F9 and Ctrl+F10 shortcuts (Windows) and the Cmd+F9 and Cmd+F10 shortcuts (Macintosh) because they are used in Dreamweaver UltraDev to open the Server Behaviors and Data Bindings panels.

You can export the current shortcut set using the Export Set as HTML icon in the Keyboard Shortcuts dialog box. The exported HTML file displays all menu commands, including those with keyboard shortcuts. The document can be printed from your browser or printed from Microsoft Word. Search for "Keyboard Shortcut Matrix" in the Dreamweaver Help (F1) to find unused keyboard shortcut combinations.

The Rename Set icon (see Figure 19-1) renames the currently selected custom keyboard set but does not permit you to rename a factory set. The Delete Set icon does not delete the current keyboard set; rather, it displays the Delete Set dialog box, which lists keyboard sets that can be deleted. Factory sets cannot be deleted, so they are not shown in the list. The currently active set cannot be deleted either, so switch to another set before attempting to delete the set currently in use.

Custom keyboard shortcut sets are stored in *.xml* files in the *Dreamweaver 4/ Configuration/Menus/Custom Sets* folder. To share your keyboard shortcuts with others, copy the corresponding *.xml* files to the correct folder on another computer.

Keyboard Shortcuts in the menus.xml File

You can also modify keyboard shortcuts by editing the *menus.xml* file directly. Earlier, we saw how to define keyboard shortcuts using the key attribute of a <menuitem> tag. The *menus.xml* file also defines keyboard shortcuts using the <shortcutlist> and <shortcut> tags as shown in Example 19-2.

Example 19-2: Sample keyboard shortcut definitions

```
<shortcutlist id="DWMainWindow">
  <shortcut key="Cmd+Shift+Z" file="Menus/MM/Edit_Clipboard.htm"
    arguments="'redo'" id="DWShortcuts_Edit_Redo" />
  <shortcut key="Opt+BkSp"    file="Menus/MM/Edit_Clipboard.htm"
    arguments="'undo'" id="DWShortcuts_Edit_Undo" />
  <shortcut key="Opt+F4" command="dw.quitApplication()"
    name="Quit Application" id="DWShortcuts_Main_Quit" />
  <shortcut key="Cmd+U" command="dw.showPreferencesDialog()"
    id="DWShortcuts_Edit_Preferences" />
```

Example 19-2: Sample keyboard shortcut definitions (continued)

```
  <shortcut key="Cmd+Right" file="Menus/MM/Accelerators_Main.htm"
    arguments="'right', false" name="Go to Next Word"
    id="DWShortcuts_Main_CmdRight" />
</shortcutlist>
```

The <shortcutlist> tag

The <shortcutlist> element is used to define a group of keyboard shortcuts. It has three attributes:

id (required)

> The required shortcut list id must identify each shortcut list uniquely and should match the id of the corresponding menu bar or contextual menu with which the shortcuts are associated. Do not change the ids of the built-in shortcuts lists—DWMainWindow, DWMainSite, DWTimelineContext, and DWHTMLContext—as doing so prevents them from working.

app

> Specifies whether to enable the shortcut list in **dreamweaver** (Dreamweaver) or **ultradev** (UltraDev) only. If this attribute is omitted, the shortcuts list is available in both applications.

platform

> Specifies whether to enable the shortcut list on either **mac** (Macintosh) or **win** (Windows) only. If this attribute is omitted, the shortcuts list is available on both platforms.

The <shortcutlist> tag can contain one or more <shortcut> tags. It can also contain one or more comments of the form <!-- -->.

The <shortcut> tag

The <shortcut> element identifies an individual keyboard shortcut that is associated with a Dreamweaver command or menu item. Eight attributes can be set for a <shortcut> element:

id (required)

> The required shortcut id must identify each shortcut uniquely. If you add a shortcut, ensure that its id doesn't match the id of existing shortcuts. Do not change the ids of built-in shortcuts, as doing so prevents them from working.

name

> The shortcut name, such as "Open", appears in the Keyboard Shortcuts dialog box for the benefit of users. Dreamweaver identifies shortcuts by id, not name, but you should provide a meaningful name as well.

key

> Specifies the key combination for this shortcut as described earlier in the "Adding a menu item" section.

app

Specifies whether to enable the shortcut in dreamweaver (Dreamweaver) or ultradev (UltraDev) only. If this attribute is omitted, the shortcut is available in both applications.

platform

Specifies whether to enable the shortcut on either mac (Macintosh) or win (Windows) only. If this attribute is omitted, the shortcut is available on both platforms.

command

Specifies a JavaScript command that is executed when this keyboard shortcut is used. A shortcut must include either a file or command attribute.

file

Specifies an HTML file that controls the function of the keyboard shortcut, as described earlier in the "Adding a menu item" section.

arguments

Provides a comma-separated list of arguments passed to the file specified by the file attribute. Enclose string arguments within single quotes (') inside the double quotes used to delimit the attribute's value, such as arguments="'right', false" (see Example 19-2).

A <shortcutlist> can contain as many <shortcut> elements as desired. Save the *menus.xml* file changes in your text editor and then restart Dreamweaver for the changes to take effect.

Customizing the Objects Panel

In earlier chapters, we used the Objects panel to insert many built-in objects into an HTML document. You can add a custom icon to the Objects panel to insert any object. The Objects panel offers greater flexibility than library items, which insert HTML code only. To create a new object for the Objects panel, create an HTML document, including JavaScript that inserts your object into the current document.

Basing your new object on one of the existing objects in the *Dreamweaver 4/ Configuration/Objects* folder is your most convenient option. Within that folder are subfolders corresponding to the seven default categories of the Objects panel (Characters, Common, Forms, Frames, Head, Invisibles, and Special) plus a Tools folder for the Draw Layout Table and Draw Layout Cell tools that are always visible in the Objects panel

---

 The subfolder in which an object file is placed determines the category under which it appears in the Objects panel. Items can be moved between folders, and folders can be renamed.

Search for "Creating a simple object" under Help → Using Dreamweaver (F1) for an example of adding a simple object to the Objects panel. Example 19-3 shows the *Button.htm* file from the *Configuration/Objects/Forms* directory.

Example 19-3: A sample object definition file

```
<HTML><HEAD>
<!-- Copyright 1999 Macromedia, Inc. All rights reserved. -->
<TITLE>Insert Button</TITLE>
<SCRIPT LANGUAGE="javascript" SRC="../../Shared/MM/Scripts/CMN/docInfo.js">
</SCRIPT>
<SCRIPT LANGUAGE="javascript" SRC="../../Shared/MM/Scripts/CMN/localText.js">
</SCRIPT>
<SCRIPT LANGUAGE="javascript" SRC="formInsert.js"></SCRIPT>
<SCRIPT LANGUAGE="javascript">
function isDOMRequired() {
    // Return false, indicating that this object is available in code view.
    return false;
}
function objectTag() {
  return returnFormTag(document.body.innerHTML);
}
</SCRIPT>
</HEAD>
<BODY>
<INPUT TYPE="submit" NAME="Submit" VALUE="Submit">
</BODY>
</HTML>
```

Each object file uses JavaScript, often in an external *.js* file, to implement the object's functionality. For example, the JavaScript file *formInsert.js* contains code that controls the insertion of form objects. The <body> element of Example 19-3 specifies the HTML to be inserted into the Document window (in this case, a Submit button) when the object is accessed from the Objects panel.

An image (*.gif*) file is associated with each HTML file. This *.gif* file contains the graphic icon to appear in the Objects panel and can be created in Fireworks, for example. Icons should be no larger than 18 × 18 pixels (oversized icons are cropped). The *.gif* file must have the same name as the *.htm* file, except for the extension. For example, the image associated with the *Button.htm* file is named *Button.gif.*

With your *.gif* and *.htm* files saved in the desired subfolder of the *Configuration/ Objects* folder, restart Dreamweaver. Your custom object button should appear in the Objects panel under the category corresponding to the folder in which it is stored. Clicking your custom icon should insert the custom object into your page. The Objects panel can be configured to show icons, text, or both using the preferences under Edit → Preferences → General → Objects Panel.

Downloadable extensions that insert an object, such as the Atomz Search extension described in Chapter 22, typically add new categories and icons to the Objects panel. Extensions may also add new entries to the Insert menu or Command menu to insert an object or access the extension's features. After installation, the Extension Manager tells you if you must restart Dreamweaver to access the new features provided by an extension. Some extensions can be reloaded by Ctrl-clicking (Windows) or Opt-clicking (Macintosh) the category selector in the Objects panel and choosing Reload Extensions.

Adding Characters to the Objects Panel

The icons in the Objects panel's Characters category insert special characters, such as a copyright symbol, as described in the "Characters" section of Chapter 2. Procedure 7 demonstrates how to add a custom character, such as þ (a small Icelandic thorn character), to the Objects panel's Character category.

Procedure 7

1. Use File → Open to open one of the *.htm* files, such as *Copyright.htm*, from the *Dreamweaver4/Configuration/Objects/Characters* directory.

2. Use Code view (View → Code) to examine the JavaScript that inserts a named entity, such as ©, into your document.

3. Modify line 18 of the script, such as return "þ";. (Activate line numbers using View → Code View Options → Line Numbers.)

4. Resave the file in the same directory, but with a new name, such as *thorn.htm*.

5. Create an 18 × 18–pixel GIF image, perhaps using Fireworks, to act as an icon in the Character category view of the Objects panel.

6. Save the GIF file in the same directory with a name to match the *.htm* file, such as *thorn.gif*.

When you restart Dreamweaver, your new icon will appear in the Objects panel's Character category. Use only valid named entities or character entity codes, approved by the World Wide Web Consortium (W3C). Invalid entities will appear incorrectly, or not at all, when viewed in a web browser. Not all web browsers and operating systems display entities in the same way. See Appendix B for details.

The next chapter covers customizing Dreamweaver's dialog boxes and default document template.

CHAPTER 20

Customizing the Document Template and Dialog Boxes

You can customize Dreamweaver's default document template and the options that appear in Dreamweaver's dialog boxes. Both of the customizations covered in this chapter apply globally to your entire Dreamweaver installation, not just the current site.

Customizing the Default Document

New, blank documents are actually based on a default document template; therefore, any modification to the document template affects every newly created document. You can modify the default document template to reflect the basic page design of your site. If you work on multiple sites, you may prefer to create custom templates for each one (see Chapter 8).

Dreamweaver's default document template is stored in the file named *Dreamweaver 4/Configuration/Templates/default.html*. Prior to overwriting your default document template, make a backup copy, rename it to *old_default.html*, and store it in the same folder as the original. Then open *default.html* in Dreamweaver (use File → Open, not File → New From Template).

As you can see in Figure 20-1, the default document template includes <title>, <head>, and <meta> tags, and an empty <body> tag. It uses a white background and black text.

Edit the *default.html* file as you would any HTML file; add any content that you want to include in all documents (text, images, or stylesheet information). If you work on multiple sites, make only changes that are common to all sites. After you customize *default.html* and restart Dreamweaver, every newly created document will inherit your changes.

Figure 20-2 shows a new document based on a modified template. Note the copyright notice, a meta tag that identifies the developer, and the modified text and background colors.

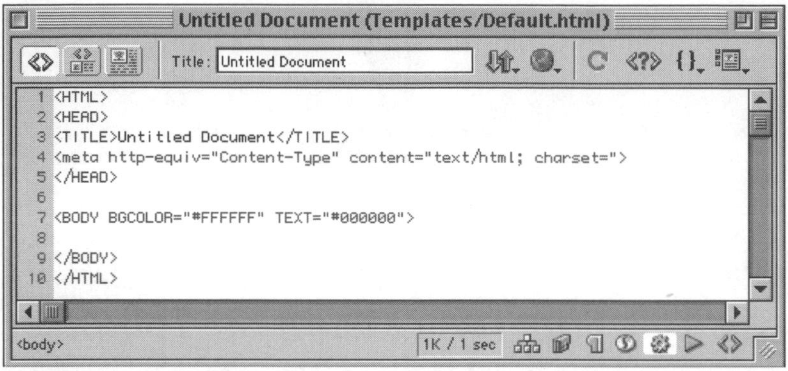

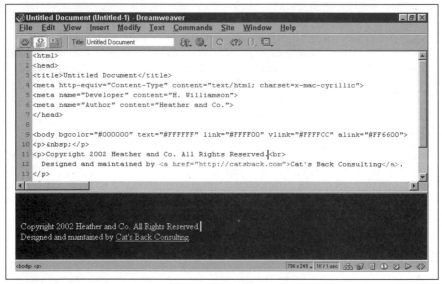

Figure 20-1: The default.html Dreamweaver document template

Figure 20-2: Document based on revised template

Although the changes shown in Figure 20-2 are minimal, you can make much more elaborate changes, as shown in Figure 20-3. Save your changes to the default document template using File → Save, not File → Save As Template.

Remember that you can save any file as a template using File → Save As Template and then base a new document on the template using File → New From Template. Modifying the *default.html* file is just an easy way to get a head start each time you create a new document, or even a document template.

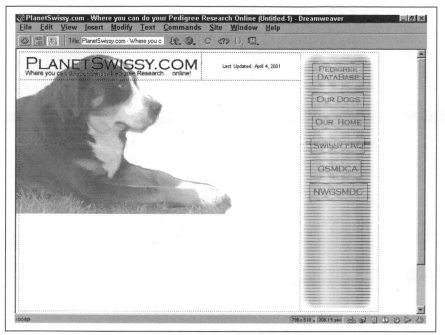

Figure 20-3: Document based on extensively modified template

![owl icon] You can modify the *default.html* file to act as the basis for creating XHTML-compliant pages as described in Appendix C.

The *default.html* file does not include locked and editable regions like the templates described in Chapter 8. When a new document is derived from it, all items are editable and unwanted items can be deleted.

Customizing Dreamweaver Dialog Boxes

Dreamweaver dialog boxes are created using HTML forms stored in the *Dreamweaver 4/Configuration/Commands* directory. You can modify these HTML files to alter the appearance of Dreamweaver's dialog boxes permanently. Alterations to these dialog boxes are reflected across all Dreamweaver sites.

Table 20-1 lists the files used to implement many of Dreamweaver's menu options. JavaScript within the HTML file, and in external *.js* files, controls the dialog boxes' functionality. You can edit these files to change the appearance and behavior of Dreamweaver's dialog boxes and menu commands. Most of these files are stored in the *Dreamweaver 4/Configuration/Commands* directory. Files whose paths begin with *Shared* are located in the *Dreamweaver 4/Configuration/Shared* directory and are used by multiple dialog boxes.

Table 20-1: Dialog box HTML and JS files

Menu command or dialog box	HTML and JS files used
File → Save	_afterSave.htm _beforeSave.htm
File → Open	_onOpen.htm
Commands → Add/Remove Netscape Resize Fix	Add Remove NS Resize Fix.htm addNSResizeFix.htm Add Remove NS Resize Fix.js Shared/MM/Scripts/CMN/localText.js Shared/MM/Scripts/CMN/DOM.js
Alert dialog boxes	AlertDS.htm AlterDS.js
Commands → Apply Source Formatting	Apply Source Formatting.htm Source Formatting.js
Commands → Check Page for Accessibility	Check for Accessibility.htm Check for Accessibility.js
Commands → Clean Up HTML	Clean Up HTML.htm Clean Up HTML.js Shared/MM/Scripts/CMN/DOM.js Shared/MM/Scripts/CMN/localText.js Shared/MM/Scripts/CMN/errMsg.js
Commands → Clean Up Word HTML	Clean Up Word HTML.htm Clean Up Word HTML.js Source Formatting.js Shared/MM/Scripts/CMN/displayHelp.js Shared/MM/Scripts/CMN/UI.js Shared/MM/Scripts/CMN/DOM.js Shared/MM/Scripts/Class/classCheckbox.js Shared/MM/Scripts/Class/TabControlClass.js Shared/MM/Scripts/CMN/localText.js Shared/MM/Scripts/CMN/errMsg.js
Confirmation dialog boxes	confirmDS.htm confirmDS.js
Commands → Create Web Photo Album	Create Web Photo Album.htm Create Web Photo Album.js Shared/MM/Scripts/CMN/localText.js Shared/MM/Scripts/CMN/UI.js Shared/MM/Scripts/CMN/string.js Shared/MM/Scripts/CMN/displayHelp.js
Insert → Date	Date.htm Date.js Date_beforeSave.htm Shared/MM/Scripts/CMN/localText.js Shared/MM/Scripts/CMN/UI.js Shared/MM/Scripts/CMN/dateID.js Shared/MM/Scripts/CMN/displayHelp.js
File → Debug in Browser	debugSyntaxResults.htm debugSyntaxResults.js

Table 20-1: Dialog box HTML and JS files (continued)

Menu command or dialog box	HTML and JS files used
Edit → Keyboard Shortcuts	*delete set.htm* *delete set.js* *duplicate set.htm* *duplicate set.js* *Keyboard Shortcuts.html* *Keyboard Shortcuts.js* *Processing.htm* *rename set.htm* *rename set.js*
File → Design Notes	*Design Notes.js* *Design Notes_onOpen.htm* *Design Notes_onOpen.js* *DesignNotesMultiFile.htm* *DesignNotesMultiFile.js*
File → Export → Export Table	*Export Table.htm* *Export Table.js* *Shared/MM/Scripts/CMN/UI.js* *Shared/MM/Scripts/CMN/localText.js* *Shared/MM/Scripts/CMN/displayHelp.js*
Help → Extension Manager	*Extension Help.htm* *Extension Help.js* *Manage Extensions.htm* *Manage Extensions.js*
Insert → Interactive Image → Fireworks HTML	*Fireworks HTML.htm* *Fireworks HTML.js* *PasteFireworksHTML.htm* *PasteFireworksHTML.js* *Shared/MM/Scripts/CMN/string.js* *Shared/MM/Scripts/insertFireworksHTML.js* *Shared/MM/Scripts/Class/FileClass.js* *Shared/MM/Scripts/CMN/localText.js* *Shared/MM/Scripts/CMN/displayHelp.js*
Insert → Interactive Image → Flash Button	*Flash Button.htm* *Flash Button.js* *Flash Button.xml* *Shared/MM/Scripts/CMN/docInfo.js* *Shared/MM/Scripts/Class/FileClass.js* *Shared/MM/Scripts/Class/ListControlClass.js* *Shared/MM/Scripts/CMN/localText.js* *Shared/MM/Scripts/CMN/string.js* *Shared/MM/Scripts/CMN/displayHelp.js* *Shared/MM/Scripts/flashObjects.js*
Insert → Interactive Image → Flash Text	*Flash Text.htm* *Flash Text.js* *Shared/MM/Scripts/Class/ListControlClass.js* *Shared/MM/Scripts/Class/ImageButtonClass.js* *Shared/MM/Scripts/CMN/displayHelp.js* *Shared/MM/Scripts/flashObjects.js* *Shared/MM/Scripts/CMN/localText.js*

Table 20-1: Dialog box HTML and JS files (continued)

Menu command or dialog box	HTML and JS files used
Commands → Format Table	*Format Table.btm* *Format Table.js* *Shared/MM/Scripts/CMN/localText.js* *Shared/MM/Scripts/CMN/docInfo.js* *Shared/MM/Scripts/CMN/displayHelp.js*
File → Import → Import Table Data	*Import Table Data.btm* *Tabular Data.btm* *TabularData.js* *Shared/MM/Scripts/CMN/UI.js* *Shared/MM/Scripts/CMN/file.js* *Shared/MM/Scripts/CMN/localText.js*
Insert → Interactive Image → Rollover Image	*Rollover.btm* *Rollover.js* *Shared/MM/Scripts/CMN/errmsg.js* *Shared/MM/Scripts/CMN/string.js* *Shared/MM/Scripts/CMN/localText.js*
Insert → Interactive Image → Navigation Bar	*Insert Nav Bar.btm* *Modify Nav Bar.btm* *NavigationBar.js* *Shared/MM/Scripts/Class/ListControlClass.js* *Shared/MM/Scripts/navBar.js* *Shared/MM/Scripts/CMN/localText.js* *Shared/MM/Scripts/CMN/UI.js* *Shared/MM/Scripts/CMN/string.js* *Shared/MM/Scripts/CMN/Handler.js*
Insert → Special Characters → Other	*InsertEnt.btm* *InsertEnt.js* *Shared/MM/Scripts/CMN/localText.js* *Shared/MM/Scripts/CMN/displayHelp.js*
Insert → Form Objects → Jump Menu	*Jump Menu.btm* *Jump Menu.js* *Shared/MM/Scripts/CMN/localText.js* *Shared/MM/Scripts/jumpMenuUI.js* *Shared/MM/Scripts/CMN/docInfo.js* *Shared/MM/Scripts/CMN/string.js* *Shared/MM/Scripts/CMN/form.js* *Shared/MM/Scripts/CMN/file.js*
View → Table View → Layout View	*Layout Cell.btm* *Layout Table.btm* *layoutViewIntro.btm* *layoutViewIntro.js,* *layoutViewIntroStandard.gif*
Help → Lessons	*Lessions.btm*
Command → Optimize Image in Fireworks	*Optimize Image in Fireworks.html* *Optimize Image in Fireworks.js*
Commands → Set Color Scheme	*Set Color Scheme.btm* *colorSchemes.js* *Set Color Scheme.js* *Shared/MM/Scripts/CMN/localText.j*

Table 20-1: Dialog box HTML and JS files (continued)

Menu command or dialog box	HTML and JS files used
Commands → Sort Table	*Sort Table.btm*
	Sort Table.js
	Shared/MM/Scripts/CMN/docInfo.js
	Shared/MM/Scripts/CMN/localText.js

Consider the Insert Rollover Image dialog box implemented with the *Rollover.btm* file shown in Figure 20-4.

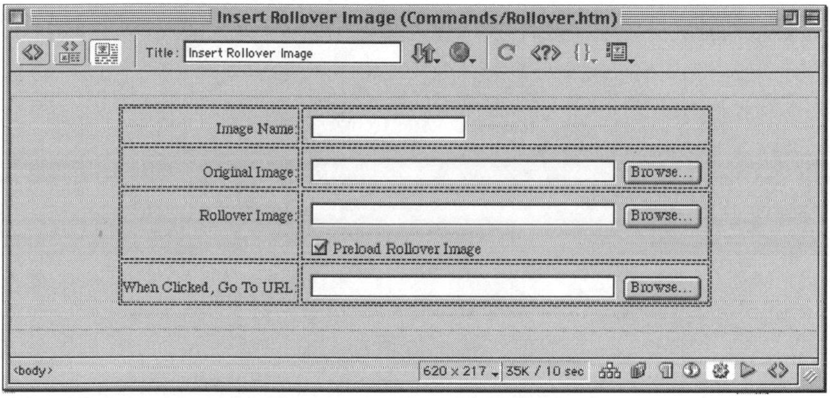

Figure 20-4: The Rollover.htm file

Notice that the options in this form match those used in the Insert Rollover Image dialog box shown in Figure 20-5.

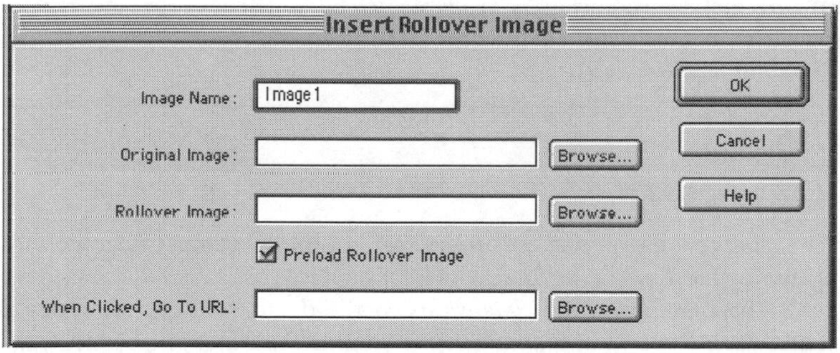

Figure 20-5: The Insert Rollover Image dialog box

Open the *Rollover.btm* file in Dreamweaver to see the HTML code used to implement the dialog box and the JavaScript used to manipulate the contents of this form (*Rollover.btm* can be found in the *Dreamweaver 4/Configuration/Commands* folder).

Figure 20-6 shows a modified version of the dialog box created by adding the following HTML code to the *Rollover.htm* file. As always, you should make a backup copy of your original files before making any changes.

```
<p><i><b>
   Do not place any rollover images in documents intended
   for 3.0 and earlier browsers.
</b></i></p>
```

You must save the file and restart Dreamweaver before the changes will be reflected in the dialog box, as seen in Figure 20-6.

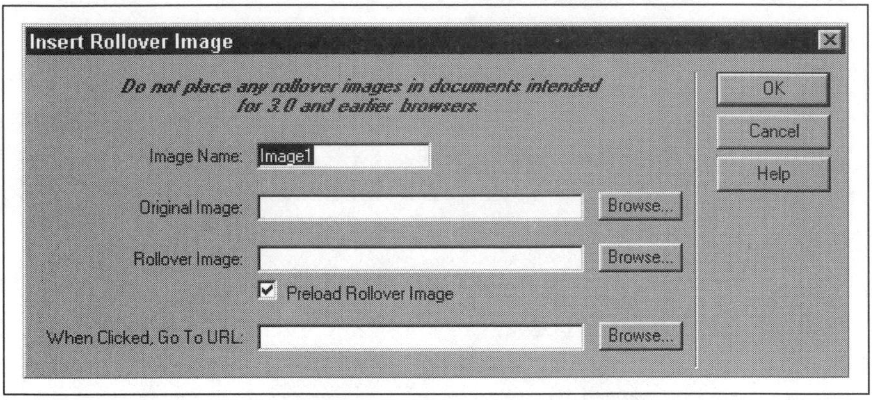

![Insert Rollover Image dialog box with the message "Do not place any rollover images in documents intended for 3.0 and earlier browsers." Image Name: Image1, Original Image with Browse button, Rollover Image with Browse button, Preload Rollover Image checkbox checked, When Clicked, Go To URL with Browse button, and OK, Cancel, Help buttons.]

Figure 20-6: Modified Insert Rollover Image dialog box

You can modify any dialog box to add functionality, remove functionality, or add helpful information as we did in the Insert Rollover Image dialog box.

 To make customization available to other users, copy the revised files manually to each computer's *Dreamweaver 4/Configuration/ Commands* folder.

The Extensions.txt File

The *Extensions.txt* file in the *Dreamweaver 4/Configuration* folder controls the pop-up list of file types available in the Open file dialog box (accessed via File → Open). The first line of the *Extensions.txt* file determines the file types shown by default. Each line of the file contains a comma-separated list of file extensions (in capital letters) followed by a colon and a description. For example, you can add this line to the *Extensions.txt* file to create a new category called Image Files:

```
JPG,JPE,JPEG,GIF,PNG:Image Files
```

Note that the All Documents category shows a more limited range of extensions than the All Files (*.*) category. Remember to back up the *Extensions.txt* file before making changes, and restart Dreamweaver to put the changes into effect.

As you can see, Dreamweaver's interface is extremely flexible and extensible. In Chapter 22, we'll cover some behaviors used to extend Dreamweaver. Carried to its logical extreme, you can build an entirely new application on top of the Dreamweaver platform, as was done in the case of Dreamweaver UltraDev.

The next chapter covers Dreamweaver's integration with server-side languages.

CHAPTER 21

Displaying Third-Party Tags

Server-side processing technologies such as Active Server Pages (ASP), ColdFusion (CF), JavaServer Pages (JSP), and PHP insert non-HTML code into HTML documents and other standalone files. Dreamweaver uses third-party tag definition files to display these non-HTML tags. If using ASP, JSP, or ColdFusion, consider using Dreamweaver UltraDev, which offers a simplified interface for creating server-side scripts. (Future versions of UltraDev will probably offer support for PHP.)

Third-Party Tag Files

The *Dreamweaver 4/Configuration/ThirdPartyTags* folder contains the tag definition files that support ASP, JSP, ColdFusion and PHP tags. (This folder also contains GIF images used as placeholder icons for third-party tags.) The tag definition files are in XML format and can be modified to enhance Dreamweaver's recognition of server-side language tags.

If you are using a server-side language not supported by Dreamweaver, you can create additional tag files that tell Dreamweaver how to read and display third-party tags. (If creating a new tag definition file, give it an *.xml* extension and place it in the *ThirdPartyTag* folder.) After creating or updating a tag definition file, restart Dreamweaver to load the new tag definitions. To prevent Dreamweaver from rewriting code in external files, add the third-party script's file extension to the "Never Rewrite Code in File with Extensions" field under Edit → Preferences → Code Rewriting. See the section "Code Rewriting Preferences" in Chapter 18 for more information. The formatting options for third-party tags are also controlled by the *SourceFormat.txt* file, discussed in the "Code Format Preferences" section in Chapter 18.

<tagspec> Elements

Each tag definition file contains one or more <tagspec> elements. A <tagspec> element does not define a third-party tag (that's up to the third-party language itself), it just tells Dreamweaver how to interpret and display third-party tags. See "Customizing the interpretation of third-party tags" under Help → Extending Dreamweaver for additional guidance.

Dreamweaver can interpret two types of third-party tags:

HTML-style tags
So-called normal *HTML-style tags* are third-party tags that look like typical HTML tags. HTML-style tags may use an opening and closing tag such as `<tagname>` and `</tagname>` to enclose data (similar to matching HTML block tags such as `<p></p>`). HTML-style tags can also be empty. In this case, similar to an HTML `<img>` tag, they can contain attributes but do not surround content and do not use a closing tag. ColdFusion uses HTML-style tags.

String-delimited tags
String-delimited tags are third-party tags that are delimited by different characters than HTML tags. For example, ASP tags start with `<%` and end with `%>`. Therefore, the `<tagspec>` for string-delimited tags includes the `start_string` and `end_string` attributes to specify the delimiters that mark the beginning and end of the tag. Dreamweaver ignores the information between these delimiters. String-delimited tags are similar to empty HTML-style tags (such as `<img>`) because they do not surround content and do not use a closing tag.

The valid attributes and their values within the `<tagspec>` differ depending on whether the `<tagspec>` element describes an HTML-style tag or a string-delimited tag. Dreamweaver uses the attributes to validate or parse the third-party tags (or refrain from doing so, if instructed). The attributes are as follows:

tag_name
Specifies the name for the tag. For HTML-style tags, this attribute is the name of the tag, such as `CFABORT`. For string-delimited tags, the `tag_name` is used solely to determine if a Property inspector can edit the tag. (Custom Property inspectors can be written to display and adjust third-party tags, as described in the "A simple Property inspector example" section under Help → Extending Dreamweaver.) A Property inspector can indicate that it understands a tag by including its `tag_name` surrounded by asterisks on its first line of code. For example, because ASP tags use `tag_name="asp"`, Property inspectors that can understand ASP tags should include `*asp*` on their first line.

tag_type
Specifies whether an HTML-style tag can include contents between its opening and closing tags (`"nonempty"`) or is empty (`"empty"`). This attribute is ignored for string-delimited tags.

render_contents
Specifies whether to display the tag's contents (`"true"`) or a placeholder icon (`"false"`) in Design view. This attribute is required if you are using `tag_type="nonempty"`, but is ignored for string-delimited tags.

content_model
Specifies where a tag can appear in an HTML file and what type of content it can contain. Four values are possible:

block_model
> A tag that can contain block-level elements and appear in the HTML document body only.

head_model
> A tag that can contain text and appear in the HTML document head only.

marker_model
> A tag that can appear anywhere in the HTML document, such as in the head or body section, and can contain any HTML code that is valid within that section.

script_model
> A tag that contains third-party script information and can be located anywhere in the document. Dreamweaver ignores the content of tags that use this model, such as ColdFusion tags.

start_string
> Specifies the starting delimiter for a string-delimited tag, such as `"<%"` for ASP tags. This attribute is required for string-delimited tags.

end_string
> Specifies the ending delimiter for a string-delimited tag, such as `"%>"` for ASP tags. This attribute is required for string-delimited tags.

detect_in_attribute
> Specifies whether Dreamweaver ignores everything between `start_string` and `end_string` (for a string-delimited tag) or between opening and closing tags (for an HTML-style tag), even inside attribute names and values. Use `true` for string-delimited tags. The default is `false`.

parse_attributes
> Specifies whether to parse element attributes. The default is `true`. Set it to `false` if the element's attributes don't use the typical `name="value"` format and thus cannot be parsed by Dreamweaver. For example, the CFIF tag, which implements a logical *if* statement in ColdFusion, has attributes that aren't name/value pairs and instead look like `<CFIF x is 5>`. Regardless, this option does not apply to string-delimited tags, whose attributes are never parsed.

icon
> Specifies the filename of the GIF image that serves as the placeholder icon in Design view. (The *.gif* files are typically stored in the *ThirdPartyTag* folder alongside the tag definition files.)

icon_width
> Specifies the icon width, in pixels. Most icons are no more than 18 pixels wide.

icon_height
> Specifies the icon height, in pixels. Most icons are no more than 18 pixels high.

Custom Tag Display in Design View

The `tag_type` and `render_contents` attributes of the `<tagspec>` element determine how Dreamweaver displays third-party tags in the Document window's Design view. If `tag_type="empty"` or `render_contents="false"`, Dreamweaver displays the placeholder icon specified by the `icon` attribute (depending on the preferences set under View → Visual Aids → Invisible Elements and Edit → Preferences → Invisible Elements → Server Markup Tags (ASP, CFML, etc.)).

The contents of nonempty tags for which `render_contents="true"` are displayed in Design view. The content is highlighted according to the preference set under Edit → Preferences → Highlighting → Third-Party Tags.

ASP Tags

Microsoft Active Server Pages (ASP) is a server-side product offered by most ISPs using Microsoft IIS web servers. ISPs using Unix- or Solaris-based servers typically offer an ASP knock-off such as Chili!Soft's ASP. ASP processes server-side scripts and delivers HTML pages to the user's browser dynamically. For an overview of ASP, see *http://msdn.microsoft.com/workshop/server/asp/ASPover.asp*.

For more information on ASP, see A. Keyton Weissinger's *ASP in a Nutshell* (O'Reilly).

ASP files have an *.asp* extension. Blocks of ASP code start with <% and end with %>. Therefore, the following excerpt from the *ASP.xml* file identifies ASP code as string-delimited:

```
<tagspec tag_name="asp" detect_in_attribute="true"
  start_string="<%" end_string="%>"
  icon="ASP.gif" icon_width="17" icon_height="15">
</tagspec>
```

The *ASPScripts.xml* file identifies additional ASP scripts tags. For example, it identifies the MM_CMD tag as being an HTML-style tag that is empty, not rendered, and that can appear anywhere in the document:

```
<tagspec tag_name="MM_CMD" tag_type="empty"
  render_contents="false" content_model="marker_model"
  icon="ASP.gif" icon_width="17" icon_height="15">
</tagspec>
```

The ASP-related tags recognized by Dreamweaver are listed in Table 21-1.

Table 21-1: Recognized ASP tags

Opening delimiter or tag	Closing delimiter or tag	Description
<%	%>	Delimits all ASP code
<MM_CMD>	N/A	Inserts a server command
<MM_CMDRECSET>	N/A	Performs a command on a record set
<MM_RECORDSET>	</MM_RECORDSET>	Manipulates the contents of a record set
<MM_ASPSCRIPT>	N/A	Inserts ASP Script into the document
<MM_VARIABLES>	</MM_VARIABLES>	Identifies variables

JSP Tags

Sun JavaServer Pages (JSP) is a server-side product offered by most ISPs. Like ASP, it processes server-side scripts and dynamically delivers HTML pages to the user's browser. For an overview of JSP, see *http://java.sun.com/products/jsp/*.

For more information on JSP, see Hans Bergsten's *JavaServer Pages* (O'Reilly) and *JavaServer Pages Pocket Reference* (O'Reilly).

JSP files have a *.js* or *.jsp* extension. JSP code begins with <% and ends with %>, the same delimiters as ASP; therefore, Dreamweaver displays the *ASP.gif* icon for JSP code, as configured by the *ASP.xml* file described in the preceding section. If you use JSP but not ASP, you can edit the *ASP.xml* file to specify the *JSP.gif* file as the icon instead. Dreamweaver also recognizes the JSP-related tags identified in the *JPSScripts.xml* file and listed in Table 21-2.

Table 21-2: Recognized JSP tags

Opening delimiter or tag	Closing delimiter or tag
<%	%>
<MM_RESULTSET>	</MM_RESULTSET>
<MM_PREPARED>	</MM_PREPARED>
<MM_CALL>	N/A
<MM_CALLRESSET>	N/A
<MM_JSPSCRIPT>	N/A
<jsp:getProperty>	N/A
<INCLUDEIF>	</INCLUDEIF>

PHP Tags

PHP is another server-side scripting language that delivers HTML pages to the user's browser. For an overview of PHP, see *http://www.php.net/*.

For more information on PHP see *PHP Pocket Reference* by Rasmus Lerdorf (O'Reilly). Also see *Webmaster in a Nutshell* by Stephen Spainhour and Robert Eckstein (O'Reilly).

PHP files have a *.php*, *.php3* or *.php4* extension. Blocks of PHP code start with <? and end with ?>. Therefore, the *PHP.xml* file includes the following <tagspec> element that identifies PHP code as string–delimited:

```
<tagspec tag_name="php" detect_in_attribute="true"
  start_string="<?" end_string="?>"
  icon="PHP.gif" icon_width="17" icon_height="15">
</tagspec>
```

ColdFusion Tags

Macromedia ColdFusion (formerly Allaire ColdFusion) also processes server-side scripts and delivers HTML pages to the user's browser dynamically. For an overview of ColdFusion, see *http://www.macromedia.com/software/coldfusion/*.

For more on ColdFusion, see *Programming ColdFusion* by Rob Brooks-Bilson (O'Reilly).

ColdFusion Markup Language (CFML) uses HTML-style tags, as defined in the *ColdFusion.xml* file. For example, the following `<tagspec>` element tells Dreamweaver how to display a CFML tag named `CFABORT`:

```
<tagspec tag_name="CFABORT" tag_type="empty" render_contents="false"
   content_model="script_model" detect_in_attribute="true"
   icon="ColdFusion.gif" icon_width="16" icon_height="16">
</tagspec>
```

ColdFusion files have a *.cfm* or *.cfml* extension and can contain both CFML elements and HTML elements. CFML tag names begin with `CF`. For example, CFML offers a `<CFFORM>` element analogous to the HTML `<form>` element. Table 21-3 lists the CFML tags recognized in Dreamweaver by default. Many ColdFusion tags are not listed, but you can add them to the *ColdFusion.xml* file, as described earlier. With Macromedia's recent acquisition of ColdFusion, expect to see greater support for CFML tags in future versions of Dreamweaver and UltraDev.

Table 21-3: Recognized ColdFusion tags

Opening tag	Closing tag	Description
`<CFABORT>`	N/A	Aborts processing of CFML
`<CFAPPLICATION>`	N/A	Defines an application and activates its variables
`<CFAPPLET>`	N/A	Embeds Java applets in a CFFORM
`<CFBREAK>`	N/A	Breaks out of a loop
`<CFCOL>`	N/A	Defines a column in a CFTABLE
`<CFCONTENT>`	N/A	Defines the content type of an inserted file
`<CFCOOKIE>`	N/A	Sets cookie variables
`<CFDIRECTORY>`	N/A	Performs directory handling
`<CFELSE>`	N/A	Logical *else* (used with CFIF)
`<CFELSEIF>`	N/A	Logical *else-if* (used with CFIF)
`<CFERROR>`	N/A	Displays an error message
`<CFFTP>`	N/A	Performs FTP file transfers
`<CFFORM>`	`</CFFORM>`	Creates a CFML form
`<CFGRID>`	`</CFGRID>`	Creates a CFFORM grid
`<CFGRIDCOLUMN>`	N/A	Defines columns in CFGRID
`<CFGRIDROW>`	N/A	Defines rows in CFGRID
`<CFHEADER>`	N/A	Creates HTTP headers
`<CFHTMLHEAD>`	N/A	Writes an HTML page with `<head>` content
`<CFHTTP>`	`</CFHTTP>`	Performs HTTP GET or POST
`<CFHTTPPARAM>`	N/A	Sets parameters for CFHTTP POST
`<CFIF>`	`</CFIF>`	Logical *if* construct
`<CFINCLUDE>`	N/A	Includes another CFML file
`<CFINDEX>`	N/A	Creates Verity search index

Table 21-3: Recognized ColdFusion tags (continued)

Opening tag	Closing tag	Description
<CFINPUT>	N/A	CFFORM input elements (radio buttons, etc.)
<CFINSERT>	N/A	Inserts record in ODBC data source
<CFLDAP>	N/A	LDAP directory services
<CFMAIL>	</CFMAIL>	Sends email
<CFMODULE>	N/A	Custom tag invocation
<CFOBJECT>	N/A	Used for COM, CORBA, or JAVA objects
<CFOUTPUT>	</CFOUTPUT>	Displays results
<CFPARAM>	N/A	Defines a parameter
<CFPOP>	N/A	Retrieves email
<CFQUERY>	</CFQUERY>	Performs a SQL query
<CFREPORT>	</CFREPORT>	Embeds Crystal Reports report
<CFROW>	</CFROW>	Defines a row in a CFTABLE
<CFSCHEDULE>	N/A	Schedules a page execution
<CFSCRIPT>	</CFSCRIPT>	Adds CFScript elements
<CFSEARCH>	N/A	Executes a search (used with CFINDEX)
<CFSELECT>	</CFSELECT>	Creates a selection element in a CFFORM
<CFSET>	N/A	Defines a variable
<CFSETTING>	N/A	Controls template settings
<CFSLIDER>	N/A	Creates a slider control in a CFFORM
<CFTABLE>	</CFTABLE>	Creates a table
<CFTEXTINPUT>	N/A	Creates a single-line text entry box in a CFFORM
<CFTRANSACTION>	</CFTRANSACTION>	Groups a batch of CFQUERY statements
<CFTREE>	</CFTREE>	Creates a tree control element in a CFFORM
<CFTREEITEM>	N/A	Creates a single tree item in a CFTREE element
<CFUPDATE>	N/A	Updates a data source

The next chapter shows how to extend Dreamweaver by using Extensions available through the Dreamweaver Exchange.

CHAPTER 22

Extending Dreamweaver

Dreamweaver is highly extensible. You can download new functions and commands (known collectively as *extensions*) from the Dreamweaver Exchange on Macromedia's web site. Although many extensions are written by Macromedians, hundreds more are written by third-party companies and users.

Dreamweaver Extensions

By definition, an infinite number of extensions are possible and we can't cover them all here. For those using extensions created by others, this chapter covers some of the most useful extensions. For those creating their own extensions, see the "Writing Your Own Extensions" section at the end of this chapter.

The Dreamweaver Exchange

You can search for, learn about, and download extensions using the Dreamweaver Exchange web site. If you develop your own extensions, you can upload them to the Exchange for others to use.

Using Dreamweaver extensions requires four steps:

1. Pick an extension from the Dreamweaver Exchange.

2. Download the extension to your local hard drive.

3. Install the extension with the Extension Manager. (Installing an extension will update one or more parts of Dreamweaver's UI, such as the Objects panel, Insert Menu, Commands menu, Help menu, or the Add Behavior pop-up menu in the Behaviors panel.)

4. Access the extension as you would access built-in features from the Objects panel, Commands menu, or elsewhere in the UI.

You can access the Dreamweaver Exchange in several ways:

- Choose the Help → Dreamweaver Exchange option from Dreamweaver's main menu bar.

- Choose the Commands → Get More Commands option from Dreamweaver's main menu bar.

- Choose the Get More Behaviors option from the Add Behavior (+) pop-up menu in the Behaviors panel.

- Choose File → Go To Macromedia Exchange from the Extension Manager's menu bar (or press Cmd-G on the Macintosh while the Extension Manager application is active).

- Click the Go To Macromedia Exchange icon in the Extension Manager's toolbar (Windows only).

- Click the Get More Styles button in the Insert Flash Button dialog box, accessible using Insert → Interactive Images → Flash Button.

- Visit the Exchange directly by pointing your browser to *http://www.macromedia.com/exchange/dreamweaver/*.

Although no separate exchange exists for Fireworks extensions, there is a Fireworks category on the Dreamweaver Exchange. UltraDev and Flash extensions both have separate exchanges.

Visit the UltraDev Exchange at:

http://www.macromedia.com/exchange/ultradev/

Visit the Flash Exchange at:

http://www.macromedia.com/exchange/flash/

Picking an Extension

The Dreamweaver Exchange includes a description page and discussion forum for each extension. Extensions typically include documentation explaining their use. You can get additional help from the resources cited in the preface. Extensions are grouped into the categories listed in Table 22-1. You can find an extension by searching the Dreamweaver Exchange or browsing extensions by category. Many extensions are not in the category you might expect, so peruse them or use the Exchange's search option.

Table 22-1: Extension categories

Category	Description and sample extensions
Accessibility	Enhance accessibility for portable devices and users with disabilities, such as adding `alt` attributes to `<img>` tags, setting DOCTYPE elements, managing cookies, and assessing accessibility.
App Servers	Query, view, and format dynamic data accessed with ASP, JSP, ColdFusion, and PHP server-side languages.
Browsers	Scripts for browser detection and redirection, adding pages to favorites lists, and creating SMIL profiles.
DHTML/ Layers	DHTML objects and behaviors (including updated Show-Hide Layers and Set Text of Layers behaviors for NN6).

Table 22-1: Extension categories (continued)

Category	Description and sample extensions
eCommerce	Transaction processing, shopping carts, and catalogs.
Fireworks	Fireworks integration with Dreamweaver; Firework image effects.
Flash Media	Flash object integration; additional Flash buttons or text styles.
Learning	Objects for learning and courseware, such as CourseBuilder (see Chapter 23).
Navigation	Additional styles of navigation bars, menu options, and frames effects.
Productivity	Authoring time utilities that improve integration with other products, clean up HTML, and import site definition files.
Rich Media	Support for third-party multimedia plugins such as QuickTime, RealVideo, RealAudio, banner images, three-dimensional objects, and NetMeeting links.
Scripting	Tools to assist in writing Dreamweaver extensions and browser scripts in JavaScript, ASP, and PHP.
Security	Add security elements to your pages and prevent your site from being framed by another site.
Style/Format	Custom styles, custom formatting, and advanced CSS effects, such as floating frames, nonbreaking text, and CSS color changes.
Tables	Enhanced table creation, formatting, and manipulation, such as changing the table axis and populating a table with ODBC data.
Text	Advanced text editing and formatting features, such as spellcheckers, character case changes, math symbols, and text coloring.

Extending Dreamweaver

Downloading an Extension

Instructions for downloading extensions are given on the Dreamweaver Exchange. You will be asked to register (for free) before downloading an extension. Most Dreamweaver extensions are free. Commercial extensions are identified on the extension explanation page and may offer a free lite version or 30-day trial.

Extensions, usually comprised of HTML and JavaScript (*.js*) files, are packaged in Macromedia Extension Package (*.mxp*) files, which include a compressed version of the extension plus documentation and related files. Downloaded *.mxp* files are installed in a separate step by using the *Extension Manager*. When downloading an Extension (*.mxp* file), save it in a directory that is not within your site's root folder, thereby making it easier to delete the *.mxp* files when they are no longer needed. By convention, downloaded *.mxp* files are placed in a folder called *Downloaded Extensions* within the Dreamweaver 4 installation folder.

The Extension Manager

The *Extension Manager*, shown in Figure 22-1 and formerly known as the Package Manager, is a standalone application that manages extensions.

There are several ways to launch the Extension Manager:

- Choose the Help → Manage Extensions option from Dreamweaver's main menu bar.

- Choose the Commands → Manage Extensions option from Dreamweaver's main menu bar.

- In Windows, choose Programs → Macromedia Extension Manager → Macromedia Extension Manager from the Windows Start menu.

- On the Macintosh, double-click the Extension Manager application in the Macromedia Extension Manager installation folder.

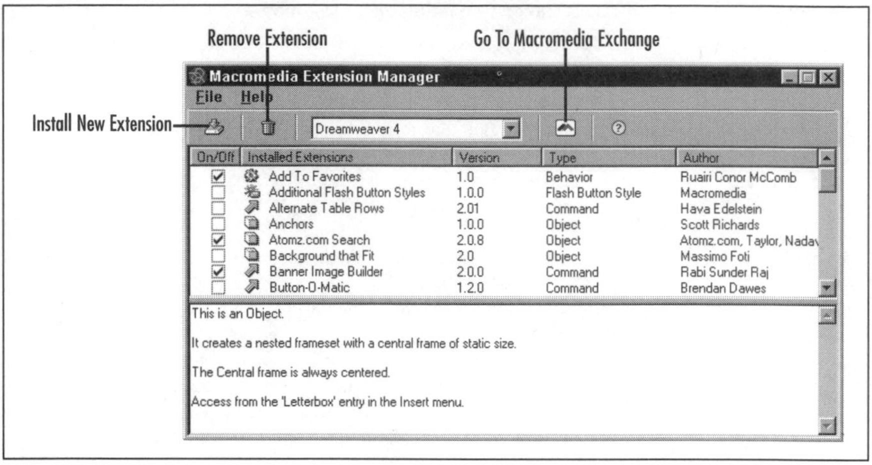

Figure 22-1: Extension Manager

The Extension Manager is included with DW4, but DW3 and DW2 users must download the extension manager from Macromedia's site. Not all DW4 extensions work with prior versions of Dreamweaver and not all extensions support all browsers (the documentation for each extension includes compatibility information).

Installing an Extension

Download an extension from the Dreamweaver Exchange prior to installation. Install an Extension (*.mxp*) file that was downloaded previously by:

- Choosing the File → Install Extension from the Extension Manager menu bar.

- Pressing Ctrl+I (Windows) or Cmd+O (Macintosh) while the Extension Manager is the active application.

- Clicking the Install New Extension icon in the Extension Manager's toolbar (Windows only).

- On Windows, you can double-click an *.mxp* file to initiate installation (on the Macintosh, this works only if the *.mxp* file's hidden file type is set to MmXm).

- Extensions can be imported from other Dreamweaver or UltraDev installations by choosing File → Import Extensions from the Extension Manager menu bar (or by pressing Cmd-I on the Macintosh).

When prompted, select the *.mxp* file to install and answer any other questions that may be posed during installation (such as questions about a license agreement).

After installation, the Extension Manager tells you if you must restart Dreamweaver to access the new features provided by the extension. Some extensions can be reloaded by Ctrl-clicking (Windows) or Opt-clicking (Macintosh) the category selector in the Objects panel and choosing Reload Extensions.

Active extensions are indicated in the Installed Extensions list in the Extension Manager window by a checkmark in the On/Off field. When you select an extension, the Extension Manager displays brief instructions for the extension and explains how to access it in Dreamweaver.

Disabling Extensions

Disable an extension temporarily by unchecking the on/off checkbox next to its name in the Extension Manager window.

Excessive numbers of extensions can slow Dreamweaver's startup time. To reduce the application's startup time, disable extensions that you don't need.

Remove an extension to disable it permanently by:

* Choosing File → Remove Extension from the Extension Manage menu bar.

* Pressing Ctrl+R (Windows) or Cmd+- (Macintosh) while the Extension Manager is the active application.

* Clicking the Remove Extension icon from the Extension Manager toolbar (Windows only).

Useful Extensions

The Dreamweaver Exchange contains over 480 extensions. Each extension has its own page containing a download link, a general description, a link to a discussion panel, reviews, compatibility information, and a link to ask questions of the extension developer. Most extensions are available for both the Macintosh and Windows. Some extensions enhance authoring-time capabilities, whereas others affect the visitors' browsing experience.

Check the Dreamweaver Exchange periodically for new extensions, especially browser profiles used to support new versions of the major browsers. The Netscape 6 Pack update is part of the 4.01 update and can be downloaded from *http://www.macromedia.com/support/dreamweaver/downloads/*. Unzip (Windows) or unstuff (Macintosh) the downloadable Netscape 6 Pack to extract the *.mxp* file that can be installed as described earlier.

Ten useful extensions, a small fraction of those available, are listed next. These extensions must be downloaded from the Dreamweaver Exchange site and installed before they will be available on your installation of Dreamweaver. Each extension's category is indicated in parentheses following its name.

Add to Favorites (Browsers category)

The Add to Favorites extension, by Rvairi Conor McComb, opens the Add to Favorites dialog box when IE users visit a web page (visitors must respond to the dialog to complete the operation). This extension adds the IE → Add to Favorites behavior to the Add Behavior (+) pop-up menu of the Behaviors panel.

The Add To Favorites action is typically triggered by an onClick event associated with a hyperlink. When you apply the behavior during authoring, specify the title to be used for the entry in the favorites list.

Atomz Search (App Servers category)

The Atomz Search extension, by Atomz, Taylor, and Nadav Savio, lets you add an Atomz search engine to your web site, which allows visitors to search your site for keywords. You will need to create an Atomz account before using this extension.

Installing the Atomz extension adds an Atomz category to the Objects panel, as shown in Figure 22-2.

Figure 22-2: The Objects panel's Atomz category

Add a search engine to your page by using the Insert Atomz.com Search button in the Objects panel's Atomz category or by selecting Insert → Atomz.com Search.

The Atomz Search extension requires a username and password that identifies your site (which is why you must first create an account with Atomz). Without the account information, the Atomz extension cannot insert the search engine. Once you've filled in the questions in the Atomz extension dialog box (not shown) Dreamweaver inserts the Atomz search field into your document, as shown in Figure 22-3.

The HTML code inserted by the Atomz behavior for the standard search form is as follows:

```
<!-- Atomz Search HTML for Wagonboss.net -->
<form method="get" action="http://search.atomz.com/search/">
<input size=15 name="sp-q"><br>
<input type=submit value="Search">
<input type=hidden name="sp-a" value="ab23456h89">
</form>
```

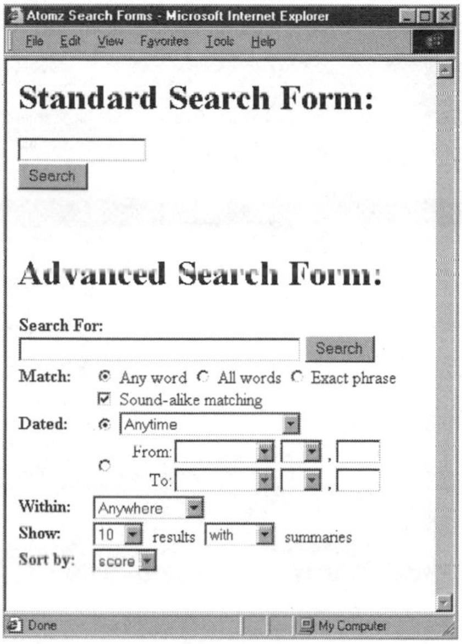

Figure 22-3: Atomz standard and advanced search forms on a web page

Other utilities that add a search feature to your site include Simple Search from Matt's Script Archive (*http://www.worldwidemart.com/scripts/search.shtml*).

Banner Image Builder (Rich Media category)

The Banner Image Builder extension, by Rabi Sunder Raj, creates rotating banners ads with links. Once the extension is installed, use the Commands → Banner Image Builder option to open the Banner Image Builder dialog box, shown in Figure 22-4.

In the Banner Image Builder dialog box, select the images and destination URLs, transition duration, and target frame. The code necessary to manage up to ten banner ad images is inserted into your document automatically.

External Link Checker (Navigation category)

Dreamweaver's built-in link checker (Site → Check Links Sitewide) does not verify external links (see Chapters 6 and 7 for details). However, the External Link Checker extension, by Scott Richards, automatically checks external links (therefore, it requires an active Internet connection).

After installing the extension, check external links in the current document by using Command → Check External Links. Check external links for all files selected in the Site window by using Site → Check External Links in the Site window (Windows) or main menu bar (Macintosh). These options open the External Link Checker dialog box, shown in Figure 22-5.

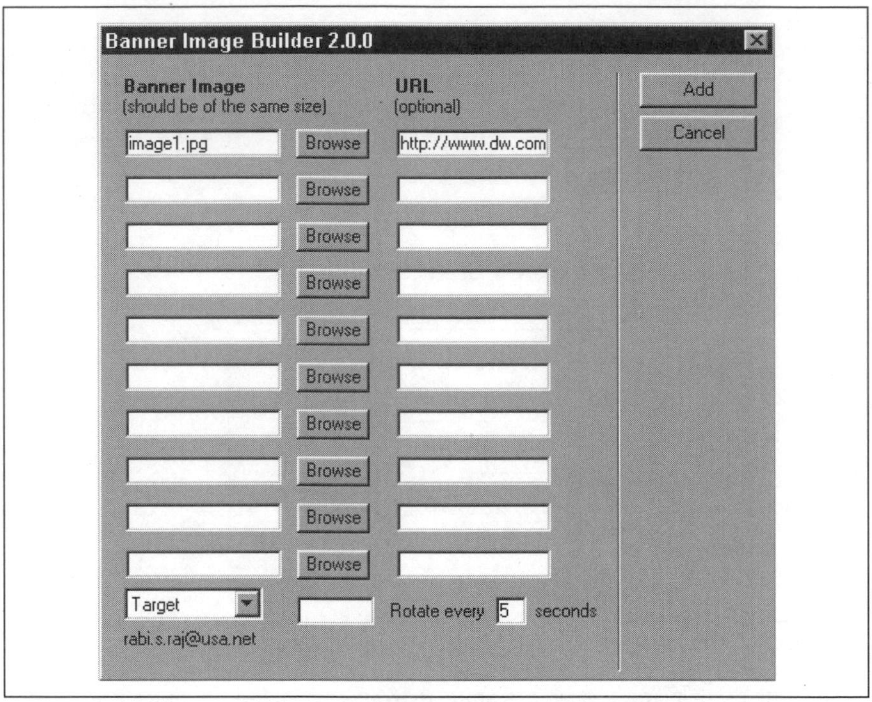

Figure 22-4: The Banner Image Builder dialog box

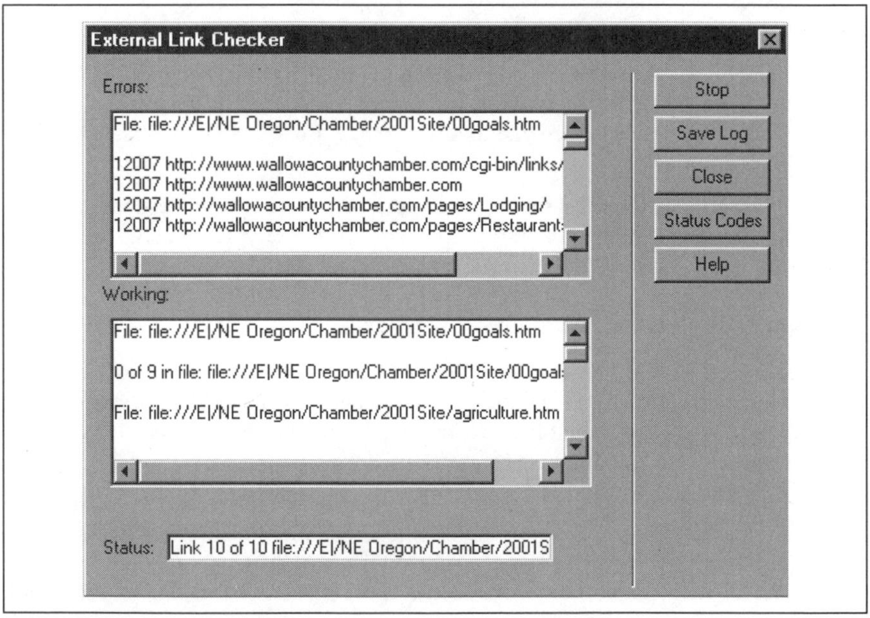

Figure 22-5: The External Link Checker extension

Version 1.0.0 of the External Link Checker extension is often unreliable and may fail to validate all external links in the chosen documents. It also does not verify email address links. You may prefer to use Dreamweaver's built-in link checker to generate a list of external URLs that you can verify by hand. Avoid linking to pages deep within other web sites, as site structures change often. Consider linking to the home page of other sites instead.

In the External Link Checker dialog box, click the Save Log button to copy the verification results to a file. Click the Status Codes button to display a list of HTTP status codes, as shown in Figure 22-6 (these codes help diagnose the cause of unreachable external links).

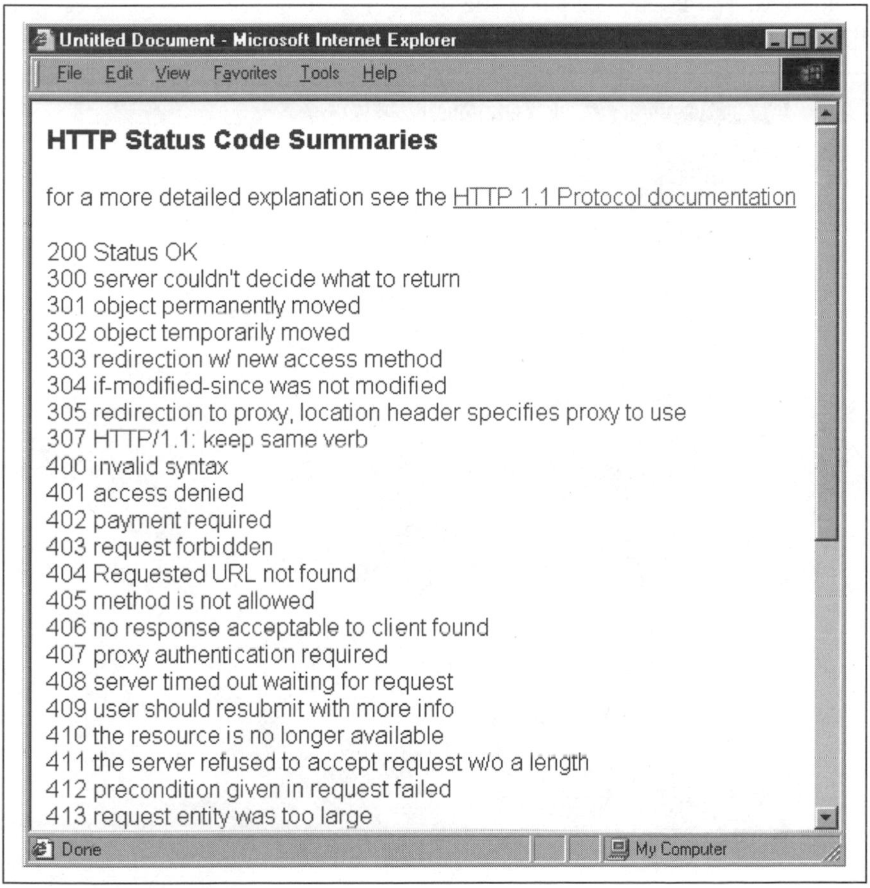

Untitled Document - Microsoft Internet Explorer

File   Edit   View   Favorites   Tools   Help

HTTP Status Code Summaries

for a more detailed explanation see the HTTP 1.1 Protocol documentation

200 Status OK
300 server couldn't decide what to return
301 object permanently moved
302 object temporarily moved
303 redirection w/ new access method
304 if-modified-since was not modified
305 redirection to proxy, location header specifies proxy to use
307 HTTP/1.1: keep same verb
400 invalid syntax
401 access denied
402 payment required
403 request forbidden
404 Requested URL not found
405 method is not allowed
406 no response acceptable to client found
407 proxy authentication required
408 server timed out waiting for request
409 user should resubmit with more info
410 the resource is no longer available
411 the server refused to accept request w/o a length
412 precondition given in request failed
413 request entity was too large

Done   My Computer

Figure 22-6: HTTP status codes

The External Link Checker does not alter your HTML document or allow you to correct links automatically, but it does identify the HTML documents containing unreachable links. If the problem is a bad URL, correct the link by hand (remember that a site might be temporarily unavailable even if the URL is correct).

dHTML Scrollable Area (DHTML/Layers category)

Creating scrollable layers is difficult due to differences in Netscape and Internet Explorer. The dHTML Scrollable Area behavior, by David G. Miles, creates scrollable layers that work in 4.0+ browsers using four separate <div> elements. (Note that this extension is listed at the end of the DHTML/Layers category, and not in alphabetical order, in the Dreamweaver Exchange.) After installing the extension, insert a scrollable layer by using Insert → AP Scrollable Area or the Insert Absolutely Positioned Scrolling Layer icon in the Objects panel's Goodies category. Configure the object settings in the Create Absolutely Positioned Scrollable Layer dialog box. The Positioning tab of the dialog box, shown in Figure 22-7, controls the size, placement, and scrolling speed of the layer.

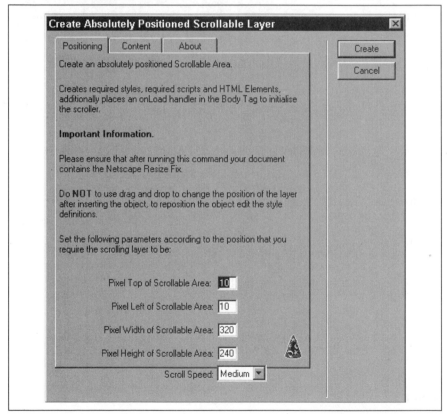

Figure 22-7: Create Absolutely Positioned Scrollable Layer Positioning tab

The dialog box's Content tab (not shown) allows you to enter the layer's content, which can be any content other than nested layers (which aren't supported in NN4). When using this extension, use the Commands → Add/Remove Netscape Resize Fix option to ensure that Netscape browsers will refresh properly when the browser window is resized.

Check Page for Accessibility (Accessibility category)

The Check Page for Accessibility extension, by Macromedia, checks whether special-needs browsers can view your web pages. Site accessibility is important not just for disabled users, but also for alternative devices and text-based browsers. For example, a site that is readable by text-based browsers that then convert the text to audio is useful for both blind users and car drivers who can't take their eyes off the road. Sites than comply with accessibility standards are more likely to work with existing browsers and are less likely to fail in future browsers (reducing maintenance costs).

Once you install the extension, run it by selecting Commands → Check Page for Accessibility, which opens the dialog box shown in Figure 22-8. Select the accessibility standard conformance options in this dialog box and click OK to analyze the page.

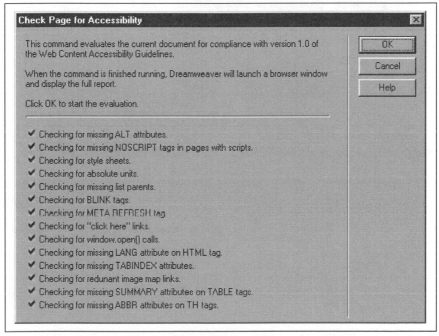

Figure 22-8: The Check Page for Accessibility extension

Dreamweaver displays an evaluation report listing the line number, element, and accessibility problems within the document.

Dreamweaver Platform SDK (Scripting category)

The Dreamweaver Platform SDK extension, by Macromedia, helps you create extensions for Dreamweaver, Fireworks, and UltraDev. This extension helps you add objects, scripts, and behaviors to your Dreamweaver UI. The extension adds the SDK Samples category to the Objects panel and adds the Insert → SDK Samples menu to Dreamweaver's menu bar, as shown in Figure 22-9.

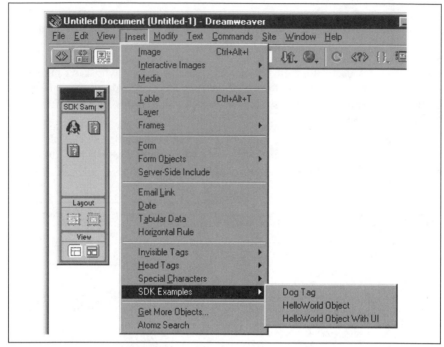

Figure 22-9: Locations of SDK samples additions in Dreamweaver's UI

The SDK extension also adds tools under the Commands → SDK Tools submenu. Figure 22-10 shows the Show Document Structure dialog box, opened by selecting Commands → SDK Tools → Show Document Structure. This dialog box allows you to view the actual structure of your document, including comments but excluding content.

When developing complex web sites, such as those that use HTML, XML, and JavaScript, the structure information helps you spot errors in your code. For more details on the SDK extension consult the help files it installs in the *Dreamweaver 4/SDK/Docs* directory.

Open Picture Window Fever! (Productivity category)

The Open Picture Window Fever! extension, by Drew McLellan, opens a minimalist browser pop-up window that is the same size as the selected image. Once installed, this extension adds the Fever → Open Picture Window Fever behavior to the Add Behavior (+) pop-up menu of the Behaviors panel.

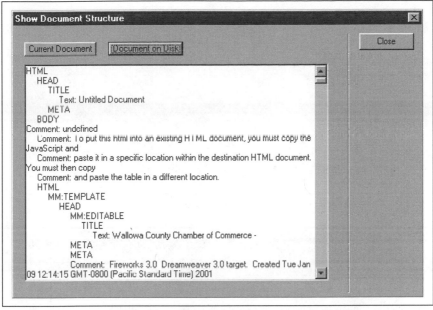

Figure 22-10: The Show Document Structure dialog box (part of Platform SDK extension)

This extension is perfect for opening large versions of thumbnail images in photo albums. Apply it to the thumbnails created with Dreamweaver's Commands → Create Web Photo Album option to open the larger photo without requiring the screen real estate associated with a full browser window.

Set Permissions (Productivity category)

The Set Permissions extension, by Jay London, allows you to set the permissions of a file on a remote Unix server. To set the permissions of a remote file, right-click (Windows) or Ctrl-click (Macintosh) on a file in the Remote Files pane of the Site Files window and select the Set Permissions option from the contextual menu. Choosing this action opens the File Access Properties dialog box, shown in Figure 22-11, where you can set the file permissions.

This command instructs the Unix file server to change the file permissions using the *chmod* command (for more information on *chmod*, see *Web Design in a Nutshell* by Jennifer Niederst (O'Reilly)). The Set Permissions command works only on Unix servers accessed through FTP connections.

Table of Contents (Navigation category)

The Table of Contents extension, by Scott Richards, converts a series of named anchors or headings into a linked table of contents (TOC). After installing the extension, you can insert a TOC into your document by using Commands → Create Table of Contents. The Create Table of Contents dialog box, shown in Figure 22-12, allows you to select what types of HTML elements to use for the TOC.

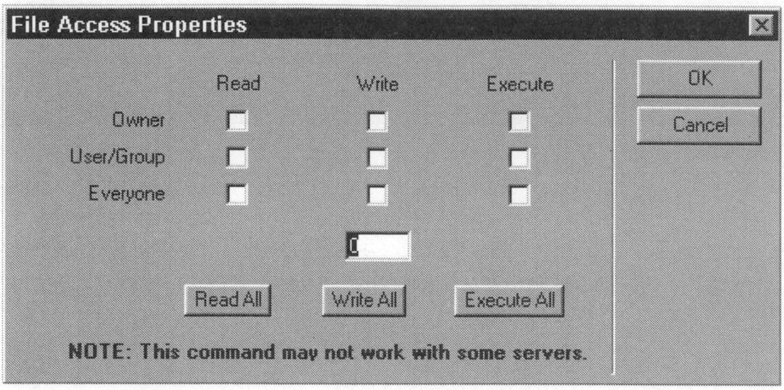

Figure 22-11: The File Access Properties dialog box

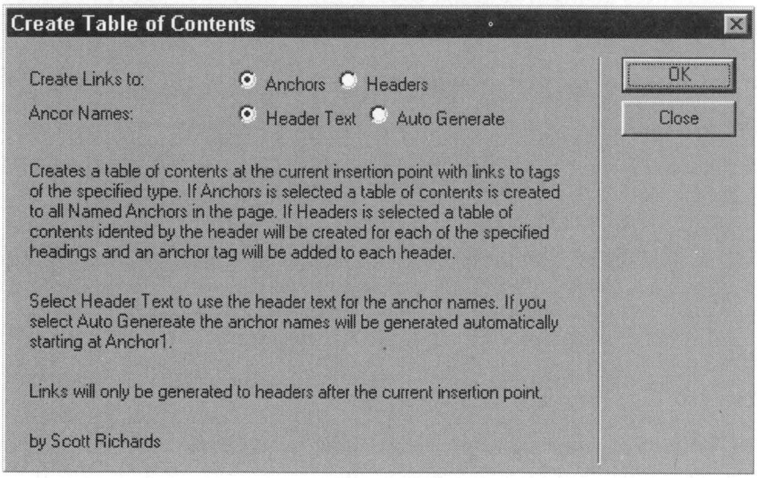

Figure 22-12: The Create Table of Contents dialog box

A TOC is a great complement to a graphical site map. You can also use the extension to generate a TOC for a lengthy HTML document, such as an online user manual.

Password Protection and eCommerce

There are hundreds of extensions that we don't have room to cover here. Furthermore, we didn't cover several commonly requested features for which Dreamweaver UltraDev is better suited than Dreamweaver. Features that depend on the web server software, such as password protection and eCommerce, are better implemented using UltraDev.

UltraDev's Server Behaviors panel includes server-side behaviors for user authentication, such as the Restrict Access To Page behavior. If you implement password protection yourself, be aware that different servers use different methods for password protection. The ColdFusion Server's password mechanism is described in *Programming ColdFusion* by Rob Brooks-Bilson (O'Reilly). The Apache server uses an *.htpasswd* file to password protect a directory, as described in Stephen Spainhour and Robert Eckstein's *Webmaster in a Nutshell* (O'Reilly). If you are using other servers, such as IIS, consult your webmaster, ISP, or server documentation for details on password protecting your site or a portion of your site.

The UltraCart extension, available from *http://www.powerclimb.com/powerclimb/ Behaviors.htm*, is an eCommerce shopping cart solution. See the eCommerce category in the Dreamweaver Exchange and UltraDev Exchange for the UltraCart Patch for UD4 extension by Joseph Scavitto and other third-party eCommerce solutions.

Dreamweaver and UltraDev extensions aren't the only way to add functionality to your site. For example, freely available CGI scripts implement many useful functions even though they aren't well-integrated into Dreamweaver's UI (see the resources cited in the preface).

Writing Your Own Extensions

If you can write HTML and JavaScript, you can write Dreamweaver extensions. In earlier chapters, we saw how to add custom objects to the Objects panel, create custom dialog boxes, and add commands to the Commands menu. Dreamweaver extensions are merely customized menu options, behaviors, and objects that have been packaged to make them easily shareable.

Resources for Extension Developers

Macromedia provides several resources to help you write Dreamweaver extensions:

- For a thorough discussion of creating extensions, the Help → Extending Dreamweaver option from the Dreamweaver main menu bar accesses the full text of Macromedia's *Extending Dreamweaver* manual. (The PDF version of the manual, *Extending Dreamweaver.pdf*, is included in the *Extending the Studio* folder of the Dreamweaver 4 installation CD-ROM. The same folder includes *Extending Fireworks.pdf*, which documents how to extend Fireworks.)

- The Help → Creating and Submitting Extensions option in the Extension Manager window's menu bar gives an overview of how to create extensions and submit them to the Dreamweaver Exchange.

- Visit *http://www.macromedia.com/support/dreamweaver/extend.html* for more detail on customizing and extending Dreamweaver

- Avail yourself of the Dreamweaver Exchange and the resources cited in the preface.

- Also see *Building Dreamweaver 4 and Dreamweaver UltraDev 4 Extensions* by Ray West and Tom Muck (Osborne).

Overview of Developing an Extension

The following steps will help you start creating and distributing your own extensions:

1. Create the JavaScript, HTML, and icons required for your extension. Use the built-in Dreamweaver objects and commands as a starting point. Consult the resources cited previously for information on the API and Document Object Model (DOM) used by Dreamweaver.

2. Comply with the Macromedia UI Guidelines as described at *http://dynamic. macromedia.com/MM/exchange/ui_guidelines.jsp*.

3. Test your extension thoroughly on multiple configurations, including various flavors of Windows, the Mac OS, and different browsers. See the Macromedia web page "About Extension Testing and Approval" at *http://dynamic. macromedia.com/MM/exchange/about_testing.jsp* for a testing plan and steps necessary to receive Macromedia Approval certification for your extension.

4. Move the relevant files to a staging area so they are easily accessible when creating the package for distribution.

5. Write the installation file (an *.mxi* file) that controls extension installation. For a sample, see the *Blank.mxi* file in the *Extension ManagerSamples/ Dreamweaver* folder. The *.mxi* file also defines how a developer accesses the extensions features, such as via a keyboard shortcut, menu item, or the Objects panel. For details on the *.mxi* file format, see "The Macromedia Extension Installation File Format," available at *http://download.macromedia. com/pub/exchange/mxi_file_format.pdf*.

6. Use the Extension Manager's File → Package Extension command to create an Extension package (*.mxp* file) from the *.mxi* file created in Step 5. The same package is used on both platforms in most cases. (Use a filename that is valid on both Windows and Macintosh and does not contain spaces.) The *.mxp* file contains compressed versions of the necessary files, plus installation instructions used by the Extension Manager.

7. Install the *.mxp* file on your own machine using the Extension Manager's File → Install Extension command to ensure that the extension installs properly (preferably, you should test it on a fresh machine to ensure that the necessary files are installed by the package and are not simply left over from your development efforts). Retest the extension's features to verify that the installation is correct.

8. Submit the extension to the Exchange by using the Extension Manager's File → Submit Extension command by or going directly to *http://dynamic. macromedia.com/bin/MM/exchange/about_submission.jsp*. This action accesses the Macromedia Exchange site where you must log in and follow on-screen instructions to submit your extension.

The next chapter covers the CourseBuilder extension, which simplifies the creation of web-based training courses.

CHAPTER 23

CourseBuilder

CourseBuilder for Dreamweaver simplifies the creation of web-based instructional materials. It helps you create tests, surveys, quizzes, and other courseware for Internet distribution. CourseBuilder *interactions* insert elements, such as multiple-choice questions, that consitute your courseware. You can also add customized logic and interactivity to your pages built with CourseBuilder.

Installing CourseBuilder

The CourseBuilder extension for Dreamweaver is free from Macromedia's site at *http://www.macromedia.com/software/coursebuilder*. The Macromedia site also contains information about using CourseBuilder and provides tutorials and support information for this extension.

To install CourseBuilder:

1. Download it from the preceding URL or the Macromedia Exchange (accessible using the Commands → Get More Commands option).

2. Once you have downloaded CourseBuilder, open the Extension Manager by selecting Commands → Manage Extensions.

3. Within the Extension Manager use the File → Install Extension option to select the CourseBuilder extension you downloaded (it is named *cb_dw_ud.mxp*).

4. Restart Dreamweaver to make the CourseBuilder interactions available in the newly created Learning category in Dreamweaver's Objects panel.

5. Installing CourseBuilder also adds a Modify → CourseBuilder submenu to Dreamweaver's Modify menu from which you can add interactions, edit interactions, and more.

CourseBuilder Interactions

CourseBuilder interactions allow you to easily build a project from basic elements. After installing CourseBuilder you can access the full CourseBuilder documentation under Help → Using CourseBuilder. The elaborate help files documents each interaction type. Help buttons also appear in each tab of the CourseBuilder Interaction dialog box (see Figure 23-2). If you installed CourseBuilder in the *Dreamweaver 4/ CourseBuilder* folder, a sample CourseBuilder project is at *Dreamweaver 4/ CourseBuilder/Tutorial/cb_tutorial/discover_comp/discover_nav.htm*. More online information can be found at the resources listed under Help → Welcome to CourseBuilder.

If you are developing highly interactive courseware, you should consider using other Macromedia products, such as Flash, Director, or Authorware, in combination with Dreamweaver. Authorware is designed for creating computer-based training (CBT) and is bundled with Dreamweaver in the eLearning Studio (see *http://www.macromedia.com/software/elearningstudio/*). For an overview of eLearning solutions, see the eLearning product matrix at *http://www.macromedia. com/resources/elearning/matrix.pdf.*

Inserting and Editing Interactions

To insert a CourseBuilder interaction into an HTML document use Insert → CourseBuilder Interaction or click the Insert CourseBuilder Interaction icon in the Objects panel's Learning category, shown in Figure 23-1.

Figure 23-1: The Learning category of the Objects panel

Inserting an interaction opens the CourseBuilder Interaction dialog box, shown in Figure 23-2. Click the Help button in the CourseBuilder Interaction dialog box to open context-sensitive help for the currently selected interaction.

CourseBuilder requires that support files be installed in the folder in which the HTML document is saved. To avoid redundant copies of the support files, keep all your HTML pages that use CourseBuilder in the same folder. If necessary, Dreamweaver prompts you to copy support files to the needed location automatically. (You can copy the support files manually using Modify → CourseBuilder → Copy Support Files.) These support files must be uploaded to your web server as described in "What to put on the web server" under Help → Using CourseBuilder.

Select an interaction type from the Category list and then choose an interaction in the dialog box's Gallery tab. By default, the CourseBuilder Interaction dialog box shows interactions available for 4.0+ browsers. Targeting 3.0 browsers limits you to Multiple Choice, Text Entry, and Action Manager interactions. Because CourseBuilder is extensible, you can add your own interactions to the built-in ones using Modify → CourseBuilder → Add Interaction to Gallery.

Some features of the Drag and Drop, Slider, and Explorer interactions may not work in Netscape 6. For more information, see "CourseBuilder interactive compatibility with browsers" under Help → Using CourseBuilder.

Click OK to insert an interaction, which adds an <interaction> tag to your HTML document. You can select the <interaction> tag using the Tag Selector. You can open the Property inspector by double-clicking the CourseBuilder placeholder icon that represents each interaction in the Document window (the placeholder looks like the icon shown in Figure 23-1). To edit the selected interaction, use Modify → CourseBuilder → Edit Interaction, Ctrl+Alt+E (Windows), Cmd+Opt+E (Macintosh), or the Edit button in the Property inspector.

Interactions automatically add HTML <form> tags to your document. There can be more than one interaction per page, each with its own <form> tag. An HTML page can contain both CourseBuilder interactions and standard HTML elements. As shown in the CourseBuilder tutorial, you can also augment an interaction with HTML elements from the Objects panel. For example, you might add a button with a link to the next page of a quiz. However, don't add more <form> tags to existing interactions and don't nest <interaction> tags.

Use the "Insert in Layer (4.0+ browsers only)" checkbox in the Property inspector to place the CourseBuilder interaction within a layer, which allows you to position it on the page. If you insert an interaction within a layer, avoid nesting layers within the interaction, as NN4 doesn't handle nested layers very well.

Let's take a brief look at each type of built-in interaction before covering the Action Manager interaction, which ties them all together. At the end of the chapter we'll describe how to configure interactions.

Multiple Choice

Multiple Choice interactions, shown in Figure 23-2, create input buttons that are more attractive than standard radio buttons or checkboxes. Select a Multiple Choice interaction from the Gallery tab. Use the General, Choices, and Action Mgr tabs to configure the interaction, and click the OK button to insert it. See the "Configuring Interactions" section later in this chapter for details on configuring Multiple Choice interactions

You can use a Multiple Choice interaction to create a menu as demonstrated in the CourseBuilder tutorial under Help → Using CourseBuilder. The tutorial also shows how to create test questions using Multiple Choice interactions. You can't test interactions in Dreamweaver. Preview your pages in a browser using File → Preview in Browser (F12).

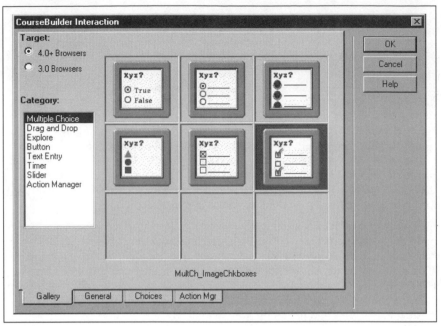

Figure 23-2: Multiple Choice interactions in the CourseBuilder Interaction dialog box's Gallery tab

Drag and Drop

Drag and Drop interactions, shown in Figure 23-3, require the site visitor to drag an object to a target location. For example, you could use it to let students sort animals into herbivore and carnivore categories. Select a Drag and Drop interaction from the Gallery tab. Use the General, Elements, Pairs, and Action Mgr tabs to configure the interaction, and click the OK button to insert it. (The Elements tab configures the draggable objects and their targets. The Pairs tab specifies correct and incorrect pairings among drag and drop objects.)

The CourseBuilder tutorial under Help → Using CourseBuilder demonstrates how to use a Drag and Drop interaction.

Explore

Explore interactions, shown in Figure 23-4, allow visitors to select among multiple hotspots in an image to access more information about an item. Select an Explore interaction from the Gallery tab. Use the General, Hot Areas, and Action Mgr tabs to configure the interaction, and click the OK button to insert it.

The CourseBuilder tutorial under Help → Using CourseBuilder demonstrates how to use an Explore interaction.

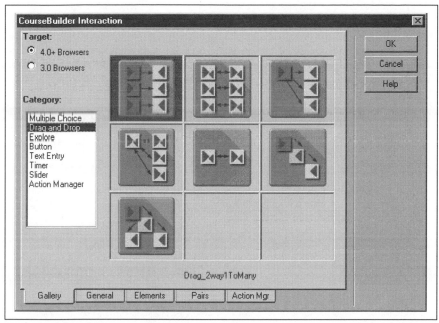

Figure 23-3: Drag and Drop interactions

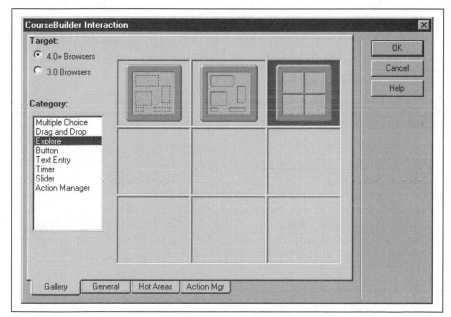

Figure 23-4: Explore interactions

Button

Button interactions, shown in Figure 23-5, allow visitors to set a button's state. Choose between the two basic button styles on the Gallery tab, and then configure the button's appearance on the General tab. Use the Action Mgr tab to configure the interaction, and click the OK button to insert it.

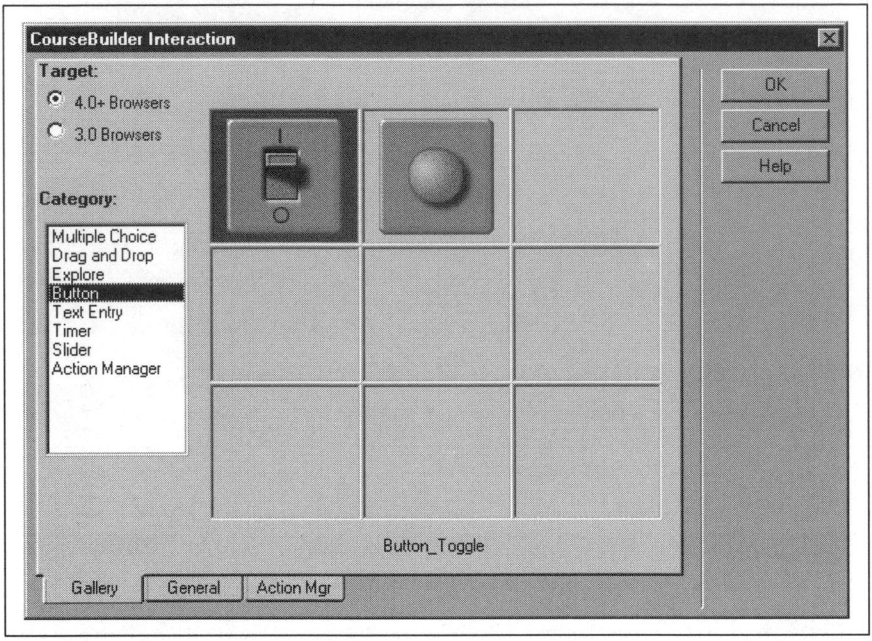

Figure 23-5: Button interactions

The documentation under Help → Using CourseBuilder includes extensive details on configuring Button interactions.

Text Entry

Text Entry interactions, shown in Figure 23-6, implement single- or multiline entry fields. You can evaluate the accuracy of text responses by searching the response for chosen words or phrases. You can also provide a list of correct and incorrect responses to a question. Select one of the two Text Entry interactions from the Gallery tab. Use the General, Responses, and Action Mgr tabs to configure the interaction, and click the OK button to insert it.

Timer

Timer interactions, shown in Figure 23-7, can limit the time allowed for a user action and provide a timer that counts up or down. You can choose between single- and multiple-target timers. Choose between the two basic Timer styles on the Gallery tab, and configure the timer's appearance with the General tab. Use the Triggers and Action Mgr tabs to configure the interaction, and click the OK button to insert it.

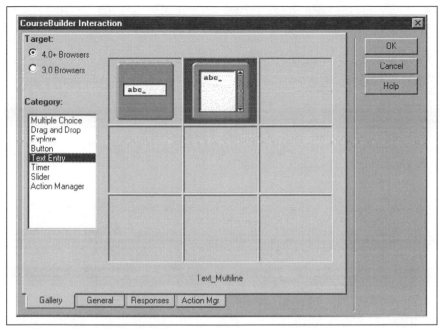

Figure 23-6: Text Entry interactions

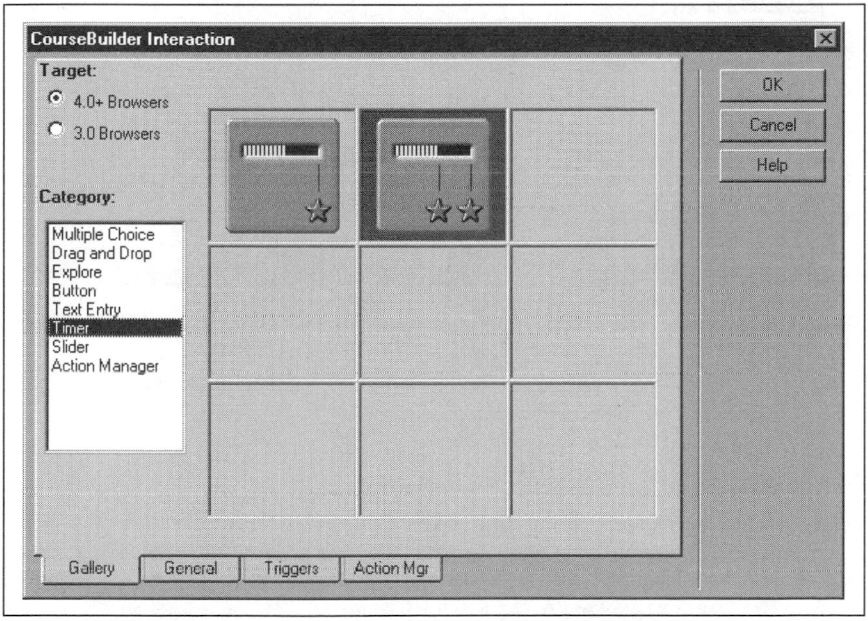

Figure 23-7: Timer interactions

The documentation under Help → Using CourseBuilder includes extensive details on using and configuring Timer interactions.

Slider

Slider interactions, shown in Figure 23-8, allow users to provide input using a slider bar. For example, slider bars can be used to rate how users feel about a specific test question or to set the volume of background music. You can choose between single- and multiple-selection range sliders. Choose between the two basic Slider styles on the Gallery tab, and configure the slider's appearance on the General tab. Use the Ranges and Action Mgr tabs to configure the interaction, and click the OK button to insert it.

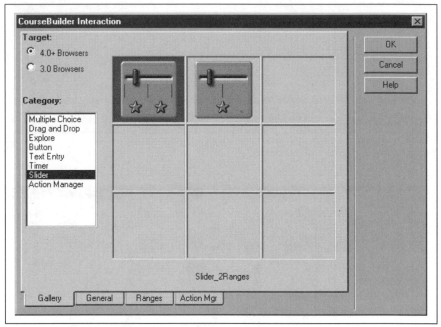

Figure 23-8: Slider interactions

The documentation under Help → Using CourseBuilder includes extensive details on using and configuring Slider interactions.

Action Manager Template

An Action Manager object can manage other CourseBuilder interactions on a page. It can collect the results of other interactions, such as multiple-choice questions, and submit those results to a computer-managed instruction (CMI) system. Don't confuse an Action Manager object, which defines actions regarding other Course-Builder interactions on the page, with the Action Mgr tab, which defines the conditions and actions for each individual interaction

Figure 23-9 shows the General tab of the Action Manager interaction (a.k.a. the Action Manager template). The General tab can be used, for example, to tell CourseBuilder to judge the other interactions on the page when the user clicks a button (such as a Submit button). The documentation under Help → Using Course-Builder includes suggestions and guidelines for using Action Manager interactions, including using multiple Action Manager objects on a single page. Use the Action Mgr tab to specify how an Action Manager object will judge other interactions, as described in the section "The Actions Mgr Tab" later in this chapter.

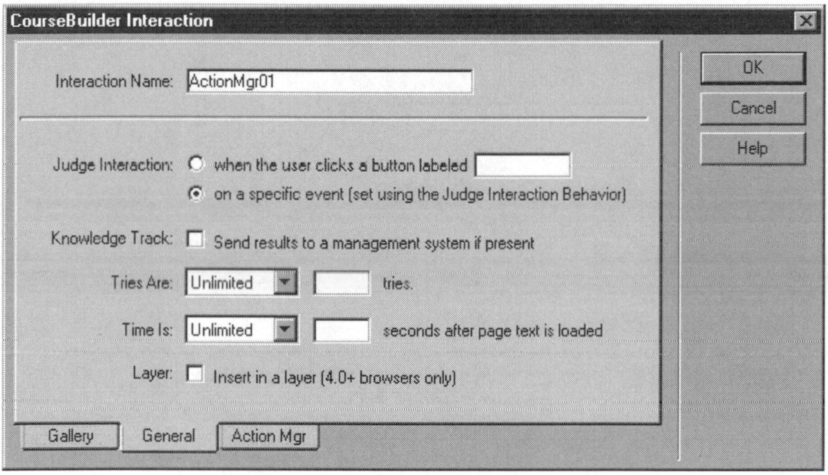

Figure 23-9: General tab of the default Action Manager interaction

Configuring Interactions

CourseBuilder interactions are designed speed courseware development, but you must configure each interaction for your unique needs. If you select one of the Multiple Choice interactions, for example, you must specify a question and possible answers. Customize each interaction's options using the tabs at the bottom of the CourseBuilder Interaction dialog box (these tabs differ depending on the class of interaction selected from the Gallery tab). For example, the General tab of the MultCh_ImageChkboxes01 interaction, shown in Figure 23-10, lets you configure the Multiple Choice object.

The General tab is present for all interactions, and the contents of the tab are highly similar for each class of interaction. The top of the General tab includes the interaction's name and some interaction-specific configuration options. For multiple choice questions, for example, specify the text of the question to ask.

The lower portion of the General tab includes options that determine when the interaction is judged, what constitutes a correct answer, whether to send the results to a Knowledge Track system, how many attempts (tries) to allow the user, the time limit, whether to provide a reset button, and whether to place the interaction's contents within a layer (the last option is also available in the Property inspector).

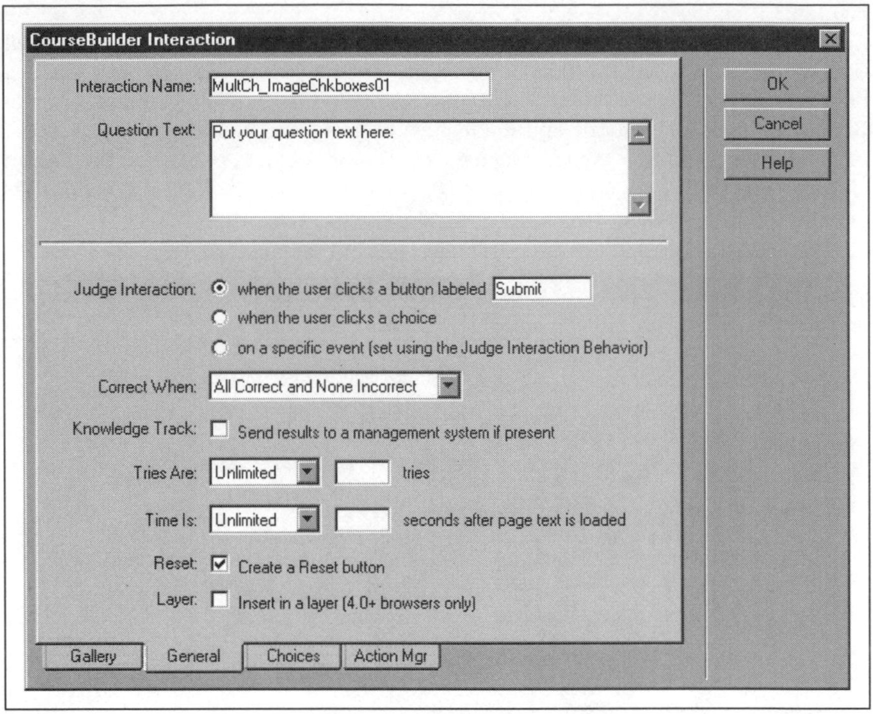

Figure 23-10: General tab for Multiple Choice interactions

Other tabs in the CourseBuilder Interaction dialog box vary in scope and number for each type of interaction. For example, Multiple Choice interactions have a Choices tab, shown in Figure 23-11, that let you specify the multiple choice answers and other options.

The other classes of interactions include tabs specific to their requirements as described under Help → Using CourseBuilder.

The Actions Mgr Tab

Each CourseBuilder interaction (including Action Manager objects) includes an Action Mgr tab similar to the one shown in Figure 23-12. The Action Mgr tab contains the Actions list that controls how the objects interact and how they are affected by different conditions.

The Action list contains one or more *segments*, as seen in Figure 23-12, and segments are evaluated from top to bottom. Actions can be triggered by a user event (such as clicking a Submit button), a Judge Interaction event (as configured in an interaction's General tab), or a timer expiration event (when the user exceeds the allowed time).

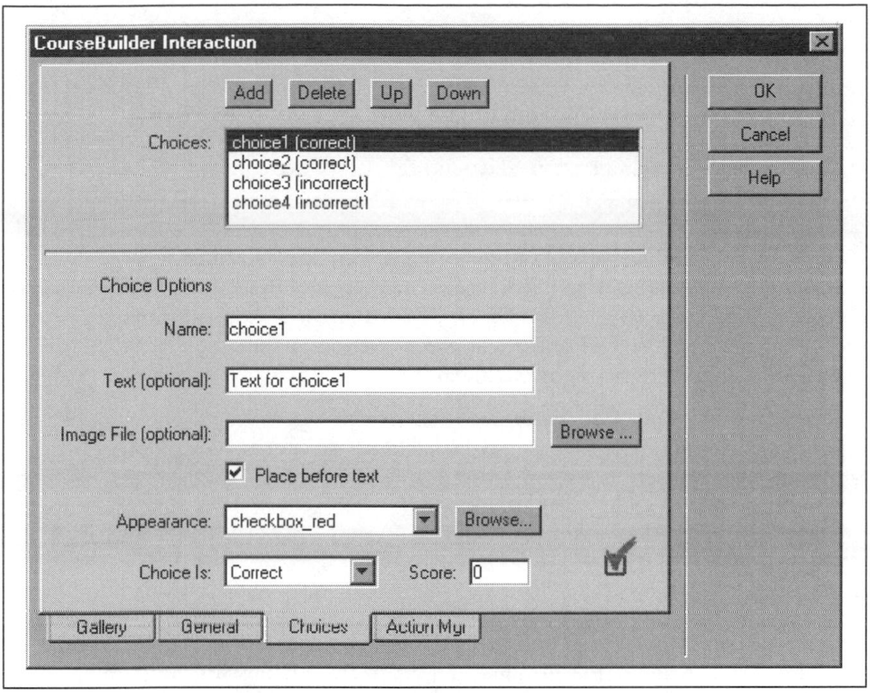

Figure 23-11: Choices tab for Multiple Choice interactions

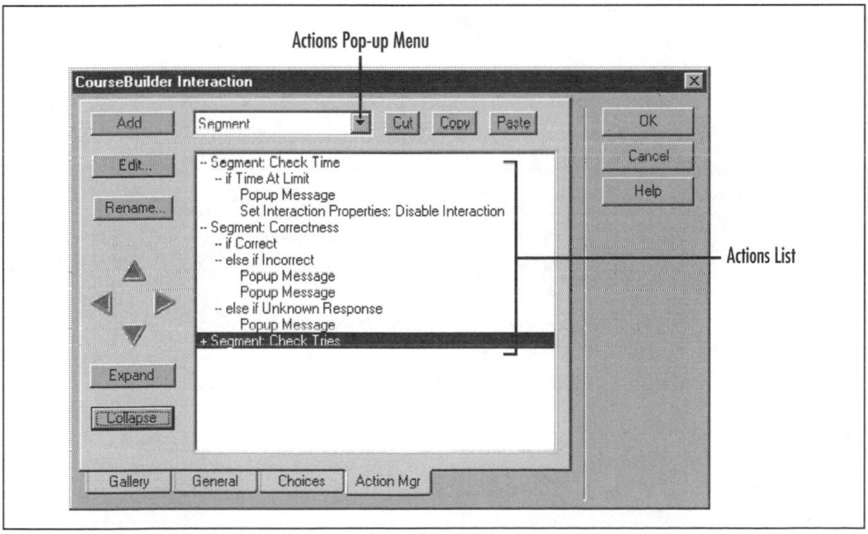

Figure 23-12: Action Mgr tab for Multiple Choice interactions

The Actions list contains logic to implement your courseware, such as displaying a message when the user gets the wrong answer. By default, most interactions display a pop-up message when a condition is met. You will usually delete the Popup Message behavior and replace it with a customized action.

Use the Expand and Collapse buttons in the Action Mgr tab to expand or collapse portions of the Actions list. Use the Cut, Copy, and Paste buttons to move or delete an item in the list. Use the Up and Down arrow buttons to move an item in the hierarchy. Use the Left and Right arrow buttons to indent or outdent a line item (i.e., change its position in the hierarchy).

There are several supported action types as seen in Figure 23-12. The Actions pop-up menu includes entries for Segments, logical structures (Condition, Else, and Stop), behaviors (such as Popup Message), CourseBuilder actions (such as Judge Interaction), and Tracking actions (to submit data). To add a new item to the Actions list, select the action type from the Actions pop-up menu and click the Add button.

Segments

Segments are containers for all other actions in the Actions list. Most interactions include three segments by default, which check the correctness of the user entry (Correctness), whether time has expired (Check Time), and whether the user has exceeded the allowed number of attempts (Check Tries). The Check Time and Check Tries segments are ignored if the General tab options specify unlimited tries and time. To add a segment, select Segment from the Actions pop-up menu and click the Add button. To open the Segment Editor, shown in Figure 23-13, select a segment from the Actions list (see Figure 23-12) and click the Edit button.

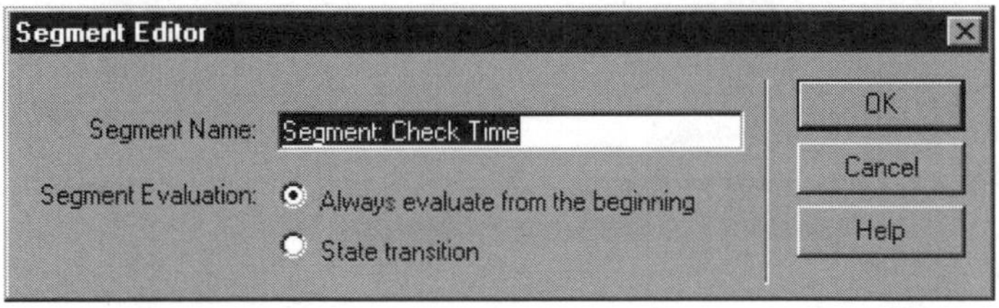

Segment Editor	☒
Segment Name: Segment: Check Time	OK
Segment Evaluation: ⊙ Always evaluate from the beginning	Cancel
○ State transition	Help

Figure 23-13: Segment Editor

In the Segment Editor, specify the segment's name. The Segment Evaluation field is typically set to Always Evaluate From The Beginning, except for Timer interactions, which use the State Transition option.

Logical structures

Three logical options—Condition, Else, and Stop—can be added by selecting one of them in the Actions pop-up menu and clicking the Add button.

Condition

Use the Condition option to create logical if statements. If an if statement already exists within a segment, this option adds an else if statement automatically. Conditional statements can be modified using the Condition Editor, shown in Figure 23-14, which is opened by selecting a condition from the Actions list and clicking the Edit button.

Else

Use the Else option to create an else clause following an if or else if statement.

Stop

Use the Stop option to halt logical processing (skip the rest of the actions in the Actions list)

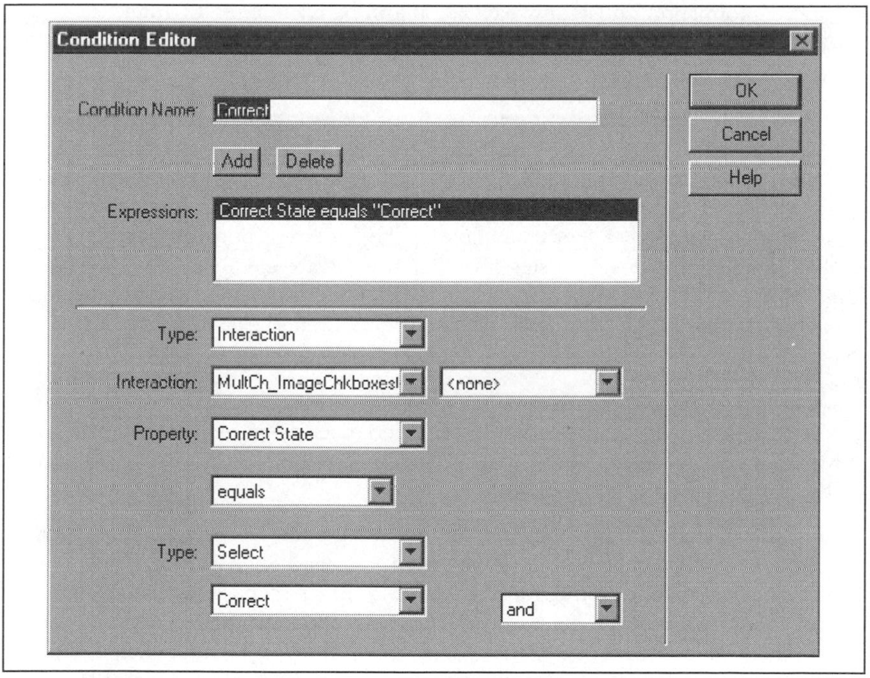

Figure 23-14: Condition Editor

Behaviors

The behaviors available in the Actions pop-up menu are the same ones available in the Dreamweaver Behaviors panel. To add a behavior, select its name from the Actions pop-up menu and click the Add button. By default, most interactions trigger the Popup Message behavior, which simply displays a message to the user. You'll typically replace the Popup Message behavior with something more interesting such as a Go To URL action. To replace a behavior in the Actions list (see Figure 23-12), delete it using the Cut button, and then insert a new behavior using the Add button.

When you edit a behavior using the Edit button, Dreamweaver displays the behaviors parameters dialog box specific to that behavior (the same one used when editing a behavior in the Behaviors panel). For example, the Popup Message dialog box, shown in Figure 23-15, lets you edit a message displayed to the user.

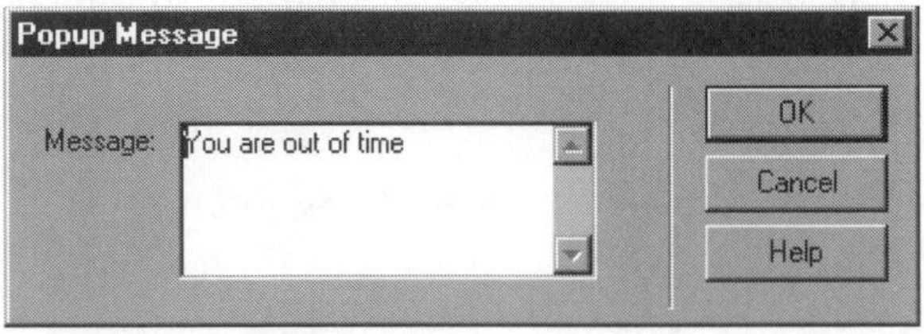

Figure 23-15: The Popup Message dialog box

For more information on Dreamweaver's built-in behaviors, see Chapter 12.

CourseBuilder actions

There are three CourseBuilder-specific actions—Judge Interaction, Reset Interaction, and Set Interaction Properties—which can be added by selecting one of them in the Actions pop-up menu and clicking the Add button. These actions initiate the judging of other CourseBuilder interactions, reset the state of an interaction, or set an interaction's properties. For example, use the Set Interaction Properties action to enable, disable, or change the state of other courseware elements. To open the Set Interaction Properties dialog box, shown in Figure 23-16, select a Set Interaction Properties item from the Actions list (see Figure 23-12) and click the Edit button.

Tracking actions

Tracking actions allow CourseBuilder to send data to a remote database or a computer-managed instruction (CMI) system such as IBM LearningSpace (formerly Lotus LearningSpace and Pathware).

There are eight tracking-specific actions, including Send Core Data, Send Interaction Info, Send Lesson Status, Send Objective Info, and Send Score, which can be added by selecting one of them in the Actions pop-up menu and clicking the Add button. These actions can be used to communicate to a remote server running appropriate middleware. See "Scoring and Data Tracking" under Help → Using CourseBuilder for information on the tracking actions. See the CourseBuilder web site for information about interfacing to a database using CGI, ASP, ColdFusion, or other database server software. Refer also to the "Knowledge Track: Sends Results to a Management System If Present" option under the General tab.

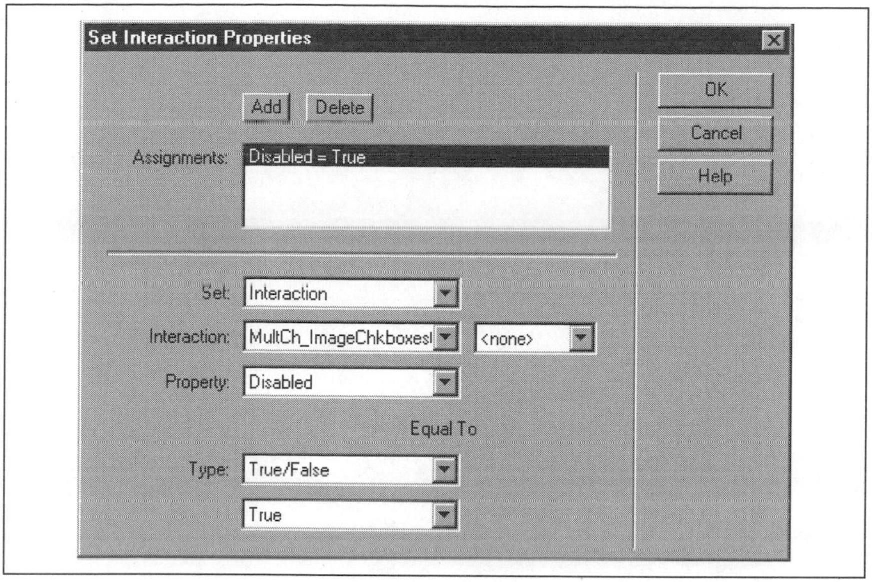

Figure 23-16: Set Interaction Properties dialog box

We've covered a lot of territory in this book. You should now be well on your way to mastering Dreamweaver and developing sites with it efficiently. The appendixes collate reference material to help keep your development on track. Pay special attention to the development and deployment guidelines in Appendix C. Good luck!

PART V

Appendixes

The appendixes include important reference information you'll need during site development.

APPENDIX A

Keyboard Shortcuts

Macromedia has standardized keyboard shortcuts across many of their products. As described in Chapter 20, you can save and print the keyboard shortcuts using the Export Set as HTML button in the Keyboard Shortcuts dialog box (accessible under Edit → Keyboard Shortcuts. This appendix lists keyboard shortcuts in the Macromedia Standard keyboard shortcut set for both Macintosh and Windows. The meaning assigned to a keyboard shortcut may vary depending on which Dreamweaver window is active. Some shortcuts may not work on some computers, particularly laptops, which intercept some function keys. If a shortcut does not work on the Macintosh, such as F12 to launch the primary browser, turn off the Hot Function Key option in the Keyboard Control Panel.

Window Menu and Panels

The Window menu allows you to open the myriad of panels available in Dreamweaver, as listed in Table A-1. Table A-1 is an enhanced version of Table 1-4.

Table A-1: Dreamweaver panels and shortcuts

Action	Menu	Windows	Macintosh
Objects panel	Window → Object	Ctrl+F2	Cmd+F2
Property inspector	Window → Properties or Modify → Selection Properties	Ctrl+F3, Ctrl+Shift+J	Cmd+F3, Cmd+Shift+J
Launcher	Window → Launcher	Alt+W, U	N/A
Site Files view	Window → Site Files or Site → Site Files	F8	F8
Site Map view	Window → Site Map or Site → Site Map	Alt+F8	Opt+F8
Assets panel	Window → Assets	F11	F11
Behaviors panel	Window → Behaviors	Shift+F3	Shift+F3

Table A-1: Dreamweaver panels and shortcuts (continued)

Action	Menu	Windows	Macintosh
Code Inspector	Window → Code Inspector	F10	F10
CSS Styles panel	Window → CSS Styles	Shift+F11	Shift+F11
Frames panel	Window → Frames	Shift+F2	Shift+F2
History panel	Window → History	Shift+F10	Shift+F10
HTML Styles panel	Window → HTML Styles	Ctrl+F11	Cmd+F11
Layers panel	Window → Layers	F2	F2
Library category of Assets panel	Window → Library	Alt+W, I	N/A
Reference panel (open or close)	**Window** → Reference	Ctrl+Shift+F1	Cmd+Shift+F1
Reference tab	Help → Reference	Shift+F1	Shift+F1
Timelines panel	Window → Timelines	Shift+F9	Shift+F9
Templates category of Assets panel	Window → Templates	Alt+W, M	N/A
Arrange panels	Window → Arrange Panels	Alt+W, G	N/A
Show/Hide panels	Window → Show/Hide Panels	F4	F4
Minimize all panels	Window → Minimize All (Windows only)	Shift+F4	Not supported
Restore all panels	Window → Restore All (Windows only)	Alt+Shift+F4	Not supported
Document window	Window → *document*	N/A	N/A
Quick Tag Editor	Modify → Quick Tag Editor	Ctrl+T	Cmd+T

Help Menu

The Help menu provides access to outstanding help resources, including the full text of Macromedia's *Using Dreamweaver* and *Extending Dreamweaver* manuals, the O'Reilly Reference panel (HTML, CSS, and JavaScript documentation), tutorials, and online resources. Its options are listed in Table A-2. Some options without keyboard shortcuts are not shown.

Table A-2: Help menu options and shortcuts

Action	Menu	Windows	Macintosh
What's New, Guided Tour, Tutorial, Lessons	Help → Welcome	Alt+H, W	N/A
Help on using Dreamweaver	Help → Using Dreamweaver	F1	F1
Open or close Reference panel	Window → Reference	Ctrl+Shift+F1	Cmd+Shift+F1
Activate Reference tab	Help → Reference	Shift+F1	Shift+F1
Technical support (web site)	Help → Dreamweaver Support Center	Alt+H, D	N/A

Action	Menu	Windows	Macintosh
Macromedia forums (newsgroups)	Help → Macromedia Online Forums	Alt+H, M, M	N/A
Help on extending Dreamweaver	Help → Extending Dreamweaver	Alt+H, E	N/A

File and Edit Menu

The document manipulation options, found primarily on the File and Edit menus, are shown in Table A-3. Some options without keyboard shortcuts are not shown.

Table A-3: Document manipulation options and shortcuts

Action	Menu	Windows	Macintosh
New document	File → New	Ctrl+N	Cmd+N
New document from template	File → New from Template	Alt+F, W	N/A
Open an HTML file	File → Open	Ctrl+O	Cmd+O
Open in frame	File → Open in Frame	Ctrl+Shift+O	Cmd+Shift+O
Close File	File → Close	Ctrl+W Ctrl+F4	Cmd+W
Save File	File → Save	Ctrl+S	Cmd+S
Save (frameset) as	File → Save As, or File → Save Frameset As	Ctrl+Shift+S	Cmd+Shift+S
Save all (frames)	File → Save All, or File → Save All Frames	Alt+F, L	N/A
Preview in primary browser	File → Preview in Browser → *primary*	F12	F12
Preview in secondary browser	File → Preview in Browser → *secondary*	Ctrl+F12, Shift+F12	Cmd+F12, Shift+F12
Debug in primary browser	File → Debug in Browser → *primary*	Alt+F12	Opt+F12
Debug in secondary browser	File → Debug in Browser → *secondary*	Ctrl+Alt+F12	Cmd+Opt+F12
Check links	File → Check Links	Shift+F8	Shift+F8
Check links sitewide	Site ▸ Check Links Sitewide	Ctrl+F8	Cmd+F8
Exit (quit application)	File → Exit	Ctrl+Q Alt+F4	Cmd+Q Opt+F4
Undo	Edit → Undo	Ctrl+Z, Alt+BkSp	Cmd+Z, Opt+BkSp
Redo	Edit → Redo	Ctrl+Y, Ctrl+Shift+Z	Cmd+Y, Cmd+Shift+Z
Cut	Edit → Cut	Ctrl+X, Shift+Del	Cmd+X, Shift+Del
Copy	Edit → Copy	Ctrl+C, Ctrl+Ins	Cmd+C, Cmd+Ins
Paste	Edit → Paste	Ctrl+V, Shift+Ins	Cmd+V, Shift+Ins
Clear	Edit → Clear	Del or BkSp	Del or BkSp

Table A-3: Document manipulation options and shortcuts (continued)

Action	Menu	Windows	Macintosh
Copy HTML	Edit → Copy HTML	Ctrl+Shift+C	Cmd+Shift+C
Paste HTML	Edit → Paste HTML	Ctrl+Shift+V	Cmd+Shift+V
Select all	Edit → Select All	Ctrl+A	Cmd+A
Select parent tag	Edit → Select Parent Tag	Ctrl+Shift+<	Cmd+Shift+<
Select child tag	Edit → Select Child	Ctrl+Shift+>	Cmd+Shift+>
Find and replace	Edit → Find and Replace	Ctrl+F Ctrl+H	Cmd+F Cmd+H
Find next/again	Edit → Find Next (Windows) Edit → Find Again (Macintosh)	F3	Cmd+G
Launch external editor	Edit → Edit with *editor*	Ctrl+E	Cmd+E
Preferences	Edit → Preferences	Ctrl+U	Cmd+U
Open History panel	Window → History	Shift+F10	Shift+F10
Page properties	Modify → Page Properties	Ctrl+J	Cmd+J

Document View Options

The document view options control the appearance of your document within the document. The options shown in Table A-4 are found on the View menu.

Table A-4: Document view options and shortcuts

Action	Menu	Windows	Macintosh
Switch views	View → Switch Views	Ctrl+Tab	Opt+Tab
Refresh Design view	View → Refresh Design View	F5	F5
Head Content bar	View → Head Content	Ctrl+Shift+W	Cmd+Shift+W
Switch to standard table view	View → Table View → Standard	Ctrl+Shift+F6	Cmd+Shift+F6
Switch to layout table view	View → Table View → Layout	Ctrl+F6	Cmd+F6
Toggle visibility of all elements	View → Visual Aids → Hide All	Ctrl+Shift+I	Cmd+Shift+I
Show rulers	View → Rulers → Show	Ctrl+Alt+R	Cmd+Opt+R
Show gridlines	View → Grid → Show Grid	Ctrl+Alt+G	Cmd+Opt+G
Snap to gridlines	View → Grid → Snap to Grid	Ctrl+Alt+Shift+G	Cmd+Opt+Shift+G
Show/hide panels	View → Show/Hide Panels	F4	F4
Plugins	View → Plugins	See Table A-14	See Table A-14
Document window toolbar	View → Toolbar	Ctrl+Shift+T	Cmd+Shift+T

Insert Menu

The Insert menu inserts HTML objects into a document, as indicated in Table A-5. Also see the Objects panel and Table 1-1 in Chapter 1, the discussion of core objects in Chapter 2, the insertion of external assets in Chapter 5, and the coverage of forms in Chapter 3.

Table A-5. Insert menu options and shortcuts

Insert	Menu	Windows	Macintosh
Hyperlink	Modify → Make Link	Ctrl+L	Cmd+L
Image	Insert → Image	Ctrl+Alt+I	Cmd+Opt+I
Rollover image	Insert → Interactive Images → Rollover Image	Alt+I, N, R	N/A
Navigation bar	Insert → Interactive Images → Navigation Bar	Alt+I, N, G	N/A
Flash Button	Insert → Interactive Images → Flash Button	Alt+I, N, F	N/A
Flash Text	Insert → Interactive Images → Flash Text	Alt+I, N, L	N/A
Fireworks HTML	Insert → Interactive Images → Fireworks HTML	Alt+I, N, I	N/A
Flash media	Insert → Media → Flash	Ctrl+Alt+F	Cmd+Opt+F
Shockwave media	Insert → Media → Shockwave	Ctrl+Alt+D	Cmd+Opt+D
Generator media	Insert → Media → Generator	Alt+I, M, G	N/A
Java Applet	Insert → Media → Applet	Alt+I, M, A	N/A
Plugin	Insert → Media → Plugin	Alt+I, M, P	N/A
ActiveX control	Insert → Media → ActiveX	Alt+I, M, C	N/A
HTML table	Insert → Table	Ctrl+Alt+T	Cmd+Opt+T
Layer	Insert → Layer	Alt+I, Y	N/A
Insert frames	Insert → Frames	Alt+I, S	N/A
Form	Insert → Form	Alt+I, F	N/A
Text field	Insert → Form Objects → Text Field	Alt+I, B, T	N/A
Button	Insert → Form Objects → Button	Alt+I, B, B	N/A
Checkbox	Insert → Form Objects → Check Box	Alt+I, B, C	N/A
Radio button	Insert → Form Objects → Radio Button	Alt+I, B, R	N/A
List/menu	Insert → Form Objects → List/Menu	Alt+I, B, L	N/A
File field	Insert → Form Objects → File Field	Alt+I, B, F	N/A
Image field	Insert → Form Objects → Image Field	Alt+I, B, I	N/A
Hidden field	Insert → Form Objects → Hidden Field	Alt+I, B, H	N/A
Jump menu	Insert → Form Objects → Jump Menu	Alt+I, B, J	N/A

Insert	Menu	Windows	Macintosh
Server-side include	Insert → Server-Side Include	Alt+I, E	N/A
Email link	Insert → Email Link	Alt+I, L	N/A
Date	Insert → Date	Alt+I, D	N/A
Tabular data	Insert → Tabular Data	Alt+I, A	N/A
Horizontal rule	Insert → Horizontal Rule	Alt+I, Z	N/A
Named anchor	Insert → Invisible Tags → Named Anchor	Ctrl+Alt+A	Cmd+Opt+A
Script	Insert → Invisible Tags → Script	Alt+I, V, P	N/A
Comment	Insert → Invisible Tags → Comment	Alt+I, V, O	N/A
Meta tag	Insert → Head Tags → Meta	Alt+I, H, M	N/A
Keywords	Insert → Head Tags → Keywords	Alt+I, H, K	N/A
Description	Insert → Head Tags → Description	Alt+I, H, D	N/A
Refresh	Insert → Head Tags → Refresh	Alt+I, H, R	N/A
Base tag	Insert → Head Tags → Base	Alt+I, H, B	N/A
Link tag	Insert → Head Tags → Link	Alt+I, H, L	N/A
Line break	Insert → Special Characters → Line Break	Shift+Return	Shift+Return
Nonbreaking space	Insert → Special Characters → Non-Breaking Space	Ctrl+Shift+Space	Cmd+Shift+Space
Copyright symbol	Insert → Special Characters → Copyright	Alt+I, C, C	N/A
Registered trade-mark symbol	Insert → Special Characters → Registered	Alt+I, C, R	N/A
Trademark symbol	Insert → Special Characters → Trademark	Alt+I, C, T	N/A
Pound symbol	Insert → Special Characters → Pound	Alt+I, C, P	N/A
Yen symbol	Insert → Special Characters → Yen	Alt+I, C, Y	N/A
Euro symbol	Insert → Special Characters → Euro	Alt+I, C, U	N/A
Left quote	Insert → Special Characters → Left Quote	Alt+I, C, L	N/A
Right quote	Insert → Special Characters → Right Quote	Alt+I, C, I	N/A
Em-dash	Insert → Special Characters → Em-Dash	Alt+I, C, M	N/A
Other characters	Insert → Special Characters → Other	Alt+I, C, O	N/A
More object types from Exchange	Insert → Get More Objects	Alt+I, G	N/A

Editing and Formatting Text

The options in Table A-6 control text formatting. See Table A-16 for text editing shortcuts.

Table A-6: Text editing and formatting keyboard shortcuts

Action	Menu or Keyboard	Windows	Macintosh
Left-align objects	Modify → Align → Left	Ctrl+Shift+1	Cmd+Shift+1
Right-align objects	Modify → Align → Right	Ctrl+Shift+3	Cmd+Shift+3
Align object tops	Modify → Align → Top	Ctrl+Shift+4	Cmd+Shift+4
Align object bottoms	Modify → Align → Bottom	Ctrl+Shift+6	Cmd+Shift+6
Make objects same width	Modify → Align → Make Same Width	Ctrl+Shift+7	Cmd+Shift+7
Make objects same height	Modify → Align → Make Same Height	Ctrl+Shift+9	Cmd+Shift+9
Indent text	Text → Indent	Ctrl+Alt+]	Cmd+Opt+]
Outdent text	Text → Outdent	Ctrl+Alt+[	Cmd+Opt+[
Paragraph format	Text → Paragraph Format	Ctrl+Shift+P	Cmd+Shift+P
No paragraph formatting	Text → Paragraph Format → None	Ctrl+0	Cmd+0
Heading 1	Text → Paragraph Format → Heading 1	Ctrl+1	Cmd+1
Heading 2	Text → Paragraph Format → Heading 2	Ctrl+2	Cmd+2
Heading 3	Text → Paragraph Format → Heading 3	Ctrl+3	Cmd+3
Heading 4	Text → Paragraph Format → Heading 4	Ctrl+4	Cmd+4
Heading 5	Text → Paragraph Format → Heading 5	Ctrl+5	Cmd+5
Heading 6	Text → Paragraph Format → Heading 6	Ctrl+6	Cmd+6
Left-align text	Text → Align → Left	Ctrl+Alt+Shift+L	Cmd+Opt+Shift+L
Center text	Text → Align → Center	Ctrl+Alt+Shift+C	Cmd+Opt+Shift+C
Right-align text	Text → Align → Right	Ctrl+Alt+Shift+R	Cmd+Opt+Shift+R
Bold	Text → Style → Bold	Ctrl+B	Cmd+B
Italic	Text → Style → Italic	Ctrl+I	Cmd+I
Edit CSS stylesheet	Text → CSS Styles → Edit CSS Style Sheet	Ctrl+Shift+E	Cmd+Shift+E
Check spelling	Text → Check Spelling	Shift+F7	Shift+F7

Hyperlinks

The options in Table A-7 control hyperlinks in Dreamweaver. You can read more about managing hyperlinks in Chapter 2.

Table A-7: Hyperlink options

Action	Menu	Windows	Macintosh
Make/change link	Modify → Make/Change Link	Ctrl+L	Cmd+L
Remove link	Modify → Remove Link	Ctrl+Shift+L	Cmd+Shift+L
Modify link in Property inspector	Modify → Selection Properties	Ctrl+Shift+J	Cmd+Shift+J
Insert email link	Insert → Email Link	Alt+I, L	N/A
Insert named anchor	Insert → Invisible Tags → Named Anchor	Ctrl+Alt+A	Cmd+Opt+A

Tables

Table A-8 documents the options for manipulating tables. You can read more about managing tables in Chapter 3.

Table A-8: Options for manipulating tables

Action	Menu or description	Windows	Macintosh
Select table	Modify → Table → Select Table	Ctrl+A	Cmd+A
Merge cells	Modify → Table → Merge Cells	Ctrl+Alt+M	Cmd+Opt+M
Split cells	Modify → Table → Split Cells	Ctrl+Alt+S	Cmd+Opt+S
Insert row	Modify → Table → Insert Row	Ctrl+M	Cmd+M
Insert column	Modify → Table → Insert Column	Ctrl+Shift+A	Cmd+Shift+A
Insert rows and columns	Modify → Table → Insert Rows and Columns	Alt+M, T, I	N/A
Delete row	Modify → Table → Delete Row	Ctrl+Shift+M	Cmd+Shift+M
Delete column	Modify → Table → Delete Column	Ctrl+Shift+-	Cmd+Shift+-
Increase row span	Modify → Table → Increase Row Span	Alt+M, T, R	N/A
Increase cell column span	Modify → Table → Increase Column Span	Ctrl+Shift+]	Cmd+Shift+]
Decrease row span	Modify → Table → Decrease Row Span	Alt+M, T, W	N/A
Decrease cell column span	Modify → Table → Decrease Column Span	Ctrl+Shift+[	Cmd+Shift+[
Clear cell heights	Modify → Table → Clear Cell Heights	Alt+M, T, H	N/A
Clear cell widths	Modify → Table → Clear Cell Widths	Alt+M, T, T	N/A
Convert column widths to pixels	Modify → Table → Convert Widths to Pixels	Alt+M, T, X	N/A
Convert column widths to percent	Modify → Table → Convert Widths to Percent	Alt+M, T, O	N/A

Action	Menu or description	Windows	Macintosh
Left-align object	Modify → Align → Left	Ctrl+Shift+1	Cmd+Shift+1
Right-align object	Modify → Align → Right	Ctrl+Shift+3	Cmd+Shift+3
Top-align object	Modify ▸ Align ▸ Top	Ctrl+Shift+4	Cmd+Shift+4
Bottom-align object	Modify → Align → Bottom	Ctrl+Shift+6	Cmd+Shift+6
Make objects same width	Modify → Align → Make Same Width	Ctrl+Shift+7	Cmd+Shift+7
Make objects same height	Modify → Align → Make Same Height	Ctrl+Shift+9	Cmd+Shift+9
Defer table update	Edit → Preferences → General → Faster Table Updating	Ctrl+Space	Cmd+Space
Standard view	View → Table View → Standard View	Ctrl+Shift+F6	Cmd+Shift+F6
Layout view	View → Table View → Layout View	Ctrl+F6	Cmd+F6
Insert table in Standard view	Insert → Table	Ctrl+Alt+T	Cmd+Opt+T
Draw multiple tables or cells in Layout view	Use Draw Layout Table or Draw Layout Cell tool in Objects panel without reselecting tool	Hold down Ctrl key while drawing	Hold down Cmd key while drawing
Don't snap to grid in Layout view	Prevent tables and cells from snapping to nearby elements (within 8 pixels)	Hold down Alt key while drawing	Hold down Opt key while drawing
Select rectangular area of cells	Click in upper-left corner, then Shift-click in lower-right corner	Shift-click	Shift-click
Contextual menu	Displays contextual popup menu	Right-click	Ctrl-click
Nudge cell by one pixel	Move cells in Layout view	Arrow keys	Arrow keys
Nudge cell by ten pixels	Move cells in Layout view	Shift+arrow keys	Shift+arrow keys
Next cell	Move insertion point to next cell (adds a new row if necessary)	Tab	Tab
Previous cell	Move insertion point to previous cell	Shift+Tab	Shift+Tab
Format table	Commands → Format Table	Alt+C, F	N/A
Sort table	Commands → Sort Table	Alt+C, S	N/A
Import tabular data	File → Import → Import Tabular Data	Alt+F, I, T	N/A
Export tabular data	File → Export → Export Table	Alt+F, E, T	N/A
Create layers from a table	Modify → Convert → Tables to Layers	Alt+M, C, T	N/A
Create a table from layers	Modify → Convert → Layers to Table	Alt+M, C, L	N/A

Keyboard
Shortcuts

Frames

Table A-9 documents the options for manipulating frames. You can read more about managing frames in Chapter 4.

Table A-9: Options for manipulating frames

Action	Menu or command	Windows	Macintosh
Open Frames panel	Window → Frames	Shift+F2	Shift+F2
Open a document in current frame	File → Open in Frame	Ctrl+Shift+O	Cmd+Shift+O
Save (frameset) as	File → Save Frameset As	Ctrl+Shift+S	Cmd+Shift+S
Save all (frames)	File → Save All Frames	Alt+F, L	N/A
Left frame	Insert → Frames → Left	Alt+I, S, L	N/A
Right frame	Insert → Frames → Right	Alt+I, S, R	N/A
Top frame	Insert → Frames → Top	Alt+I, S, T	N/A
Bottom frame	Insert → Frames → Bottom	Alt+I, S, B	N/A
Left and top frames	Insert → Frames → Left and Top	Alt+I, S, E	N/A
Left top frame	Insert → Frames → Left Top	Alt+I, S, F	N/A
Top left frame	Insert → Frames → Top Left	Alt+I, S, O	N/A
Split into frames	Insert → Frames → Split	Alt+I, S, S	N/A
Modify content of noframes tag	Modify → Frameset → Edit NoFrames content	Alt+M, F, E	N/A
Create frame on right	Modify → Frameset → Split Frame Left	Alt+M, F, L	N/A
Create frame on left	Modify → Frameset → Split Frame Right	Alt+M, F, R	N/A
Create frame on bottom	Modify → Frameset → Split Frame Up	Alt+M, F, U	N/A
Create frame on top	Modify → Frameset → Split Frame Down	Alt+M, F, D	N/A
Select a frame	Click from in Frames panel	Alt-click in frame	Opt+Shift-click in frame
Select next frame or frameset	Click different frame in Frames panel	Alt+Right	Cmd+Right
Select previous frame or frameset	Click different frame in Frames panel	Alt+Left	Cmd+Left
Select parent frameset	Click edge of in Frames panel	Alt+Up	Cmd+Up
Select first child frame or frameset	Click child frame in Frames panel	Alt+Down	Cmd+Down

Table A-9: Options for manipulating frames (continued)

Action	Menu or command	Windows	Macintosh
Add a new frame to frameset	See Frames category in Objects panel	Alt-drag frame border	Opt-drag frame border
Add a new frame to frameset using push method	Modify → Frameset submenu	Alt+Ctrl-drag frame border	Cmd+Opt-drag frame border

Layers

Table A-10 documents the options for manipulating layers. You can read more about managing layers in Chapters 2, 14, and 17.

Table A-10: Options for manipulating layers

Action	Windows	Macintosh
Select layer	Ctrl+Shift-click	Cmd+Shift-click
Select and move layer	Ctrl+Shift-drag	Cmd+Shift-drag
Add or remove layer from selection	Shift-click layer	Shift-click layer
Move selected layer by 1 pixel	Arrow keys	Arrow keys
Move selected layer by 10 pixels	Shift+Arrow keys	Shift+Arrow keys
Resize selected layer by 1 pixel	Ctrl+Arrow keys	Opt+Arrow keys Cmd+Arrow keys
Resize selected layer by 10 pixels	Ctrl+Shift+Arrow keys	Opt+Shift+Arrow keys Cmd+Shift+Arrow keys
Align selected layers to the Top/Bottom/Left/Right of the last selected layer	Ctrl+Up/Down/Left/Right Arrow	Cmd+Up/Down/Left/ Right Arrow
Make selected layers the same width	Ctrl+Shift+[	Cmd+Shift+[
Make selected layers the same height	Ctrl+Shift+]	Cmd+Shift+]
Modify → Convert → Tables to Layers	Alt+M, C, T	N/A
Modify → Convert → Layers to Table	Alt+M, C, L	N/A
Toggle nesting preference on or off when creating a layer	Ctrl-drag	Cmd-drag
Toggle the display of the grid	Ctrl+Alt+Shift+G	Cmd+Opt+Shift+G
Snap To grid	Ctrl+Alt+G	Cmd+Opt+G
Add keyframe to timeline	F6	F6
Remove keyframe from timeline	Shift+F6	Shift+F6

Site Menu in Main Menu Bar

Table A-11 documents the options and shortcuts for the Site menu in the main menu bar (i.e., the Document window). See Table A-12 for details on the Site window menu bar, which applies to Windows only. See Table A-13 for details on the Site → Site Files View and Site → Site Map View submenus, which apply to Macintosh only. Some options without shortcuts are not shown (see Chapter 6 for details).

Table A-11: Site menu options

Action	Menu	Windows	Macintosh
Site Files view	Site → Site Files	F8	F8
Site Map view	Site → Site Map	Alt+F8	Opt+F8
Define new site	Site → New Site[a]	Alt+S, N	N/A
Open site	Site → Open Site → *site from list*[a]	Alt+S, O	N/A
Define or edit sites	Site → Define Sites[a]	Alt+S, D	N/A
Connect/disconnect from server	Site → Connect/Disconnect[a]	Ctrl+Alt+Shift+F5	N/A
Download files	Site → Get[a]	Ctrl+Shift+D	Cmd+Shift+D
Check out files	Site → Check Out[a]	Ctrl+Alt+Shift+D	Cmd+Opt+Shift+D
Upload files	Site → Put[a]	Ctrl+Shift+U	Cmd+Shift+U
Check in files	Site → Check In[a]	Ctrl+Alt+Shift+U	Cmd+Opt+Shift+U
Undo file check out	Site → Undo Check Out[a]	Alt+S, U	N/A
Reports	Site → Reports[a]	Alt+S, T	N/A
Check links sitewide	Site → Check Links Sitewide[a]	Ctrl+F8	Cmd+F8
Check links for current file	Site → Check Links	Shift+F8	Shift+F8
Locate in Local Site	Site → Locate in Local Site[b]	Alt+S, L	N/A
Locate in Remote Site	Site → Locate in Remote Site[b]	Alt+S, R	N/A

[a] Also available from Site menu of Site window (Windows only).
[b] Also available from Edit menu of Site window (Windows only).

Site Window Menus

Table A-12 documents the options and shortcuts available in the Site window (the Site window has a menu bar in Windows only). See Table A-11 for details on the Document window's Site menu. Also see Chapters 6 and 7.

Table A-12: Site window menu options

Action	Menu (Windows only)	Windows	Macintosh
Open new Document window	New → Window	Ctrl+N	Cmd+N
Create new document from template	New from Template	Alt+F, M	N/A
Create and link to new file[a]	File → New File	Ctrl+Shift+N	Cmd+Shift+N
Create new folder	File → New Folder	Ctrl+Alt+Shift+N	Cmd+Opt+Shift+N
Open existing file	File → Open	Ctrl+O	Cmd+O
Open selected file	File → Open Selection	Ctrl+Alt+Shift+O; Enter	Cmd+Opt+Shift+O, Return
Close Site window	File → Close	Ctrl+W; Ctrl+F4	Cmd+W
Save site map picture[a]	File → Save Site Map	Alt+F, V (saves as BMP or PNG)	Saves as PICT or JPEG
Rename file	File → Rename	F2	F2
Delete file	File → Delete	Del	Del
Check links	Site → Check Links	Shift+F8	Shift+F8
Preview in primary browser	File → Preview in Browser → *browser1*	F12	F12
Preview in secondary browser	File → Preview in Browser → *browser2*	Ctrl+F12, Shift+F12	Cmd+F12, Shift+F12
Refresh[b]	View → Refresh	F5	F5
Refresh Local Site[b]	View → Refresh Local	Shift+F5	Shift+F5
Refresh Remote Site[b]	View → Refresh Remote	Alt+F5	Opt+F5
View file as root[a]	View → View as Root	Ctrl+Shift+R	Cmd+Shift+R
Show/hide link[a]	View → Show/Hide Link	Ctrl+Shift+Y	Cmd+Shift+Y
Show page titles[a]	View → Show Page Titles	Ctrl+Shift+T	Cmd+Shift+T
Connect/disconnect from server	Site → Connect Site → Disconnect	Ctrl+Alt+Shift+F5	Cmd+Opt+Shift+F5
Download files	Site → Get	Ctrl+Shift+D	Cmd+Shift+D
Check out files	Site → Check Out	Ctrl+Alt+Shift+D	Cmd+Opt+Shift+D
Upload files	Site → Put	Ctrl+Shift+U	Cmd+Shift+U
Check in files	Site → Check In	Ctrl+Alt+Shift+U	Cmd+Opt+Shift+U
Check links sitewide	Site → Check Links Sitewide	Ctrl+F8	Cmd+F8
Link to new file[a]	Site → Link to New File	Ctrl+Shift+N	Cmd+Shift+N
Link to existing file[a]	Site → Link to Existing	Ctrl+Shift+K	Cmd+Shift+K
Change link[a]	Site → Change Link	Ctrl+L	Cmd+L
Remove link[a]	Site → Remove Link	Ctrl+Shift+L, Delete	Cmd+Shift+L, Delete

Keyboard Shortcuts

Table A-12: Site window menu options (continued)

Action	Menu (Windows only)	Windows	Macintosh
Site Files view	Window → Site Files	F8	F8
Site Map view	Window → Site Map	Alt+F8	Opt+F8
Assets panel	Window → Assets	F11	F11
Minimize all	Window → Minimize All	Shift+F4	N/A
Restore all	Window → Restore All	Alt+Shift+F4	N/A
Help	Help → Using Dreamweaver	F1	F1
Reference panel	Help → Reference	Shift+F1	Shift+F1
Zoom in site map	N/A	Ctrl+ + (plus)	Cmd+ + (plus)
Zoom out site map	N/A	Ctrl+ - (hyphen)	Cmd+ - (hyphen)
Cancel FTP Transfer	N/A	Esc	Esc
Open Code Inspector	N/A	F10	F10

a Also available under Site → Site Map View menu of the main menu bar (Macintosh only).
b Also available under Site → Site Files View menu of the main menu bar (Macintosh only).

Commands Menu

Table A-13 lists the two Commands menu shortcuts (see Chapter 7 for details). Because Dreamweaver does not have a print function, the Ctrl+P (Windows) and Cmd+P (Macintosh) commands typically used for printing play recorded macro commands.

Table A-13: Commands menu shortcuts

Action	Menu	Windows	Macintosh
Record a command	Commands → Start Recording	Ctrl+Shift+X	Cmd+Shift+X
Play a recorded command	Commands → Play Recorded Command	Ctrl+P	Cmd+P

Plugins Options

Table A-14 lists the options for working with plugins. See Chapter 5.

Table A-14: Plugin option shortcuts

Action	Menu	Windows	Macintosh
Play plugins	View → Plugins → Play	Ctrl+Alt+P	Cmd+Opt+P
Stop plugins	View → Plugins → Stop	Ctrl+Alt+X	Cmd+Opt+X
Play all plugins	View → Plugins → Play All	Ctrl+Alt+Shift+P	Cmd+Opt+Shift+P
Stop all plugins	View → Plugins → Stop All	Ctrl+Alt+Shift+X	Cmd+Opt+Shift+X
Insert Plugin	Insert → Media → Plugin	Alt+I, M, P	N/A

Templates and Libraries

Table A-15 lists the shortcuts for templates and library features. See Chapters 8 and 9.

Table A-15: Template and Library option shortcuts

Action	Menu	Windows	Macintosh
Add Object to Library	Modify → Library → Add Object to Library	Ctrl+Shift+B	Cmd+Shift+B
Make New Editable Template Region	Modify → Template → New Editable Region	Ctrl+Alt+V	Cmd+Opt+V

Document Editing Shortcuts

Table A-16 lists the options and shortcuts that control document editing. Also see Chapters 1 and 7.

Table A-16: HTML option shortcuts

Action	Menu	Windows	Macintosh
Undo	Edit → Undo	Ctrl+Z, Alt+BkSp	Cmd+Z, Opt+BkSp
Redo	Edit → Redo	Ctrl+Y, Ctrl+Shift+Z	Cmd+Y, Cmd+Shift+Z
Cut	Edit → Cut	Ctrl+X, Shift+Del	Cmd+X, Shift+Del
Copy	Edit → Copy	Ctrl+C; Ctrl+Ins	Cmd+C, Cmd+Ins
Paste	Edit → Paste	Ctrl+V, Shift+Ins	Cmd+V, Shift+Ins
Copy HTML	Edit → Copy HTML	Ctrl+Shift+C	Cmd+Shift+C
Paste HTML	Edit → Paste HTML	Ctrl+Shift+V	Cmd+Shift+V
Select all	Edit → Select All	Ctrl+A	Cmd+A
Select parent tag	Edit → Select Parent Tag	Ctrl+Shift+<	Cmd+Shift+<
Select child tag	Edit → Select Child	Ctrl+Shift+>	Cmd+Shift+>
Find and replace	Edit → Find and Replace	Ctrl+F	Cmd+F
Find next/again	Edit → Find Next/Again	F3	Cmd+G
Open Quick Tag Editor	Modify → Quick Tag Editor	Ctrl+T	Cmd+T
Balance braces	N/A	Ctrl+'	Cmd+'
Toggle views	View → Switch Views	Ctrl+Tab	Cmd+Tab
Toggle breakpoint	See {} icon in Code view toolbar	Ctrl+Alt+B	Cmd+Opt+B
Delete word left	Modifier+Backspace	Ctrl+BkSp	Cmd+BkSp
Delete word right	Modifier+Delete key	Ctrl+Del	Cmd+Del
Select line up	Shift+up arrow	Shift+Up	Shift+Up
Select line down	Shift+down arrow	Shift+Down	Shift+Down
Select previous character	Shift+left arrow	Shift+Left	Shift+Left
Select next character	Shift+right arrow	Shift+Right	Shift+Right

Table A-16: HTML option shortcuts (continued)

Action	Menu	Windows	Macintosh
Previous page	Page up	PgUp	PgUp
Next page	Page down	PgDn	PgDn
Select previous page	Shift+Page up	Shift+PgUp	Shift+PgUp
Select next page	Shift+Page down	Shift+PgDn	Shift+PgDn
Go to next word	Modfier+right arrow	Ctrl+Right	Cmd+Right
Go to previous word	Modfier+left arrow	Ctrl+Left	Cmd+Left
Go to previous paragraph	Modfier+up arrow	Ctrl+Up	Cmd+Up
Go to next paragraph	Modfier+down arrow	Ctrl+Down	Cmd+Down
Move to start of line	Home	Home	Home
Move to end of line	End	End	End
Select to start of line	Shift+Home	Shift+Home	Shift+Home
Select to end of line	Shift+End	Shift+End	Shift+End
Top of file	Modfier+Home	Ctrl+Home	Cmd+Home
Bottom of file	Modfier+End	Ctrl+End	Cmd+End
Select to start of file	Modfier+Shift+Home	Ctrl+Shift+Home	Cmd+Shift+Home
Select to end of file	Modfier+Shift+End	Ctrl+Shift+End	Cmd+Shift+End
Select until next word	Modfier+Shift+right arrow	Ctrl+Shift+Right	Cmd+Shift+Right
Select from previous word	Modfier+Shift+left arrow	Ctrl+Shift+Left	Cmd+Shift+Left
Select from previous paragraph	Modfier+Shift+up arrow	Ctrl+Shift+Up	Cmd+Shift+Up
Select until next paragraph	Modfier+Shift+down arrow	Ctrl+Shift+Down	Cmd+Shift+Down
Indent code	Edit → Indent Code	Ctrl+]	Cmd+]
Outdent code	Edit → Outdent Code	Ctrl+[	Cmd+[
Launch external editor	Edit → Launch External Editor	Ctrl+E	Cmd+E
Refresh Design View	View → Refresh Design View	F5	F5
View Head Content	View → Head Content	Ctrl+Shift+W	Cmd+Shift+W
Document window toolbar	View → Toolbar	Ctrl+Shift+T	Cmd+Shift+T

Manipulating Timelines

Table A-17 shows the option and shortcuts used to manipulating timelines. Also see Chapter 17.

Table A-17: Timelines options and shortcuts

Action	Menu	Windows	Macintosh
Open Timelines panel	Window → Timelines	Shift+F9	Shift+F9
Add object to timeline	Modify → Timeline → Add Object to Timeline	Ctrl+Alt+Shift+T	Cmd+Opt+Shift+T
Add keyframe to timeline	Modify → Timeline → Add Keyframe	F6	F6
Remove keyframe from timeline	Modify → Timeline → Remove Keyframe	Shift+F6	Shift+F6

APPENDIX B

HTML Character Entities

HTML Character Entities

To insert special characters into your document, use the icons in the Objects panel's Characters category, as shown in Figure B-1, or the Insert → Special Characters menu. (See Chapter 2 for details on using the Characters category of the Objects panel.)

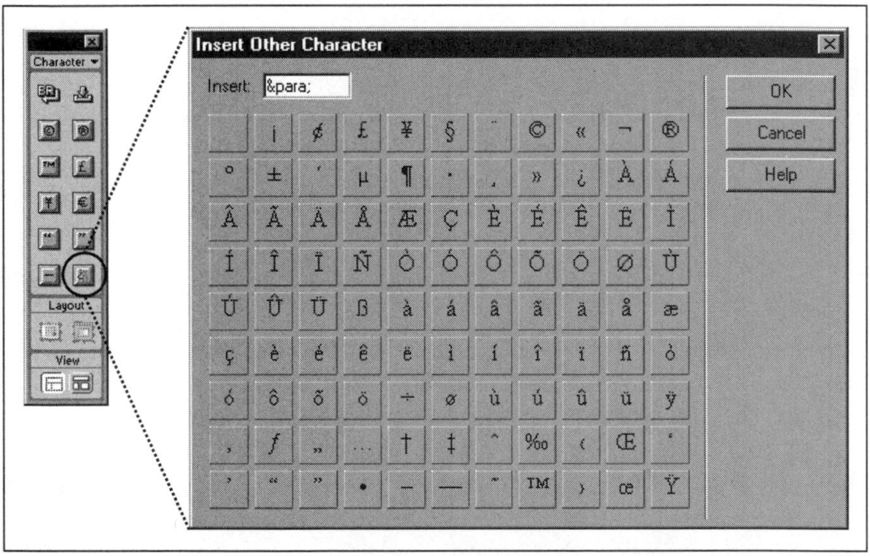

Figure B-1: Objects panel's Character category and the Insert Other Category dialog box

Other special characters and foreign characters, such as umlauts and accents, are inserted using the Insert Other Character dialog box (shown in Figure B-1). Open the Insert Other Character dialog box using the Other Characters icon in the Objects panel or Insert → Special Characters → Other. If you use special characters frequently, Procedure 7 in Chapter 19 demonstrates how to add a custom character icon to the Objects panel.

If the built-in characters entities are insufficient, you can enter so-called *HTML character entities* in the Insert field of the Insert Other Character dialog box, as seen in Figure B-1 (or you can hand-edit the HTML code). The Entity column of Table B-1 shows three-digit HTML character entity codes (of the form &#*nnn*;) for commonly needed characters. For example, > represents the greater-than sign (>). Note the leading &# characters and the terminating ; character. Also note the zero used to pad numbers under 100 to three digits. If a more convenient name, such as >, exists for the character entity, it is shown in the Named Entity column. Notice that named entities start with & and end with ; but do not include a # symbol.

You don't always need to use an HTML character entity code to display a character, even though a code exists. Common characters, such as letters, numbers, !, and %, are displayed properly when entered directly into the Design pane of the Document window. Conversely, not all character entity codes are supported in all browsers. Dreamweaver displays unrecognized characters as a square box. Browsers typically display unrecognized characters literally. For example, Ž is displayed as a greater-than-or-equal-to sign in some browsers, but many browsers display it as "Ž".

The entities shown in Table B-1 work in the latest version of the major browsers (although the character displayed by the browser may depend on the font and language coding in use). Table B-1 groups characters according to their similarity. Tables of HTML character entity sorted by the entity number are available widely, including in *Webmaster in a Nutshell*, *HTML/XHTML: The Definitive Guide*. and *XML in a Nutshell*. However, many special characters are difficult to reproduce accurately in print, so you may notice errors in printed versions.

A complete table of HTML character entities, both for reference and for testing with different browsers, is available at *http://www.dwian.com/char_entities.html*. An extended discussion of HTML character entities is available at *http://www. bbsinc.com/iso8859.html*.

Table B-1: Commonly needed HTML character entities

Entity	Named entity	Symbol	Description
		Invisible space	Nonbreaking space
©	©	©	Copyright
®	®	®	Registered trademark
™		™	Trademark
“		"	Left double quotes (curly)
”		"	Right double quotes (curly)
"	"	"	Straight double quotes (also indicates inches)
'		'	Straight single quote or straight apostrophe (also indicates feet)

Entity	Named entity	Symbol	Description
‘		'	Left single curly quote
’		'	Right single curly quote (curly apostrophe)
#		#	Hash mark
$		$	Dollar sign
&#162	¢	¢	Cent sign
&#163	£	£	Pound (money)
&#165	¥	¥	Yen (money)
&#128	&euro	See Figure B-1	Euro (money)
!		!	Exclamation point
%		%	Percent sign
&	&amp	&	Ampersand
<	<	<	Less-than sign
>	>	>	Greater-than sign
=		=	Equals sign
&#247,	÷	÷	Division sign
¼	¼	1/4	Fraction one-fourth
½	½	1/2	Fraction one-half
¾	¾	1/3	Fraction three-fourths
*		*	Asterisk
+		+	Plus sign
±	±	±	Plus/minus sign (+/-)
-		-	Hyphen or minus sign
­	­	-	Soft hyphen
–		–	En dash
—		—	Em dash
—		_	Underscore
/		/	Slash
\		\	Backslash
(		(	Left parenthesis
)		)	Right parenthesis
[		[	Left square bracket
]		]	Right square bracket
{		{	Left curly brace
}		}	Right curly brace
•		●	Bullet
·	·	·	Middle dot
¹	¹	^{1}	Superscript 1
²	²	^{2}	Superscript 2
³	³	^{3}	Superscript 3
°	°	º	Degree sign (temperature)

APPENDIX C

Site Construction Checklist

This appendix consolidates guidelines used for planning, constructing, and deploying your web site using Dreamweaver.

Browser and Platform Support

Deciding which features, browsers, and platforms to support is an iterative process. While trying to cast as wide a net as possible, you might find yourself limited by browser incompatibilities with necessary features. On the other hand, you might design a less ambitious site for greater compatibility or provide alternate versions of the site for different browsers. Take inventory of both the site's goals and likely user base to make an initial decision on platform and browser support. Test a prototype as early as possible to decide if you must change your initial design decision.

Here are the broad strokes:

- Define your target audience, which dictates the browsers and platforms you'll support and which plugins you can use (or avoid). Corporate clients tend to use Internet Explorer on Windows and also tend to be resistant to requiring their users to download plugins. On the other hand, some corporate intranets support Netscape exclusively. You should support IE for the Mac and Netscape on both platforms if at all possible, because Dreamweaver makes it easy to do so. Sites targeting schools and Macintosh users should support Macintosh browsers more aggressively. Most clients don't understand browser compatibility issues so they'll need your guidance.

- Settle on the browsers you intend to support. For a general interest site, remember that most people use Windows and the majority of those users have Internet Explorer 4.0 or later. It is probably unnecessary to support 3.0 browsers. Requiring a 4.0+ browser allows you to use CSS, as discussed in Chapter 10, and layers, as discussed in Chapters 4, 14, and 17. Macintosh users account for less than 10 percent of the total market, but may make up a larger percentage of your target audience. Netscape browsers have less than 20 percent market share according to most web surveys (some list Netscape with less than 10 percent). AOL customers can use any browser, but the default AOL browser is a derivative of Internet Explorer. Opera is the most prevalent minor browser on Windows and iCab is the most prevalent minor browser on the Macintosh. Test on Linux and Unix browsers, especially if catering to developers; although the Linux market share is small, the user base is growing and extremely vocal. The marginal cost of supporting these browsers is usually negligible.

- Determine which plugins are required, if any. Flash 4 support is ubiquitous (over 95 percent of the installed base) and Flash 5 support is over 70 percent. For example, in a recent online financial calculator, we needed to print the results for the user. Flash 4 didn't offer adequate printing support, so we decided to require Flash 5 rather than eliminate this crucial feature (or have it perform unreliably). According to the Media Metrix survey at *http://www. macromedia.com/software/player_census/flashplayer/tech_breakdown.html*, about 98 percent of users have the Flash plugin, 69 percent have the Acrobat Reader plugin, 69 percent have the QuickTime plugin, and 44 percent have the RealPlayer plugin (not all users have the latest version of the plugin). See Chapter 5 for important information regarding plugins and see Chapter 12 for details on the Check Plugin behavior.

- Determine whether you will use frames and layers. Almost all browsers support tables and frames (and you can provide a no-frames alternative) and the basic features of layers are supported in all 4.0+ browsers. More esoteric features of layers aren't supported as consistently, but that isn't a reason to avoid layers altogether. Refer to the section "Layers and Tables and Frames, Oh My!" in the preface for more details. Also see Chapters 3 and 4.

- Pick a minimum connection speed. It is usually unnecessary to design for less than a 56 Kbps connection unless targeting rural and international customers. On the other hand, expecting users to have connections faster than 56K is unrealistic. Unless targeting users whom you know to have ISDN, satellite, cable, DSL, or faster connections, gear your site towards 56 Kbps modem users. The status bar shows the estimated downloaded time for the connection speed set under Edit → Preferences → Status Bar. Use the 28 Kbps setting to approximate the download time on 56 Kbps modems, because actual connection speeds are about half the ideal speed.

- Pick a minimum browser window size and test your pages at that resolution using the Window Size Selector pop-up menu in the status bar. Designing for 800 × 600 pixels (the most common monitor resolution) leaves a working area of 760 × 420 pixels after subtracting for the browser's borders and toolbars. Also test on monitors with a larger resolution to ensure that titles are centered on a wide screen, for example.

- Test your graphics on different platforms and at different color depths. You can safely assume that most users have 16-bit monitors (thousands of colors) but not necessarily millions of colors. Older computers may support only 8-bit graphics (256 colors). Graphics tend to appear darker under Windows than on the Mac, so test your graphics for sufficient contrast and brightness. On the Macintosh, use Fireworks' View → Windows Gamma option to approximate a graphic's appearance under Windows. Under Windows, use Fireworks' View → Macintosh Gamma to approximate a graphic's appearance on the Mac.

Site Construction Tasks

Constructing a successful web site requires a series of steps to ensure both its visibility and its effectiveness (often in regard to sales).

- Define your graphics. Sketch them out so that you're not the only one who can see what they look like. Be sure to get client approval of the basic design before producing all your graphics.

- Define your navigational system using navigation bars, frames, jump menus, or something fancier such as Flash.

- Design your directory structure and create a standard file naming system. See Chapter 6 for more site-planning tips.

- Define your site using Site → Define so you have easy access to all your site's assets. (See Chapter 6 for more details.)

- Focus the development of your site on its primary goal (making money, building community, or disseminating information) and not on dynamic effects for their own sake.

- Design templates for your site's pages (see Chapter 8).

- Convert repetitive images, HTML, and links into Library items that can be reused and updated across the site quickly (see Chapter 9).

- Define CSS stylesheets for your site (see Chapter 10).

- Use HTML styles to speed the application of text styles. (See Chapter 11).

Deployment Guidelines

You'll ordinarily preview individual pages and your entire site in a browser using File → Preview in Browser (F12), not in Dreamweaver itself.

 Preview your pages as you develop them so that problems are spotted early. Test early, test often, test on all target platforms in all target browsers (TETOTOATPIATB).

Hire a testing company or ask colleagues and friends to perform an informal site check (ask them to report any glaring problems along with their browser and OS versions). The Dreamweaver 4 CD-ROM includes installers for the NN4.7 and IE5.5 browsers. You can download others browser versions from the vendors' sites.

Test your site thoroughly by taking the following steps:

- Check your pages in all targeted web browsers on all target platforms. Test Versions 4.x, 5.x, and 6.x of Internet Explorer and Netscape Navigator, plus less popular browsers such as the AOL browser, Opera, and iCab.

- Test on all supported platforms, including different versions of the Mac OS (7.x, 8.x, 9.x, and OS X) and Windows (95, 98, 98SE, Me, NT, 2000, and XP). Test on Linux and Unix browsers, if appropriate.

- Always support (and test) the browser used by the site owner. If the site doesn't work when decision makers use it, they will rapidly lose confidence. Saying "It looks great on my machine" will not suffice.

- Test whether users behind a firewall can access your site.

- Test all passwords and their corresponding privileges for password-protected sites (and don't leave sensitive information unprotected).

- Test whether your site deals gracefully with unsupported browsers. If applicable, test pages that use frames, layers, and CSS in browsers that don't support these features. Use the File → Check Target Browsers option to detect possible unsupported features. Verify that the no-frames version of your site appears as intended or that users with older browsers can see an appropriate error message. Use the Check Browser behavior to redirect users with older browsers accordingly.

- Test whether your page deals gracefully with users who don't have a necessary plugin or who have an outdated version of a plugin. Be sure that the server MIME types are set for all files that require plugins. Verify that plugins can be downloaded or upgraded as needed (either automatically or manually). Plugin detection differs markedly on Netscape and Internet Explorer on Macintosh and Windows, so test them each separately. Some plugins suffer incompatibilities when used with the AOL browser, so test versions of AOL on both Macintosh and Windows if you are supporting that browser. See Chapters 5, 12, and 16 for details on plugins and MIME types.

- Check the spelling on every page of your site using Dreamweaver's spellchecker (Text → Check Spelling).

- Check all links on all pages of your site using Site → Check Links Sitewide. Check external links using the External Link Checker extension (see Chapter 22) or other external link checking program.

- Run Dreamweaver's site reports regularly to ensure that there are no missing files or hidden errors.

- Check web accessibility (See Chapter 22) for text-only browsers (such as Lynx) or speech-based browsers (those that read web pages to the blind).

Web Address and Email Address Tips

The following tips help maximize the utility of your site and convey an air of professionalism to your visitors. Contact your webmaster or ISP for assistance with these items.

- Ensure that your site is accessible both with and without the *www* server name, such as with the URLs *http://www.mydomain.com* and *http://mydomain.com*.

- Ensure that the email addresses *webmaster@mydomain.com* and *postmaster@mydomain.com* are forwarded to appropriate administrators. Mail directed to incorrect email addresses, such as *nobody@mydomain.com*, should be redirected to an administrator rather than ignored or bounced back to the user.

- Configure your server to display a custom page if a link is broken. A custom error page can give the user more information than the default 404 (file not found) error. Include a search feature on the page (see Chapter 22).

- Check your server logs periodically for reports of broken links. (Most servers can log attempts to reach nonexistent URLs.)

- Ensure that every folder, including the site root, has a default file, such as *index.htm,* to prevent visitors from viewing your directory structure or receiving an error message. The filename of your site's home page depends on your server. Some servers assume *index.htm* or *index.html* as the default home page. Other servers assume *home.htm, home.html, default.htm,* or *default.html* as the default home page. Consult your webmaster for details.

Navigation Methods

Pay attention to how your users navigate your site. If the interface isn't simple, visitors will leave or fail to find the information they need to make a purchase decision.

- Just as graphical user interfaces offer a consistent user experience, your entire site should share a common navigation system. Don't ask a visitor to select from a drop-down menu at the top of one page and then from a series of images at the bottom of the next page.

- Every web page should include the answer to your visitors' two main questions: "Where am I?" and "Where am I going?" Include a navigation bar or navigation panel that indicates the visitor's current location and gives easy access to other portions of the site. Such an approach keeps the user oriented and motivated to explore your site further.

- Navigational elements should be easily discernable. Buttons should have a raised appearance and text links should be separated with pipes (|) or other characters to delimit user choice visually.

- Use rollover text or graphics with your buttons to provide more information to the visitor while maintaining an uncluttered page design. Use the Set Text of Status Bar behavior to provide help on the status bar of the user's browser. Both techniques help to engage the user through interactivity.

- Make a search mechanism readily available, as described in Chapter 22.

- Test your site on real users, then refine your design.

Content

You have heard the phrase, "Content is king," and it remains true for the Web. Despite cost pressures, superior design and content can make your site stand out.

- Your clients know their business and their customers. Encourage your client or marketing staff to participate fully in the high-level design of the site. That said, you should provide guidance as to what works and doesn't work on the Web. In other words, ask clients what they want to get across to their customers, and then help them achieve that goal.

- Employ a professional copywriter with knowledge of the client's industry and a flair for writing copy that sells and inspires.

- Check grammar, spelling, and punctuation carefully. Keep articles under 1,000 words, if possible. Break longer articles onto multiple pages.

- Check the page layout in various browsers and different resolutions. Look for potentially misaligned images.

- Performance, performance, performance! Don't overload your page with so much content that it slows down performance. Potential visitors will leave before ever seeing your beautiful design. Try to keep page load times under 10 seconds, and certainly no more than 30 seconds (an eternity for a user).

Colors

Color can communicate very effectively when used properly, but can be a real eyesore when used improperly. The following tips will help you to use color effectively.

- Use the Commands → Set Color Scheme option to select a color scheme for your site.

- Pick a combination of foreground and background colors that has adequate contrast and improves legibility. Telephone books use yellow pages because black text on a light yellow background offers the highest contrast on printed paper. Experiment with different colors, as monitor brightness and contrast settings differ markedly. Also pick a san serif font and an adequate point size to make the text easy to read on screen.

- Avoid inverse text (light text on a dark background) especially if you expect the page to be printed.

- Avoid color schemes that make text illegible to colorblind visitors. Remember that there are different types of color-blindness, including an inability to distinguish red from green and an inability to discern shades of gray.

- Avoid color schemes that seem so retro or modern that they obscure your message.

- Avoid oversaturated and cliché colors, such as pure red (#FF0000), green (#00FF00), and blue (#0000FF). Tone down pure white (#FFFFFF) to a shade of gray if nearby colors appear to bleed into the white area.

- Be aware of the emotions that colors can evoke and how they reflect on your message. Colors such as pale pinks and blues tend toward a softer appearance, while browns and reds have a stronger, rustic appearance. Don't use colors that provoke anxiety if you want to put your audience at ease. See Table C-1 for details.

Table C-1 summarizes the emotions loosely associated with different colors.

Table C-1: The meaning of colors

Color	Interpretations
Black	Dark or heavy; balance it with other colors to look chic instead of morbid.
White	Avoid pure white, as it can be too brash. Use it for accents or tone it down by combining it with other colors.
Dark blue	Distant, authoritative, or reserved. Avoid pure blue (#0000FF), which may be too intense. Use navy blue instead.
Aqua blue	Peacefulness and relaxation. Nature and water.
Green	Encourages interest and exploration; engaging. Combine with subtle yellows for contrast. Avoid drab green unless selling camouflage gear or alligator bait.
Yellow	Fiery and emotional with raised expectations.
Light brown	Rustic strength and history (sienna photographs).
Brown	Cultivation and distinction (brick and wood).
Red	Alertness and intensity. Avoid pure red, which conveys emergency rather than urgency.
Magenta	Cool and artificial.

Any color can be specified as a hexadecimal RGB triplet (#RRGGBB). Some colors can also be specified by name, such as `<body bgcolor="red">`, but support varies by browser. The most widely supported named colors are listed in Table C-2.

Table C-2: Color names defined in the HTML 3.2 standard

Color name	RGB equivalent
aqua	#00FFFF
black	#000000
blue	#0000FF
fuchsia	#FF00FF
gray	#808080
green	#008000
lime	#00FF00
maroon	#800000
navy	#000080
olive	#808000
purple	#800080
red	#FF0000
silver	#C0C0C0
teal	#008080
yellow	#FFFF00
white	#FFFFFF

XHTML Compliance

XHTML represents the evolution of HTML 4.01 into an XML-compliant standard. XHTML is the next step in the development of HTML and will be slowly adopted as the default language of most browsers. For a full discussion of XHTML, see *HTML & XHTML: The Definitive Guide* by Chuck Musciano and Bill Kennedy (O'Reilly). This appendix covers the steps to ensure that your HTML complies with the XHTML standard. When converting from HTML to XHTML you must follow more rigid rules:

- All element and attribute names must be in lowercase. You can set them to lowercase by using the Case for Tags and Case for Attributes preferences under Edit → Preferences → Code Format.

- All attribute values must be enclosed in quotation marks. Dreamweaver encloses attributes in quotes by default, and you should use quotes when hand-editing HTML in Code view or the Quick Tag Editor.

- The root element of the document must be <html>. Dreamweaver uses the <html> element as the root element of all newly created documents (unless you change the *default.html* file on which all new documents are based).

- The <!DOCTYPE> declaration must precede the root element in the document, as in:

```
<!DOCTYPE html PUBLIC "-//W3C//DTD XHTML 1.0 Transitional//EN"
"http://www.w3.org/TR/xhtml1/DTD/xhtml1-transitional.dtd">
```

 Dreamweaver does not include the <!DOCTYPE> element in its documents. You can add this element by modifying the default document template, *default.html* (see Chapter 21).

- The default namespace associated with the root element must be:

```
http://www.w3.org/1999/xhtml
```

 Dreamweaver does not include any reference to a default namespace in the default document template. You can add this reference by modifying the *default.html* file.

- All elements must be closed. Empty elements must be closed with a forward slash before the closing >, such as in <br /> and <img.../>. Nonempty elements must be closed using a standard end tag.

 Dreamweaver does not include the closing slash with empty elements. This deficiency can be remedied by editing the appropriate object insertion files located in the */Configuration/Objects* folder.

- If an element is not normally empty, use a closing tag, even if a particular instance is empty. For example, use `<p></p>` instead of `<p />`.

- The use of external stylesheets is suggested if the stylesheet uses any of the following characters: <, &,],], >, or –.

- The use of external scripts is suggested if your script uses any of the following characters: <, &,],], >, or –.

 Because XHTML parsers can remove comments from content, enclosing scripts and stylesheets within comment delimiters may not hide the stylesheet or script from browsers that don't support those features.

- Line breaks and extra whitespace found within attribute values are handled inconsistently and should therefore be avoided.

- When creating transitional documents, use both the `lang` and `xml:lang` attributes when specifying the language of an element. The `lang` attribute allows older browsers to view the document properly. When used together, the value of the `xml:lang` attribute will take precedence.

- Use the `id` attribute, not the `name` attribute, to identify elements. The `name` attribute isn't supported in XHTML documents because it is not defined as an attribute of type ID. The `id` attribute isn't supported in all browsers, so provide redundant `id` and `name` attributes to support older browsers.

 Dreamweaver uses the `name` attribute, rather than the `id` attribute, in all instances. Add the `id` attribute manually by using the Quick Tag Editor.

- Use both the XML declaration `<?xml version="1.0" encoding="EUC-JP"?>` and a matching `meta http-equiv` element, such as `<meta http-equiv="Content-type" content="text/html; charset="EUC-JP"' />` to specify the character encoding used in your XHTML document. When these attributes are used together, XML-compliant applications use the XML declaration.

 Dreamweaver uses the `<meta http-equiv>` element/attribute combination. You can modify the *default.html* file to include the `<?xml?>` declaration.

- Boolean attributes that are not assigned a value, such as `checked`, `nowrap`, `compact`, and `resize`, are not supported in XHTML browsers, although they will continue to be used for HTML browsers. To comply with XHTML standards (and still support HTML browsers) set Boolean values to themselves, such as `checked="checked"`.

Dreamweaver follows the old HTML standard in which a Boolean attribute without a value implies an assignment to true. You can change the default by modifying HTML files in the */Configuration/ Objects* directory.

- When an ampersand (&) appears in an attribute value, it must be displayed as the character entity &. This requirement creates problems when working with addresses containing ampersands within href attributes, since they would need to be expressed as *http://website.com/cgi-bin/sendmail. pl?id=guest&name=user* rather than as *http://website.dom/cgi-bin/ sendmail.pl?id=guest&name=user.*

 Dreamweaver displays ampersands found within URLs as the ampersand rather than the & entity.

Search Engines

Most search engines are moving toward a pay-to-play business model. The site that pays the most money appears at the top of the search results listing, and only sites that pay a fee are listed at all. This system undermines everything you may have learned previously about search engine rankings, but the following tips are good for optimizing page placement in any search engine. Because each search engine determines relevancy differently, one <meta> tag won't gain your prominent placement in all the search engines. Use a combination of tags and keywords on different pages to increase your overall chance of success.

- Provide a different <title> for each web page.
- Create a description tag containing keywords or key phrases—including those used in the <title> tag—by using Insert → Head Tags → Description. Write a clear, compelling description of each page in 25 words or less. Do not repeat your key phrase several times; instead, use it with other related key phrases not included in that page's <title> tag.
- Create one keyword tag for each page on your site by using Insert → Head Tags → Keywords. Add the best key phrase for the page in the <meta name="keywords"> tag and use only one or two key phrases in this tag (not the 1,000 characters allowed).
- Make your key phrase part of the first sentence of your page content, which should be the same as your description <meta> tag. (This technique covers you for robots that index the first sentence and those that don't.)
- Create a site map with text links and a "How to Link to This Site" page. Both are simple and effective ways to encourage individuals and search engines to link to your site.

<title>

Although not all search engines use the `<title>` element to help index HTML pages, many do. Each title should contain no more than ten words and should begin with one keyword or key phrase. Each page should use a different keyword or key phrase in its title. The objective is to use each indexed page on your web site as a separate entry in the search engine, increasing your opportunity to attract an audience to your site. For example, you could make the title of your page "Foundation American Quarter Horses for Rodeos, Ranches, and Ropings."

Dreamweaver allows over 300 characters in the `<title>` field and HTML itself has no limitation, but most search engines index the first 256 characters only. Many search engines use the document title as the description of the site, while others use the first sentence of the document.

Graphics and Performance

To decrease page load times, use a graphics optimization program, such as Macromedia Fireworks, to ensure that your graphics are as small as possible. Here are some sure-fire suggestions:

Crop images
> By reducing the dimensions of an image, you reduce its size and therefore its download time.

Use GIFs for graphic elements
> GIF graphics are more efficient than JPEG files for graphical elements using 256 colors or less, such as simple graphics and line drawings.

Use JPEGs for photographs
> JPEG files are the most efficient format for photographic images. Reduce the JPEG quality setting for greater compression.

Reduce number of colors
> Reduce the number of colors in each image to the smallest number possible.

Display low-resolution images while loading larger images
> The total load time of the page increases, although the visitor sees an image in less time.

Interlace GIF images
> Interlaced GIF images provide an idea of what the image looks like before it has loaded fully.

Specify height and width attributes for `<img>` elements
> Specifying the height and width attributes of the `<img>` element allow the remaining text to load, correctly formatted, while the image is downloaded to the browser. (Theoretically, it is also required by the HTML 4.0 specification.)

Trim down animations
> Crop all animations so they take up as little space as possible. Avoid including static areas in the animation (separate animated elements from the background).

Use thumbnail images when possible

Use small, clear thumbnail images rather than full-size images so visitors have the option (but are not obligated) to look at larger images.

Break images into reusable parts

Judiciously break an image into multiple parts that can be reused, which saves the time it takes to download the full image again.

Provide text alternatives

Provide text descriptions of your images in the `alt` attributes of the `<img>` element (required for HTML 4 compliance). You can also provide a text-only version of your site, which users can access at their discretion.

Use vector graphics

For various performance and compatibility reasons, most developers use Flash for compact vector-based graphics. Internet Explorer 5 and Netscape Navigator 6 also support XML-based Scalable Vector Graphics (SVG), but SVG is not supported in earlier versions of these browsers.

Index

We'd like to hear your suggestions for improving our indexes. Send email to *index@oreilly.com*.

Behaviors icon, 241
Behaviors panel, 241
  browser configuration behaviors
      and, 255
  Drag Layer behavior and, 270
  Set Text of Layer behavior and, 273
Block category, 216
.bmp files, saving site map as, 128
<body> tag
  attaching behaviors to, 242
  library items and, 195
  <noframes> tag and, 83
  Page Properties dialog box and, 46
Border category, 218
borders
  for browsers, 59
  cross-hatched, 79
  CSS Border category and, 218
  for frames, 81
  for framesets, 80
  nested framesets and, 83
Box category, 217

 tag, text placement and, 50
broken links, 151–152
  displayed in red, 136
  web site planning and, 407
browsers
  animations and, 299
  border settings and, 59
  checking compatibility and, 181
  configuration behaviors for, 255–259
  CourseBuilder interactive compatibility
      and, 367
  CSS Extensions category and, 221
  default behaviors and, 244
  events and, 246
  extensions and, 353
  external resources and, 92
  JavaScript-capable, 239
  layers and, 66, 84, 269
  older, xviii
    layers and, xx
    Layout view and, 61
    nested framesets and, 79
  preferences for, 318
  previewing HTML documents in, 180
  primary/secondary, 181
    preferences for, 318
  special characters and, 401
  special-needs, 359
  support for CSS and, 201

  timelines and, 292, 296
  viewing Shockwave objects in, 106
  web site planning and, 403–405
Browsers extension category, 354
built-in behaviors, 242–247
bulleted lists, 44
bullets, CSS List category and, 219
Button interactions, 370
buttons, 73
  attaching sound behavior to, 283
  image fields and, 74
  images acting as, 277
  Swap Image behavior and, 262

C

Call JavaScript behavior, 248
Cascading Style Sheets (see CSS)
case sensitivity
  anchor names and, 23, 28
  links and, 28
  URLs and, 23, 140
categories
  asset, 161
  of extensions in Dreamweaver
      Exchange, 350
  in Objects panel, 7
  in Preferences dialog box, 307–320
  in Site Definition dialog box, 120–130
  in Style Definition dialog box, 214–222
.cct files, 107
cells, 54–64
  background images and, 59
  creating, 61
  deleting, 63
  editable regions and, 187
  formatting
    in Layout view, 62–64
    in Standard view, 54–60
  merging/splitting, 60
  padding for, 64
  preference for editing, 308
  selecting, 55
  spanning/unspanning, 60
  wrapping text within, 64
.cfm files, 104
CFML (ColdFusion Markup
      Language), 346
CGI scripts
  broken links and, 152
  site functionality and, 363
Change Property behavior, 272–275, 281

Change Property dialog box, 272, 281
character entities (see special characters)
character sets, <meta> element and, 18
characters
    formatting, HTML styles and, 232
    special, 48, 332, 400–402
    (see also fonts)
Characters category, 8, 330
Check Browser behavior, 256
Check In button/Check Out button, 143
check in/check out feature (see File
        Check In/Check Out feature)
Check Page for Accessibility
        extension, 359
Check Plugin behavior, 256
Check Target Browsers dialog box, 181
Check Time/Check Tries segments, 376
checkboxes, 73
checklist for web site construction, xiv,
        403–414
    specific tasks for (list), 405
checkmark icon, 136, 142
Chinese, preference for double-byte
        characters and, 308
chmod command, 361
Choose Editable Region for Orphaned
        Content dialog box, 192
circle with slash, 190
<cite> tag, 41
.class files, 107
Class IDs, 109
class selectors, 174, 203, 209–213
    applying/clearing, 223
Clean Up FrontPage HTML dialog
        box, 168
Clean Up HTML dialog box, 164
Clean Up Word HTML dialog box, 166
Cleanup FrontPage HTML Sitewide
        extension, 168
Clear Paragraph Style, 232
Clear Selection Style, 232
clickable regions, 31
client-side image maps, 28–37
Clip option (layers), 88
Cmd key (Macintosh), xxiii
CMI system (see computer-managed
        instruction)
Code and Design view, 4
Code Colors category, 309
code editors, external, 177
Code Format category, 309–312

Code inspector, 6
    editing HTML in, 164
    (see also Code view)
Code pane, 4, 5
    editing HTML in, 164
Code Rewriting category, 312
code (see HTML code)
<code> tag, 41
Code view, 4
    code colors preferences and, 309
    code format preferences and, 309–312
ColdFusion Markup Language
        (CFML), 346
ColdFusion Server, password protection
        and, 363
ColdFusion tags, 346–348
ColdFusion.xml file, 347
colors/background colors
    for cells/tables, 58, 64
        defaults for, 318
    CSS Background property and, 216
    custom, maintaining for individual web
        sites, 44
    for Flash Buttons, 101
    for Flash Text, 103
    for layers, 85, 88
    preferences
        for highlighting colors, 315
        for HTML code, 309
    of text, 42–44
    web site planning and, 408
    web-safe, 42–44
columns, 56, 65
    File View Columns category and, 128
Command key (Macintosh), xxiii
commands
    copying, 179
    custom, 179
    Dreamweaver extensions and, 349
    exporting, 328
    Fireworks and, 93, 267
    paragraph-formatting, 38
    pop-up menus and, 138
    recording, 180
    table-related, 53
    text-formatting, 41
    time-related, 303
Commands → Apply Source
        Formatting, 177
Commands → Banner Image Builder, 355
Commands → Check External Links, 355

.js files (*continued*)
   for implementing menu
      options, 335–339
   opening, 250
   (see also JavaScript)
JScript (Microsoft), 239
JSP (JavaServer Pages), 346
Judge Interaction, 378
Jump Menu behavior, 287
Jump Menu dialog box, 74
Jump Menu Go dialog box, 289
jump menus, 74
   behaviors and, 287–289

K

<kbd> tag, 41
keyboard shortcuts, xxiii, 383–399
   customizing, 325–330
      Clean Up HTML command and, 166
   duplicating, 327
   finding unused, 328
   for frameset options, 77
   for inserting objects, 10
   list of, 180
   for panels, 13, 383
   for Quick Tag Editor, 176
   recorded by Dreamweaver, 179
   for tables, 53
keyframes, 293, 294
   properties and, 296, 298
keywords
   editing, 18
   for Rel/Rev attributes, 22
keywords attribute, 18

L

language attribute, 250
languages
   Chinese/Japanese, double-byte
      characters and, 308
   ColdFusion, 346
   Java, 239
   special characters for, 400
   (see also ActionScript; Lingo)
Launcher bar, 13
   preference for icons in, 318
Layer Preferences dialog box, 84
<layer> tag, 84
layers, xix, 84–91
   adding to timelines, 294
   altering dynamically, 273–275

animating images and, 299
behaviors and, 269–275
converting to tables, 66, 84
creating, 86
CSS Background category and, 215
CSS Border category and, 218
deleting, 91
dragging/dropping, 270–272
formatting, 84–86, 87, 91
   keyboard shortcuts for, 393
hiding/showing, 301
inserting into editable regions, 191
position of, 84, 87–89
   animating, 297
preferences for, 317
properties of, changing
   with Property inspector, 298
   with timelines, 296–298
resizing, 272
scrollable, 358
web site planning and, 404
Layers category, 317
Layers panel, 89
layout tables (see tables)
Layout view
   preferences for, setting, 64
   properties available in, 64
   switching to, 61
   tables and, 61–67
Layout View button, 61
Layout View category, 317
.lbi files, 196
.lck files, 143
Learning category, 366
letters in lists, 45
Library folder, 196
Library icon, 194
library items, 194–199
   deleting, 198
   highlighting preference for, 315
   inserting into documents, 195
   keyboard shortcuts for, 397
   vs. Objects panel, 330
   table summarizing operations, 198
Library panel/Library category, 161, 194
line breaks, 50
   keyboard shortcut for inserting, 10
Line Number option, 5
line numbering, 160
Lingo scripting language, 105
   Shockwave movies and, 285

About the Authors

Heather Williamson has authored several best-selling web-authoring books. She has spent the last five years designing and developing corporate intranets and Internet sites. Since 1997, she has managed a small web-development and consulting company that provides programming and development services, including web-page development, graphic design, multimedia development, technical training, and applications development.

Bruce Epstein wrote O'Reilly's *Director in a Nutshell* and *Lingo in a Nutshell* and was the editor for *ActionScript: The Definitive Guide*. He has been a multimedia programmer and consultant for 10 years, specializing in Macromedia technologies such as Director, Dreamweaver, and Flash.

Colophon

Our look is the result of reader comments, our own experimentation, and feedback from distribution channels. Distinctive covers complement our distinctive approach to technical topics, breathing personality and life into potentially dry subjects.

The animal on the cover of *Dreamweaver in a Nutshell* is a cobra. Cobras are members of the endangered Elapidae family, which includes the king, Asian, and spitting cobras and the asp. Cobras are known for their aggressive behavior, deadly venom, and the hood that appears when the cobra is in a striking position. The hood itself is attached to a set of ribs that extends behind the cobra's head. With a habitat ranging from Africa to South Asia, the Philippines, and Indonesia, cobras generally live near streams, forests, bamboo thickets, agricultural areas, and mangrove swamps.

The king cobra, a native of South Asia, is the largest species, ranging from 10 to 18 feet long. This cobra usually feeds on other types of reptiles, including pythons, and is more aggressive than most other cobras. The king cobra female lays up to 40 eggs and makes a nest for her young out of leaves and branches. Though most cobras rarely attack if left alone, the king cobra female attacks with little provocation if she feels that her eggs are threatened. The Asian cobra, found mostly in India and Pakistan, is valued for eating rodents that feed on crops. It is also used by snake charmers for entertainment. The cobra doesn't actually respond to music, but follows movements of the snake charmer's hands and pipe after being provoked to a striking position. The spitting cobra, a native of Africa, is unusual because it spits its venom accurately up to eight feet. The asp, also from Africa, is the most common type of cobra.

Cobra venom is considered dangerous because of its neurotoxic effects. Victims of cobra bites often die from respiratory arrest and heart failure, but sometimes survive if given an antivenom that reverses the neurotoxin. In the future, drugs made from cobra venom may have pharmaceutical value as painkillers and anticancer drugs.

Ann Schirmer was the production editor and copyeditor for *Dreamweaver in a Nutshell*. Colleen Gorman was the proofreader. Melanie Wang and Matt Hutchinson provided quality control. Brenda Miller wrote the index.

Ellie Volckhausen designed the cover of this book, based on a series design by Edie Freedman. The cover image is a 19th-century engraving from the Dover Pictorial Archive. Emma Colby produced the cover layout with QuarkXPress 4.1 using Adobe's ITC Garamond font.

Melanie Wang designed the interior layout based on a series design by Nancy Priest. Mihaela Maier converted the files from Microsoft Word to FrameMaker 5.5.6 using tools created by Mike Sierra. The text and heading fonts are ITC Garamond Light and Garamond Book. The illustrations that appear in the book were produced by Robert Romano and Jessamyn Read using Macromedia FreeHand 9 and Adobe Photoshop 6. This colophon was written by Ann Schirmer.

Whenever possible, our books use a durable and flexible lay-flat binding.

More Titles from O'Reilly

Web Authoring and Design

Designing Web Audio

By Josh Beggs & Dylan Thede
1st Edition January 2001
398 pages, ISBN 1-56592-353-7

Designing Web Audio is the most complete Internet audio guide on the market, loaded with informative real-world case studies and interviews with some of the world's leading audio and web producers. Its step-by-step instructions on how to use the most popular web audio formats to stream music make it an invaluable resource for web developers and web music enthusiasts.

Learning WML & WMLScript

By Martin Frost
1st Edition October 2000
208 pages, ISBN 1-56592-947-0

The next generation of mobile communicators is here, and delivering content will mean programming in WML and WMLScript. *Learning WML & WMLScript* gets developers up to speed quickly on these technologies, mapping out in detail the Wireless Application Environment (WAE), and its two major components: Wireless Markup Language (WML), and WMLScript. With these two technologies, developers can format information in almost all applications for display by mobile devices.

Dreamweaver 4: The Missing Manual

By Dave McFarland
1st Edition July 2001
480 pages, ISBN 0-596-00097-9

Dreamweaver 4: The Missing Manual is the ideal companion to this complex software. Following an anatomical tour of a web page to orient new users, author Dave McFarland walks you through the process of creating and designing a complete web site. Armed with this handbook, both first-time and experienced web designers can easily use DreamWeaver to bring stunning, interactive web sites to life.

Web Design in a Nutshell, 2nd Edition

By Jennifer Niederst
2nd Edition September 2001
640 pages, ISBN 0-596-00196-7

Web Design in a Nutshell contains the nitty-gritty on everything you need to know to design Web pages. Written by veteran Web designer Jennifer Niederst, this book provides quick access to the wide range of technologies and techniques from which Web designers and authors must draw. Topics include understanding the Web environment, HTML, graphics, multimedia and interactivity, and emerging technologies.

Learning Web Design

By Jennifer Niederst
1st Edition March 2001
418 pages, ISBN 0-596-00036-7

In *Learning Web Design*, Jennifer Niederst shares the knowledge she's gained from years of experience as both web designer and teacher. She starts from the very beginning – defining the Internet, the Web, browsers, and URLs – assuming no previous knowledge of how the Web works. Jennifer helps you build the solid foundation in HTML, graphics, and design principles that you need for crafting effective web pages.

ActionScript: The Definitive Guide

By Colin Moock
1st Edition May 2001
720 pages, ISBN 1-56592-852-0

ActionScript: The Definitive Guide is for web developers and web authors who want to go beyond simple Flash animations to create enhanced Flash-driven sites. Regardless of your level of programming expertise, this combination of ActionScript fundamentals, applications, and handy quick-reference will have you scripting like a pro.

O'REILLY®

TO ORDER: **800-998-9938** • *order@oreilly.com* • *http://www.oreilly.com/*
OUR PRODUCTS ARE AVAILABLE AT A BOOKSTORE OR SOFTWARE STORE NEAR YOU.
FOR INFORMATION: **800-998-9938** • **707-829-0515** • *info@oreilly.com*

Web Authoring and Design

HTML & XHTML: The Definitive Guide, 4th Edition

By Chuck Musciano & Bill Kennedy
4th Edition August 2000
680 pages, ISBN 0-596-00026-X

This complete guide is full of examples, sample code, and practical hands-on advice for creating truly effective web pages and mastering advanced features. Web authors learn how to insert images, create useful links and searchable documents, use Netscape extensions, design great forms, and much more. The fourth edition covers XHTML 1.0, HTML 4.01, Netscape 6.0, and Internet Explorer 5.0, plus all the common extensions.

Information Architecture for the World Wide Web

By Louis Rosenfeld & Peter Morville
1st Edition February 1998
224 pages, ISBN 1-56592-282-4

Learn how to merge aesthetics and mechanics to design Web sites that "work." This book shows how to apply principles of architecture and library science to design cohesive Web sites and intranets that are easy to use, manage, and expand. Covers building complex sites, hierarchy design and organization, and techniques to make your site easier to search. For Webmasters, designers, and administrators.

Cascading Style Sheets:The Definitive Guide

By Eric A. Meyer
1st Edition May 2000
470 pages, ISBN 1-56592-622-6

CSS is the HTML 4.0-approved method for controlling visual presentation on Web pages. *Cascading Style Sheets: The Definitive Guide* offers a complete, detailed review of CSS1 properties and other aspects of CSS1. Each property is explored individually in detail with discussion of how each interacts with other properties. There is also information on how to avoid common mistakes in interpretation. This book is the first major title to cover CSS in a way that acknowledges and describes current browser support, instead of simply describing the way things work in theory. It offers both advanced and novice Web authors a comprehensive guide to implementation of CSS.

O'REILLY®

TO ORDER: **800-998-9938** • **order@oreilly.com** • **http://www.oreilly.com/**
OUR PRODUCTS ARE AVAILABLE AT A BOOKSTORE OR SOFTWARE STORE NEAR YOU.
FOR INFORMATION: **800-998-9938** • **707-829-0515** • **info@oreilly.com**

How to stay in touch with O'Reilly

1. Visit Our Award-Winning Site

http://www.oreilly.com/

★ "Top 100 Sites on the Web" —*PC Magazine*
★ "Top 5% Web sites" —*Point Communications*
★ "3-Star site" —*The McKinley Group*

Our web site contains a library of comprehensive product information (including book excerpts and tables of contents), downloadable software, background articles, interviews with technology leaders, links to relevant sites, book cover art, and more. File us in your Bookmarks or Hotlist!

2. Join Our Email Mailing Lists

New Product Releases

To receive automatic email with brief descriptions of all new O'Reilly products as they are released, send email to:
ora-news-subscribe@lists.oreilly.com
Put the following information in the first line of your message (*not* in the Subject field):
subscribe ora-news

O'Reilly Events

If you'd also like us to send information about trade show events, special promotions, and other O'Reilly events, send email to:
ora-news-subscribe@lists.oreilly.com
Put the following information in the first line of your message (*not* in the Subject field):
subscribe ora-events

3. Get Examples from Our Books via FTP

There are two ways to access an archive of example files from our books:

Regular FTP

- ftp to:
  ftp.oreilly.com
  (login: anonymous
  password: your email address)
- Point your web browser to:
  ftp://ftp.oreilly.com/

FTPMAIL

- Send an email message to:
  ftpmail@online.oreilly.com
  (Write "help" in the message body)

4. Contact Us via Email

order@oreilly.com
To place a book or software order online. Good for North American and international customers.

subscriptions@oreilly.com
To place an order for any of our newsletters or periodicals.

books@oreilly.com
General questions about any of our books.

software@oreilly.com
For general questions and product information about our software. Check out O'Reilly Software Online at **http://software.oreilly.com/** for software and technical support information. Registered O'Reilly software users send your questions to:
website-support@oreilly.com

cs@oreilly.com
For answers to problems regarding your order or our products.

booktech@oreilly.com
For book content technical questions or corrections.

proposals@oreilly.com
To submit new book or software proposals to our editors and product managers.

international@oreilly.com
For information about our international distributors or translation queries. For a list of our distributors outside of North America check out:
http://www.oreilly.com/distributors.html

5. Work with Us

Check out our website for current employment opportunites:
http://jobs.oreilly.com/

O'Reilly & Associates, Inc.
101 Morris Street, Sebastopol, CA 95472 USA
TEL   707-829-0515 or 800-998-9938
       (6am to 5pm PST)
FAX   707-829-0104

Titles from O'Reilly

International Distributors

http://international.oreilly.com/distributors.html • international@oreilly.com

UK, EUROPE, MIDDLE EAST AND AFRICA (EXCEPT FRANCE, GERMANY, AUSTRIA, SWITZERLAND, LUXEMBOURG, AND LIECHTENSTEIN)

INQUIRIES
O'Reilly UK Limited
4 Castle Street
Farnham
Surrey, GU9 7IIS
United Kingdom
Telephone: 44-1252-711776
Fax: 44-1252-734211
Email: information@oreilly.co.uk

ORDERS
Wiley Distribution Services Ltd.
1 Oldlands Way
Bognor Regis
West Sussex PO22 9SA
United Kingdom
Telephone: 44-1243-843294
UK Freephone: 0800-243207
Fax: 44-1243-843302 (Europe/EU orders)
or 44-1243-843274 (Middle East/Africa)
Email: cs-books@wiley.co.uk

GERMANY, SWITZERLAND, AUSTRIA, LUXEMBOURG, AND LIECHTENSTEIN

INQUIRIES & ORDERS
O'Reilly Verlag
Balthasarstr. 81
D-50670 Köln, Germany
Telephone: 49-221-973160-91
Fax: 49-221-973160-8
Email: anfragen@oreilly.de (inquiries)
Email: order@oreilly.de (orders)

FRANCE

INQUIRIES & ORDERS
Éditions O'Reilly
18 rue Séguier
75006 Paris, France
Tel: 33-1-40-51-71-89
Fax: 33-1-40-51-72-26
Email: france@oreilly.fr

CANADA (FRENCH LANGUAGE BOOKS)
Les Éditions Flammarion ltée
375, Avenue Laurier Ouest
Montréal (Québec) H2V 2K3
Tel: 1-514-277-8807
Fax: 1-514-278-2085
Email: info@flammarion.qc.ca

HONG KONG
City Discount Subscription Service, Ltd.
Unit A, 6th Floor, Yan's Tower
27 Wong Chuk Hang Road
Aberdeen, Hong Kong
Tel: 852-2580-3539
Fax: 852-2580-6463
Email: citydis@ppn.com.hk

KOREA
Hanbit Media, Inc.
Chungmu Bldg. 210
Yonnam-dong 568-33
Mapo-gu
Seoul, Korea
Tel: 822-325-0397
Fax: 822-325-9697
Email: hant93@chollian.dacom.co.kr

PHILIPPINES
Global Publishing
G/F Benavides Garden
1186 Benavides St
Manila, Philippines
Tel: 632-254-8949/632-252-2582
Fax: 632-734-5060/632-252-2733
Email: globalp@pacific.net.ph

TAIWAN
O'Reilly Taiwan
1st Floor, No. 21, Lane 295
Section 1, Fu-Shing South Road
Taipei, 106 Taiwan
Tel: 886-2-27099669
Fax: 886-2-27038802
Email: mori@oreilly.com

CHINA
O'Reilly Beijing
SIGMA Building, Suite B809
No. 49 Zhichun Road
Haidian District
Beijing 100031, P.R. China
Tel: 86-10-8809-7475
Fax: 86-10-8809-7463
Email: beijing@oreilly.com

INDIA
Shroff Publishers & Distributors Pvt. Ltd.
12, "Roseland", 2nd Floor
180, Waterfield Road, Bandra (West)
Mumbai 400 050
Tel: 91-22-641-1800/643-9910
Fax: 91-22-643-2422
Email: spd@vsnl.com

JAPAN
O'Reilly Japan, Inc.
Yotsuya Y's Building
7 Banch 6, Honshio-cho
Shinjuku-ku
Tokyo 160-0003 Japan
Tel: 81-3-3356-5227
Fax: 81-3-3356-5261
Email: japan@oreilly.com

SINGAPORE, INDONESIA, MALAYSIA AND THAILAND
TransQuest Publishers Pte Ltd
30 Old Toh Tuck Road #05-02
Sembawang Kimtrans Logistics Centre
Singapore 597654
Tel: 65-4623112
Fax: 65-4625761
Email: wendiw@transquest.com.sg

ALL OTHER COUNTRIES
O'Reilly & Associates, Inc.
101 Morris Street
Sebastopol, CA 95472 USA
Tel: 707-829-0515
Fax: 707-829-0104
Email: order@oreilly.com

AUSTRALIA
Woodslane Pty., Ltd.
7/5 Vuko Place
Warriewood NSW 2102
Australia
Tel: 61-2-9970-5111
Fax: 61-2-9970-5002
Email: info@woodslane.com.au

NEW ZEALAND
Woodslane New Zealand, Ltd.
21 Cooks Street (P.O. Box 575)
Waganui, New Zealand
Tel: 64-6-347-6543
Fax: 64-6-345-4840
Email: info@woodslane.com.au

ARGENTINA
Distribuidora Cuspide
Suipacha 764
1008 Buenos Aires
Argentina
Phone: 54-11-4322-8868
Fax: 54-11-4322-3456
Email: libros@cuspide.com

O'REILLY®

TO ORDER: **800-998-9938** • **order@oreilly.com** • **http://www.oreilly.com/**
OUR PRODUCTS ARE AVAILABLE AT A BOOKSTORE OR SOFTWARE STORE NEAR YOU.
FOR INFORMATION: **800-998-9938** • **707-829-0515** • **info@oreilly.com**